THE
OFFICIAL
FOOTBALL
ASSOCIATION
YEARBOOK

1996-97

THE FOOTBALL ASSOCIATION

Patron: Her Majesty The Queen
President: HRH The Duke of Kent, KG

Council
Chairman: KStJ Wiseman (Southampton FC)
Vice-Chairman: CH Willcox MBE JP (Gloucestershire)
Chief Executive: RHG Kelly FCIS

WT Annable, Nottinghamshire
MM Armstrong, Huntingdonshire
RE Barston, Leicestershire and Rutland
KW Bates, FA Premier League, Chelsea FC
RD Bayley, Division 3, Leek Town FC
RG Berridge, Bedfordshire
MR Berry, English Schools
K Boyer, North Riding
AW Brett, Shropshire
BW Bright, Kent
EA Brown, Suffolk
CD Bullen, Cambridgeshire
A Burbidge, Cheshire
RF Burden, Gloucestershire
RI Burr, Division 7, Millwall FC
DG Champion, Cornwall
JA Christopher, Berks and Bucks
A Clark, Division 1, Whitley Bay FC
JW Coad ATII, Cambridgeshire
P Coates, Division 4, Stoke City FC
K Compton, Derbyshire
Lt Cdr PJW Danks RN, Royal Navy
JE Davey, Sussex
D Dein, FA Premier League, Arsenal FC
HD Ellis, FA Premier League, Aston Villa FC
ST Farmer JP, Shropshire
JB Fleming, Westmorland
DSR Gillard, Division 10, Ashford Town FC
WP Goss MSc, ARCS DIC, Amateur Football
   Alliance
DG Hammond FCA, MIHGT, The Football
   League, Swansea City FC
F Hannah CEng MIMechE ARTCS,
   Manchester
Miss J Hemsley, Women's Football Alliance
DJ Henson, Devon
Sir David Hill-Wood Bt, Australia
Gp Capt PW Hilton, Royal Air Force
AJ Hobbs, Somerset and Avon (South)
PS Hough, Dorset
FLJ Hunter, Liverpool
DJ Insole CBE, Cambridge University
RG Kibble, Hertfordshire
RW Kiddell JP ACII, Norfolk
P Kirby, New Zealand
Major TC Knight, Army
PJ Ladbrook, Oxfordshire
MR Leggett, Worcestershire
DJ Lewin, Lancashire
WG McKeag BA (Cantab), The Football
   League

AD McMullen MBE, Bedfordshire
K Marsden, Division 6, Gainsborough
   Trinity FC
MH Matthews, Oxford University
RE Maughan, Northumberland
Sir Bert Millichip, Division 4, West Bromwich
   Albion FC
BW Moore, Division 8, Yeovil Town FC
T Myatt, Staffordshire
S Nathan, London
RG Noades, The Football League, Crystal
   Palace FC
AK Odell, Middlesex
EM Parry, Wiltshire
FD Pattison, Durham
EG Powell, Herefordshire
ER Prescott, Herefordshire
MH Rawding, East Riding
KJ Reames, The Football League, Lincoln
   City FC
R Redmond, Bedfordshire
DG Richards, FA Premier League, Sheffield
   Wednesday FC
BA Richardson, FA Premier League, Coventry
   City FC
GL Ricketts, Birmingham
T Robinson, The Football League, Bury FC
P Rushton, Worcestershire
JM Ryder, Cornwall
CJ Saunders, Independent Schools
LFJ Smith, Surrey
GAJ Snell, Essex
WM Steward ACIS, Suffolk
IH Stott, Division 2, Oldham
   Athletic FC
AC Taylor MBE, West Riding
CB Taylor, Division 5, Barnsley FC
JC Thomas, Durham
G Thompson JP, Sheffield and
   Hallamshire
R Tinkler, Lincolnshire
ACF Turvey MCIM, Division 9, Hayes FC
PJ Vine, Hampshire
B Walden, Northamptonshire
JJ Waterall, Nottinghamshire
N White FSCA, Division 3, Liverpool FC
W Wilson, Cumberland
JF Wiseman, Birmingham City FC

THE OFFICIAL FOOTBALL ASSOCIATION YEARBOOK

1996- 97

PAN BOOKS

This edition published 1996 by Pan Books
an imprint of Macmillan Publishers Limited
25 Eccleston Place, London SW1W 9NF
and Basingstoke

Associated companies throughout the world

ISBN 0-330-347675

Copyright © 1996 by The Football Association

Fixtures 1996–1997 © FA Premier League

Fixtures 1996–1997 © The Football League
Reproduced under Licence No. NCH11296

1 3 5 7 9 8 6 4 2

A CIP catalogue record for this book is available from the British Library

Typeset by Spottiswoode Ballantyne Printers Ltd
Printed and bound in Great Britain by BPC Hazell Books Ltd
A member of The British Printing Company Ltd

CONTENTS

1 ● CHIEF EXECUTIVE'S REPORT

By most standards the recent European Championship, held in England for the first time, was a major success; the warm, friendly and humorous atmosphere surrounding all the matches was a real throwback to the old days of good-natured banter between rival fans. Eight cities went continental. Euphoria built as the England team again went so close to a final.

I said before Euro 96 that, even were England to finish champions, the need for a technical director to take the game forward in techniques and tactics would remain paramount. I still believe that.

Moreover, the remarkable interest generated last June provides a superb opportunity for football to capitalise on the progress it has made in recent years. Consider the facts:
- participation by 16–59 year old males has increased by 80.4% in ten years
- attendances at League matches increased from 16.5 million in 1985 to 22 million in 1996
- over 5,000 staff provide programmes or courses for over one million students per year
- since 1984 there have been established 147 centres of excellence caring for 10,000 children between the ages of 9 to 16.
- The Football Association National School at Lilleshall in Shropshire is producing top-quality international players

- participation and attendance by girls and women is rising dramatically
- commercial revenue from the business side of professional football – particularly from television – is going through the roof

Thus, we already have a base upon which – with the aid of Euro 96 – we can build.

We must rectify the shortcomings that have become apparent in schools, with the reduction in scope for the teaching of football.

We must sizeably increase the numbers of children playing small sided football, particularly mini-soccer.

We must put in place procedures to develop talented players from as early as age seven.

We must help clubs to develop suitable facilities for coaching and training.

Only by developing far-sighted policies for the development of the game will we be able to capitalise on the success of the European Championship and withstand the threat posed by the Bosman case to the fabric of the game in England.

We owe it to those lovely English supporters to do nothing less.

Graham Kelly

2 ● WORLD CUP FINALS 1930–1994

Year	Venue	Winner		Runner-up	Result	
1930	Montevideo	Uruguay	v	Argentina	4–2	
1934	Rome	Italy	v	Czechoslovakia	2–1	*
1938	Paris	Italy	v	Hungary	4–2	
1950	Rio de Janeiro	Uruguay	v	Brazil	2–1	
1954	Berne	West Germany	v	Hungary	3–2	
1958	Stockholm	Brazil	v	Sweden	5–2	
1962	Santiago	Brazil	v	Czechoslovakia	3–1	
1966	Wembley	England	v	West Germany	4–2	*
1970	Mexico City	Brazil	v	Italy	4–1	
1974	Munich	West Germany	v	Holland	2–1	
1978	Buenos Aires	Argentina	v	Holland	3–1	*
1982	Madrid	Italy	v	West Germany	3–1	
1986	Mexico City	Argentina	v	West Germany	3–2	
1990	Rome	West Germany	v	Argentina	1–0	
1994	Los Angeles	Brazil	v	Italy	0–0	†

* after extra time
† won on penalty-kicks

3 ● EUROPEAN CHAMPIONSHIP FINALS 1960–1996

Year	Venue	Winner		Runner-up	Result	
1960	Paris	USSR	v	Yugoslavia	2–1	
1964	Madrid	Spain	v	USSR	2–1	
1968	Rome	Italy	v	Yugoslavia	2–0	†
1972	Brussels	West Germany	v	USSR	3–0	
1976	Belgrade	Czechoslovakia	v	West Germany	2–2	††
1980	Rome	West Germany	v	Belgium	2–1	
1984	Paris	France	v	Spain	2–0	
1988	Munich	Holland	v	USSR	2–0	
1992	Gothenburg	Denmark	v	Germany	2–0	
1996	Wembley	Germany	v	CzechRepublic	2–1	*

† *after 1–1 draw*
†† *won on penalty-kicks*
* *won with "golden goal"*

Paul Gascoigne pursued by Scottish captain McAllister at Euro 96.

4 ● EUROPEAN CHAMPION CLUBS' CUP WINNERS 1956–1996

Year	Venue	Winner		Runners-up	Result	
1956	Paris	Real Madrid	v	Stade de Rheims	4–3	
1957	Madrid	Real Madrid	v	AC Fiorentina	2–0	
1958	Brussels	Real Madrid	v	AC Milan	3–2	*
1959	Stuttgart	Real Madrid	v	Stade de Rheims	2–0	
1960	Glasgow	Real Madrid	v	Eintracht Frankfurt	7–3	
1961	Berne	Benfica	v	Barcelona	3–2	
1962	Amsterdam	Benfica	v	Real Madrid	5–3	
1963	Wembley	AC Milan	v	Benfica	2–1	
1964	Vienna	Inter-Milan	v	Real Madrid	3–1	
1965	Madrid	Inter-Milan	v	Benfica	1–0	
1966	Brussels	Real Madrid	v	Partizan Belgrade	2–1	
1967	Lisbon	Celtic	v	Inter-Milan	2–1	
1968	Wembley	Manchester United	v	Benfica	4–1	*
1969	Madrid	AC Milan	v	Ajax Amsterdam	4–1	
1970	Milan	Feyenoord	v	Celtic	2–1	*
1971	Wembley	Ajax Amsterdam	v	Panathinaikos	2–0	
1972	Rotterdam	Ajax Amsterdam	v	Inter-Milan	2–0	
1973	Belgrade	Ajax Amsterdam	v	Juventus	1–0	
1974	Brussels	Bayern Munich	v	Atletico Madrid	1–1	
	Brussels	Bayern Munich	v	Atletico Madrid	4–0	
1975	Paris	Bayern Munich	v	Leeds United	2–0	
1976	Glasgow	Bayern Munich	v	St Etienne	1–0	
1977	Rome	Liverpool	v	Borussia Mönchengladbach	3–1	
1978	Wembley	Liverpool	v	FC Bruges	1–0	
1979	Munich	Nottingham Forest	v	Malmö	1–0	
1980	Madrid	Nottingham Forest	v	Hamburg	1–0	
1981	Paris	Liverpool	v	Real Madrid	1–0	
1982	Rotterdam	Aston Villa	v	Bayern Munich	1–0	
1983	Athens	Hamburg	v	Juventus	1–0	
1984	Rome	Liverpool	v	Roma	1–1	**
1985	Brussels	Juventus	v	Liverpool	1–0	
1986	Seville	Steaua Bucharest	v	Barcelona	0–0	**
1987	Vienna	Porto	v	Bayern Munich	2–1	
1988	Stuttgart	PSV Eindhoven	v	Benfica	0–0	**
1989	Barcelona	AC Milan	v	Steaua Bucharest	4–0	
1990	Vienna	AC Milan	v	Benfica	1–0	
1991	Bari	Red Star Belgrade	v	Marseille	0–0	**
1992	Wembley	Barcelona	v	Sampdoria	1–0	*
1993	Munich	Marseille	v	AC Milan	1–0	
1994	Athens	AC Milan	v	Barcelona	4–0	
1995	Vienna	Ajax Amsterdam	v	AC Milan	1–0	
1996	Rome	Juventus	v	Ajax Amsterdam	1–1	**

* after extra time
** won on penalty-kicks

5 ● EUROPEAN CUP WINNERS' CUP WINNERS 1961–1996

Year	Venue	Winner		Runners-up	Result	
1961		AC Fiorentina	v	Glasgow Rangers	4–1	†
1962	Glasgow	Atletico Madrid	v	AC Fiorentina	1–1	
	Stuttgart	Atletico Madrid	v	AC Fiorentina	3–0	
1963	Rotterdam	Tottenham Hotspur	v	Atletico Madrid	5–1	
1964	Brussels	Sporting Lisbon	v	MTK Budapest	3–3	*
	Antwerp	Sporting Lisbon	v	MTK Budapest	1–0	
1965	Wembley	West Ham United	v	Munich 1860	2–0	
1966	Glasgow	Borussia Dortmund	v	Liverpool	2–1	*
1967	Nuremberg	Bayern Munich	v	Rangers	1–0	*
1968	Rotterdam	AC Milan	v	Hamburg	2–0	
1969	Basle	Slovan Bratislava	v	Barcelona	3–2	
1970	Vienna	Manchester City	v	Gornik Zabrze	2–1	
1971	Athens	Chelsea	v	Real Madrid	1–1	*
	Athens	Chelsea	v	Real Madrid	2–1	
1972	Barcelona	Glasgow Rangers	v	Moscow Dynamo	3–2	
1973	Salonika	AC Milan	v	Leeds United	1–0	
1974	Rotterdam	Magdeburg	v	AC Milan	2–0	
1975	Basle	Dynamo Kiev	v	Ferencvaros	3–0	
1976	Brussels	Anderlecht	v	West Ham United	4–2	

Kanu of Ajax hurdles Jugovic's challenge in Rome.

Year	Venue	Winner	v	Runners-up	Result	
1977	Amsterdam	Hamburg	v	Anderlecht	2–0	
1978	Paris	Anderlecht	v	Austria Vienna	4–0	
1979	Basle	Barcelona	v	Fortuna Düsseldorf	4–3	*
1980	Brussels	Valencia	v	Arsenal	0–0	**
1981	Düsseldorf	Dynamo Tbilisi	v	Carl Zeiss Jena	2–1	
1982	Barcelona	Barcelona	v	Standard Liège	2–1	
1983	Gothenburg	Aberdeen	v	Real Madrid	2–1	*
1984	Basle	Juventus	v	Porto	2–1	
1985	Rotterdam	Everton	v	Rapid Vienna	3–1	
1986	Lyon	Dynamo Kiev	v	Atletico Madrid	3–0	
1987	Athens	Ajax Amsterdam	v	Lokomotiv Leipzig	1–0	
1988	Strasbourg	Mechelen	v	Ajax Amsterdam	1–0	
1989	Berne	Barcelona	v	Sampdoria	2–0	
1990	Gothenburg	Sampdoria	v	Anderlecht	2–0	*
1991	Rotterdam	Manchester United	v	Barcelona	2–1	
1992	Lisbon	Werder Bremen	v	Monaco	2–0	
1993	Wembley	Parma	v	Royal Antwerp	3–1	
1994	Copenhagen	Arsenal	v	Parma	1–0	
1995	Paris	Real Zaragoza	v	Arsenal	2–1	*
1996	Brussels	Paris St-Germain	v	Rapid Vienna	1–0	

† *aggregate over two legs*
* *after extra time*
** *won on penalty-kicks*

6 ● UEFA CUP WINNERS 1958–1996

Known also as the Inter Cities Fairs' Cup until 1971. Two-leg finals except in 1964 and 1965.
Aggregate scores.

Year	Winner		Runners-up	Result	
1958	Barcelona	v	London	8–2	
1960	Barcelona	v	Birmingham	4–1	
1961	Roma	v	Birmingham	4–2	
1962	Valencia	v	Barcelona	7–3	
1963	Valencia	v	Dynamo Zagreb	4–1	
1964	Real Zaragoza	v	Valencia	2–1	
1965	Ferencvaros	v	Juventus	1–0	
1966	Barcelona	v	Real Zaragoza	4–3	
1967	Dynamo Zagreb	v	Leeds United	2–0	
1968	Leeds United	v	Ferencvaros	1–0	
1969	Newcastle United	v	Ujpest Dozsa	6–2	
1970	Arsenal	v	Anderlecht	4–3	
1971	Leeds United	v	Juventus	3–3	*
1972	Tottenham Hotspur	v	Wolverhampton Wanderers	3–2	
1973	Liverpool	v	Borussia Mönchengladbach	3–2	
1974	Feyenoord	v	Tottenham Hotspur	4–2	
1975	Borussia Mönchengladbach	v	Twente Enschede	5–1	
1976	Liverpool	v	FC Bruges	4–3	
1977	Juventus	v	Bilbao	2–2	*
1978	PSV Eindhoven	v	Bastia	3–0	
1979	Borussia Mönchengladbach	v	Red Star Belgrade	2–1	
1980	Eintracht Frankfurt	v	Borussia Mönchengladbach	3–3	*
1981	Ipswich Town	v	AZ 67 Alkmaar	5–4	
1982	IFK Gothenburg	v	Hamburg	4–0	
1983	Anderlecht	v	Benfica	2–1	
1984	Tottenham Hotspur	v	Anderlecht	2–2	†
1985	Real Madrid	v	Videoton	3–1	
1986	Real Madrid	v	Cologne	5–3	
1987	IFK Gothenburg	v	Dundee United	2–1	
1988	Bayer Leverkusen	v	Espanol	3–3	†
1989	Napoli	v	Stuttgart	5–4	
1990	Juventus	v	AC Fiorentina	3–1	
1991	Inter-Milan	v	Roma	2–1	
1992	Ajax Amsterdam	v	Torino	2–2	*
1993	Juventus	v	Borussia Dortmund	6–1	
1994	Inter-Milan	v	Casino Salzburg	2–0	
1995	Parma	v	Juventus	2–1	
1996	Bayern Munich	v	Bordeaux	5–1	

* won on away goals rule
† won on penalty-kicks

7 ● REVIEW OF THE EUROPEAN SEASON 1995–96

The two-year plan of Juventus coach Marcello Lippi came to fruition in Rome's Olympic Stadium as the Italian giants won the Champion Clubs' Cup Final a year after breaking the Milan "monopoly" in Serie A. Striker Ravanelli and goalkeeper Peruzzi – both in Italy's squad for Euro 96 – were key contributors to one of the greatest moments in Juventus' colourful history. The former scored on 12 minutes from an "impossible" angle to boost their clear resolve to win the trophy and the latter was superb in the penalty shootout, saving kicks from Davids and Silooy to help Juventus to an ultimate 4–2 shootout advantage after the teams had been locked at 1–1 after extra time.

Litmanen, the Finn, equalised Ravanelli's effort on 40 minutes but Juventus finished the stronger. For captain Gianluca Vialli it was the perfect climax to years of endeavour in this prestigious competition – four seasons ago, for example, his Sampdoria team had lost out to Koeman's stunning free-kick for Barcelona at Wembley. It was also a fitting climax to Vialli's career in Serie A. He will begin the new season in the Premiership with Chelsea.

French football, enjoying a renaissance after Marseille's disgrace of three seasons ago, celebrated its best-ever season on the European club stage. Nantes reached the Champions' League semi-final, Bordeaux featured in the UEFA Cup Final and Paris Saint-Germain became only the second French winners ever in Europe by winning the Cup Winners' Cup in Brussels. Bruno N'Gotty struck home the only goal in the King Baudouin Stadium in the 28th minute, his shot after a short free-kick taking a deflection and skidding past Rapid Vienna goalkeeper Konsel's right hand. The final scoreline of 1–0 had scarcely reflected PSG's technical superiority.

Franz Beckenbauer, legendary player and coach for club and country in Germany, completed a set of major triumphs when the club which he now serves in the joint role of president and coach, Bayern Munich, won the UEFA Cup Final over two legs against Bordeaux. Beckenbauer had already been a winner in the World Cup, European Championship, World Club Cup, Champions' Cup, Cup

Winners' Cup, plus domestic titles in Germany and America.

Bayern had taken full advantage of the home leg to grab a 2–0 lead. They exerted virtually all the pressure in the first half-hour without any tangible reward and then Helmer's 35th-minute breakthrough was followed by another successful strike from Scholl on the hour. They survived the expected Bordeaux charge in the second leg and then hit them twice on the break in the first twenty minutes of the second half through Scholl and the Bulgarian Kostadinov. Jurgen Klinsmann's goal that wrapped it up at 3–1 was his fifteenth of the campaign – a record for the UEFA Cup.

For a country whose clubs had won the Champions' Cup six times in a row (1977–82), the results in the three main European club competitions in season 1995–96 were hugely disappointing. Blackburn Rovers were brought back to earth after the euphoria of winning the Championship for the first time since 1914 by finishing fourth out of four in their Champions' League group. An opening home defeat to Moscow Spartak (0–1) was followed by another two weeks later in Trondheim as Norwegian champions Rosenborg scored a clinching goal (2–1) with four minutes left. The writing was on the wall after that.

Everton accounted for KR Reykjavik 6–3 on aggregate in their opening round of the Cup Winners' Cup and then went out to Feyenoord of Rotterdam without finding the net in either leg. Of England's four entries in the UEFA Cup only one, Nottingham Forest, made it through to the quarter-finals. Manchester United fell at the first to Rotor Volgograd on the away goals rule, Liverpool got past Spartak Vladikavkaz (2–1 on aggregate) before the Danes from Brondby beat them at Anfield for a 1–0 aggregate advantage and Leeds United, who had impressed in Monaco, were dumped out by PSV Eindhoven in the next round by an aggregate score of 8–3. Forest had put out Malmo, Auxerre and Lyon, but when Bayern Munich came to the City Ground they scored five – just as PSV had done at Elland Road. England will have one less place in the coming season's UEFA Cup.

THE TEAMS AND PLAYERS

Group A

ENGLAND
1 David Seaman (Arsenal)
2 Gary Neville (Manchester United)
3 Stuart Pearce (Nottingham Forest)
4 Paul Ince (Inter Milan)
5 Tony Adams (Arsenal)
6 Gareth Southgate (Aston Villa)
7 David Platt (Arsenal)
8 Paul Gascoigne (Rangers)
9 Alan Shearer (Blackburn Rovers)
10 Teddy Sheringham (Tottenham)
11 Darren Anderton (Tottenham)
12 Steve Howey (Newcastle)
13 Tim Flowers (Blackburn Rovers)
14 Nick Barmby (Middlesbrough)
15 Jamie Redknapp (Liverpool)
16 Sol Campbell (Tottenham)
17 Steve McManaman (Liverpool)
18 Les Ferdinand (Newcastle)
19 Philip Neville (Manchester United)
20 Steve Stone (Nottingham Forest)
21 Robbie Fowler (Liverpool)
22 Ian Walker (Tottenham)

SWITZERLAND
1 Marco Pascolo (Servette)
2 Marc Hottiger (Everton)
3 Yvan Quentin (Sion)
4 Stephane Henchoz (Hamburg)
5 Alain Geiger (Grasshoppers)
6 Raphael Wicky (Sion)
7 Sebastien Fournier (Sion)
8 Christophe Ohrel (St Etienne)
9 Marco Grassi (Rennes to Monaco)
10 Ciriaco Sforza (Bayern Munich)
11 Stephane Chapuisat (B. Dortmund)
12 Stephane Lehmann (Sion)
13 Sebastien Jeanneret (Neuchatel Xamax)
14 Kubilay Turkyilmaz (Grasshoppers)
15 Ramon Vega (Grasshoppers)
16 Marcel Koller (Grasshoppers)
17 Johann Vogel (Grasshoppers)
18 Regis Rothenbuhler (Neuchatel Xamax)
19 David Sesa (Servette)
20 Alexandre Comisetti (Grasshoppers)
21 Christophe Bonvin (Sion)
22 Joel Corminboeuf (Xamax)

HOLLAND
1 Edwin van der Sar (Ajax)
2 Michael Reiziger (Ajax to AC Milan)
3 Danny Blind (Ajax)
4 Clarence Seedorf (Sampdoria to
   Real Madrid)
5 Frank de Boer (Ajax)
6 Ronald de Boer (Ajax)
7 Gaston Taument (Feyenoord)
8 Edgar Davids (Ajax to AC Milan)
9 Patrick Kluivert (Ajax)
10 Dennis Bergkamp (Arsenal)
11 Peter Hoekstra (Ajax)
12 Aron Winter (Lazio to Inter Milan)
13 Arthur Numan (PSV Eindhoven)
14 Richard Witschge (Bordeaux to Ajax)
15 Winston Bogarde (Ajax)
16 Ed de Goey (Feyenoord)
17 Jordi Cruyff (Barcelona)
18 Johan de Kock (Roda JC)
19 Youri Mulder (Schalke 04)
20 Phillip Cocu (PSV Eindhoven)
21 Ruud Hesp (Roda JC)
22 John Veldman (Sparta Rotterdam)

SCOTLAND
1 Jim Leighton (Hibernian)
2 Stewart McKimmie (Aberdeen)
3 Tom Boyd (Celtic)
4 Colin Calderwood (Tottenham)
5 Colin Hendry (Blackburn Rovers)
6 Derek Whyte (Middlesbrough)
7 John Spencer (Chelsea)
8 Stuart McCall (Rangers)
9 Ally McCoist (Rangers)
10 Gary McAllister (Leeds)
11 John Collins (Celtic to Monaco)
12 Andrew Goram (Rangers)
13 Tosh McKinlay (Celtic)
14 Gordon Durie (Rangers)
15 Eoin Jess (Coventry)
16 Craig Burley (Chelsea)
17 Billy McKinlay (Blackburn Rovers)
18 Kevin Gallacher (Blackburn Rovers)
19 Darren Jackson (Hibernian)
20 Scott Booth (Aberdeen)
21 Scot Gemmill (Nottingham Forest)
22 Nicky Walker (Partick)

Group B

BULGARIA
1 Borislav Mihaylov (Reading)
2 Radostin Kischischev (Neftochimik)
3 Trifon Ivanov (Rapid Wien)
4 Ilian Kiriakov (Famagusta to Aberdeen)
5 Petar Hubchev (Hamburg)
6 Zlatko Iankov (Bayer Verdingen)
7 Emil Kostadinov (Bayern Munich)
8 Hristo Stoichkov (Parma)
9 Luboslav Penev (Atletico Madrid)
10 Krassimir Balakov (Stuttgart)
11 Iordan Lechkov (Hamburg)
12 Dimitar Popov (CSKA Sofia)
13 Bontcho Guentchev (Luton)
14 Nasko Sirakov (Slavia Sofia)
15 Ivaylo Iordanov (Sporting Lisbon)
16 Daniel Borimirov (TSV 1860 Munich)
17 Emil Kremenliev (Olympiakos)
18 Tzanko Tzvetanov (W. Mannheim)
19 Gosho Guinchev (Denizlispor)
20 Gueorgui Donkov (CSKA Sofia)
21 Ivo Gueorguiev (Spartak Varna)
22 Zdravko Zdravkov (Slavia Sofia)

SPAIN
1 Andoni Zubizarreta (Valencia)
2 Juan Manuel Lopez (Atletico Madrid)
3 Alberto Belsue (Real Zaragoza)
4 Rafael Alkorta (Real Madrid)
5 Abelardo Fernandez (Barcelona)
6 Fernando Hierro (Real Madrid)
7 Jose Emilio Amavisca (Real Madrid)
8 Julen Guerrero (Athletic Bilbao)
9 Juan Antonio Pizzi (Tenerife)
10 Donato Gama da Silva (D La Coruna)
11 Alfonso Perez Munoz (Betis to Real Madrid)
12 Sergi Barjuan (Barcelona)
13 Santiago Canizares (Real Madrid)
14 Francisco Narvaez KIKO (A. Madrid)
15 Jose Luis Perez Caminero (A. Madrid)
16 Jorge Otero (Valencia)
17 Javier Manjarin (Dep La Coruna)
18 Guillermo Amor (Barcelona)
19 Julio Salinas (Sporting Gijon)
20 Miguel Angel Nadal (Barcelona)
21 Luis Enrique Martinez (Real Madrid to Barcelona)
22 Jose Francisco Molina (Atletico Madrid)

ROMANIA
1 Bogdan Stelea (Steaua Bucharest)
2 Dan Petrescu (Chelsea)
3 Daniel Claudiu Prodan (St Bucharest)
4 Miodrag Belodedici (Villareal)
5 Ioan Angelo Lupescu (B. Leverkusen)
6 Gheorghe Popescu (Barcelona)
7 Marius Mihai Lacatus (St Bucharest)
8 Ovidiu Ioan Sabau (Brescia Calcio)
9 Florin Raducioiu (Espanyol)
10 Gheorghe Hagi (Barcelona)
11 Dorinel Munteanu (Cologne)
12 Florin Prunea (Dynamo Bucharest)
13 Tibor Selymes (Cercle Brugge)
14 Constantin Galca (Steaua Bucharest)
15 Anton Dobos (Steaua Bucharest)
16 Gheorghe Mihali (Guingamp)
17 Iulian Filipescu (Steaua Bucharest)
18 Ovidiu Stinga (Salamanca)
19 Adrian Ilie (Steaua Bucharest)
20 Viorel Moldovan (Neuchatel Xamax)
21 Ion Vladoiu (Steaua Bucharest)
22 Florin Tene (Rapid Bucharest)

FRANCE
1 Bernard Lama (Paris St Germain)
2 Jocelyn Angloma (Torino to Inter Milan)
3 Eric Di Meco (Monaco)
4 Franck Lebouef (Strasbourg)
5 Laurent Blanc (Auxerre to Barcelona)
6 Vincent Guerin (Paris St Germain)
7 Didier Deschamps (Juventus)
8 Marcel Desailly (AC Milan)
9 Youri Djorkaeff (Paris St Germain to Inter Milan)
10 Zinedine Zidane (Bordeaux to Juventus)
11 Patrice Loko (Paris St Germain)
12 Bixente Lizarazu (Bordeaux)
13 Christophe Dugarry (Bordeaux)
14 Sabri Lamouchi (Auxerre)
15 Lilian Thuram (Monaco to Parma)
16 Fabien Barthez (Monaco)
17 Mickael Madar (Monaco)
18 Reynald Pedros (Nantes)
19 Christian Karembeu (Sampdoria)
20 Alain Roche (Paris St Germain)
21 Corentin Martins (Auxerre)
22 Bruno Martini (Montpellier)

Group C

GERMANY
1 Andreas Kopke (Eintracht Frankfurt)
2 Stefan Reuter (Borussia Dortmund)
3 Marco Bode (Werder Bremen)
4 Steffen Freund (Borussia Dortmund)
5 Thomas Helmer (Bayern Munich)
6 Matthias Sammer (Borussia Dortmund)
7 Andreas Moller (Borussia Dortmund)
8 Mehmet Scholl (Bayern Munich)
9 Fredi Bobic (Stuttgart)
10 Thomas Hassler (Karlsruhe)
11 Stefan Kuntz (Besiktas)
12 Oliver Kahn (Bayern Munich)
13 Mario Basler (Werder Bremen to Bayern Munich)
14 Markus Babbel (Bayern Munich)
15 Jurgen Kohler (Borussia Dortmund)
16 Rene Schneider (Hansa Rostock)
17 Christian Ziege (Bayern Munich)
18 Jurgen Klinsmann (Bayern Munich)
19 Thomas Strunz (Bayern Munich)
20 Oliver Bierhoff (Udinese)
21 Dieter Eilts (Werder Bremen)
22 Oliver Reck (Werder Bremen)

CZECH REPUBLIC
1 Petr Kouba (Sparta Prague)
2 Radek Latal (Schalke 04)
3 Jan Suchoparek (Slavia Prague)
4 Pavel Nedved (Sparta Prague)
5 Miroslav Kadlec (Kaiserslautern)
6 Vaclav Nemecek (Servette)
7 Jiri Nemec (Schalke 04)
8 Karel Poborsky (Slavia Prague)
9 Pavel Kuka (Kaiserslautern)
10 Radek Drulak (Petra Drnovice)
11 Martin Frydek (Sparta Prague)
12 Lubos Kubik (Petra Drnovice)
13 Radek Bejbl (Slavia Prague)
14 Patrik Berger (Borussia Dortmund)
15 Michal Hornak (Sparta Prague)
16 Pavel Srnicek (Newcastle)
17 Vladimir Smicer (Slavia Prague)
18 Martin Kotulek (Sigma Olomouc)
19 Karel Rada (Sigma Olomouc)
20 Pavel Novotny (Slavia Prague)
21 Milan Kerbr (Sigma Olomouc)
22 Ladislav Maier (Slovan Liberec)

ITALY
1 Angelo Peruzzi (Juventus)
2 Luigi Apolloni (Parma)
3 Paolo Maldini (AC Milan)
4 Amedeo Carboni (Roma)
5 Alessandro Costacurta (AC Milan)
6 Alessandro Nesta (Lazio)
7 Roberto Donadoni (NY/NJ MetroStars)
8 Roberto Mussi (Parma)
9 Moreno Torricelli (Juventus)
10 Demetrio Albertini (AC Milan)
11 Dino Baggio (Parma)
12 Francesco Toldo (Fiorentina)
13 Fabio Rossitto (Udinese)
14 Alessandro Del Piero (Juventus)
15 Angelo Di Livio (Juventus)
16 Roberto Di Matteo (Lazio)
17 Diego Fuser (Lazio)
18 Pierluigi Casiraghi (Lazio)
19 Enrico Chiesa (Sampdoria to Parma)
20 Fabrizio Ravanelli (Juventus)
21 Gianfranco Zola (Parma)
22 Luca Bucci (Parma)

RUSSIA
1 Dmitri Kharine (Chelsea)
2 Omar Tetradze (Alania Vladikavkaz)
3 Yuri Nikiforov (Spartak Moscow)
4 Iliya Tsymbalar (Spartak Moscow)
5 Yuri Kovtun (Dynamo Moscow)
6 Valeri Karpin (Real Sociedad)
7 Viktor Onopko (Real Oviedo)
8 Andrei Kanchelskis (Everton)
9 Igor Kolyvanov (Foggia)
10 Alexandr Mostovoi (Strasbourg)
11 Sergei Kiriyakov (Karlsruhe)
12 Stanislav Cherchesov (FC Tirol)

13 Yevgeni Bushmanov (CSKA Moscow)
14 Igor Dobrovolsky (unattached)
15 Igor Shalimov (Udinese)
16 Igor Simutenkov (Reggiana)
17 Vladimir Bestchastnykh (Werder Bremen)
18 Igor Yanovski (Alania Vladikavkaz)
19 Vladislav Radimov (CSKA Moscow)
20 Sergei Gorlukovich (Spartak Moscow)
21 Dmitri Khokhlov (CSKA Moscow)
22 Sergei Ovchinnikov (Lokomotiv Moscow)

Group D
PORTUGAL
1 Vitor Baia (Porto)
2 Carlos Secretario (Porto)
3 Joao Santos (Porto)
4 Oceano Cruz (Sporting Lisbon)
5 Fernando Couto (Parma)
6 Jose Tavares (Boavista)
7 Vitor Araujo (Vitoria)
8 Joao Pinto (Benfica)
9 Ricardo Pinto (Sporting Lisbon)
10 Rui Costa (Fiorentina)
11 Jorge Cadete (Celtic)
12 Alfredo Castro (Boavista)
13 Dimas Teixeira (Benfica)
14 Pedro Barbosa (Sporting Lisbon)
15 Domingos Oliviera (Porto)
16 Helder Cristovao (Benfica)
17 Hugo Porifio (Leiria)
18 Antonio Folha (Porto)
19 Paulo Sousa (Juventus)
20 Luis Figo (Barcelona)
21 Paulo Madeira (Belenenses)
22 Rui Correia (Braga)

CROATIA
1 Drazen Ladic (Croatia Zagreb)
2 Nikola Jurcevic (Freiburg)
3 Robert Jarni (Real Betis)
4 Igor Stimac (Derby County)
5 Nikola Jerkan (Real Oviedo)
6 Slaven Bilic (West Ham)
7 Aljosa Asanovic (Hajduk Split)
8 Robert Prosinecki (Barcelona)
9 Davor Suker (Sevilla to Real Madrid)
10 Zvonimir Boban (AC Milan)
11 Alen Boksic (Lazio to Juventus)
12 Marijan Mrmic (Varteks Varazdin)
13 Mario Stanic (FC Bruges)
14 Zvonimir Soldo (Croatia Zagreb)
15 Dubravko Pavlicic (Alicante)
16 Mladen Mladenovic (Salzburg to Osaka)
17 Igor Parnic (Osijek)
18 Elvis Brajkovic (1860 Munich)
19 Goran Vlaovic (Padova)
20 Dario Simic (Croatia Zagreb)
21 Igor Cvitanovic (Croatia Zagreb)
22 Tonci Gabric (Hajduk Split)

TURKEY
1 Adnan Erkan (Ankaragucu)
2 Recep Cetin (Besiktas)
3 Alpay Ozalan (Besiktas)
4 Vedat Inceefe (Karabukspor)
5 Tugay Kerimoglu (Galatasaray)
6 Ertugrul Saglam (Besiktas)
7 Hami Mandirali (Trabzonspor)
8 Ogun Temizkanoglu (Trabzonspor)
9 Hakan Sukur (Galatasaray)
10 Oguz Cetin (Fenerbahce)
11 Orhan Cikirikci (Trabzonspor)
12 Faruk Yigit (Kocaelispor)
13 Rahim Zafer (Genclerbirligi)
14 Saffet Sancakli (Kocaelispor)
15 Tayfun Korkut (Fenerbahce)
16 Sergen Yalcin (Besiktas)
17 Abdullah Ercan (Trabzonspor)
18 Arif Erdem (Galatasaray)
19 Tolunay Kafkas (Trabzonspor)
20 Bulent Korkmaz (Galatasaray)
21 Sanver Goymen (Altay)
22 Rustu Recber (Fenerbahce)

DENMARK
1 Peter Schmeichel (Manchester United)
2 Thomas Helveg (Udinese)
3 Marc Rieper (West Ham)
4 Lars Olsen (Brondby)
5 Jes Hogh (Fenerbahce)
6 Michael Schjonberg (Odense)
7 Brian Steen Nielsen (Odense)
8 Claus Thomsen (Ipswich Town)
9 Mikkel Beck (Fortuna Cologne)
10 Michael Laudrup (Real Madrid to V Kobe)
11 Brian Laudrup (Rangers)
12 Torben Piechnik (Aarhus)
13 Henrik Larsen (Lyngby)
14 Jens Risager (Brondby)
15 Erik Bo Andersen (Rangers)
16 Lars Hogh (Odense)
17 Allan Nielsen (Brondby)
18 Kim Vilfort (Brondby)
19 Stig Tofting (Aarhus)
20 Jacob Laursen (Silkeborg)
21 Soren Andersen (Aalborg)
22 Mogens Krogh (Brondby)

EURO 96: MATCH DETAILS

Group A – Wembley/Villa Park
England, Switzerland, Holland, Scotland

Group B – Elland Road/St James' Park
Spain, Bulgaria, Romania, France

Group C – Old Trafford/Anfield
Germany, Czech Republic, Italy, Russia

Group D – Hillsborough/City Ground
Denmark, Portugal, Turkey, Croatia

Date	(time)	Venue	Result (scorers)		Att
8.6	(15.00)	Wembley	England 1 v 1 Switzerland		76,567
			(Shearer)	(Turkyilmaz pen)	
9.6	(14.30)	Elland Road	Spain 1 v 1 Bulgaria		26,006
			(Alfonso)	(Stoichkov pen)	
9.6	(17.00)	Old Trafford	Germany 2 v 0 Czech Republic		37,300
			(Ziege, Moller)		
9.6	(19.30)	Hillsborough	Denmark 1 v 1 Portugal		34,993
			(Laudrup B.)	(Sa Pinto)	
10.6	(16.30)	Villa Park	Holland 0 v 0 Scotland		34,363
10.6	(19.30)	St James' Park	Romania 0 v 1 France		26,323
				(Dugarry)	
11.6	(16.30)	Anfield	Italy 2 v 1 Russia		35,120
			(Casiraghi 2)	(Tsymbalar)	
11.6	(19.30)	City Ground	Turkey 0 v 1 Croatia		22,460
				(Vlaovic)	
13.6	(16.30)	St James' Park	Bulgaria 1 v 0 Romania		19,107
			(Stoichkov)		
13.6	(19.30)	Villa Park	Switzerland 0 v 2 Holland		36,800
				(Cruyff, Bergkamp)	
14.6	(16.30)	City Ground	Porgugal 1 v 0 Turkey		22,670
			(Couto)		
14.6	(19.30)	Anfield	Czech Republic 2 v 1 Italy		37,320
			(Nedved, Bejbl)	(Chiesa)	
15.6	(15.00)	Wembley	Scotland 0 v 2 England		76,864
				(Shearer, Gascoigne)	

Date	(time)	Venue	Result (scorers)	Att
15.6	(18.00)	Elland Road	France 1 v 1 Spain (Djorkaeff) (Caminero)	35,626
16.6	(15.00)	Old Trafford	Russia 0 v 3 Germany (Klinsmann 2, Sammer)	50,760
16.6	(18.00)	Hillsborough	Croatia 3 v 0 Denmark (Suker 2 – 1 pen, Boban)	33,671
18.6	(16.30)	St James' Park	France 3 v 1 Bulgaria (Blanc, Penev o.g., Loko) (Stoichkov)	26,976
18.6	(16.30)	Elland Road	Romania 1 v 2 Spain (Raducioiu) (Manjarin, Amor)	32,719
18.6	(19.30)	Villa Park	Scotland 1 v 0 Switzerland (McCoist)	34,926
18.6	(19.30)	Wembley	Holland 1 v 4 England (Kluivert) (Shearer 2 – 1 pen, Sheringham 2)	76,798
19.6	(16.30)	City Ground	Croatia 0 v 3 Portugal (Figo, Joao Pinto, Domingos)	20,484
19.6	(16.30)	Hillsborough	Turkey 0 v 3 Denmark (Laudrup B. 2, Nielsen A.)	28,951
19.6	(19.30)	Anfield	Russia 3 v 3 Czech Republic (Mostovoi, Tetradze, (Suchoparek, Kuka, Beschastnykh) Smicer)	21,128
19.6	(19.30)	Old Trafford	Italy 0 v 0 Germany	53,740

Final Tables

Group A	P	W	D	L	F	A	Pts
England	3	2	1	0	7	2	7
Holland	3	1	1	1	3	4	4
Scotland	3	1	1	1	1	2	4
Switzerland	3	0	1	2	1	4	1

Group B	P	W	D	L	F	A	Pts
France	3	2	1	0	5	2	7
Spain	3	1	2	0	4	3	5
Bulgaria	3	1	1	1	3	4	4
Romania	3	0	0	3	1	4	0

Group C	P	W	D	L	F	A	Pts
Germany	3	2	1	0	5	0	7
Czech Rep	3	1	1	1	5	6	4
Italy	3	1	1	1	3	3	4
Russia	3	0	1	2	4	8	1

Group D	P	W	D	L	F	A	Pts
Portugal	3	2	1	0	5	1	7
Croatia	3	2	0	1	4	3	6
Denmark	3	1	1	1	4	4	4
Turkey	3	0	0	3	0	5	0

Quarter-Finals

Date	(time)	Venue	Result (scorers)	Att
22.6	(15.00)	Wembley	*England 0 v 0 Spain	75,440
22.6	(18.30)	Anfield	†France 0 v 0 Holland	37,465
23.6	(15.00)	Old Trafford	Germany 2 v 1 Croatia (Klinsmann pen, Sammer) (Suker)	43,412
23.6	(18.30)	Villa Park	Portugal 0 v 1 Czech Republic (Poborsky)	26,832

* England won 4–2 on penalties
† France won 5–4 on penalties

Semi-Finals

Date	(time)	Venue	Result (scorers)	Att
26.6	(16.00)	Old Trafford	France 0 v 0 Czech Republic*	43,877
26.6	(19.30)	Wembley	England 1 v 1 Germany† (Shearer) (Kuntz)	75,862

* Czech Republic won 6–5 on penalties
† Germany won 6–5 on penalties

Final

Date	(time)	Venue	Result (scorers)	Att
30.6	(19.00)	Wembley	*Germany 2 v 1 Czech Republic (Bierhoff 2) (Berger pen)	73,611

* Germany won with "golden goal"

9 ● FIFA WORLD CUP: FRANCE 98

UEFA – QUALIFYING COMPETITION

Group 1: DEN/GRE/HRV/SVN/BIH
24.04.96 Greece v Slovenia
01.09.96 Greece v Bosnia-Herzegovina
01.09.96 Slovenia v Denmark
09.10.96 Denmark v Greece
09.10.96 Bosnia-Herzegovina v Croatia
10.11.96 Croatia v Greece
29.03.97 Croatia v Denmark
02.04.97 Croatia v Slovenia
02.04.97 Bosnia-Herzegovina v Greece
30.04.97 Denmark v Slovenia
30.04.97 Greece v Croatia
08.06.97 Denmark v Bosnia-Herzegovina
20.08.97 Bosnia-Herzegovina v Denmark
06.09.97 Croatia v Bosnia-Herzegovina
10.09.97 Denmark v Croatia
10.09.97 Bosnia-Herzegovina v Slovenia
11.10.97 Greece v Denmark
11.10.97 Slovenia v Croatia

Group 2: ITA/ENG/POL/GEO/MOL
01.09.96 Moldova v England
05.10.96 Moldova v Italy
09.10.96 England v Poland
09.10.96 Italy v Georgia
09.11.96 Georgia v England
10.11.96 Poland v Moldova
12.02.97 England v Italy
29.03.97 Italy v Moldova
02.04.97 Poland v Italy
30.04.97 England v Georgia
30.04.97 Italy v Poland
31.05.97 Poland v England
07.06.97 Georgia v Moldova
14.06.97 Poland v Georgia
10.09.97 England v Moldova
10.09.97 Georgia v Italy
24.09.97 Moldova v Georgia
07.10.97 Moldova v Poland
11.10.97 Italy v England
11.10.97 Georgia v Poland

Group 3: NOR/SUI/FIN/HUN/AZE
02.06.96 Norway v Azerbaijan
31.08.96 Azerbaijan v Switzerland
01.09.96 Hungary v Finland
06.10.96 Finland v Switzerland
09.10.96 Norway v Hungary
10.11.96 Switzerland v Norway
10.11.96 Azerbaijan v Hungary
02.04.97 Azerbaijan v Finland
30.04.97 Norway v Finland
30.04.97 Switzerland v Hungary
08.06.97 Finland v Azerbaijan
08.06.97 Hungary v Norway
20.08.97 Finland v Norway
20.08.97 Hungary v Switzerland
06.09.97 Switzerland v Finland
06.09.97 Azerbaijan v Norway
10.09.97 Hungary v Azerbaijan
10.09.97 Norway v Switzerland
11.10.97 Finland v Hungary
11.10.97 Switzerland v Azerbaijan

Group 4: SWE/SCO/AUT/LVA/BLR/EST
01.06.96 Sweden v Belarus
31.08.96 Austria v Scotland
31.08.96 Belarus v Estonia
01.09.96 Latvia v Sweden
05.10.96 Estonia v Belarus
05.10.96 Latvia v Scotland
09.10.96 Sweden v Austria
09.10.96 Estonia v Scotland
09.10.96 Belarus v Latvia
09.11.96 Austria v Latvia
10.11.96 Scotland v Sweden
29.03.97 Scotland v Estonia
02.04.97 Scotland v Austria
30.04.97 Austria v Estonia
30.04.97 Sweden v Scotland
30.04.97 Latvia v Belarus
18.05.97 Estonia v Latvia
08.06.97 Estonia v Sweden
08.06.97 Latvia v Austria
08.06.97 Belarus v Scotland
20.08.97 Estonia v Austria
20.08.97 Belarus v Sweden
06.09.97 Austria v Sweden
06.09.97 Scotland v Belarus
06.09.97 Latvia v Estonia
10.09.97 Sweden v Latvia
10.09.97 Belarus v Austria
11.10.97 Austria v Belarus
11.10.97 Scotland v Latvia
11.10.97 Sweden v Estonia

Group 5: RUS/BGR/ISR/CYP/LUX
01.09.96 Israel v Bulgaria
01.09.96 Russia v Cyprus
08.10.96 Luxembourg v Bulgaria
09.10.96 Israel v Russia
10.11.96 Cyprus v Israel
10.11.96 Luxembourg v Russia
14.12.96 Cyprus v Bulgaria
15.12.96 Israel v Luxembourg
29.03.97 Cyprus v Russia
30.03.97 Luxembourg v Israel
02.04.97 Bulgaria v Cyprus

30.04.97 Israel v Cyprus
30.04.97 Russia v Luxembourg
08.06.97 Bulgaria v Luxembourg
08.06.97 Russia v Israel
20.08.97 Bulgaria v Israel
07.09.97 Luxembourg v Cyprus
10.09.97 Bulgaria v Russia
11.10.97 Cyprus v Luxembourg
11.10.97 Russia v Bulgaria

Group 6: ESP/CZE/SVK/YUG/MLT/FRO
12.02.97 Spain v Malta
31.03.97 Malta v Slovakia
02.04.97 Czech Republic v Yugoslavia
30.04.97 Yugoslavia v Spain
30.04.97 Malta v Faroe Islands
21.05.97 Slovakia v Czech Republic
08.06.97 Yugoslavia v Slovakia
08.06.97 Faroe Islands v Malta
08.06.97 Spain v Czech Republic
20.08.97 Czech Republic v Faroe Islands
06.09.97 Faroe Islands v Czech Republic
10.09.97 Slovakia v Yugoslavia
24.09.97 Malta v Czech Republic
24.09.97 Slovakia v Spain
11.10.97 Malta v Yugoslavia
11.10.97 Czech Republic v Slovakia
11.10.97 Spain v Faroe Islands

Group 7: HOL/BEL/TUR/WAL/SMR
02.06.96 San Marino v Wales
31.08.96 Belgium v Turkey
31.08.96 Wales v San Marino
05.10.96 Wales v Netherlands
09.10.96 San Marino v Belgium
09.11.96 Netherlands v Wales
10.11.96 Turkey v San Marino
14.12.96 Belgium v Netherlands
29.03.97 Netherlands v San Marino
29.03.97 Wales v Belgium
02.04.97 Turkey v Netherlands
30.04.97 Turkey v Belgium
30.04.97 San Marino v Netherlands
07.06.97 Belgium v San Marino
20.08.97 Turkey v Wales
06.09.97 Netherlands v Belgium
10.09.97 San Marino v Turkey
11.10.97 Belgium v Wales
11.10.97 Netherlands v Turkey

Group 8: ROM/IRL/LTU/ISL/MKD/LIE
24.04.96 Macedonia v Liechtenstein
01.06.96 Iceland v Macedonia
31.08.96 Liechtenstein v Ireland Republic
31.08.96 Romania v Lithuania
05.10.96 Lithuania v Iceland
09.10.96 Iceland v Romania
09.10.96 Ireland Republic v Macedonia
09.10.96 Lithuania v Liechtenstein
09.11.96 Liechtenstein v Macedonia

10.11.96 Ireland Republic v Iceland
14.12.96 Macedonia v Romania
29.03.97 Romania v Liechtenstein
02.04.97 Lithuania v Romania
02.04.97 Macedonia v Ireland Republic
30.04.97 Liechtenstein v Lithuania
30.04.97 Romania v Ireland Republic
07.06.97 Ireland Republic v Liechtenstein
07.06.97 Macedonia v Iceland
11.06.97 Iceland v Lithuania
19.08.97 Liechtenstein v Iceland
20.08.97 Ireland Republic v Lithuania
20.08.97 Romania v Macedonia
06.09.97 Iceland v Ireland Republic
06.09.97 Liechtenstein v Romania
06.09.97 Lithuania v Macedonia
10.09.97 Romania v Iceland
10.09.97 Lithuania v Ireland Republic
11.10.97 Iceland v Liechtenstein
11.10.97 Ireland Republic v Romania
11.10.97 Macedonia v Lithuania

Group 9: GER/POR/NIR/UKR/ALB/ARM
31.08.96 Northern Ireland v Ukraine
31.08.96 Armenia v Portugal
05.10.96 Northern Ireland v Armenia
05.10.96 Ukraine v Portugal
09.10.96 Albania v Portugal
09.10.96 Armenia v Germany
09.11.96 Albania v Armenia
09.11.96 Germany v Northern Ireland
09.11.96 Portugal v Ukraine
14.12.96 Northern Ireland v Albania
14.12.96 Portugal v Germany
29.03.97 Albania v Ukraine
29.03.97 Northern Ireland v Portugal
02.04.97 Albania v Germany
02.04.97 Ukraine v Northern Ireland
30.04.97 Germany v Ukraine
30.04.97 Armenia v Northern Ireland
07.05.97 Ukraine v Armenia
07.06.97 Portugal v Albania
07.06.97 Ukraine v Germany
20.08.97 Northern Ireland v Germany
20.08.97 Portugal v Armenia
20.08.97 Ukraine v Albania
06.09.97 Germany v Portugal
06.09.97 Armenia v Albania
10.09.97 Albania v Northern Ireland
10.09.97 Germany v Armenia
11.10.97 Germany v Albania
11.10.97 Portugal v Northern Ireland
11.10.97 Armenia v Ukraine

QUALIFICATION FOR THE FINALS (WORLDWIDE)

EUROPE
Fourteen qualifiers plus France, who qualify
automatically as hosts

Group one: Denmark, Greece, Croatia, Slovenia, Bosnia.

Group two: Italy, England, Poland, Georgia, Moldavia.

Group three: Norway, Switzerland, Finland, Hungary, Azerbaijan.

Group four: Sweden, Scotland, Austria, Latvia, Belarus, Estonia.

Group five: Russia, Bulgaria, Israel, Cyprus, Luxembourg.

Group six: Spain, Czech Republic, Slovakia, Yugoslavia, Malta, Faroe Islands.

Group seven: Holland, Belgium, Turkey, Wales, San Marino.

Group eight: Romania, Ireland Republic, Lithuania, Iceland, Macedonia, Liechtenstein.

Group nine: Germany, Portugal, Northern Ireland, Ukraine, Albania, Amenia.

Nine group winners and the best runner-up (method to be determined) qualify for the finals. The other eight runners-up will be paired for play-offs with the winners qualifying.

SOUTH AMERICA

Four qualifiers plus Brazil, who qualify automatically as champions

Argentina, Bolivia, Chile, Colombia, Ecuador, Paraguay, Peru, Uruguay and Venezuela.

ASIA

Three qualifiers plus one to play-off with Oceania winner

First round

Group one: Saudi Arabia, Malaysia, Bangladesh, Taiwan

Group two: Iran, Syria, Maldive Islands, Kirghizistan.

Group three: United Arab Emirates, Bahrain, Jordan.

Group four: Japan, Oman, Nepal, Macao.

Group five: Uzbekistan, Indonesia, Yemen, Cambodia.

Group six: South Korea, Thailand, Hong Kong.

Group seven: Kuwait, Lebanon, Singapore.

Group eight: China, Turkmenistan, Vietnam, Tajikistan.

Group nine: Iraq, Kazakhstan, Pakistan.

Group ten: Qatar, India, Sri Lanka, Philippines.

Second round

Group winners drawn into two groups of five; top two in each group qualify for semi-finals.

Semi-finals

Winners qualify for 1998 finals; losers to play-off. Play-off winner qualifies, loser to play-off with Oceania winner.

OCEANIA

Winner to play-off with fourth Asian team for place in finals.

First round

Melanesian group: Papua New Guinea, Solomon Islands, Vanuatu.

Polynesian group: Cook Islands, Tonga, Western Samoa. Winner qualifies for second round with winner of play-off between Melanesian group runner-up and Polynesian group winner.

Second round

Group one: Australia, Tahiti, play-off winner.

Group two: New Zealand, Fiji, Melanesian group winner.

Third round

Winner group one v winner group two. Winner into play-off with fourth Asian team.

NORTH AND CENTRAL AMERICA

Three qualifiers

Caribbean zone

First round: Aruba v Dominican Republic; Bahamas v St Kitts and Nevis; Guyana v Grenada; Dominica v Antigua.

Second round: Bermuda v Trinidad and Tobago; Puerto Rico v St Vincent; Cayman Islands v Cuba; Bahamas or St Kitts and Nevis v St Lucia; Guyana or Grenada v Haiti; Surinam v Jamaica; Dominica or Antigua v Barbados; Aruba or Dominican Republic v Dutch Antilles.

Third round: Teams drawn into pairs with winners to semi-finals.

Central American zone

Nicaragua v Guatemala; Belize v Panama. Winners qualify for semi-finals.

Semi-finals

Group one: United States, Costa Rica plus two qualifiers.

Group two: Canada, El Salvador plus two qualifiers.

Group three: Mexico, Honduras plus two qualifiers. Top two in each group go to final phase; top three in final phase qualify for France.

AFRICA

Five qualifiers

First round: Sudan v Zambia; Namibia v Mozambique; Tanzania v Ghana; Swaziland v Gabon; Uganda v Angola; Mauritius v Zaire; Malawi v South Africa; Madagascar v Zimbabwe; Guinea-Bissau v Guinea; Rwanda v Tunisia; Congo v Ivory Coast; Kenya v Algeria; Burundi v Sierra Leone; Mauritania v Burkina Faso; Togo v Senegal; Gambia v Liberia.

Second round: First-round winners plus Cameroon, Nigeria, Egypt and Morocco drawn in five groups of four with group winners qualifying for France.

10 ● ENGLAND'S FULL INTERNATIONAL RECORD 1872–1996

(Up to and including 1st July 1996)

	HOME						AWAY					
	P	W	D	L	F	A	P	W	D	L	F	A
Albania	1	1	0	0	5	0	1	1	0	0	2	0
Argentina	5	3	2	0	10	6	5	1	2	2	5	5
Australia	–	–	–	–	–	–	5	3	2	0	5	2
Austria	5	3	1	1	18	9	10	5	2	3	36	16
Belgium	4	3	1	0	17	3	14	10	3	1	50	21
Bohemia	–	–	–	–	–	–	1	1	0	0	4	0
Brazil	8	2	4	2	10	10	10	1	3	6	6	15
Bulgaria	3	2	1	0	4	1	3	2	1	0	4	0
Cameroon	1	1	0	0	2	0	1	1	0	0	3	2
Canada	–	–	–	–	–	–	1	1	0	0	1	0
Chile	1	0	1	0	0	0	3	2	1	0	4	1
China	–	–	–	–	–	–	1	1	0	0	3	0
Colombia	2	0	2	0	1	1	1	1	0	0	4	0
Croatia	1	0	1	0	0	0	–	–	–	–	–	–
Cyprus	1	1	0	0	5	0	1	1	0	0	1	0
Czechoslovakia	5	4	1	0	13	6	7	3	2	2	12	9
Denmark	6	5	0	1	9	3	8	4	4	0	18	8
Ecuador	–	–	–	–	–	–	1	1	0	0	2	0
Egypt	–	–	–	–	–	–	2	2	0	0	5	0
FIFA	1	0	1	0	4	4	–	–	–	–	–	–
Finland	2	2	0	0	7	1	7	6	1	0	27	5
France	8	6	2	0	23	4	14	9	1	4	39	23
Germany, East	2	2	0	0	4	1	2	1	1	0	3	2
Germany (and West)	9	5	1	3	16	10	13	4	4	5	22	19
Greece	3	2	1	0	8	0	3	3	0	0	7	1
Holland	7	3	3	1	18	9	6	2	2	2	4	6
Hungary	8	7	0	1	21	9	11	6	1	4	29	18
Iceland	–	–	–	–	–	–	1	0	1	0	1	1
Ireland, Northern	49	40	6	3	169	36	47	34	10	3	150	44
Ireland, Republic of	6	3	2	1	11	6	7	2	4	1	8	6
Israel	–	–	–	–	–	–	2	1	1	0	2	1
Italy	6	3	2	1	9	5	11	3	3	5	16	17
Japan	1	1	0	0	2	1	–	–	–	–	–	–
Kuwait	–	–	–	–	–	–	1	1	0	0	1	0
Luxembourg	3	3	0	0	18	1	4	4	0	0	20	2
Malaysia	–	–	–	–	–	–	1	1	0	0	4	2
Malta	1	1	0	0	5	0	1	1	0	0	1	0
Mexico	2	2	0	0	10	0	4	1	1	2	4	3
Morocco	–	–	–	–	–	–	1	0	1	0	0	0
New Zealand	–	–	–	–	–	–	2	2	0	0	3	0
Nigeria	1	1	0	0	1	0	–	–	–	–	–	–
Norway	4	2	2	0	9	1	6	3	1	2	17	6
Paraguay	–	–	–	–	–	–	1	1	0	0	3	0
Peru	–	–	–	–	–	–	2	1	0	1	5	4
Poland	5	3	2	0	10	2	6	2	3	1	6	4
Portugal	7	5	2	0	13	5	9	3	4	2	23	13

	HOME						AWAY					
	P	*W*	*D*	*L*	*F*	*A*	*P*	*W*	*D*	*L*	*F*	*A*
Rest of Europe	1	1	0	0	3	0	–	–	–	–	–	–
Rest of the World	1	1	0	0	2	1	–	–	–	–	–	–
Romania	4	0	4	0	3	3	5	2	2	1	4	2
San Marino	1	1	0	0	6	0	1	1	0	0	7	1
Saudi Arabia	–	–	–	–	–	–	1	0	1	0	1	1
Scotland	54	26	11	17	117	87	54	18	13	23	73	81
Spain	7	5	1	1	19	6	11	5	2	4	16	14
Sweden	5	2	2	1	12	9	10	4	3	3	15	10
Switzerland	7	4	3	0	16	5	10	7	0	3	25	9
Tunisia	–	–	–	–	–	–	1	0	1	0	1	1
Turkey	4	4	0	0	18	0	4	3	1	0	11	0
USA	1	1	0	0	2	0	6	4	0	2	29	7
USSR (and CIS)	4	2	1	1	10	5	8	3	3	2	11	10
Uruguay	4	1	2	1	3	3	5	1	1	3	5	9
Wales	49	32	9	8	126	46	48	30	12	6	113	44
Yugoslavia	7	4	3	0	15	7	7	1	2	4	8	13
TOTAL	318	201	74	43	804	306	407	210	100	97	876	458

GRAND TOTAL

Played	*Won*	*Drawn*	*Lost*	*For*	Goals *Against*
725	411	174	140	1683	764

The England squad for the Croatia match in April.

11 ● ENGLAND'S GOALSCORERS 1946–1996

(Up to and including 1st July 1996)

49	Charlton, R	5	Anderton	2	Cowans
48	Lineker	5	Atyeo	2	Eastham
44	Greaves	5	Baily	2	Froggatt, J
30	Finney	5	Brooking	2	Froggatt, R
30	Lofthouse	5	Carter	2	Haines
27	Platt	5	Edwards	2	Hancocks
26	Robson, B	5	Hitchens	2	Hunter
24	Hurst	5	Latchford	2	Ince
23	Mortensen	5	Neal	2	Lee, S
21	Channon	5	Pearce	2	Moore
21	Keegan	5	Pearson, S C (Stan)	2	Perry
20	Peters	5	Pearson, J S (Stuart)	2	Pointer
18	Haynes	5	Pickering, F	2	Royle
18	Hunt, R	5	Wright, I	2	Smith, A
16	Lawton	4	Adams	2	Stone
16	Taylor, T	4	Barnes, P	2	Taylor, P
16	Woodcock	4	Bull	2	Tueart
13	Chivers	4	Dixon, K	2	Wignall
13	Mariner	4	Ferdinand	2	Worthington
13	Smith, R	4	Hassall	1	A'Court
12	Francis, T	4	Revie	1	Astall
11	Douglas	4	Robson, R	1	Beattie
11	Mannion	4	Sheringham	1	Bowles
11	Barnes, J	4	Steven	1	Bradford
10	Clarke, A	4	Watson, D	1	Bridges
10	Flowers, R	4	Webb	1	Chamberlain
10	Lee, F	3	Baker	1	Crawford
10	Milburn	3	Blissett	1	Dixon, L
10	Shearer	3	Butcher	1	Goddard
10	Wilshaw	3	Currie	1	Hirst
9	Beardsley	3	Elliott	1	Hughes, E
9	Bell	3	Francis, G	1	Kay
9	Bentley	3	Grainger	1	Keown
9	Hateley	3	Kennedy, R	1	Kidd
8	Ball	3	McDermott	1	Langton
8	Broadis	3	Matthews, S	1	Lawler
8	Byrne, J	3	Morris	1	Lee, J
8	Gascoigne	3	O'Grady	1	Lee, R
8	Hoddle	3	Peacock	1	Le Saux
8	Kevan	3	Ramsey	1	Mabbutt
7	Connelly	3	Sewell	1	Marsh
7	Coppell	3	Wilkins	1	Medley
7	Paine	3	Wright, W	1	Melia
6	Charlton, J	2	Allen, R	1	Merson
6	Johnson	2	Anderson	1	Mullery
6	Macdonald	2	Barmby	1	Nicholls
6	Mullen	2	Bradley	1	Nicholson
6	Rowley	2	Broadbent	1	Palmer
6	Waddle	2	Brooks	1	Parry

Paul Gascoigne (second from right) scores stylishly in Beijing's Workers' Stadium.

12 ● ENGLAND CAPS 1872–1996

(Up to and including 1st July 1996)

1	Abbott W (Everton)
5	A'Court A (Liverpool)
45	Adams T (Arsenal)
5	Adcock H (Leicester City)
1	Alcock C (Wanderers)
1	Alderson J (C Palace)
2	Aldridge A (WBA, Walsall Town Swifts)
3	Allen A (Stoke)
1	Allen A (Aston Villa)
5	Allen C (QPR, Spurs)
5	Allen H (Wolves)
2	Allen J (Portsmouth)
5	Allen R (WBA)
1	Alsford W (Spurs)
2	Amos A (Old Carthusians)
1	Anderson R (Old Etonians)
2	Anderson S (Sunderland)
30	Anderson V (Nottm Forest, Arsenal, Man Utd)
16	Anderton D (Spurs)
1	Angus J (Burnley)
43	Armfield J (Blackpool)
1	Armitage G (Charlton)
3	Armstrong D (Middlesbrough, Southampton)
1	Armstrong K (Chelsea)
1	Arnold J (Fulham)
7	Arthur J (Blackburn)
3	Ashcroft J (Woolwich Arsenal)
1	Ashmore G (WBA)
1	Ashton C (Corinthians)
5	Ashurst W (Notts County)
2	Astall G (Birmingham)
5	Astle J (WBA)
17	Aston J (Man Utd)
12	Athersmith W (Aston Villa)
6	Atyeo J (Bristol City)
1	Austin S (Man City)
1	Bach P (Sunderland)
7	Bache J (Aston Villa)
5	Baddeley T (Wolves)
1	Bagshaw J (Derby County)
2	Bailey G (Man Utd)
5	Bailey H (Leicester Fosse)
2	Bailey M (Charlton)
19	Bailey N (Clapham Rovers)
9	Baily E (Spurs)
1	Bain J (Oxford Univ)
1	Baker A (Arsenal)
2	Baker B (Everton, Chelsea)
8	Baker J (Hibernian, Arsenal)
72	Ball A (Blackpool, Everton, Arsenal)

1	Ball J (Bury)
1	Balmer W (Everton)
1	Bamber J (Liverpool)
3	Bambridge A (Swifts)
18	Bambridge E C (Swifts)
1	Bambridge E H (Swifts)
73	Banks G (Leicester, Stoke)
1	Banks H (Millwall)
6	Banks T (Bolton)
2	Bannister W (Burnley, Bolton)
3	Barclay R (Sheff Wed)
2	Bardsley D (QPR)
2	Barham M (Norwich City)
5	Barkas S (Man City)
11	Barker J (Derby County)
1	Barker R (Herts Rangers)
1	Barker R R (Casuals)
1	Barlow R (WBA)
9	Barmby N (Spurs, Middlesbrough)
79	Barnes J (Watford, Liverpool)
22	Barnes P (Man City, WBA, Leeds Utd)
1	Barnet H (Royal Engineers)
3	Barrass M (Bolton)
1	Barrett A (Fulham)
3	Barrett E (Oldham, Aston Villa)
1	Barrett J (West Ham Utd)
5	Barry L (Leicester City)
1	Barson F (Aston Villa)
1	Barton J (Blackburn)
7	Barton P (Birmingham)
3	Barton W (Wimbledon, Newcastle)
16	Bassett W (WBA)
1	Bastard S (Upton Park)
21	Bastin C (Arsenal)
17	Batty D (Leeds Utd, Blackburn)
2	Baugh R (Stafford Road, Wolves)
1	Bayliss A (WBA)
3	Baynham R (Luton)
59	Beardsley P (Newcastle, Liverpool)
2	Beasant D (Chelsea)
1	Beasley A (Huddersfleld)
2	Beats W (Wolves)
9	Beattie K (Ipswich)
2	Becton F (Preston, Liverpool)
2	Bedford H (Blackpool)
48	Bell C (Man City)
2	Bennett W (Sheff Utd)
1	Benson R (Sheff Utd)
12	Bentley R (Chelsea)
1	Beresford J (Aston Villa)
1	Berry A (Oxford Univ)
4	Berry J (Man Utd)

1 Bestall J (Grimsby)	2 Brown A S (Sheff Utd)
1 Betmead H (Grimsby)	9 Brown G (Huddersfield, Aston Villa)
1 Betts M (Old Harrovians)	5 Brown J (Blackburn)
1 Betts W (Sheff Wed)	6 Brown J H (Sheff Wed)
3 Beverley J (Blackburn)	1 Brown K (West Ham)
1 Birkett R H (Clapham Rovers)	1 Brown T (WBA)
1 Birkett R (Middlesbrough)	1 Brown W (West Ham)
2 Birley F (Oxford Univ, Wanderers)	3 Bruton J (Burnley)
3 Birtles G (Nottm Forest)	1 Bryant W (Clapton)
4 Bishop S (Leicester City)	6 Buchan C (Sunderland)
3 Blackburn F (Blackburn)	1 Buchanan W (Clapham Rovers)
1 Blackburn G (Aston Villa)	1 Buckley F C (Derby County)
26 Blenkinsop E (Sheff Wed)	13 Bull S (Wolves)
1 Bliss H (Spurs)	1 Bullock F E (Huddersfield)
14 Blissett L (Watford)	3 Bullock N (Bury)
1 Blockley J (Arsenal)	4 Burgess H (Man City)
23 Bloomer S (Derby County, Middlesbrough)	4 Burgess H (Sheff Wed)
5 Blunstone F (Chelsea)	1 Burnup C (Cambridge Univ)
8 Bond R (Preston, Bradford City)	3 Burrows H (Sheff Wed)
7 Bonetti P (Chelsea)	1 Burton F E (Nottm Forest)
2 Bonsor A (Wanderers)	2 Bury L (Cambridge Univ, Old Etonians)
1 Booth F (Man City)	77 Butcher T (Ipswich, Rangers)
2 Booth T (Blackburn, Everton)	1 Butler J (Arsenal)
2 Bould S (Arsenal)	1 Butler W (Bolton)
6 Bowden E (Arsenal)	2 Byrne G (Liverpool)
5 Bower A (Corinthians)	11 Byrne J J (C Palace, West Ham)
3 Bowers J (Derby County)	33 Byrne R (Man Utd)
5 Bowles S (QPR)	
1 Bowser S (WBA)	4 Callaghan I (Liverpool)
1 Boyer P (Norwich)	1 Calvey J (Nottm Forest)
3 Boyes W (WBA, Everton)	8 Campbell A (Blackburn, Huddersfield)
1 Boyle T (Burnley)	2 Campbell S (Spurs)
3 Brabrook P (Chelsea)	9 Camsell, G (Middlesbrough)
3 Bracewell P (Everton)	1 Capes A (Stoke)
1 Bradford G (Bristol Rovers)	2 Carr J (Middlesbrough)
12 Bradford J (Birmingham)	2 Carr J (Newcastle)
3 Bradley W (Man Utd)	1 Carr W H (Owlerton)
1 Bradshaw F (Sheff Wed)	13 Carter H S (Sunderland, Derby County)
1 Bradshaw T (Liverpool)	3 Carter J H (WBA)
4 Bradshaw W (Blackburn)	5 Catlin A E (Sheff Wed)
3 Brann G (Swifts)	2 Chadwick A (Southampton)
2 Brawn W (Aston Villa)	7 Chadwick E (Everton)
6 Bray J (Man City)	8 Chamberlain M (Stoke)
1 Brayshaw E (Sheff Wed)	8 Chambers H (Liverpool)
4 Bridges B (Chelsea)	46 Channon M (Southampton, Man City)
11 Bridgett A (Sunderland)	2 Charles G (Nottm Forest)
2 Brindle T (Darwen)	35 Charlton J (Leeds Utd)
5 Brittleton J (Sheff Wed)	106 Charlton R (Man Utd)
9 Britton C (Everton)	1 Charnley R (Blackpool)
7 Broadbent P (Wolves)	1 Charnsley C (Small Heath)
14 Broadis I (Man City, Newcastle)	8 Chedgzoy S (Everton)
1 Brockbank J (Cambridge Univ)	3 Chenery C (C Palace)
3 Brodie J B (Wolves)	27 Cherry T (Leeds Utd)
5 Bromilow T G (Liverpool)	2 Chilton A (Man Utd)
2 Bromley-Davenport W E (Oxford Univ)	1 Chippendale H (Blackburn)
18 Brook E (Man City)	24 Chivers M (Spurs)
47 Brooking T (West Ham)	1 Christian E (Old Etonians)
3 Brooks J (Spurs)	4 Clamp E (Wolves)
7 Broome F H (Aston Villa)	1 Clapton D (Arsenal)
3 Brown A (Aston Villa)	4 Clare T (Stoke)

19 Clarke A (Leeds Utd)
1 Clarke H (Spurs)
4 Clay T (Spurs)
35 Clayton R (Blackburn)
1 Clegg J (Sheff Wed)
2 Clegg W (Sheff Wed, Sheff Albion)
61 Clemence R (Liverpool, Spurs)
5 Clement D (QPR)
2 Clough B (Middlesbrough)
14 Clough N (Nottm Forest)
4 Coates R (Burnley, Spurs)
9 Cobbold W (Cambridge Univ,
   Old Carthusians)
2 Cock J (Huddersfield, Chelsea)
13 Cockburn H (Man Utd)
37 Cohen G (Fulham)
1 Colclough H (C Palace)
1 Cole A (Man Utd)
1 Coleman E (Dulwich Hamlet)
1 Coleman J (Woolwich Arsenal)
2 Collymore S (Nottm Forest)
3 Common A (Sheff Utd, Middlesbrough)
2 Compton L H (Arsenal)
1 Conlin J (Bradford City)
20 Connelly J (Burnley, Man Utd)
1 Cook T E (Brighton)
2 Cooper C (Nottm Forest)
1 Cooper N C (Cambridge Univ)
15 Cooper T (Derby County)
20 Cooper T (Leeds Utd)
42 Coppell S (Man Utd)
20 Copping W (Leeds Utd, Arsenal)
1 Corbett B (Corinthians)
1 Corbett R (Old Malvernians)
3 Corbett W (Birmingham)
9 Corrigan J (Manchester C.)
7 Cottee A (West Ham, Everton)
4 Cotterill G (Cambridge Univ,
   Old Brightonians)
1 Cottle J (Bristol City)
3 Cowan S (Man City)
10 Cowans G (Aston Villa, Bari)
1 Cowell A (Blackburn)
3 Cox J (Liverpool)
1 Cox J D (Derby County)
14 Crabtree J (Burnley, Aston Villa)
1 Crawford J F (Chelsea)
2 Crawford R (Ipswich)
10 Crawshaw T (Sheff Wed)
8 Crayston W (Arsenal)
1 Creek N (Corinthians)
7 Cresswell W (South Shields,
   Sunderland, Everton)
41 Crompton R (Blackburn)
26 Crooks S (Derby County)
1 Crowe C (Wolves)
2 Cuggy F (Sunderland)
12 Cullis S (Wolves)
2 Cunliffe A (Blackburn)
1 Cunliffe D (Portsmouth)

1 Cunliffe J (Everton)
6 Cunningham L (WBA, Real Madrid)
3 Curle K (Man City)
2 Currey E (Oxford Univ)
17 Currie A (Sheff Utd, Leeds Utd)
6 Cursham A (Notts County)
8 Cursham H (Notts County)

5 Daft H (Notts County)
7 Daley A (Aston Villa)
1 Danks T (Nottm Forest)
2 Davenport J (Bolton)
1 Davenport P (Nottm Forest)
2 Davis G (Derby County)
3 Davis H (Sheff Wed)
1 Davison J (Sheff Wed)
2 Dawson J (Burnley)
3 Day S (Old Malvernians)
16 Dean W (Everton)
3 Deane B (Sheffield Utd)
2 Deeley N (Wolves)
2 Devey J (Aston Villa)
8 Devonshire A (West Ham)
9 Dewhurst F (Preston)
1 Dewhurst G (Liverpool Ramblers)
48 Dickinson J (Portsmouth)
3 Dimmock J (Spurs)
6 Ditchburn E (Spurs)
1 Dix R (Derby County)
1 Dixon J (Notts County)
8 Dixon K (Chelsea)
21 Dixon L (Arsenal)
4 Dobson A (Notts County)
1 Dobson C (Notts County)
5 Dobson M (Burnley, Everton)
1 Doggart A (Corinthians)
15 Dorigo T (Chelsea, Leeds Utd)
4 Dorrell A (Aston Villa)
36 Douglas B (Blackburn)
1 Downs R (Everton)
5 Doyle M (Manchester C.)
5 Drake E (Arsenal)
6 Ducat A (Woolwich Arsenal, Aston Villa)
4 Dunn A T (Cambridge Univ, Old Etonians)
1 Duxbury M (Man Utd)

2 Earle S (Clapton, West Ham)
19 Eastham G (Arsenal)
1 Eastham G R (Bolton)
17 Eckersley W (Blackburn)
18 Edwards D (Man Utd)
1 Edwards J (Shropshire Wanderers)
16 Edwards W (Leeds Utd)
1 Ehiogu U (Aston Villa)
2 Ellerington W (Southampton)
3 Elliott G (Middlesbrough)
5 Elliott W (Burnley)
4 Evans R (Sheff Utd)
2 Ewer F (Casuals)
1 Fairclough P (Old Foresters)

1	Fairhurst D (Newcastle)
1	Fantham J (Sheff Wed)
2	Fashanu J (Wimbledon)
1	Felton W (Sheff Wed)
1	Fenton M (Middlesbrough)
20	Fenwick T (QPR, Spurs)
10	Ferdinand L (QPR, Newcastle)
2	Field E (Clapham Rovers)
76	Finney T (Preston)
11	Fleming H (Swindon)
2	Fletcher A (Wolves)
49	Flowers R (Wolves)
8	Flowers T (Southampton, Blackburn)
9	Forman F (Nottm Forest)
3	Forman F R (Nottm Forest)
11	Forrest J (Blackburn)
1	Fort J (Millwall)
5	Foster R (Oxford Univ, Corinthians)
3	Foster S (Brighton & Hove Albion)
1	Foulke W (Sheff Utd)
1	Foulkes W (Man Utd)
5	Fowler, R (Liverpool)
1	Fox F (Gillingham)
12	Francis G (QPR)
52	Francis T (Birmingham, Nottm Forest, Man City, Sampdoria)
27	Franklin C (Stoke)
5	Freeman B (Everton, Burnley)
13	Froggatt J (Portsmouth)
4	Froggatt R (Sheff Wed)
1	Fry C (Corinthians)
1	Furness W (Leeds Utd)
2	Galley T (Wolves)
2	Gardner T (Aston Villa)
1	Garfield B (WBA)
1	Garratty W (Aston Villa)
3	Garrett T (Blackpool)
43	Gascoigne P (Spurs, Lazio, Rangers)
2	Gates E (Ipswich)
3	Gay L (Cambridge Univ, Old Brightonians)
2	Geary F (Everton)
1	Geaves R (Clapham Rovers)
3	Gee C (Everton)
4	Geldard A (Everton)
1	George C (Derby County)
3	George W (Aston Villa)
2	Gibbins W (Clapton)
1	Gidman J (Aston Villa)
3	Gillard I (QPR)
1	Gilliat W (Old Carthusians)
1	Goddard P (West Ham)
25	Goodall F (Huddersfield)
14	Goodall J (Preston, Derby County)
3	Goodhart H (Old Etonians)
1	Goodwyn A (Royal Engineers)
1	Goodyer A (Nottm Forest)
5	Gosling R (Old Etonians)
1	Gosnell A (Newcastle)
1	Gough H (Sheff Utd)

14	Goulden L (West Ham)
2	Graham L (Millwall)
2	Graham T (Nottm Forest)
7	Grainger C (Sheff Utd, Sunderland)
1	Gray A (Crystal Palace)
57	Greaves J (Chelsea, Spurs)
8	Green G (Sheff Utd)
1	Green T (Wanderers)
2	Greenhalgh E (Notts County)
18	Greenhoff B (Man Utd, Leeds Utd)
2	Greenwood D (Blackburn)
6	Gregory J (QPR)
6	Grimsdell A (Spurs)
3	Grosvenor A (Birmingham)
2	Gunn W (Notts County)
1	Gurney R (Sunderland)
3	Hacking J (Oldham)
1	Hadley N (WBA)
1	Hagan J (Sheffield U.)
1	Haines J (WBA)
1	Hall A (Aston Villa)
10	Hall G (Spurs)
17	Hall J (Birmingham)
1	Halse H (Man Utd)
1	Hammond H (Oxford Univ)
3	Hampson J (Blackpool)
4	Hampton H (Aston Villa)
3	Hancocks J (Wolves)
30	Hapgood E (Arsenal)
1	Hardinge H (Sheff Utd)
4	Hardman H (Everton)
13	Hardwick G (Middlesbrough)
1	Hardy H (Stockport County)
21	Hardy S (Liverpool, Aston Villa)
2	Harford M (Luton Town)
3	Hargreaves F (Blackburn)
2	Hargreaves J (Blackburn)
1	Harper E (Blackburn)
1	Harris G (Burnley)
2	Harris P (Portsmouth)
6	Harris S (Cambridge Univ, Old Westminsters)
2	Harrison A (Old Westminsters)
2	Harrison G (Everton)
2	Harrow J (Chelsea)
8	Hart E (Leeds Utd)
1	Hartley F (Oxford City)
1	Harvey A (Wednesbury Strollers)
1	Harvey C (Everton)
5	Hassall H (Huddersfield, Bolton)
32	Hateley M (Portsmouth, AC Milan, Monaco, Rangers)
5	Hawkes R (Luton)
5	Haworth G (Accrington)
2	Hawtrey J (Old Etonians)
1	Haygarth E (Swifts)
56	Haynes J (Fulham)
2	Healless H (Blackburn)
2	Hector K (Derby County)

1 Hedley G (Sheff Utd)
4 Hegan K (Corinthians)
2 Hellawell M (Birmingham)
5 Henfrey A (Cambridge Univ, Corinthians)
1 Henry R (Spurs)
1 Heron F (Wanderers)
5 Heron G (Uxbridge, Wanderers)
1 Hibbert W (Bury)
25 Hibbs H (Birmingham)
2 Hill F (Bolton)
6 Hill G (Man Utd)
11 Hill J (Burnley)
3 Hill R (Luton)
1 Hill R H (Millwall)
1 Hillman J (Burnley)
1 Hills A (Old Harrovians)
8 Hilsdon G (Chelsea)
6 Hine E (Leicester City)
3 Hinton A (Wolves, Nottm Forest)
3 Hirst D (Sheff Wed)
7 Hitchens G (Aston Villa, Inter-Milan)
2 Hobbis H (Charlton)
53 Hoddle G (Spurs, Monaco)
24 Hodge S (Aston Villa, Spurs, Nottm Forest)
6 Hodgetts D (Aston Villa)
5 Hodgkinson A (Sheffield U)
3 Hodgson G (Liverpool)
3 Hodkinson J (Blackburn)
3 Hogg W (Sunderland)
2 Holdcroft G (Preston)
5 Holden A (Bolton)
4 Holden G (Wednesbury OA)
2 Holden-White C (Corinthians)
1 Holford T (Stoke)
10 Holley G (Sunderland)
3 Holliday E (Middlesbrough)
1 Hollins J (Chelsea)
7 Holmes R (Preston)
10 Holt J (Everton, Reading)
14 Hopkinson E (Bolton)
2 Hossack A (Corinthians)
7 Houghton W (Aston Villa)
5 Houlker A (Blackburn, Portsmouth,
   Southampton)
5 Howarth R (Preston, Everton)
23 Howe D (WBA)
3 Howe J (Derby)
1 Howell L (Wanderers)
2 Howell R (Sheff Utd, Liverpool)
4 Howey S (Newcastle)
2 Hudson A (Stoke)
1 Hudson J (Sheffield)
1 Hudspeth F (Newcastle)
6 Hufton A (West Ham)
62 Hughes E (Liverpool, Wolves)
3 Hughes L (Liverpool)
9 Hulme J (Arsenal)
1 Humphreys P (Notts County)
3 Hunt G (Spurs)
2 Hunt Rev. K (Leyton)

34 Hunt R (Liverpool)
2 Hunt S (WBA)
7 Hunter J (Sheff Heeley)
28 Hunter N (Leeds Utd)
49 Hurst G (West Ham)

23 Ince P (Man Utd, Inter Milan)
2 Iremonger J (Nottm Forest)

9 Jack D (Bolton, Arsenal)
1 Jackson E (Oxford Univ)
3 Jarrett B (Cambridge Univ)
2 Jefferis F (Everton)
2 Jezzard B (Fulham)
8 Johnson D (Ipswich, Liverpool)
2 Johnson E (Saltley Coll, Stoke)
5 Johnson J (Stoke)
5 Johnson T (Man City, Everton)
6 Johnson W (Sheff Utd)
10 Johnston H (Blackpool)
3 Jones A (Walsall Swifts, Great Lever)
6 Jones H (Blackburn)
1 Jones H (Nottm Forrest)
3 Jones M (Sheffield U, Leeds Utd)
8 Jones R (Liverpool)
1 Jones W (Bristol City)
2 Jones W (Liverpool)
1 Joy B (Casuals)

3 Kail E (Dulwich Hamlet)
1 Kay T (Everton)
9 Kean F (Sheff Wed, Bolton)
63 Keegan K (Liverpool, SV Hamburg,
   Southampton)
4 Keen E (Derby County)
14 Kelly R (Burnley, Sunderland, Huddersfield)
2 Kennedy A (Liverpool)
17 Kennedy R (Liverpool)
1 Kenyon-Slaney W (Wanderers)
11 Keown M (Everton, Arsenal)
14 Kevan D (WBA)
2 Kidd B (Man Utd)
1 King R (Oxford Univ)
1 Kingsford R (Wanderers)
1 Kingsley M (Newcastle)
4 Kinsey G (Wolves, Derby County)
3 Kirchen A (Arsenal)
1 Kirton W (Aston Villa)
1 Knight A (Portsmouth)
4 Knowles C (Spurs)

26 Labone B (Everton)
2 Lampard F (West Ham)
3 Langley J (Fulham)
11 Langton R (Blackburn, Preston, Bolton)
12 Latchford R (Everton)
2 Latheron E (Blackburn)
4 Lawler C (Liverpool)
23 Lawton T (Everton, Chelsea, Notts County)
2 Leach T (Sheff Wed)

5 Leake A (Aston Villa)
1 Lee E (Southampton)
27 Lee F (Manchester C.)
1 Lee J (Derby)
7 Lee R (Newcastle)
14 Lee S (Liverpool)
1 Leighton J (Nottm Forest)
12 Le Saux G (Blackburn)
6 Le Tissier M (Southampton)
1 Lilley H (Sheff Utd)
2 Linacre H (Nottm Forest)
13 Lindley T (Cambridge Univ, Nottm Forest)
4 Lindsay A (Liverpool)
1 Lindsay W (Wanderers)
80 Lineker G (Leicester, Everton,
   Barcelona, Spurs)
7 Lintott E (QPR, Bradford City)
1 Lipsham H (Sheff Utd)
1 Little B (Aston Villa)
4 Lloyd L (Liverpool, Nottm Forest)
1 Lockett A (Stoke)
5 Lodge L (Cambridge Univ, Corinthians)
7 Lofthouse J (Blackburn, Accrington)
33 Lofthouse N (Bolton)
5 Longworth E (Liverpool)
1 Lowder A (Wolves)
3 Lowe E (Aston Villa)
3 Lucas T (Liverpool)
2 Luntley E (Nottm Forest)
1 Lyttelton Hon A (Cambridge Univ)
1 Lyttelton Hon E (Cambridge Univ)

16 Mabbutt G (Spurs)
1 Macauley R (Cambridge Univ)
14 Macdonald M (Newcastle)
6 Macrae S (Notts County)
5 McCall J (Preston)
25 McDermott T (Liverpool)
8 McDonald C (Burnley)
28 McFarland R (Derby County)
4 McGarry W (Huddersfield)
2 McGuinness W (Man Utd)
1 McInroy A (Sunderland)
17 McMahon S (Liverpool)
15 McManaman S (Liverpool)
4 McNab R (Arsenal)
2 McNeal R (WBA)
9 McNeil M (Middlesbrough)
1 Maddison F (Oxford Univ)
24 Madeley P (Leeds Utd)
5 Magee T (WBA)
4 Makepeace H (Everton)
19 Male G (Arsenal)
26 Mannion W (Middlesbrough)
35 Mariner P (Ipswich, Arsenal)
1 Marsden J (Darwen)
3 Marsden W (Sheff Wed)
9 Marsh R (QPR, Manchester C)
2 Marshall T (Darwen)
17 Martin A (West Ham)

1 Martin H (Sunderland)
3 Martyn N (Crystal Palace)
1 Marwood B (Arsenal)
1 Maskrey H (Derby County)
3 Mason C (Wolves)
5 Matthews R (Coventry)
54 Matthews S (Stoke, Blackpool)
2 Matthews V (Sheff Utd)
2 Maynard W (1st Surrey Rifles)
1 Meadows J (Man City)
6 Medley L (Spurs)
1 Meehan T (Chelsea)
2 Melia J (Liverpool)
2 Mercer D (Sheff Utd)
5 Mercer J (Everton)
23 Merrick G (Birmingham)
14 Merson P (Arsenal)
2 Metcalfe V (Huddersfield)
1 Mew J (Man Utd)
1 Middleditch B (Corinthians)
13 Milburn J (Newcastle)
1 Milier B (Burnley)
1 Miller H (Charlton)
3 Mills G (Chelsea)
42 Mills M (Ipswich)
14 Milne G (Liverpool)
1 Milton A (Arsenal)
4 Milward A (Everton)
5 Mitchell C (Upton Park)
1 Mitchell J (Man City)
1 Moffat H (Oldham)
4 Molyneux G (Southampton)
7 Moon W (Old Westminsters)
2 Moore H (Notts County)
1 Moore J (Derby County)
108 Moore R (West Ham)
1 Moore W (West Ham)
2 Mordue J (Sunderland)
1 Morice C (Barnes)
6 Morley A (Aston Villa)
1 Morley H (Notts County)
1 Morren T (Sheff Utd)
2 Morris F (WBA)
3 Morris J (Derby)
3 Morris W (Wolves)
1 Morse H (Notts County)
3 Mort T (Aston Villa)
1 Morten A (C Palace)
25 Mortensen S (Blackpool)
1 Morton J (West Ham)
9 Mosforth W (Sheff Wed, Sheff Albion)
4 Moss F (Arsenal)
5 Moss F (Aston Villa)
2 Mosscrop E (Burnley)
3 Mozley B (Derby)
12 Mullen J (Wolves)
35 Mullery A (Spurs)

50 Neal P (Liverpool)
16 Needham E (Sheff Utd)

14 Neville G (Man Utd)
1 Neville P (Man Utd)
27 Newton K (Blackburn, Everton)
2 Nicholls J (WBA)
1 Nicholson W (Spurs)
5 Nish D (Derby)
23 Norman M (Spurs)
3 Nuttall H (Bolton)

16 Oakley W (Oxford Univ, Corinthians)
3 O'Dowd J (Chelsea)
2 O'Grady M (Huddersfield, Leeds Utd)
1 Ogilvie R (Clapham Rovers)
1 Oliver L (Fulham)
2 Olney B (Aston Villa)
4 Osborne F (Fulham, Spurs)
1 Osborne R (Leicester City)
4 Osgood P (Chelsea)
11 Osman R (Ipswich)
2 Ottaway C (Oxford Univ)
1 Owen J (Sheffield)
3 Owen S (Luton)

7 Page L (Burnley)
19 Paine T (Southampton)
20 Pallister G (Middlesbrough, Man Utd)
18 Palmer C (Sheff Wed)
1 Pantling H (Sheff Utd)
3 Paravacini P J de (Cambridge Univ)
19 Parker P (QPR, Man Utd)
1 Parker T (Southampton)
1 Parkes P (QPR)
2 Parkinson J (Liverpool)
1 Parr P (Oxford Univ)
3 Parry E (Old Carthusians)
2 Parry R (Bolton)
2 Patchitt B (Corinthians)
2 Pawson F (Cambridge Univ, Swifts)
1 Payne J (Luton)
6 Peacock A (Middlesbrough, Leeds Utd)
3 Peacock J (Middlesbrough)
70 Pearce S (Nottm Forest)
1 Pearson H (WBA)
1 Pearson J H (Crewe)
15 Pearson J S (Stuart) (Man Utd)
8 Pearson S C (Stan) (Man Utd)
1 Pease W (Middlesbrough)
1 Pegg D (Man Utd)
4 Pejic M (Stoke)
3 Pelly F (Old Foresters)
25 Pennington J (WBA)
5 Pentland F (Middlesbrough)
3 Perry C (WBA)
1 Perry T (WBA)
3 Perry W (Blackpool)
1 Perryman S (Spurs)
67 Peters M (West Ham, Spurs)
1 Phelan M (Man Utd)
3 Phillips L (Portsmouth)
3 Pickering F (Everton)

1 Pickering J (Sheff Utd)
1 Pickering N (Sunderland)
1 Pike T (Cambridge Univ)
1 Pilkington B (Burnley)
1 Plant J (Bury)
62 Platt D (Aston Villa, Bari, Juventus, Sampdoria, Arsenal)
1 Plum S (Charlton)
3 Pointer R (Burnley)
1 Porteous T (Sunderland)
1 Priest A (Sheff Utd)
1 Prinsep J (Clapham Rovers)
2 Puddefoot S (Blackburn)
1 Pye J (Wolves)
3 Pym R (Bolton)

4 Quantrill A (Derby County)
5 Quixall A (Sheffield W.)

2 Radford J (Arsenal)
4 Raikes G (Oxford Univ)
32 Ramsey A (Southampton, Spurs)
1 Rawlings A (Preston)
2 Rawlings W (Southampton)
1 Rawlinson J (Cambridge Univ)
1 Rawson H (Royal Engineers)
2 Rawson W (Oxford Univ)
1 Read A (Tufnell Park)
1 Reader J (WBA)
3 Reaney P (Leeds Utd)
5 Redknapp J (Liverpool)
2 Reeves K (Norwich, Man City)
5 Regis C (WBA, Coventry)
13 Reid P (Everton)
6 Revie D (Manchester C.)
8 Reynolds J (WBA, Aston Villa)
1 Richards C (Nottm Forest)
1 Richards G (Derby County)
1 Richards J (Wolves)
2 Richardson J (Newcastle)
1 Richardson K (Aston Villa)
1 Richardson W (WBA)
1 Rickaby S (WBA)
5 Rigby A (Blackburn)
4 Rimmer E (Sheff Wed)
1 Rimmer J (Arsenal)
1 Ripley S (Blackburn)
17 Rix G (Arsenal)
1 Robb G (Spurs)
3 Roberts C (Man Utd)
4 Roberts F (Man City)
6 Roberts G (Spurs)
1 Roberts H (Arsenal)
1 Roberts H (Millwall)
3 Roberts R (WBA)
2 Roberts W (Preston)
4 Robinson J (Sheff Wed)
11 Robinson J W (Derby County, New Brighton Tower, Southampton)
90 Robson B (WBA, Man Utd)

20	Robson R (WBA)
14	Rocastle D (Arsenal)
5	Rose W (Wolves, Preston)
2	Rostron T (Darwen)
1	Rowe A (Spurs)
6	Rowley J (Man Utd)
2	Rowley W (Stoke)
6	Royle J (Everton, Manchester C)
3	Ruddlesdin H (Sheff Wed)
1	Ruddock N (Liverpool)
6	Ruffell J (West Ham)
1	Russell B (Royal Engineers)
11	Rutherford J (Newcastle)

4	Sadler D (Man Utd)
2	Sagar C (Bury)
4	Sagar E (Everton)
5	Salako J (Crystal Palace)
1	Sandford E (WBA)
5	Sandilands R (Old Westminsters)
1	Sands J (Nottm Forest)
86	Sansom K (C Palace, Arsenal)
1	Saunders F (Swifts)
1	Savage A (C Palace)
1	Sayer J (Stoke)
3	Scales J (Liverpool)
1	Scattergood E (Derby County)
3	Schofield J (Stoke)
17	Scott L (Arsenal)
1	Scott W (Brentford)
29	Seaman D (QPR, Arsenal)
6	Seddon J (Bolton)
5	Seed J (Spurs)
5	Settle J (Bury, Everton)
6	Sewell J (Sheffield W.)
1	Sewell W (Blackburn)
5	Shackleton L (Sunderland)
2	Sharp J (Everton)
8	Sharpe L (Man Utd)
1	Shaw G E (WBA)
5	Shaw G L (Sheff Utd)
2	Shea D (Blackburn)
28	Shearer A (Southampton, Blackburn)
1	Shellito K (Chelsea)
6	Shelton A (Notts County)
1	Shelton C (Notts Rangers)
2	Shepherd A (Bolton, Newcastle)
20	Sheringham T (Spurs)
125	Shilton P (Leicester, Stoke, Nottm Forest, Southampton, Derby County)
1	Shimwell E (Blackpool)
1	Shutt G (Stoke)
3	Silcock J (Man Utd)
3	Sillett P (Chelsea)
1	Simms E (Luton)
8	Simpson J (Blackburn)
12	Sinton A (QPR)
12	Slater W (Wolves)
1	Smalley T (Wolves)
5	Smart T (Aston Villa)

3	Smith A (Nottm Forest)
1	Smith A K (Oxford Univ)
13	Smith A M (Arsenal)
2	Smith B (Spurs)
1	Smith C E (C Palace)
20	Smith G O (Oxford Univ, Old Carthusians, Corinthians)
4	Smith H (Reading)
2	Smith J (WBA)
5	Smith Joe (Bolton)
2	Smith J C R (Millwall)
3	Smith J W (Portsmouth)
1	Smith Leslie (Brentford)
6	Smith Lionel (Arsenal)
15	Smith R A (Spurs)
1	Smith S (Aston Villa)
1	Smith S C (Leicester City)
2	Smith T (Birmingham)
1	Smith T (Liverpool)
3	Smith W H (Huddersfield)
1	Sorby T (Thursday Wanderers)
9	Southgate G (Aston Villa)
3	Southworth J (Blackburn)
3	Sparks F (Herts Rangers, Clapham Rovers)
2	Spence J (Man Utd)
2	Spence R (Chelsea)
2	Spencer C (Newcastle)
6	Spencer H (Aston Villa)
7	Spiksley F (Sheff Wed)
3	Spilsbury B (Cambridge Univ)
1	Spink N (Aston Villa)
1	Spouncer W (Nottm Forest)
33	Springett R (Sheffield W.)
11	Sproston B (Leeds Utd, Spurs, Man City)
3	Squire R (Cambridge Univ)
1	Stanbrough M (Old Carthusians)
8	Staniforth R (Huddersfield)
2	Starling R (Sheff Wed, Aston Villa)
3	Statham D (WBA)
6	Steele F (Stoke)
1	Stein B (Luton)
1	Stephenson C (Huddersfield)
3	Stephenson G (Derby County, Sheff Wed)
2	Stephenson J (Leeds Utd)
1	Stepney A (Man Utd)
1	Sterland M (Sheffield Wed)
36	Steven T (Everton, Rangers, Marseille)
7	Stevens G A (Spurs)
46	Stevens G (Everton, Rangers)
3	Stewart J (Sheff Wed, Newcastle)
3	Stewart P (Spurs)
28	Stiles N (Man Utd)
3	Stoker J (Birmingham)
9	Stone S (Nottm Forest)
2	Storer H (Derby County)
19	Storey P (Arsenal)
1	Storey-Moore I (Nottm Forest)
20	Strange A (Sheff Wed)
1	Stratford A (Wanderers)
1	Streten B (Luton)

2	Sturgess A (Sheff Utd)	
8	Summerbee M (Man City)	
1	Sunderland A (Arsenal)	
5	Sutcliffe J (Bolton, Millwall)	
19	Swan P (Sheffield Wed)	
6	Swepstone H (Pilgrims)	
19	Swift F (Manchester C)	
1	Tait G (Birmingham Excelsior)	
6	Talbot B (Ipswich, Arsenal)	
3	Tambling R (Chelsea)	
3	Tate J (Aston Villa)	
1	Taylor E (Blackpool)	
8	Taylor E H (Huddersfield)	
2	Taylor J (Fulham)	
3	Taylor P H (Liverpool)	
4	Taylor P J (C Palace)	
19	Taylor T (Man Utd)	
1	Temple D (Everton)	
2	Thickett H (Sheff Utd)	
2	Thomas D (Coventry)	
8	Thomas D (QPR)	
9	Thomas G (Crystal Palace)	
2	Thomas M (Arsenal)	
16	Thompson P (Peter) (Liverpool)	
42	Thompson P (Phil) (Liverpool)	
2	Thompson T (Aston Villa, Preston)	
8	Thomson R (Wolves)	
4	Thornewell G (Derby County)	
1	Thornley I (Man City)	
4	Tilson S (Man City)	
2	Titmuss F (Southampton)	
27	Todd C (Derby)	
2	Toone G (Notts County)	
1	Topham A (Casuals)	
2	Topham R (Wolves, Casuals)	
3	Towers A (Sunderland)	
2	Townley W (Blackburn)	
2	Townrow J (Clapton Orient)	
1	Tremelling D (Birmingham)	
2	Tresadern J (West Ham)	
6	Tueart D (Man City)	
7	Tunstall F (Sheff Utd)	
1	Turnbull R (Bradford City)	
2	Turner A (Southampton)	
2	Turner H (Huddersfield)	
3	Turner J (Bolton, Stoke, Derby County)	
1	Tweedy G (Grimsby)	
1	Ufton D (Charlton)	
2	Underwood A (Stoke)	
1	Unsworth D (Everton)	
4	Urwin T (Middlesbrough, Newcastle)	
1	Utley G (Barnsley)	
5	Vaughton O (Aston Villa)	
6	Veitch C (Newcastle)	
1	Veitch J (Old Westminsters)	
2	Venables T (Chelsea)	
2	Venison B (Newcastle)	
1	Vidal R (Oxford Univ)	

2	Viljoen C (Ipswich)
2	Viollet D (Man Utd)
2	Von Donop P (Royal Engineers)
3	Wace H (Wanderers)
62	Waddle C (Newcastle, Spurs, Marseille)
9	Wadsworth S (Huddersfield)
1	Wainscoat W (Leeds Utd)
5	Waiters A (Blackpool)
2	Walden F (Spurs)
59	Walker D (Nottm Forest, Sampdoria, Sheff Wed)
2	Walker I (Spurs)
18	Walker W (Aston Villa)
7	Wall G (Man Utd)
3	Wallace C (Aston Villa)
1	Wallace D (Southampton)
5	Walsh P (Luton)
9	Walters A (Cambridge Univ, Old Carthusians)
1	Walters M (Rangers)
13	Walters P (Oxford Univ, Old Carthusians)
1	Walton N (Blackburn)
1	Ward J (Blackburn Olympic)
1	Ward P (Brighton and Hove Albion)
2	Ward T (Derby County)
5	Waring T (Aston Villa)
1	Warner C (Upton Park)
22	Warren B (Derby County, Chelsea)
1	Waterfield G (Burnley)
12	Watson D (Norwich, Everton)
65	Watson D (Sunderland, Man City, Werder Bremen, Southampton, Stoke)
5	Watson V (West Ham)
3	Watson W (Burnley)
4	Watson W (Sunderland)
3	Weaver S (Newcastle)
2	Webb G (West Ham)
26	Webb N (Nottm Forest, Man Utd)
3	Webster M (Middlesbrough)
26	Wedlock W (Bristol City)
2	Weir D (Bolton)
2	Welch R de C (Wanderers, Harrow Chequers)
4	Weller K (Leicester)
3	Welsh D (Charlton)
3	West G (Everton)
6	Westwood R (Bolton)
2	Whateley O (Aston Villa)
1	Wheeler J (Bolton)
4	Wheldon G (Aston Villa)
1	White D (Man City)
1	White T (Everton)
2	Whitehead J (Accrington, Blackburn)
1	Whitfield H (Old Etonians)
1	Witham M (Sheff Utd)
7	Whitworth S (Leicester)
1	Whymark T (Ipswich)
1	Widdowson S (Nottm Forest)
2	Wignall F (Nottm Forest)
1	Wilcox J (Blackburn)

Darren Anderton (second from left) puts England ahead against Hungary in the May friendly.

13 ● ENGLAND SENIOR CAPS 1995–96

	Colombia	Norway	Switzerland	Portugal	Bulgaria	Croatia	Hungary	China	Switzerland	Scotland	Holland	Spain	Germany
D. Seaman (Arsenal)	1	1	1	1	1	1	1		1	1	1	1	1
G. Neville (Man. United)	2	2	2	2	2	2	2	2	2	2	2	2	
G. Le Saux (Blackburn R)	3			3*									
J. Redknapp (Liverpool)	4	4	4					4		3*			
T. Adams (Arsenal)	5	5	5	5				5	5	5	5	5	5
S. Howey (Newcastle U)	6			6	6								
N. Barmby (Middlesbrough)	7	7		7				7	10*		10*	4*	
P. Gascoigne (Rangers)	8		8	8	8	8		8	8	8	8	8	8
A. Shearer (Blackburn R)	9	9	9	9			9*	9	9	9	9	9	9
S. McManaman (Liverpool)	10	10	11	7*	7	6		10	7	7	7	4	2
D. Wise (Chelsea)	11	11		4			7*						
R. Lee (Newcastle U)	4*	8	7		8*		6						
J. Barnes (Liverpool)	8*												
T. Sheringham (Tottenham H)	9*	7*	10		10	10	10		10	10	10	10	10
S. Pearce (Nottm Forest)		3	3	3	3	3	3		3	3	3	3	3
G. Pallister (Man United)		6	6										
S. Stone (Nottm Forest)		11*	4*	11	11	11		10*	7*	4*		10*	
L. Ferdinand (Newcastle U)				10	9		9						
G. Southgate (Aston Villa)				4*	5		5*	6	6	6	6	6	6
P. Beardsley (Newcastle U)				10*				7*					
P. Ince (Inter Milan)					4	4	4		4	4	4		4
R. Fowler (Liverpool)					9*	9		9*			9*	11*	
D. Platt (Arsenal)					10*	7	7		8*		4*	7	7
M. Wright (Liverpool)						5	5						
J. Wilcox (Blackburn R)							8						
D. Anderton (Tottenham H)							11	11	11	11	11	11	11
I. Walker (Tottenham H)							1*	1*					
S. Campbell (Tottenham H)							4*			3*			
T. Flowers (Blackburn R)								1					
P. Nevelle (Man. United)								3					
U. Ehiogu (Aston Villa)								5*					

* substitute

● 31

14 ● UNDER-21 INTERNATIONAL MATCHES 1976–1996

UQ   UEFA Competition Qualifier
UF   UEFA Competition Finals

v Albania

1989	7/3	Shkoder	W	2–1	UQ
1989	25/4	Ipswich	W	2–0	UQ

v Angola

1995	10/6	La Seyne	W	1–0	
1996	28/5	Cuers	L	0–2	

v Austria

1994	11/10	Kapfenberg	W	3–1	UQ
1995	14/11	Middlesbrough	W	2–1	UQ

v Belgium

1994	5/6	Berre	W	2–1	
1996	24/5	Toulon	W	1–0	

v Brazil

1993	11/6	Draguignan	D	0–0	
1995	6/6	Toulon	L	0–2	
1996	1/6	Toulon	L	1–2	

v Bulgaria

1979	5/6	Pernik	W	3–1	UQ
1979	20/11	Leicester	W	5–0	UQ
1989	5/6	Toulon	L	2–3	
1996	23/4	Sunderland	L	0–1	

v Croatia

1996	23/4	Sunderland	L	0–1	

v Czech Republic

1993	9/6	Saint Cyr	D	1–1	

v Czechoslovakia

1990	27/4	Toulon	W	2–1	
1992	26/5	Toulon	L	1–2	

v Denmark

1978	19/9	Hvidovre	W	2–1	UQ
1979	11/9	Watford	W	1–0	UQ
1982	21/9	Hvidovre	W	4–1	UQ
1983	20/9	Norwich	W	4–1	UQ
1986	12/3	Copenhagen	W	1–0	UF
1986	26/3	Manchester City	D	1–1	UF
1988	13/9	Watford	D	0–0	
1994	8/3	Brentford	W	1–0	

v Finland

1977	26/5	Helsinki	W	1–0	UQ

1977	12/10	Hull	W	8–1	UQ
1984	16/10	Southampton	W	2–0	UQ
1985	21/5	Mikkeli	L	1–3	UQ

v France

1984	28/2	Sheffield Wed	W	6–1	UF
1984	28/3	Rouen	W	1–0	UF
1987	11/6	Toulon	L	0–2	
1988	13/4	Besançon	L	2–4	UF
1988	27/4	Arsenal	D	2–2	UF
1988	12/6	Toulon	L	2–4	
1990	23/5	Aix en Provence	W	7–3	
1991	3/6	Toulon	W	1–0	
1992	28/5	Aubagne	D	0–0	
1993	15/6	Toulon	W	1–0	
1994	31/5	Aubagne	L	0–3	
1995	12/6	Cannes	L	0–2	

v East Germany

1980	16/4	Sheffield Wed	L	1–2	UF
1980	23/4	Jena	L	0–1	UF

v West Germany

1982	21/9	Sheffield United	W	3–1	UF
1982	12/10	Bremen	L	2–3	UF
1987	8/9	Lüdenscheid	L	0–2	

v Germany

1991	10/9	Scunthorpe	W	2–1	

v Greece

1982	16/11	Piraeus	L	1–0	UQ
1983	29/3	Portsmouth	W	2–1	UQ
1989	7/2	Patras	L	0–1	

v Holland

1993	27/4	Portsmouth	W	3–0	UQ
1993	12/10	Utrecht	D	1–1	UQ

v Hungary

1981	5/6	Keszthely	W	2–1	UQ
1981	17/11	Nottingham	W	2–0	UQ
1983	26/4	Newcastle	W	1–0	UQ
1983	11/10	Nyiregyhaza	W	2–0	UQ
1990	11/9	Southampton	W	3–1	
1992	12/5	Vac	D	2–2	

v Israel

1985	27/2	Tel Aviv	W	2–1	

v Italy

1978	8/3	Manchester City	W	2–1	UF
1978	5/4	Rome	D	0–0	UF
1984	18/4	Manchester City	W	3–1	UF
1984	2/5	Florence	L	0–1	UF
1986	9/4	Pisa	L	0–2	UF
1986	23/4	Swindon	D	1–1	UF

v Latvia

1995	25/4	Riga	W	1–0	UQ
1995	7/6	Burnley	W	4–0	UQ

v Malaysia

1995	8/6	Six-Fours	W	2–0	

v Mexico

1988	5/6	Toulon	W	2–1	
1991	29/5	Vitrolles	W	6–0	
1992	24/5	Six-Fours	D	1–1	

v Morocco

1987	7/6	Toulon	W	2–0	
1988	9/6	Toulon	W	1–0	

v Norway

1977	1/6	Bergen	W	2–1	UQ
1977	6/9	Brighton	W	6–0	UQ
1980	9/9	Southampton	W	3–0	
1981	8/9	Drammen	D	0–0	
1992	13/10	Peterborough	L	0–2	UQ
1993	1/6	Stavanger	D	1–1	UQ
1995	10/10	Stavanger	D	2–2	

v Poland

1982	17/3	Warsaw	W	2–1	UF
1982	7/4	West Ham	D	2–2	UF
1989	2/6	Plymouth	W	2–1	UQ
1989	10/10	Jastrzebie Zdroj	W	3–1	UQ
1990	16/10	Tottenham	L	0–1	UQ
1991	12/11	Pila	L	1–2	UQ
1993	28/5	Jastrzebie Zdroj	W	4–1	UQ
1993	7/9	Millwall	L	1–2	UQ

v Portugal

1987	13/6	Sollies-Pont	D	0–0	
1990	21/5	Six-Fours	L	0–1	
1993	7/6	Miramas	W	2–0	
1994	7/6	Toulon	W	2–0	
1994	6/9	Leicester	D	0–0	UQ
1995	2/9	Santa Maria	L	0–2	UQ
1996	30/5	Arles	L	1–3	

v Republic of Ireland

1981	25/2	Liverpool	W	1–0	
1985	25/3	Portsmouth	W	3–2	
1989	9/6	Six-Fours	D	0–0	
1990	13/11	Cork	W	3–0	UQ
1991	26/3	Brentford	W	3–0	UQ

1994	15/11	Newcastle	W	1–0	UQ
1995	27/3	Dublin	W	2–0	UQ

v Romania

1980	14/10	Ploesti	L	0–4	UQ
1981	28/4	Swindon	W	3–0	UQ
1985	30/4	Brasov	D	0–0	UQ
1985	9/9	Ipswich	W	3–0	UQ

v Russia

1994	29/5	Bandol	W	2–0	

v San Marino

1993	16/2	Luton	W	6–0	UQ
1993	17/11	San Marino	W	4–0	UQ

v Scotland

1977	27/4	Sheffield United	W	1–0	
1980	12/2	Coventry	W	2–1	UF
1980	4/3	Aberdeen	D	0–0	UF
1982	19/4	Glasgow	W	1–0	UF
1982	28/4	Manchester City	D	1–1	UF
1988	16/2	Aberdeen	W	1–0	UF
1989	22/3	Nottingham	W	1–0	UF
1993	13/6	La Ciotat	W	1–0	

v Senegal

1989	7/6	Sainte-Maxime	W	6–1	
1991	27/5	Arles	W	2–1	

v Spain

1984	17/5	Seville	W	1–0	UF
1984	24/5	Sheffield United	W	2–0	UF
1987	18/2	Burgos	W	2–1	
1992	8/9	Burgos	W	1–0	

v Sweden

1979	9/6	Vasteras	W	2–1	
1986	9/9	Oestersund	D	1–1	
1988	18/10	Coventry	D	1–1	UQ
1989	5/9	Uppsala	L	0–1	UQ

v Switzerland

1980	18/11	Ipswich	W	5–0	UQ
1981	31/5	Neuenburg	D	0–0	UQ
1988	28/5	Lausanne	D	1–1	

v Turkey

1984	13/11	Bursa	D	0–0	UQ
1985	15/10	Bristol	W	3–0	UQ
1987	28/4	Izmir	D	0–0	UQ
1987	13/10	Sheffield	D	1–1	UQ
1991	30/4	Izmir	D	2–2	UQ
1991	15/10	Reading	W	2–0	UQ
1992	17/11	Leyton	L	0–1	UQ
1993	30/3	Izmir	D	0–0	UQ

v USA

1989	11/6	Toulon	L	0–2
1994	2/6	Arles	W	3–0

v USSR

1987	9/6	La Ciotat	D	0–0
1988	7/6	Six-Fours	W	1–0
1990	25/5	Toulon	W	2–1
1991	31/5	Aix-en-Provence	W	2–1

v Wales

1976	15/12	Wolverhampton	D	0–0
1979	6/2	Swansea	W	1–0
1990	5/12	Tranmere	D	0–0

v Yugoslavia

1978	19/4	Novi Sad	L	1–2	UF
1978	2/5	Manchester City	D	1–1	UF
1986	11/11	Peterborough	D	1–1	UQ
1987	10/11	Zemun	W	5–1	UQ

England Under-21 striker Neil Shipperley slides in to tackle an Austrian defender at Middlesbrough.

15 ● ENGLAND UNDER-21 CAPS 1976–1996

(Up to and including 1st June 1996)

1 Ablett G (Liverpool)	5 Butt N (Man Utd)
1 Adams N (Everton)	3 Butters G (Spurs)
5 Adams T (Arsenal)	8 Butterworth I (Coventry City, Nottm Forest)
8 Allen B (QPR)	3 Caesar G (Arsenal)
2 Allen C (Oxford Utd)	9 Callaghan N (Watford)
3 Allen C (QPR, C Palace)	4 Campbell K (Arsenal)
2 Allen M (QPR)	11 Campbell S (Spurs)
3 Allen P (West Ham, Spurs)	1 Carbon M (Derby)
1 Anderson V (Nottm Forest)	1 Carr C (Fulham)
12 Anderton D (Spurs)	9 Carr F (Nottm Forest)
1 Andrews I (Leicester City)	1 Casper C (Man Utd)
10 Ardley N (Wimbledon)	14 Caton T (Man City, Arsenal)
6 Atkinson B (Sunderland)	2 Challis T (QPR)
1 Atherton P (Coventry)	4 Chamberlain M (Stoke)
9 Awford A (Portsmouth)	1 Chapman L (Stoke City)
14 Bailey G (Man Utd)	4 Charles G (Nottm Forest)
2 Baker G (Southampton)	12 Chettle S (Nottm Forest)
1 Bannister G (Sheff Wed)	11 Clark L (Newcastle)
4 Barker S (Blackburn)	15 Clough N (Nottm Forest)
3 Barmby N (Spurs)	8 Cole A (Arsenal, Bristol City, Newcastle)
2 Barnes J (Watford)	4 Coney D (Fulham)
9 Barnes P (Man City)	1 Connor T (Brighton & Hove Albion)
4 Barrett E (Oldham)	1 Cooke R (Spurs)
16 Bart-Williams C (Sheff Wed, Nottm Forest)	4 Cooke T (Man United)
7 Batty D (Leeds Utd)	8 Cooper C (Middlesbrough)
1 Bazeley D (Watford)	3 Corrigan J (Man City)
2 Beagrie P (Sheff Utd)	8 Cottee T (West Ham)
5 Beardsmore R (Man Utd)	3 Couzens A (Leeds Utd)
9 Beckham D (Man Utd)	5 Cowans G (Aston Villa)
1 Beeston C (Stoke)	6 Cox N (Aston Villa)
3 Bertschin K (Birmingham)	5 Cranson I (Ipswich Town)
2 Birtles G (Nottm Forest)	4 Croft G (Grimsby)
6 Blackwell D (Wimbledon)	4 Crooks G (Stoke City)
8 Blake M (Aston Villa)	3 Crossley M (Nottm Forest)
4 Blissett L (Watford)	3 Cundy J (Chelsea)
3 Booth A (Huddersfield)	6 Cunningham L (WBA)
4 Bowyer L (Charlton)	1 Curbishley A (Birmingham)
13 Bracewell P (Stoke, Sunderland, Everton)	7 Daniel P (Hull City)
4 Bradshaw P (Wolves)	2 Davis K (Luton)
1 Branch M (Everton)	11 Davis P (Arsenal)
2 Breacker T (Luton Town)	2 D'Avray M (Ipswich)
5 Brennan M (Ipswich)	3 Day C (Spurs)
4 Brightwell I (Man City)	7 Deehan J (Aston Villa)
4 Briscoe L (Sheff Wed)	3 Dennis M (Birmingham)
4 Brock K (Oxford Utd)	1 Dichio D (QPR)
4 Brown M (Man City)	1 Dickens A (West Ham)
5 Bull S (Wolves)	4 Dicks J (West Ham)
7 Burrows D (WBA, Liverpool)	5 Digby F (Swindon)
7 Butcher T (Ipswich)	1 Dillon K (Birmingham)

✗ 1	Dixon K (Chelsea)	
4	Dobson T (Coventry City)	
8	Dodd J (Southampton)	
3	Donowa L (Norwich City)	
✗ 11	Dorigo T (Aston Villa)	
9	Dozzell J (Ipswich)	
3	Draper M (Notts County)	
✗ 7	Duxbury M (Man Utd)	
7	Dyer B (C Palace)	
4	Dyson P (Coventry City)	
2	Eadie D (Norwich)	
14	Ebbrell J (Everton)	
3	Edghill R (Man City)	
✗ 15	Ehiogu U (Aston Villa)	
3	Elliott P (Luton, Aston Villa)	
2	Elliott R (Newcastle)	
7	Fairclough C (Nottm Forest, Spurs)	
1	Fairclough D (Liverpool)	
✗ 11	Fashanu Justin (Norwich, Nottm Forest)	
3	Fear P (Wimbledon)	
1	Fenton G (Aston Villa)	
✗ 11	Fenwick T (QPR)	
5	Fereday W (QPR)	
10	Flitcroft G (Man City)	
✗ 3	Flowers T (Southampton)	
1	Ford M (Leeds)	
4	Forster N (Brentford)	
1	Forsyth M (Derby County)	
1	Foster S (Brighton & Hove Albion)	
✗ 8	Fowler R (Liverpool)	
2	Froggatt S (Aston Villa)	
11	Futcher P (Luton, Man City)	
2	Gabbiadini M (Sunderland)	
1	Gale T (Fulham)	
4	Gallen K (QPR)	
✗ 13	Gascoigne P (Newcastle)	
3	Gayle H (Birmingham)	
18	Gerrard P (Oldham)	
1	Gernon I (Ipswich)	
5	Gibbs N (Watford)	
1	Gibson C (Aston Villa)	
11	Gilbert W (C Palace)	
8	Goddard P (West Ham)	
13	Gordon D (C Palace)	
4	Gordon D (Norwich)	
✗ 2	Gray A (Aston Villa)	
1	Haigh P (Hull)	
11	Hall R (Southampton)	
2	Hardyman P (Portsmouth)	
✗ 10	Hateley M (Coventry City, Portsmouth)	
3	Hayes M (Arsenal)	
1	Hazell R (Wolves)	
6	Heaney N (Arsenal)	
8	Heath A (Stoke, Everton)	
7	Hendon I (Spurs)	
1	Hendrie L (Aston Villa)	
7	Hesford I (Blackpool)	
9	Hilaire V (C Palace)	
4	Hill D (Spurs)	
1	Hillier D (Arsenal)	

1	Hinchcliffe A (Man City)	
2	Hinshelwood P (C Palace)	
✗ 7	Hirst D (Sheff Wed)	
✗ 12	Hoddle G (Spurs)	
✗ 8	Hodge S (Nottm Forest, Aston Villa)	
7	Hodgson D (Middlesbrough, Liverpool)	
1	Holdsworth D (Watford)	
7	Holland C (Newcastle)	
4	Holland P (Mansfield)	
5	Horne B (Millwall)	
2	Hucker P (QPR)	
1	Impey A (QPR)	
✗ 2	Ince P (West Ham United)	
10	Jackson M (Everton)	
✗ 10	James D (Watford)	
2	James J (Luton)	
1	Jemson N (Nottm Forest)	
9	Joachim J (Leicester)	
7	Johnson T (Notts County, Derby)	
2	Johnston C (Middlesbrough)	
1	Jones C (Spurs)	
1	Jones D (Everton)	
✗ 2	Jones R (Liverpool)	
1	Keegan G (Oldham)	
1	Kenny W (Everton)	
✗ 8	Keown M (Aston Villa)	
1	Kerslake D (QPR)	
2	Kilcline B (Notts County)	
2	King A (Everton)	
7	Kitson P (Leicester, Derby)	
2	Knight A (Portsmouth)	
2	Knight I (Sheff Wed)	
5	Lake P (Man City)	
1	Langley T (Chelsea)	
10	Lee D (Chelsea)	
✗ 2	Lee R (Charlton)	
✗ 6	Lee S (Liverpool)	
✗ 4	Le Saux G (Chelsea)	
2	Lowe D (Ipswich)	
7	Lukic J (Leeds Utd)	
3	Lund G (Grimsby)	
✗ 7	Mabbutt G (Bristol Rovers, Spurs)	
6	McCall S (Ipswich)	
5	McDonald N (Newcastle)	
1	McGrath L (Coventry City)	
3	Mackenzie S (WBA)	
1	McLeary A (Millwall)	
✗ 6	McMahon S (Everton, Aston Villa)	
✗ 7	McManaman S (Liverpool)	
5	Makin C (Oldham)	
1	Marriott A (Nottm Forest)	
2	Marshall A (Norwich)	
2	Martin L (Man Utd)	
✗ 11	Martyn N (Bristol Rovers)	
3	Matteo D (Liverpool)	
9	Matthew D (Chelsea)	
1	May A (Man City)	
✗ 4	Merson P (Arsenal)	
3	Middleton J (Nottm Forest, Derby County)	
4	Miller A (Arsenal)	

2 Mills G (Nottm Forest)
3 Mimms R (Rotherham, Everton)
6 Minto S (Charlton)
5 Moore I (Tranmere)
2 Moran S (Southampton)
2 Morgan S (Leicester)
2 Mortimer P (Charlton)
8 Moses R (WBA, Man Utd)
1 Mountfield D (Everton)
1 Muggleton C (Leicester City)
1 Mutch A (Wolves)
4 Myers A (Chelsea)
8 Nethercott S (Spurs)
✗ 6 Neville P (Man Utd)
4 Newell M (Luton Town)
2 Newton E (Chelsea)
1 Nicholls A (Plymouth)
7 Oakes M (Aston Villa)
3 O'Connor J (Everton)
1 Oldfield D (Luton)
✗ 10 Olney I (Aston Villa)
3 Ord R (Sunderland)
7 Osman R (Ipswich)
22 Owen G (Man City, WBA)
1 Painter I (Stoke)
✗ 4 Palmer C (Sheff Wed)
6 Parker G (Hull, Nottm Forest)
✗ 8 Parker P (Fulham)
✗ 1 Parkes P (QPR)
5 Parkin S (Stoke City)
12 Parlour R (Arsenal)
6 Peach D (Southampton)
1 Peake A (Leicester City)
3 Pearce I (Blackburn)
✗ 1 Pearce S (Nottm Forest)
15 Pickering N (Sunderland, Coventry City)
✗ 3 Platt D (Aston Villa)
5 Plummer C (QPR)
3 Pollock J (Middlesbrough)
12 Porter G (Watford)
1 Pressman K (Sheff Wed)
4 Proctor M (Middlesbrough, Nottm Forest)
3 Ramage C (Derby County)
10 Ranson R (Man City)
✗ 18 Redknapp J (Liverpool)
14 Redmond S (Man City)
10 Reeves K (Norwich, Man City)
✗ 6 Regis C (WBA)
6 Reid N (Man City)
✗ 6 Reid P (Bolton)
4 Richards D (Wolves)
2 Richards J (Wolves)
5 Rideout P (Aston Villa, Bari)
✗ 8 Ripley S (Middlesbrough)
1 Ritchie A (Brighton & Hove Albion)
✗ 7 Rix G (Arsenal)
5 Roberts A (Millwall, C Palace)
6 Robins M (Man Utd)
✗ 7 Robson B (WBA)
6 Robson S (Arsenal, West Ham)

✗ 14 Rocastle D (Arsenal)
4 Rodger G (Coventry City)
4 Rosario R (Norwich)
1 Rowell G (Sunderland)
✗ 4 Ruddock N (Southampton)
5 Rufus R (Charlton)
1 Ryan J (Oldham Athletic)
3 Ryder S (Walsall)
5 Samways V (Spurs)
✗ 8 Sansom K (Crystal Palace)
1 Scimeca R (Aston Villa)
✗ 10 Seaman D (Birmingham)
11 Sedgley S (Coventry City, Spurs)
3 Sellars S (Blackburn)
3 Selley I (Arsenal)
✗ 8 Sharpe L (Man Utd)
7 Shaw G (Aston Villa)
✗ 11 Shearer A (Southampton)
1 Shelton G (Sheff Wed)
✗ 1 Sheringham T (Millwall)
16 Sheron M (Man City)
4 Sherwood T (Norwich City)
7 Shipperley N (Chelsea, Southampton)
5 Simpson P (Man City)
10 Sims S (Leicester City)
13 Sinclair T (QPR)
1 Sinnott L (Watford)
4 Slade S (Spurs)
3 Slater S (West Ham)
12 Small B (Aston Villa)
10 Smith D (Coventry City)
5 Smith M (Sheff Wed)
1 Smith M (Sunderland)
4 Snodin I (Doncaster)
3 Statham B (Spurs)
✗ 6 Statham D (WBA)
✗ 3 Stein B (Luton)
✗ 7 Sterland M (Sheff Wed)
✗ 2 Steven T (Everton)
✗ 1 Stevens G (Everton)
✗ 7 Stevens G (Brighton & Hove Albion, Spurs)
✗ 1 Stewart P (Man City)
5 Stuart G (Chelsea)
4 Stuart J (Charlton)
10 Suckling P (Coventry City, Man City, C Palace)
3 Summerbee N (Swindon)
✗ 1 Sunderland A (Wolves)
4 Sutch D (Norwich)
13 Sutton C (Norwich)
1 Swindlehurst D (C Palace)
✗ 1 Talbot B (Ipswich)
1 Thatcher B (Millwall)
✗ 7 Thomas D (Coventry City, Spurs)
12 Thomas M (Arsenal)
3 Thomas M (Luton)
1 Thomas R (Watford)
2 Thompson A (Bolton)
6 Thompson G (Coventry City)
5 Thorn A (Wimbledon)

3 Thornley B (Man Utd)
13 Tiler C (Barnsley, Nottm Forest)
7 Unsworth D (Everton)
10 Venison B (Sunderland)
12 Vinnicombe C (Rangers)
1 Waddle C (Newcastle)
7 Walker D (Nottm Forest)
9 Walker I (Spurs)
14 Wallace D (Southampton)
4 Wallace Ray (Southampton)
11 Wallace Rod (Southampton)
2 Walsh G (Man Utd)
4 Walsh P (Luton Town)
9 Walters M (Aston Villa)
2 Ward P (Brighton & Hove Albion)
8 Warhurst P (Oldham, Sheff Wed)
5 Watson D (Barnsley)
7 Watson D (Norwich)
2 Watson G (Sheff Wed)
13 Watson S (Newcastle)

3 Webb N (Portsmouth, Nottm Forest)
2 Whelan N (Leeds Utd)
3 Whelan P (Ipswich)
6 White D (Man City)
4 Whyte C (Arsenal)
1 Wicks S (QPR)
1 Wilkins R (Chelsea)
4 Wilkinson P (Grimsby, Everton)
4 Williams P (Charlton)
6 Williams P (Derby County)
14 Williams S (Southampton)
1 Winterburn N (Wimbledon)
1 Wise D (Wimbledon)
2 Woodcock A (Nottm Forest)
6 Woods C (Nottm Forest, QPR, Norwich)
2 Wright A (Blackburn)
4 Wright M (Southampton)
6 Wright W (Everton)
5 Yates D (Notts County)

16 ● ENGLAND UNDER-21 CAPS 1995–96

	Portugal	Norway	Austria	Croatia	Belgium	Angola	Portugal	Brazil
P. Gerrard (Oldham Athletic)	1							
P. Neville (Man. United)	2	2*						
D. Gordon (Crystal Palace)	3	3						
R. Scimeca (Aston Villa)	4							
R. Elliott (Newcastle United)	5		3					
D. Beckham (Man. United)	6		8*		5	7	6	
N. Butt (Man. United)	7		7					
T. Sinclair (Queens Park R.)	8							
A. Thompson (Bolton Wanderers)	9							
R. Fowler (Liverpool)	10		11					
N. Shipperley (Southampton)	11	9	9					
C. Bart-Williams (Nottm. F.)	7*		10					
D. Watson (Barnsley)		1						
S. Watson (Newcastle United)		2	2					
I. Pearce (Blackburn Rovers)		4						
S. Campbell (Tottenham Hotspur)		5	4					
D. Unsworth (Everton)		6	6					
A. Roberts (Crystal Palace)		7	5					
J. Pollock (Middlesbrough)		8	8					
A. Booth (Huddersfield Town)		10						
J. Joachim (Leicester City)		11						
M. Oakes (Aston Villa)	1*	1	1					
L. Bowyer (Charlton Athletic)	5*				8		7	7
C. Holland (Newcastle United)	8*	10*	10*	8	7	2*		8
D. Dichio (Queens Park Rangers)	10*							
C. Day (Tottenham Hotspur)				1	1			1
J. O'Connor (Everton)				2		2		6
R. Rufus (Charlton Athletic)				3	3	5	4	3
B. Thatcher (Millwall)				4				
M. Brown (Manchester City)				5	6	8	2	
T. Cooke (Manchester United)				6	9	4*	8	
M. Ford (Leeds United)				7				
L. Briscoe (Sheffield Wednesday)				9	10*	9		5
K. Gallen (Queens Park Rangers)				10				
B. Dyer (Crystal Palace)				11				
K. Davis (Luton Town)				1*			1	
M. Carbon (Derby County)				2*				
C. Plummer (Queens Park Rangers)				4*	2	4	3*	2
L. Hendrie (Aston Villa)				7*				
I. Moore (Tranmere Rovers)				10*	11*	11	11	11
J. Stuart (Charlton Athletic)					4	6	5	4
S. Slade (Tottenham Hotspur)					10	10	10	10
B. Thornley (Manchester United)					11		9	9
A. Marshall (Norwich City)						1		
T. Challis (Queens Park Rangers)						3	3	
M. Branch (Everton)						11*		

*substitute

17 ● ENGLAND B INTERNATIONAL MATCHES 1949–1996

v Algeria

1990	11/12	Algiers	D	0–0

v Australia

1980	17/11	Birmingham	W	1–0

v CIS

1992	28/4	Moscow	D	1–1

v Czechoslovakia

1978	28/11	Prague	W	1–0
1990	24/4	Sunderland	W	2–0
1992	24/3	Ceske Budejovice	W	1–0

v Finland

1949	15/5	Helsinki	W	4–0

v France

1952	22/5	Le Havre	L	1–7
1992	18/2	QPR	W	3–0

v West Germany

1954	24/3	Gelsenkirchen	W	4–0
1955	23/3	Sheffield	D	1–1
1978	21/2	Augsburg	W	2–1

v Holland

1949	18/5	Amsterdam	W	4–0
1950	22/2	Newcastle	W	1–0
1950	17/5	Amsterdam	L	0–3
1952	26/3	Amsterdam	W	1–0

v Iceland

1989	19/5	Reykjavik	W	2–0
1991	27/4	Watford	W	1–0

v Italy

1950	11/5	Milan	L	0–5
1989	14/11	Brighton	D	1–1

v Luxembourg

1950	21/5	Luxembourg	W	2–1

v Malaysia

1978	30/5	Kuala Lumpur	D	1–1

v Malta

1987	14/10	Ta'Qali	W	2–0

v New Zealand

1978	7/6	Christchurch	W	4–0
1978	11/6	Wellington	W	3–1
1978	14/6	Auckland	W	4–0
1979	15/10	Leyton Orient	W	4–1
1984	13/11	Nottingham Forest	W	2–0

v Northern Ireland

1994	10/5	Sheffield	W	4–2

v Norway

1989	22/5	Stavanger	W	1–0

v Republic of Ireland

1990	27/3	Cork	L	1–4
1994	13/12	Liverpool	W	2–0

v Scotland

1953	11/3	Edinburgh	D	2–2
1954	3/3	Sunderland	D	1–1
1956	29/2	Dundee	D	2–2
1957	6/2	Birmingham	W	4–1

v Singapore

1978	18/6	Singapore	W	8–0

v Spain

1980	26/3	Sunderland	W	1–0
1981	25/3	Granada	L	2–3
1991	18/12	Castellon	W	1–0

v Switzerland

1950	18/1	Sheffield	W	5–0
1954	22/5	Basle	L	0–2
1956	21/3	Southampton	W	4–1
1989	16/5	Winterthur	W	2–0
1991	20/5	Walsall	W	2–1

v USA

1980	14/10	Manchester	W	1–0

v Wales

1991	5/2	Swansea	W	1–0

v Yugoslavia

1954	16/5	Ljubljana	L	1–2
1955	19/10	Manchester	W	5–1
1989	12/12	Millwall	W	2–1

18 ● ENGLAND B CAPS 1978–1996

1 Ablett G (Liverpool)
4 Adams T (Arsenal)
7 Anderson V (Nottingham Forest)
1 Armstrong C (Crystal Palace)
2 Armstrong D (Middlesbrough)
1 Atkinson D (Sheffield Wednesday)
2 Bailey G (Manchester United)
1 Bailey J (Everton)
1 Barmby N (Tottenham)
1 Barnes P (WBA)
4 Barrett E (Oldham Athletic)
3 Barton W (Wimbledon)
1 Bart-Williams C (Sheffield Wednesday)
3 Batson B (WBA)
5 Batty D (Leeds United)
2 Beagrie P (Everton)
2 Beardsley P (Liverpool)
7 Beasant D (Wimbledon)
2 Beresford J (Newcastle)
1 Birtles G (Nottingham Forest)
1 Bishop I (West Ham United)
1 Blissett L (Watford)
2 Bond K (Norwich and Manchester City)
1 Borrows B (Coventry City)
1 Bould S (Arsenal)
1 Brock K (QPR)
1 Bruce S (Norwich City)
5 Bull S (Wolves)
3 Burrows D (Liverpool)
1 Butcher T (Ipswich Town)
1 Callaghan N (Watford)
1 Campbell K (Arsenal)
1 Campbell S (Tottenham)
1 Chapman L (Leeds United)
3 Clough N (Nottingham Forest)
1 Cole A (Newcastle)
10 Corrigan J (Manchester City)
1 Coton T (Manchester City)
2 Cowans G (Aston Villa)
1 Crook I (Norwich City)
1 Cunningham L (WBA)
4 Curle K (Wimbledon and Manchester City)
6 Daley S (Wolves)
1 Daley T (Aston Villa)
1 Davenport P (Nottingham Forest)
1 Davis P (Arsenal)
3 Deane B (Sheffield United)
1 Devonshire A (West Ham United)
2 Dicks J (West Ham)
4 Dixon L (Arsenal)
7 Dorigo T (Chelsea, Leeds United)
1 Ebbrell J (Everton)

1 Edghill R (Manchester City)
1 Ehiogu U (Aston Villa)
1 Elliott P (Celtic)
3 Elliott S (Sunderland)
3 Eves M (Wolves)
1 Fairclough C (Tottenham)
1 Fairclough D (Liverpool)
1 Fashanu J (Nottingham Forest)
3 Flanagan M (Charlton and Crystal Palace)
3 Ford T (WBA)
1 Forsyth M (Derby County)
1 Fowler R (Liverpool)
2 Fox R (Newcastle)
1 Gabbiadini M (Sunderland)
1 Gallagher J (Birmingham)
4 Gascoigne P (Tottenham)
1 Geddis D (Ipswich Town)
1 Gibson C (Aston Villa)
2 Gidman J (Aston Villa)
1 Goddard P (West Ham United)
2 Gordon D (Norwich City)
1 Greenhoff B (Manchester United)
1 Harford M (Luton Town)
1 Hazell R (Wolves)
1 Heath A (Everton)
1 Hilaire V (Crystal Palace)
6 Hill G (Manchester Utd and Derby County)
3 Hirst D (Sheffield Wednesday)
2 Hoddle G (Tottenham)
2 Hodge S (Nottingham Forest)
1 Holdsworth D (Wimbledon)
5 Hollins J (QPR)
3 Hurlock T (Millwall)
1 Ince P (Manchester United)
1 James D (Liverpool)
2 Jobson R (Oldham)
1 Johnston C (Liverpool)
2 Joseph R (Wimbledon)
7 Kennedy A (Liverpool)
1 Keown M (Everton)
1 King P (Sheffield Wednesday)
1 Lake P (Manchester City)
3 Langley T (Chelsea)
1 Laws B (Nottingham Forest)
1 Lee R (Newcastle)
2 Le Saux G (Chelsea)
5 Le Tissier M (Southampton)
1 Lineker G (Leicester City)
4 Linighan A (Norwich City)
1 Lukic J (Leeds United)
1 Lyons M (Everton)
1 McCall S (Ipswich Town)

1 McDermott T (Liverpool)
3 McLeary A (Millwall)
2 McMahon S (Aston Villa and Liverpool)
9 Mabbutt G (Tottenham)
3 Mackenzie S (Manchester City and Charlton)
7 Mariner P (Ipswich Town)
2 Martin A (West Ham United)
6 Martyn N (Bristol Rovers and C Palace)
3 Merson P (Arsenal)
1 Money R (Liverpool)
2 Morley T (Aston Villa)
3 Mortimer D (Aston Villa)
1 Mountfield D (Everton)
3 Mowbray T (Middlesbrough)
3 Mutch A (Wolves)
3 Naylor S (WBA)
6 Needham D (Nottingham Forest)
2 Newell M (Everton)
2 Osman R (Ipswich Town)
7 Owen G (Manchester City)
9 Pallister G (Middlesbrough, Manchester Utd)
5 Palmer C (Sheffield Wednesday)
1 Parker G (Nottingham Forest)
3 Parker P (QPR)
2 Parkes P (West Ham United)
1 Peach D (Southampton)
3 Platt D (Aston Villa)
1 Power P (Manchester City)
3 Preece D (Luton Town)
2 Pressman K (Sheffield Wednesday)
1 Redknapp J (Liverpool)
3 Reeves K (Manchester City)
3 Regis C (WBA)
3 Richards J (Wolves)
3 Rix G (Arsenal)
1 Roberts G (Tottenham)
3 Robson B (WBA, Manchester United)
2 Rocastle D (Arsenal)
5 Roeder G (Orient and QPR)
1 Ruddock N (Liverpool)
2 Sansom K (Crystal Palace)

2 Scales J (Wimbledon, Liverpool)
6 Seaman D (QPR)
1 Sharpe L (Manchester United)
1 Shearer A (Southampton)
1 Sherwood T (Blackburn)
1 Sims S (Leicester City)
3 Sinton A (QPR)
2 Slater S (West Ham United)
4 Smith A (Arsenal)
2 Snodin I (Everton)
4 Speight M (Sheffield United)
2 Spink N (Aston Villa)
2 Statham D (WBA)
3 Sterland M (Sheffield Wednesday, Leeds)
1 Stevens G (Everton)
5 Stewart P (Tottenham)
1 Stubbs A (Bolton)
1 Summerbee N (Swindon)
7 Sunderland A (Arsenal)
2 Sutton C (Norwich, Blackburn)
8 Talbot B (Ipswich and Arsenal)
3 Thomas G (Crystal Palace)
5 Thomas M (Liverpool)
1 Thomas M (Tottenham Hotspur)
1 Thompson P (Liverpool)
1 Waldron M (Southampton)
1 Wallace D (Manchester United)
1 Wallace R (Southampton)
1 Walters M (Rangers)
2 Ward P (Nottingham Forest)
4 Webb N (Manchester United)
1 White D (Manchester City)
1 Wilcox J (Blackburn)
3 Williams P (Charlton Athletic)
4 Williams S (Southampton)
3 Winterburn N (Arsenal)
3 Wise D (Wimbledon)
1 Woodcock T (Cologne)
2 Woods C (Norwich, Rangers)
2 Wright B (Everton)
3 Wright I (Crystal Palace)

19 ● ENGLAND'S INTERNATIONAL MATCHES 1995–96

THE ROAD TO EURO 96

England 0   Colombia 0

6th September 1995, Wembley

A draw was a fair and encouraging outcome from a "feel good" night of football on which some newer England faces performed with distinction. Middlesbrough's Nick Barmby, winning his third cap in harness with Shearer, looked to be international class throughout and Liverpool midfielder Jamie Redknapp had a remarkably assured debut alongside Gascoigne.

The talented South Americans had been late replacements for Croatia as England's first opponents of a very significant season. Fredy Rincon and the extravagantly coiffured Carlos Valderrama were typically strong and magical respectively, although the weight of the visitors' attacking numbers – they often had Tony Adams' defence under pressure with three against two or four against three – was not translated into goals.

This relatively inexperienced England team, with seven of the starting line-up on ten or fewer caps, refused to be mesmerised by the Colombians and three times the width of the woodwork denied the home side a morale-boosting victory. Gascoigne was particularly unfortunate in a match in which his passing, trickery on the ball and general belief in his own ability were again evident. He punched the ground in frustration after striking a post and later curled a free-kick an inch or two wide of Rene Higuita's goal.

The eccentric Higuita provided the game's main talking point. When Redknapp floated the ball high towards the Colombian goal, the goalkeeper could have taken a step or two forward and made a simple catch. Instead he let the ball go over his head and kicked his legs up behind him to volley the ball away from behind his head. He called it his "scorpion kick". A linesman's flag had been raised – but the referee waved play on.

England: Seaman, Neville G., Le Saux, Redknapp (Lee), Adams, Howey, Barmby, Gascoigne (Barnes), Shearer (Sheringham), McManaman, Wise.

Colombia: Higuita, Santa, Mendoza, Bernudez, De Cali, Alvarez, Lozano (Quinones), Rincon, Valderrama, Asprilla, Valenciano.

Referee: M. Batta (France)
Attendance: 20,038

Norway 0   England 0

11th October 1995, Oslo

Another goalless international but a generally more negative match this time. England calmly absorbed Norway's long-ball game after early difficulties and threatened to end the Norwegians' four-year unbeaten home record as they grew in confidence late on. A 0–0 scoreline in a competitive away fixture would certainly have been acceptable. The Shearer-Barmby partnership didn't function quite as well but England's overall display brought compensation.

Norway, despite their unimaginative tactics, came close to winning the match with seven minutes left. They forced a corner on the left and, after the ball had been played back, Liverpool's Bjornebye drove a low cross-shot into the crowded goalmouth. Seaman, probably unsighted, went down late to turn the ball away. It was only his second save of any importance – the first being in the 11th minute when Jakobsen veered past Pallister before sending in a 25-yarder that the England 'keeper pushed round at full stretch.

Some of England's youngsters prospered again. Redknapp was steady on the left of midfield and looked the part. Steve McManaman, after a quiet first half, got the measure of his club colleague, Bjornebye, and was a constant danger in the final period. He could have won the match on 73 minutes, as Robert Lee's long cross from the right cleared the home defence and fell invitingly about six yards from goal. Alas, Macca failed to control the ball on the half-volley and the chance was gone.

England newcomer Steve Stone, whose whole-hearted displays for Nottingham Forest had finally brought him international recognition, substituted for Dennis Wise in the last twenty minutes and attacked promisingly down the right flank. He looked as though he knew where the goal was.

Norway: Thorstvedt, Loken, Johnsen, Berg, Bjornebye, Bohinen, Leonhardsen (Solbakken), Rekdal, Jakobsen, Flo, Fjortoft (Brattbakk).

England: Seaman, Neville G., Pearce, Redknapp, Adams, Pallister, Barmby (Sheringham), Lee, Shearer, McManaman, Wise (Stone).

Referee: K-E. Nilsson (Sweden)
Attendance: 21,006

Alan Shearer in the thick of the action against the talented Colombians.

Teddy Sheringham lets fly at the Swiss goal during the friendly in November.

England 3   Switzerland 1

15th November 1995, Wembley

Steve Stone, after a relatively brief but encouraging debut in Oslo, joined the action earlier than anticipated against the Swiss at Wembley. Jamie Redknapp, whose cultured start to an England career was cruelly cut short by a hamstring strain, limped off in favour of Stone after just seven minutes. The latter took his opportunity with both hands, winning the "man of the match" award and scoring the third goal in England's emphatic 3–1 success.

It was arguably the home team's best performance in 18 months and was achieved against a country whose footballing star had risen swiftly in recent years – reaching the last 16 at the 1994 World Cup and qualifying for their first European finals at Euro 96. But England had been forced to come from behind, Adrian Knup having nodded a cross from Turkyilmaz beyond a stranded Seaman four minutes before the break.

A quick England riposte was essential, if only to quieten any feelings of resentment amongst the Wembley crowd, and it arrived almost immediately via the trusty left peg of Stuart Pearce. Gascoigne's short corner was played back by McManaman and Pearce thundered a shot past Pascolo's dive, the ball clearly deflecting off Quentin on its way through. It ended something of an England scoring drought – Graeme Le Saux had been the last man on target, against Brazil in the previous summer's Umbro Cup.

England's midfield twosome of Lee and the enigmatic Gascoigne found their feet in the second half, after playing second fiddle to Switzerland's better improvisation in the first period, and suddenly it was England who started to look the class side. Neville pushed forward to Stone and his cross perfectly picked out Teddy Sheringham, the Tottenham striker glancing the ball with his head into the one place in the goal that the scrambling Pascolo couldn't reach.

Steve Stone could hardly have expected last summer that he would become an important part of Terry Venables' Euro 96 plans a few months on – but his goal after the luckless Shearer had seen his shot rebound from the 'keeper's chest was a deserved reward for the gritty north-easterner. It had been a night of satisfaction for England as a whole – and the goals had flowed at last.

England: Seaman, Neville G., Pearce, Redknapp (Stone), Adams, Pallister, Lee, Gascoigne, Shearer, Sheringham, McManaman.

Switzerland: Pascolo, Hottiger, Quentin (Vega), Henchoz, Geiger, Fournier (Wolf), Sutter (Grassi), Ohrel, Knup, Sforza, Turkyilmaz.

Referee: S. Puhl (Hungary)
Attendance: 29,874

England 1   Portugal 1

12th December 1995, Wembley

If this was not yet the England of 1966, then this was a Portuguese side which stood reasonable comparison with Eusebio, Torres and the rest of the World Cup semi-finalists of the same year. A team strong on technique and disciplined in its play had been installed as one of the Euro 96 favourites and it was not difficult to see why after this impressive Wembley showing.

Portugal's players had grown up together in European (Under-18) and World (Under-20) Championships and showed a familiarity that would logically come from constant companionship.Against a side that posed more questions than the Swiss had in November, England's man of the moment, Steve Stone, came through again with distinction. Not only that, he scored the goal that earned England a draw with a stunning shot of Bobby Charlton proportions.

Terry Venables played a "diamond" formation in midfield with Paul Gascoigne in a holding role in front of the defence, something unfamiliar which he tried manfully to get to grips with, and Nick Barmby tucked in behind a twin strike-force of Shearer and Ferdinand. Beardsley improved the supply after replacing Ferdy on 65 minutes and England could easily have been celebrating a victory. The closest they got to a match-winning goal was when new cap Gareth Southgate struck the bar with almost his first touch.

Portugal had swept forward time and time again in the first half until a goal owing much to a Forest connection put the visitors in their place a minute from half-time. Pearce crossed the ball in from the left, Ferdinand knocked it down and Stone, steaming in, cracked it in from 22 yards. Neno barely moved. Then Jose Dominguez provided the pass from which fellow substitute Paulo Alves slid home a 59th-minute Portuguese equaliser.

England: Seaman, Neville G., Pearce (Le Saux), Wise (Southgate), Adams, Howey, Barmby (McManaman), Gascoigne, Shearer, Ferdinand (Beardsley), Stone.

Portugal: Neno, Carlos Secretario, Dimas, Costa, Couto, Sousa (Dominguez), Figo (Paulo Alves), Pinto J. (Dani), Pinto S., Helder, Folha (Pedro).

Referee: R. Pedersen (Norway)
Attendance: 28,592

England 1   Bulgaria 0

27th March 1996, Wembley

England's first match of 1996 brought top quality opposition to Wembley in the shape of Bulgaria, semi-finalists in the last World Cup. Star striker Hristo Stoichkov, now with Parma, travelled to

London with the party but mysteriously failed to make the starting line-up. England, boosted by Les Ferdinand's early goal, played with a purpose and appetite that was particularly encouraging with Euro 96 just three months away.

Ferdy's match-winning strike emanated from a schoolboy's error by Bulgarian defender Kremenliev, who plays his club football for Olympiakos in Greece. He took a throw-in while off balance and made a gift of the ball to Teddy Sheringham, a couple of yards inside the Bulgarian half. The Tottenham man lofted an instant pass about forty yards forward and Ferdinand sprinted onto it, held off Ivanov's muscular challenge and drove the ball into the net via the lunging body of Mikhailov, the Reading and Bulgaria 'keeper.

The visitors played without great ambition in the first period, rendering David Seaman redundant. This was possibly because England had adeptly closed down any pretensions of world-class play by Bulgaria. Paul Ince, back in the England team for the first time since the aborted match in Dublin, was as solid as a rock alongside Gazza in midfield and England enjoyed a lot of possession through the creative play of Sheringham and the hard-working McManaman.

The home side could have been three or four goals up by half-time: McManaman forced wide with only Mikhailov to beat, Sheringham missing with a header from seven yards, the flying Ferdinand dispossessed by the 'keeper a yard or two outside the box, a brilliant Sheringham effort on the turn pushed round the post. Bulgaria had to be more competitive after the break — and they were.

England: Seaman, Neville G., Pearce, Ince, Southgate, Howey, McManaman, Gascoigne (Lee), Ferdinand (Fowler), Sheringham (Platt), Stone.

Bulgaria: Mikhailov (Popov), Hubchev, Iankov, Ivanov, Kremenliev (Kishishev), Lechkov, Kiriakov, Guintchev (Guentchev), Iordanov (Borimirov), Penev (Sirakov), Kostadinov.

Referee: G. Benkoe (Austria)
Attendance: 29,708

England 0   Croatia 0

24th April 1996, Wembley

No goals — but something of a moral victory over excellent opponents who had become many people's "dark horses" for Euro 96. Six of the Croatia team had appeared together in Yugoslavian youth teams which had enjoyed success on the world stage and the depth of their understanding was clearly illustrated early on, when fifteen consecutive Croat passes left the home side thoroughly bemused. The sequence ended with a shot from the gifted Prosinecki dipping, just too late, over Seaman's goal.

But England coped. After proving that they could

live with some of the best technical quality in Europe, they finally showed enough patience and stamina to gain the upper hand over illustrious visitors and ultimately would have won comfortably but for five missed chances. Apart from the finishing it had been a very satisfactory England performance. A new-style defence, with Mark Wright flanked by Neville and Pearce, held firm throughout and Gazza, fortunately, was in the right sort of mood to charge at a retreating Croat defence.

Chances came and went at regular intervals. Steve Stone timed his run perfectly to collect Fowler's inviting pass but made a mess of his shot from six yards. The Forest winger then released Neville down the right and captain David Platt, starting his first international of the season after injury, darted between defenders to power in a header but Mrmic beat the ball away. Robbie Fowler, compared favourably with Lineker after a Liverpool season full of lethal marksmanship, failed with a weak header from Stone's cross and then — with the Croats' willpower draining away in the second period — missed by a distance when clubmate McManaman set up a straightforward chance from six yards. McManaman himself struck a post with ten minutes to go, with Sheringham off target from the rebound. It might have gone on all night.

England: Seaman, Neville G., Pearce, Ince, Wright, McManaman, Platt, Gascoigne, Fowler, Sheringham, Stone.

Croatia: Mrmic, Pavlicic (Mladenovic), Jarni, Stimac (Soldo), Jerkan, Bilic, Asanovic, Prosinecki, Suker, Boban (Stanic), Boksic (Pamic).

Referee: Z. Przesmycki (Poland)
Attendance: 33,650

England 3   Hungary 0

18th May 1996, Wembley

England finally rattled in a few goals in their last Wembley fixture before Euro 96, even though the quality of the opposition was poor. Hungary, arguably the best team in the world in the 1950s, have fallen on hard times recently and finished fourth in their Euro 96 qualifying group — with only Iceland below them. The visitors failed to register a shot at goal in the first half and England, with Blackburn's Jason Wilcox included for the first time wide on the left, were allowed to attack more or less at will.

But it took until the 39th minute for England to achieve a breakthrough and it came from the sliding right boot of Darren Anderton, back in the team after a long lay-off to recover from a persistent hernia injury. Tottenham team-mate Sheringham swept over a low cross from the left, Ferdinand went for it but missed, and Anderton arrived on cue at the far post to knock the ball into the gaping goal.

England continued to play with the same freedom

in the second period, with the possibility of a Hungarian comeback pretty remote. On 52 minutes Paul Ince flicked a free-kick into the box while the Hungarians were still trying to organise a "wall" and Platt had plenty of time in which to set himself up for a shot. Petry rushed out to successfully block the attempt but the England captain's persistence helped him to finally force the ball home.

It was 3–0 ten minutes later. Petry flapped unconvincingly at a high ball under pressure from Ferdinand and the ball fell in front of Anderton, who despatched it with a fierce snapshot that flew into the roof of the net via Sebok's lunging boot. With the game well won, a triple substitution by Terry Venables gave two further players their England debut – goalkeeper Ian Walker for an almost totally unoccupied Seaman and Spurs team-mate Sol Campbell for Ince in the "holding" role in front of the defence. A comprehensive win for the home side – but the likes of Germany and Holland could hardly be so accommodating.

England: Seaman (Walker), Neville G., Pearce, Ince (Campbell), Wright (Southgate), Lee, Platt (Wise), Wilcox, Ferdinand (Shearer), Sheringham, Anderton.

Hungary: Petry, Sebok, Banfi, Plokai, Mracsko (Aranyos), Urban, Hahn, Balog (Illes), Nagy (Telek), Horvath (Lisztes), Vincze (Egressy).

Referee: Dr. M. Merk (Germany)

Attendance: 34,184

China 0 England 3

23rd May 1996, Beijing

England's final preparatory matches before Euro 96 took them on a short tour to the Far East and, firstly, to a stiff test against the Chinese in the massive Workers' Stadium. Two goals by Nick Barmby, essential to his ambition to make the 22-man squad for the championship, and a third from England's "man of the match", Paul Gascoigne, were apt reward for a very professional performance in trying conditions.

So much could have gone wrong on an emotional night in Beijing. A 65,000 crowd welcomed their Chinese heroes with an ear-splitting roar, accompanied by the blowing of countless little plastic trumpets, and the home team was clearly ready to "do or die" against illustrious England. The playing surface had been so suspect that the England Coach had felt the need to travel out to inspect it some weeks

before the match. In the end his charges announced that they had "played on worse".

A relatively inexperienced England line-up destroyed Chinese hopes with a surprisingly authoritative display. Particularly outstanding was Tony Adams, the captain, who came through his first competitive match in four months with great credit. Flanked by Gary and Philip Neville – the first brothers to appear in the same England side since the Charltons – Adams inspired his team-mates to move forward and harry the Chinese out of their stride.

Barmby, of course, was another major success in his first England match of 1996. Close to the half-hour mark he shot right-footed against the far post and struck the rebound clinically home with his left. Seven minutes into the second half he chipped delightfully over Ou Chouliang after Gazza's exquisite through-pass had put the bubbly striker into space. When Gascoigne himself flicked in a simple third on 64 minutes the match was effectively over. There was a spate of substitutions and Robbie Fowler, on for Shearer, looked dangerous enough to boost his own Euro 96 prospects.

China: Ou Chouliang, Xu Hong, Wei Qun, Fan Zhiyi, Li Hongjun, Xie Yuxin (Li Meng), Li Bing (Peng Weiguo), Jiang Feng (Gao Zhongxun), Ma Mingyn, Gao Feng, Hao Haidung.

England: Flowers (Walker), Neville G., Neville P., Redknapp, Adams (Ehiogu), Southgate, Barmby (Beardsley), Gascoigne, Shearer (Fowler), McManaman (Stone), Anderton.

Referee: P. Collina (Italy)

Attendance: 65,000

Three days later England beat a Hong Kong Golden Select XI 1–0 in the Hong Kong Stadium. Les Ferdinand scored England's goal with a header from eight yards in the 33rd minute. Ince and Platt worked hard in midfield and Anderton looked bright when he came on for Stone. Caps were not awarded.

HKGS XI: Hesford, van der Sander (Shing Kit), Duxbury, Watson, Fook Wing, Fairweather, Grainger, Roberts, Bullen, Grabo, Bajkusa (Cam Chuen).

England: Seaman, Neville G., Pearce, Ince, Adams, Howey (Campbell), Platt, McManaman (Wilcox), Ferdinand (Shearer), Sheringham, (Fowler), Stone (Anderton).

Referee: S. Seelarjar (Malaysia)

Attendance: 26,000

FOOTBALL CAME HOME by David Barber

England's Matches at Euro 96

The Wembley crowd's reaction to Alan Shearer's third-minute headed goal against Germany in the semi-final was measured at 128 decibels – significantly louder than the sound of Concorde taking off. But this was just one of several heart-stopping high points as Football Came Home during Euro 96. England had begun with a frustrating draw in the opening match of the tournament, exactly as they had done thirty years before. Then the Scots, at Wembley for the first time since a Rous Cup encounter in 1988, were finally vanquished after David Seaman had elbowed McAllister's penalty-kick over the bar and Gazza had netted a magical clinching goal two minutes later. Fancied Holland were swept aside on "Orange Night", allowing England to top Group A, and quarter-final opponents Spain were on their way home after more than two nerve-wracking hours that included extra time (with the prospect of a match-winning "golden goal" at any moment) and a penalty shootout. 18 million home fans were watching on television. For the lucky 75,000 in the stadium, who produced a noise and atmosphere not even experienced in 1966, there had been a clear "I was there" factor. As if there hadn't been enough excitement already, pre-tournament favourites Germany awaited England in the semi-final. The Wembley showdown with one of our greatest rivals – remembering 1966 (Wembley), 1970 (Leon) and 1990 (Turin) in particular – again went the distance. This time a record 28.2 million TV audience saw a match of almost unbearable tension. One of our prominent journalists called the extra-time period "mind-boggling".

England 1   Switzerland 1

8th June 1996, Wembley

Paul Ince threaded the ball through on 23 minutes and Alan Shearer cleverly avoided the offside trap before bludgeoning a shot between Swiss goalkeeper Pascolo and his unprotected near post. So prolific in the Premiership, the Blackburn striker had found the net for the first time since his brace against the USA in September 1994. It was an opportune time to break a barren sequence. England looked to be on their way.

But they lived on their nerves for the rest of an opening game increasingly dominated by the Swiss. Their worst fears were realized eight minutes from the end when Turkyilmaz equalized from the penalty mark. Most of the predominantly English crowd felt the award of a penalty-kick against Stuart Pearce for hands rather harsh, but the only opinion which mattered was that of the Spanish referee. David Seaman guessed right; the ball went left.

England: Seaman, Neville G., Pearce, Ince, Adams, Southgate, McManaman (Stone), Gascoigne (Platt), Shearer, Sheringham (Barmby), Anderton.

Switzerland: Pascolo, Jeanneret, Vega, Henchoz, Quentin, Geiger (Koller), Vogel, Sforza, Bonvin (Chapuisat), Grassi, Turkyilmaz.

Referee: M. Diez Vega (Spain)

Attendance: 76,567

England 2   Scotland 0

15th June 1996, Wembley

After a first half arguably shaded by Scotland, there was a new verve apparent in England at the start of the second period and the first goal wasn't long in coming. McManaman found Neville wide on the right on 53 minutes and he curled in a cross that eluded Goram and his defence but connected with Shearer's head at the far post. A simple goal but the reaction from the shirt-sleeved English fans was ear-splitting.

The Scots strived to find the goal that they had found so elusive latterly and it looked promising for them on 77 minutes as Durie fell over Adams' outstretched leg and the Italian referee pointed to the penalty mark. David Seaman became England's hero as he deflected McAllister's fierce shot well over the top. A couple of minutes after the reprieve Paul Gascoigne flicked the ball over Hendry with his left foot and buried a half-volley with his right for a delightful second English goal.

England: Seaman, Neville G., Pearce (Redknapp) (Campbell), Ince (Stone), Adams, Southgate, McManaman, Gascoigne, Shearer, Sheringham, Anderton.

Scotland: Goram, McKimmie, Boyd, Calderwood, Hendry, Spencer (McCoist), McCall, McAllister, Collins, McKinlay (Burley), Durie (Jess).

Referee: P. Pairetto (Italy)

Attendance: 76,864

England 4   Holland 1

18th June 1996, Wembley

England trounced the Dutch with a display of passion and power that left home fans feeling high on victory. It was Teddy Sheringham who sparked England's opening goal on 23 minutes, releasing the ball as if out of a catapult into McManaman's urgent stride through the inside-right channel. Ince surged into the box, using his instep to flick the ball on, and Blind sent him flying. Shearer slammed home the penalty and the stadium erupted.

Early in the second period England had a dream-like eleven minutes in which they scored three times. Gazza swung in a corner from the left and Sheringham, loitering near the penalty mark, found enough power with his header to beat Van der Sar. Gazza helped to create the next, sweeping away Winter's challenge before laying the ball on a plate for Sheringham. The Tottenham man feinted to shoot and cleverly diverted it to Shearer who drove it in with awesome force. The Dutch disarray was complete as Sheringham notched his second after the goalkeeper had pushed out Anderton's effort. On 77 minutes substitute Kluivert scored the consolation goal that kept the Dutch in the competition.

England: Seaman, Neville G., Pearce, Ince (Platt), Adams, Southgate, McManaman, Gascoigne, Shearer (Fowler), Sheringham (Barmby), Anderton.

Holland: Van der Sar, Reiziger, Blind, Bogarde, Winter, Seedorf, Witschge (De Kock), De Boer R. (Kluivert), Jordi, Bergkamp, Hoekstra (Cocu).

Referee: G. Grabher (Austria)

Attendance: 76,798

England 0   Spain 0
(England won 4–2 on penalties)

22nd June 1996, Wembley

England's quarter-final performance on the following Saturday didn't quite have the sheer exuberance of the victory over the Dutch – Spain's efficient organisation was responsible for that – but there was another sort of glory this time. Adams and Southgate showed great resilience in defence, with Pearce not far behind, and England rode their luck a couple of times to ultimately win via the shootout. Salinas had shot past Seaman after Hierro's miscue had confused the English defence on 33 minutes and the referee's offside decision was debatable. Spanish forwards fell convincingly in the box several times – but Monsieur Batta refused to be swayed.

England held firm at the back and both Shearer and Sheringham missed close-range chances in the second half. And so to penalties, with English hearts fluttering like the St. George flags all round the ground. Shearer, Platt, Pearce (bravely, after his miss at Italia '90) and Gazza scored nervelessly. Hierro, the Spanish captain, hit the bar and Seaman saved magnificently from Nadal, plunging to his left to fist

the ball away. "Three Lions on a Shirt" had never been sung so lustily.

England: Seaman, Neville G., Pearce, McManaman (Barmby), Adams, Southgate, Platt, Gascoigne, Shearer, Sheringham (Stone), Anderton (Fowler).

Spain: Zubizarreta, Alkorta (Lopez), Nadal, Abelardo, Belsue, Hierro, Amor, Sergi, Manjarin (Caminero), Kiko, Salinas (Alfonso).

Referee: M. Batta (France)

Attendance: 75,440

England 1   Germany 1
(Germany won 6–5 on penalties)

26th June 1996, Wembley

This was the "big one" in every sense and it lived up to its pre-match billing. England against Germany at Wembley, the Euro 96 semi-final, will be one of those special occasions which become part of the country's sporting history and live on in the memory forever. After a gruelling thirty minutes of extra time, during which both teams came within the proverbial whisker of snatching a match-winning "golden goal", fans at Wembley and the millions watching on television were probably as drained as the players.

England had a brilliant start to the match, Adams touching on Gazza's corner from the left for Shearer to burst through and head them in front in the third minute. It was his fifth goal of Euro 96 and he finished the tournament as leading scorer. Germany's first dangerous attack produced an equaliser on 16 minutes, Helmer sliding the ball across the face of the goal for Kuntz to dart in front of Pearce and sweep the ball past Seaman. No miracle save this time – but the Arsenal 'keeper was only beaten twice in open play in the whole of Euro 96. Sudden-death extra time produced heart-stopping action: Anderton struck a post, Kuntz had a header disallowed, Gazza missed Shearer's cross-shot right on the line, Ziege's effort curled inches wide. Shearer, Platt, Pearce (yes, again), Gazza and Sheringham survived the pressure to score in the shootout ... but it was not to be. It was Germany who went on to their fourth final.

England: Seaman, McManaman, Pearce, Ince, Adams, Southgate, Platt, Gascoigne, Shearer, Sheringham, Anderton.

Germany: Kopke, Sammer, Reuter, Babbel, Helmer (Bode), Ziege, Scholl (Hassler), Freund (Strunz), Moller, Eilts, Kuntz.

Referee: S. Puhl (Hungary)

Attendance: 75,862

UNDER-21 MATCHES

Portugal 2   England 0

2nd September 1995, Santa Maria de Lamas

Dave Sexton's Under-21s had to travel to play their talented Portuguese counterparts without the injured Campbell, Unsworth and Pearce, and were facing a severe test in front of a 10,000 full house with a makeshift (and previously uncapped) central defensive pairing of Riccardo Scimeca and Robbie Elliott. A brace of goals from Sporting Lisbon striker Dani, later loaned to West Ham, caused the damage as the home side inflicted on England their first defeat of the European Championship qualifying campaign. On a further negative note Bolton's Alan Thompson was sent off two minutes from time after appearing to kick a grounded opponent.

Portugal's expert passing and movement caused England problems from the start. Gomes missed a clear chance on 14 minutes and Elliott and Phil Neville were cautioned as a suspect-looking English defence fought to stem the tide. Gomes then raced in to head Andrade's cross beyond Paul Gerrard and against a post in the 24th minute and Dani reacted quickly to score. Fowler and Shipperley looked isolated in attack and England managed just one worthwhile attempt in the first period, a shot from the lively Thompson. But Portugal had doubled their lead by the interval, Dani cutting inside Dean Gordon before shooting under Gerrard's dive with a soft effort from 20 yards. Now England had to win their last qualifying match and hope that the Portuguese dropped points in their remaining two fixtures.

England: Gerrard, Neville P., Gordon, Scimeca, Elliott, Beckham, Butt (Bart-Williams), Sinclair Thompson, Fowler, Shipperley.

Norway 2   England 2

10th October 1995, Stavanger

England came within three minutes of victory against a team currently top of their European Champion-ship qualifying group. The highly-rated Solskjaer, said to be attracting the attention of English scouts, had put the Norwegians in front on 41 minutes as his fierce shot gave Watson no hope – but England took charge after Pedersen had been dismissed early in the second half following a foul on Andy Booth and subsequent inappropriate remarks to the referee.

Tottenham's powerful midfielder Sol Campbell survived four Norwegian challenges before firing an unstoppable equaliser past Ulla on 62 minutes, his second goal at Under-21 level, and England went ahead with 13 minutes left when Booth knocked the ball in from close range after Neil Shipperley's effort had been blocked.

England had battled back well to hold an advantage going into the final three minutes, enjoying so much possession in the second half that coach Sexton thought they were "almost drunk with it", and then all their good work was ruined by a goal from the resilient Norwegians. Hestad set up the chance and Lund struck the ball home superbly.

England: Watson D. (Oakes), Watson S. (Neville P.), Gordon, Pearce, Campbell (Bowyer), Unsworth, Roberts, Pollock (Holland), Shipperley, Booth (Dichio), Joachim.

England 2   Austria 1

14th November 1995, Middlesbrough

Liverpool scoring sensation Robbie Fowler netted one and set up another to suggest that he might be ready to take the next step up the international ladder and join Terry Venables' seniors. But England's youngsters failed to make it through to the European Championship quarter-finals – despite this convinc-ing win over Austria in front of 13,496 at the Riverside Stadium – due to Portugal's 3–1 defeat of the Republic of Ireland in Leiria which ensured that they topped Group 6 by a point.

Fowler, likened by Dave Sexton to the great Jimmy Greaves, opened the scoring on 18 minutes with his third strike in eight appearances for the Under-21s. A long ball from Steve Watson split the Austrian defence and allowed Neil Shipperley to slide a pass across to Fowler, who confidently struck a low drive into the unguarded goal. Shipperley then helped himself to his own third goal at this level, slotting home past Krassnitzer on 34 minutes after Fowler had cleverly flicked on Chris Bart-Williams' free-kick. Austria had been back in contention with Cerny's surprise equaliser two minutes after Fowler's opener but England were clear winners and could have had more goals if they had shown more composure in striking positions.

England: Oakes, Watson S., Elliott, Campbell, Roberts, Unsworth, Butt, Pollock (Beckham), Shipperley, Bart-Williams (Holland), Fowler.

England 0   Croatia 1

23rd April 1996, Sunderland

A disappointingly small Roker Park crowd (4,376) saw the home team enjoy long periods of possession to little effect and lose to a goal from Vucko, arguably the pick of a Croat side packed with home-based talent. The Croatia Under-21s were as comfortable on the ball as the seniors at Wembley on the following evening but it was Dave Sexton's team which generated several chances early on. Richard Rufus powered a header against the bar from Briscoe's corner and Runje saved Bruce Dyer's effort from Terry Cooke's near-post cross from point-blank range.

An inexperienced England side, with only three players previously capped at Under-21 level, found itself exposed twice within a minute near the half-hour mark – and on the second occasion it proved decisive as far as the result was concerned. A piece of Vugrinec trickery took him easily past O'Connor and his shot, hit almost too hard, thudded against the underside of the bar. Then Chris Day dived to keep out Covic's shot but could do nothing to prevent the unmarked Vucko from thumping the rebound into the empty goal. Vucko missed a sitter for the stylish visitors three minutes into the second half, while at the other end Chris Holland blazed Kevin Gallen's centre over the top.

England: Day (Davis), O'Connor (Carbon), Rufus, Thatcher (Plummer), Brown, Cooke, Ford (Hendrie), Holland, Briscoe, Gallen (Moore), Dyer.

TOULON TOURNAMENT

England have taken part in the annual end-of-season Toulon Under-21 tournament in every year since 1987. England have won the trophy four times and their complete record reads like this:-

- 1987: Finished in fifth place, scoring just two goals in four matches
- 1988: Finished second, losing 4–2 to France in the final
- 1989: Finished fourth, winning one match
- 1990: Winners, beating Czechoslovakia 2–1 in the final
- 1991: Winners, beating France 1–0 in the final
- 1992: Eliminated in first round without a victory
- 1993: Winners, beating France 1–0 in the final
- 1994: Winners, beating Portugal 2–0 in the final
- 1995: Lost 2–0 to France in the semi-final

Coach Dave Sexton took an England Under-21 squad out to the South of France on 22 May for the 1996 tournament, with his team having been placed in Group B alongside Angola, Belgium, Brazil and Portugal. Group A comprised Argentina, Colombia, France, Holland and Russia. The two group winners would play the final in Toulon on 3 June.

Glenn Hoddle watched as England played their opening match of the tournament against Belgium in Toulon on 24 May. He was joined by assistant John Gorman in looking at players who hope to follow in the footsteps of Gascoigne, Anderton and Shearer, who have all graced this tournament.

Sexton was being assisted by Graham Rix, Hoddle's former reserve team coach at Chelsea. The pair had to make numerous changes after 11 of the original 18-man squad withdrew because of injury. Three players won their first Under-21 caps against the Belgians – Steve Slade (Tottenham), Jamie Stuart (Charlton) and Ben Thornley (Manchester United) – though the most keenly watched player would have been United's David Beckham who had made such an impact during their double-winning season. England achieved a winning start to the competition with Steve Slade's goal on 38 minutes accounting for a Belgian team that were then hammered 7–0 by Brazil.

England were in action again four days later in the Stade P. Rocofort in Cuers and their opponents this time were Angola, beaten 1–0 by England in the previous year's tournament. Unfortunately England seemed to lack some of the urgency displayed against Belgium and a couple of mistakes cost them the match. Chris Plummer hauled down Malamba on the edge of the box after skipper Richard Rufus had lost the ball in midfield and the French referee called a penalty, converted by Muhongo. Valdo Costa made it 2–0 after robbing Stuart and slipping the ball past Andy Marshall from close in. On 30 May, in Arles, England went down 3–1 to Portugal in their next match in disappointing fashion. Slade scored again – but five players were booked and Terry Cooke saw red on the hour.

For the last group fixture with Brazil, back in Toulon's Stade Mayol on 1 June, England were down to 13 available players – due to injuries and suspensions – and three of those were goalkeepers! Sexton's youngsters bowed out of the tournament bravely, taking a surprise 50th-minute lead when Tranmere Rovers striker Ian Moore scored with a cracking shot from 25 yards but then conceding two goals in a torrid six-minute spell. Alex and Adailton netted to book Brazil's place in the final against the hosts.

Squad: Day (Tottenham), Plummer (QPR), Rufus and Stuart (Charlton), Beckham (Manchester United), Brown (Manchester City), Holland (Newcastle), Bowyer (Charlton), Cooke (Manchester United), Slade (Tottenham), Thornley (Manchester United), Davis (Luton), Marshall (Norwich), O'Connor (Everton), Briscoe (Sheffield Wednesday), Moore (Tranmere), Challis (QPR), Branch (Everton).

20 ● ENGLAND'S FULL INTERNATIONAL TEAMS 1946–1996

(Up to and including 1st July 1996)

* captain   † own goal   Small numerals goals scored   Numbers after sub player replaced

Versus	Venue	Result	1	2	3	4	5
1946–47							
Northern Ireland	A	7–2	Swift	Scott	Hardwick*	W Wright	Franklin
Republic of Ireland	A	1–0	Swift	Scott	Hardwick*	W Wright	Franklin
Wales	H	3–0	Swift	Scott	Hardwick*	W Wright	Franklin
Holland	H	8–2	Swift	Scott	Hardwick*	W Wright	Franklin
Scotland	H	1–1	Swift	Scott	Hardwick*	W Wright	Franklin
France	H	3–0	Swift	Scott	Hardwick*	W Wright	Franklin
Switzerland	A	0–1	Swift	Scott	Hardwick*	W Wright	Franklin
Portugal	A	10–0	Swift	Scott	Hardwick*	W Wright	Franklin
1947–48							
Belgium	A	5–2	Swift	Scott	Hardwick*	Ward	Franklin
Wales	A	3–0	Swift	Scott	Hardwick*	P Taylor	Franklin
Northern Ireland	H	2–2	Swift	Scott	Hardwick*	P Taylor	Franklin
Sweden	H	4–2	Swift	Scott	Hardwick*	P Taylor	Franklin
Scotland	A	2–0	Swift	Scott	Hardwick*	W Wright	Franklin
Italy	A	4–0	Swift*	Scott	J Howe	W Wright	Franklin
1948–49							
Denmark	A	0–0	Swift*	Scott	Aston	W Wright	Franklin
Ireland	A	6–2	Swift	Scott	J Howe	W Wright*	Franklin
Wales	H	1–0	Swift	Scott	Aston	Ward	Franklin
Switzerland	H	6–0	Ditchburn	Ramsey	Aston	W Wright*	Franklin
Scotland	H	1–3	Swift	Aston	J Howe	W Wright*	Franklin
Sweden	A	1–3	Ditchburn	Shimwell	Aston	W Wright*	Franklin
Norway	A	4–1	Swift	Ellerington	Aston	W Wright*	Franklin
France	A	3–1	Williams	Ellerington	Aston	W Wright*	Franklin
1949–50							
Republic of Ireland	H	0–2	Williams	Mozley	Aston	W Wright*	Franklin
Wales	A	4–1	Williams	Mozley	Aston	W Wright*	Franklin
Northern Ireland	H	9–2	Streten	Mozley	Aston	Watson	Franklin
Italy	H	2–0	Williams	Ramsey	Aston	Watson	Franklin
Scotland	A	1–0	Williams	Ramsey	Aston	W Wright*	Franklin
Portugal	A	5–3	Williams	Ramsey	Aston	W Wright*	WH Jones
Belgium	A	4–1	Williams	Ramsey	Aston	W Wright*	WH Jones
Chile	N	2–0	Williams	Ramsey	Aston	W Wright*	L Hughes
USA	N	0–1	Williams	Ramsey	Aston	W Wright*	L Hughes
Spain	N	0–1	Williams	Ramsey	Eckersley	W Wright*	L Hughes
1950–51							
Northern Ireland	A	4–1	Williams	Ramsey	Aston	W Wright*[1]	Chilton
Wales	H	4–2	Williams	Ramsey*	L Smith	Watson	L Compton
Yugoslavia	H	2–2	Williams	Ramsey*	Eckersley	Watson	L Compton
Scotland	H	2–3	Williams	Ramsey	Eckersley	Johnston	J Froggatt

6	7	8	9	10	11	Substitutes
Cockburn	Finney[1]	Carter[1]	Lawton[1]	Mannion[1]	Langton[1]	
Cockburn	Finney[1]	Carter	Lawton	Mannion	Langton	
Cockburn	Finney	Carter	Lawton[1]	Mannion[2]	Langton	
Johnston	Finney[1]	Carter[2]	Lawton[4]	Mannion[1]	Langton	
Johnston	S Matthews	Carter[1]	Lawton	Mannion	Mullen	
Lowe	Finney[1]	Carter[1]	Lawton	Mannion[1]	Langton	
Lowe	S Matthews	Carter	Lawton	Mannion	Langton	
Lowe	S Matthews[1]	Mortensen[4]	Lawton[4]	Mannion	Finney[1]	
W Wright	S Matthews	Mortensen[1]	Lawton[2]	Mannion	Finney[2]	
W Wright	S Matthews	Mortensen[1]	Lawton[1]	Mannion	Finney[1]	
W Wright	S Matthews	Mortensen	Lawton[1]	Mannion[1]	Finney	
W Wright	Finney	Mortensen[3]	Lawton[1]	Mannion	Langton	
Cockburn	S Matthews	Mortensen[1]	Lawton	Pearson	Finney[1]	
Cockburn	S Matthews	Mortensen[1]	Lawton[1]	Mannion	Finney[2]	
Cockburn	S Matthews	Hagan	Lawton	Shackleton	Langton	
Cockburn	S Matthews[1]	Mortensen[3]	Milburn[1]	Pearson[1]	Finney	
W Wright*	S Matthews	Mortensen	Milburn	Shackleton	Finney[1]	
Cockburn	S Matthews	J Rowley[1]	Milburn[1]	Haines[2]	Hancocks[2]	
Cockburn	S Matthews	Mortensen	Milburn[1]	Pearson	Finney	
Cockburn	Finney[1]	Mortensen	Bentley	J Rowley	Langton	
Dickinson	Finney[1]	Morris[1]	Mortensen	Mannion	Mullen[1]	†
Dickinson	Finney	Morris[2]	J Rowley[1]	Mannion	Mullen	
Dickinson	P Harris	Morris	Pye	Mannion	Finney	
Dickinson	Finney	Mortensen[1]	Milburn[3]	Shackleton	Hancocks	
W Wright*	Finney	Mortensen[2]	J Rowley[4]	Pearson[2]	J Froggatt[1]	
W Wright*[1]	Finney	Mortensen	J Rowley[1]	Pearson	J Froggatt	
Dickinson	Finney	Mannion	Mortensen	Bentley[1]	Langton	
Dickinson	Milburn	Mortensen[1]	Bentley	Mannion	Finney[4]	
Dickinson	Milburn	Mortensen[1]	Bentley[1]	Mannion[1]	Finney	Mullen 7[1]
Dickinson	Finney	Mannion[1]	Bentley	Mortensen[1]	Mullen	
Dickinson	Finney	Mannion	Bentley	Mortensen	Mullen	
Dickinson	S Matthews	Mortensen	Milburn	E Baily	Finney	
Dickinson	S Matthews	Mannion	J Lee[1]	E Baily[2]	Langton	
Dickinson	Finney	Mannion[1]	Milburn[1]	E Baily[2]	Medley	
Dickinson	Hancocks	Mannion	Lofthouse[2]	E Baily	Medley	
W Wright*	S Matthews	Mannion	Mortensen	Hassall[1]	Finney[1]	

Versus	Venue	Result	1	2	3	4	5
Argentina	H	2–1	Williams	Ramsey	Eckersley	W Wright*	J Taylor
Portugal	H	5–2	Williams	Ramsey*	Eckersley	Nicholson[1]	J Taylor

1951–52

Versus	Venue	Result	1	2	3	4	5
France	H	2–2	Williams	Ramsey	Willis	W Wright*	Chilton
Wales	A	1–1	Williams	Ramsey	L Smith	W Wright*	Barrass
Northern Ireland	H	2–0	Merrick	Ramsey	L Smith	W Wright*	Barrass
Austria	H	2–2	Merrick	Ramsey[1]	Eckersley	W Wright*	J Froggatt
Scotland	A	2–1	Merrick	Ramsey	Garrett	W Wright*	J Froggatt
Italy	A	1–1	Merrick	Ramsey	Garrett	W Wright*	J Froggatt
Austria	A	3–2	Merrick	Ramsey	Eckersley	W Wright*	J Froggatt
Switzerland	A	3–0	Merrick	Ramsey	Eckersley	W Wright*	J Froggart

1952–53

Versus	Venue	Result	1	2	3	4	5
Northern Ireland	A	2–2	Merrick	Ramsey	Eckersley	W Wright*	J Froggatt
Wales	H	5–2	Merrick	Ramsey	I. Smith	W Wright*	J Froggatt[1]
Belgium	H	5–0	Merrick	Ramsey	L Smith	W Wright*	J Froggatt
Scotland	H	2–2	Merrick	Ramsey	L Smith	W Wright*	Barrass
Argentina	A	0–0	Merrick	Ramsey	Eckersley	W Wright*	Johnston
Chile	A	2–1	Merrick	Ramsey	Eckersley	W Wright*	Johnston
Uruguay	A	1–2	Merrick	Ramsey	Eckersley	W Wright*	Johnston
USA	A	6–3	Ditchburn	Ramsey	Eckersley	W Wright*	Johnston

1953–54

Versus	Venue	Result	1	2	3	4	5
Wales	A	4–1	Merrick	Garrett	Eckersley	W Wright*	Johnston
FIFA	H	4–4	Merrick	Ramsey[1]	Eckersley	W Wright*	Ufton
Ireland	H	3–1	Merrick	Rickaby	Eckersley	W Wright*	Johnston
Hungary	H	3–6	Merrick	Ramsey[1]	Eckersley	W Wright*	Johnston
Scotland	A	4–2	Merrick	Staniforth	R Byrne	W Wright*	H Clarke
Yugoslavia	A	0–1	Merrick	Staniforth	R Byrne	W Wright*	Owen
Hungary	A	1–7	Merrick	Staniforth	R Byrne	W Wright*	Owen
Belgium	N	4–4	Merrick	Staniforth	R Byrne	W Wright*	Owen
Switzerland	N	2–0	Merrick	Staniforth	R Byrne	McGarry	W Wright*
Uruguay	N	2–4	Merrick	Staniforth	R Byrne	McGarry	W Wright*

1954–55

Versus	Venue	Result	1	2	3	4	5
Northern Ireland	A	2–0	Wood	Foulkes	R Byrne	Wheeler	W Wright*
Wales	H	3–2	Wood	Staniforth	R Byrne	Phillips	W Wright*
West Germany	H	3–1	Williams	Staniforth	R Byrne	Phillips	W Wright*
Scotland	H	7–2	Williams	Meadows	R Byrne	Armstrong	W Wright*
France	A	0–1	Williams	P Sillett	R Byrne	Flowers	W Wright*
Spain	A	1–1	Williams	P Sillett	R Byrne	Dickinson	W Wright*
Portugal	A	1–3	Williams	P Sillett	R Byrne	Dickinson	W Wright*

1955–56

Versus	Venue	Result	1	2	3	4	5
Denmark	A	5–1	Baynham	Hall	R Byrne	McGarry	W Wright*
Wales	A	1–2	Williams	Hall	R Byrne	McGarry	W Wright*
Northern Ireland	H	3–0	Baynham	Hall	R Byrne	Clayton	W Wright*
Spain	H	4–1	Baynham	Hall	R Byrne	Clayton	W Wright*
Scotland	A	1–1	R Matthews	Hall	R Byrne	Dickinson	W Wright*
Brazil	H	4–2	R Matthews	Hall	R Byrne	Clayton	W Wright*
Sweden	A	0–0	R Matthews	Hall	R Byrne	Clayton	W Wright*
Finland	A	5–1	Wood	Hall	R Byrne	Clayton	W Wright*
West Germany	A	3–1	R Matthews	Hall	R Byrne	Clayton	W Wright*

6	7	8	9	10	11	Substitutes
Cockburn	Finney	Mortensen[1]	Milburn[1]	Hassall	Metcalfe	
Cockburn	Finney[1]	Pearson	Milburn[2]	Hassall[1]	Metcalfe	
Cockburn	Finney	Mannion	Milburn	Hassall	Medley[1]	†
Dickinson	Finney	T Thompson	Lofthouse	E Baily[1]	Medley	
Dickinson	Finney	Sewell	Lofthouse[2]	Phillips	Medley	
Dickinson	Milton	Broadis	Lofthouse[1]	E Baily	Medley	
Dickinson	Finney	Broadis	Lofthouse	Pearson[2]	J Rowley	
Dickinson	Finney	Broadis[1]	Lofthouse	Pearson	Elliott	
Dickinson	Finney	Sewell[1]	Lofthouse[2]	E Baily	Elliott	
Dickinson	R Allen	Sewell[1]	Lofthouse[2]	E Baily	Finney	
Dickinson	Finney	Sewell	Lofthouse[1]	E Baily	Elliott[1]	
Dickinson	Finney[1]	R Froggatt	Lofthouse[2]	Bentley[1]	Elliott	
Dickinson	Finney	Bentley	Lofthouse[2]	R Froggatt[1]	Elliott[2]	
Dickinson	Finney	Broadis[2]	Lofthouse	R Froggatt	J Froggatt	
Dickinson	Finney	Broadis	Lofthouse	T Taylor	Berry	
Dickinson	Finney	Broadis	Lofthouse[1]	T Taylor	Berry	
Dickinson	Finney	Broadis	Lofthouse	T Taylor[1]	Berry	
Dickinson	Finney[2]	Broadis[1]	Lofthouse[2]	R Froggatt[1]	J Froggatt	
Dickinson	Finney	Quixall	Lofthouse[2]	Wilshaw[2]	Mullen	
Dickinson	S Matthews	Mortensen[1]	Lofthouse	Quixall	Mullen[2]	
Dickinson	S Matthews	Quixall	Lofthouse[1]	Hassall[2]	Mullen	
Dickinson	S Matthews	E Taylor	Mortensen[1]	Sewell[1]	Robb	
Dickinson	Finney	Broadis[1]	R Allen[1]	Nicholls[1]	Mullen[1]	
Dickinson	Finney	Broadis	R Allen	Nicholls	Mullen	
Dickinson	P Harris	Sewell	Jezzard	Broadis[1]	Finney	
Dickinson	S Matthews	Broadis[2]	Lofthouse[2]	T Taylor	Finney	
Dickinson	Finney	Broadis	T Taylor	Wilshaw[1]	Mullen[1]	
Dickinson	S Matthews	Broadis	Lofthouse[1]	Wilshaw	Finney[1]	
Barlow	S Matthews	Revie[1]	Lofthouse	Haynes[1]	Pilkington	
Slater	S Matthews	Bentley[3]	R Allen	Shackleton	Blunstone	
Slater	S Matthews	Bentley[1]	R Allen[1]	Shackleton[1]	Finney	
Edwards	S Matthews	Revie[1]	Lofthouse[2]	Wilshaw[4]	Blunstone	
Edwards	S Matthews	Revie	Lofthouse	Wilshaw	Blunstone	
Edwards	S Matthews	Bentley[1]	Lofthouse	Quixall	Wilshaw	
Edwards	S Matthews	Bentley[1]	Lofthouse	Wilshaw	Blunstone	Quixall 9
Dickinson	Milburn	Revie[2]	Lofthouse[2]	Bradford[1]	Finney	†
Dickinson	S Matthews	Revie	Lofthouse	Wilshaw	Finney	
Dickinson	Finney[1]	Haynes	Jezzard	Wilshaw[2]	Perry	
Dickinson	Finney[1]	Atyeo[1]	Lofthouse	Haynes	Perry[2]	
Edwards	Finney	T Taylor	Lofthouse	Haynes[1]	Perry	
Edwards	S Matthews	Atyeo	T Taylor[2]	Haynes	Grainger[2]	
Edwards	Berry	Atyeo	T Taylor	Haynes	Grainger	
Edwards	Astall[1]	Haynes[1]	T Taylor	Wilshaw[1]	Grainger	Lofthouse 9[2]
Edwards[1]	Astall	Haynes[1]	T Taylor	Wilshaw	Grainger[1]	

● 55

Versus	Venue	Result	1	2	3	4	5
1956–57							
Northern Ireland	A	1–1	R Matthews	Hall	R Byrne	Clayton	W Wright*
Wales	H	3–1	Ditchburn	Hall	R Byrne	Clayton	W Wright*
Yugoslavia	H	3–0	Ditchburn	Hall	R Byrne	Clayton	W Wright*
Denmark	H	5–2	Ditchburn	Hall	R Byrne	Clayton	W Wright*
Scotland	H	2–1	Hodgkinson	Hall	R Byrne	Clayton	W Wright*
Republic of Ireland	H	5–1	Hodgkinson	Hall	R Byrne	Clayton	W Wright*
Denmark	A	4–1	Hodgkinson	Hall	R Byrne	Clayton	W Wright*
Republic of Ireland	A	1–1	Hodgkinson	Hall	R Byrne	Clayton	W Wright*
1957–58							
Wales	A	4–0	Hopkinson	D Howe	R Byrne	Clayton	W Wright*
Northern Ireland	H	2–3	Hopkinson	D Howe	R Byrne	Clayton	W Wright*
France	H	4–0	Hopkinson	D Howe	R Byrne	Clayton	W Wright*
Scotland	A	4–0	Hopkinson	D Howe	Langley	Clayton	W Wright*
Portugal	H	2–1	Hopkinson	D Howe	Langley	Clayton	W Wright*
Yugoslavia	A	0–5	Hopkinson	D Howe	Langley	Clayton	W Wright*
USSR	A	1–1	McDonald	D Howe	T Banks	Clamp	W Wright*
USSR	N	2–2	McDonald	D Howe	T Banks	Clamp	W Wright*
Brazil	N	0–0	McDonald	D Howe	T Banks	Clamp	W Wright*
Austria	N	2–2	McDonald	D Howe	T Banks	Clamp	W Wright*
USSR	N	0–1	McDonald	D Howe	T Banks	Clayton	W Wright*
1958–59							
Northern Ireland	A	3–3	McDonald	D Howe	T Banks	Clayton	W Wright*
USSR	H	5–0	McDonald	D Howe	G Shaw	Clayton	W Wright*
Wales	H	2–2	McDonald	D Howe	G Shaw	Clayton	W Wright*
Scotland	H	1–0	Hopkinson	D Howe	G Shaw	Clayton	W Wright*
Italy	H	2–2	Hopkinson	D Howe	G Shaw	Clayton	W Wright*
Brazil	A	0–2	Hopkinson	D Howe	Armfield	Clayton	W Wright*
Peru	A	1–4	Hopkinson	D Howe	Armfield	Clayton	W Wright*
Mexico	A	1–2	Hopkinson	D Howe	Armfield	Clayton	W Wright*
USA	A	8–1	Hopkinson	D Howe	Armfield	Clayton	W Wright*
1959–60							
Wales	A	1–1	Hopkinson	D Howe	A Allen	Clayton*	T Smith
Sweden	H	2–3	Hopkinson	D Howe	A Allen	Clayton*	T Smith
Northern Ireland	H	2–1	R Springett	D Howe	A Allen	Clayton*	Brown
Scotland	A	1–1	R Springett	Armfield	Wilson	Clayton*	Slater
Yugoslavia	H	3–3	R Springett	Armfield	Wilson	Clayton*	Swan
Spain	A	0–3	R Springett	Armfield	Wilson	R Robson	Swan
Hungary	A	0–2	R Springett	Armfield	Wilson	R Robson	Swan
1960–61							
Northern Ireland	A	5–2	R Springett	Armfield	McNeil	R Robson	Swan
Luxembourg	A	9–0	R Springett	Armfield	McNeil	R Robson	Swan
Spain	H	4–2	R Springett	Armfield	McNeil	R Robson	Swan
Wales	H	5–1	Hodgkinson	Armfield	McNeil	R Robson	Swan
Scotland	H	9–3	R Springett	Armfield	McNeil	R Robson	Swan
Mexico	H	8–0	R Springett	Armfield	McNeil	R Robson[1]	Swan
Portugal	A	1–1	R Springett	Armfield	McNeil	R Robson[1]	Swan
Italy	A	3–2	R Springett	Armfield	McNeil	R Robson	Swan
Austria	A	1–3	R Springett	Armfield	Angus	Miller	Swan
1961–62							
Luxembourg	H	4–1	R Springett	Armfield*	McNeil	R Robson	Swan

6	7	8	9	10	11	*Substitutes*
Edwards	S Matthews[1]	Revie	T Taylor	Wilshaw	Grainger	
Dickinson	S Matthews	Brooks[1]	Finney[1]	Haynes[1]	Grainger	
Dickinson	S Matthews	Brooks[1]	Finney	Haynes	Blunstone	T Taylor 10[2]
Dickinson	S Matthews	Brooks	T Taylor[3]	Edwards[2]	Finney	
Edwards[1]	S Matthews	T Thompson	Finney	Kevan[1]	Grainger	
Edwards	S Matthews	Atyeo[2]	T Taylor[3]	Haynes	Finney	
Edwards	S Matthews	Atyeo[1]	T Taylor[2]	Haynes[1]	Finney	
Edwards	Finney	Atyeo[1]	T Taylor	Haynes	Pegg	
Edwards	Douglas	Kevan	T Taylor	Haynes[2]	Finney[1]	†
Edwards[1]	Douglas	Kevan	T Taylor	Haynes	A'Court[1]	
Edwards	Douglas	R Robson[2]	T Taylor[2]	Haynes	Finney	
Slater	Douglas[1]	R Charlton[1]	Kevan[2]	Haynes	Finney	
Slater	Douglas	R Charlton[2]	Kevan	Haynes	Finney	
Slater	Douglas	R Charlton	Kevan	Haynes	Finney	
Slater	Douglas	R Robson	Kevan[1]	Haynes	Finney	
Slater	Douglas	R Robson	Kevan[1]	Haynes	Finney[1]	
Slater	Douglas	R Robson	Kevan	Haynes	A'Court	
Slater	Douglas	R Robson	Kevan[1]	Haynes[1]	A'Court	
Slater	Brabrook	Broadbent	Kevan	Haynes	A'Court	
McGuinness	Brabrook	Broadbent	R Charlton[2]	Haynes	Finney[1]	
Slater	Douglas	R Charlton[1]	Lofthouse[1]	Haynes[3]	Finney	
Flowers	Clapton	Broadbent[2]	Lofthouse	Haynes	A'Court	
Flowers	Douglas	Broadbent	R Charlton[1]	Haynes	Holden	
Flowers	Bradley[1]	Broadbent	R Charlton[1]	Haynes	Holden	
Flowers	Deeley	Broadbent	R Charlton	Haynes	Holden	
Flowers	Deeley	Greaves[1]	R Charlton	Haynes	Holden	
McGuinness	Holden	Greaves	Kevan[1]	Haynes	R Charlton	Flowers 6, Bradley 7
Flowers[2]	Bradley[1]	Greaves	Kevan[1]	Haynes[1]	R Charlton[3]	
Flowers	Connelly	Greaves[1]	Clough	R Charlton	Holiday	
Flowers	Connelly[1]	Greaves	Clough	R Charlton[1]	Holliday	
Flowers	Connelly	Haynes	Baker[1]	Parry[1]	Holliday	
Flowers	Connelly	Broadbent	Baker	Parry	R Charlton[1]	
Flowers	Douglas[1]	Haynes[1]	Baker	Greaves[1]	R Charlton	
Flowers	Brabrook	Haynes*	Baker	Greaves	R Charlton	
Flowers	Douglas	Haynes*	Baker	Viollet	R Charlton	
Flowers	Douglas[1]	Greaves[2]	R Smith[1]	Haynes*	R Charlton[1]	
Flowers	Douglas	Greaves[3]	R Smith[2]	Haynes*[1]	R Charlton[3]	
Flowers	Douglas[1]	Greaves[1]	R Smith[2]	Haynes*	R Charlton	
Flowers	Douglas	Greaves[2]	R Smith[1]	Haynes*[1]	R Charlton[1]	
Flowers	Douglas[1]	Greaves[3]	R Smith[2]	Haynes*[2]	R Charlton[1]	
Flowers[1]	Douglas[2]	Kevan	Hitchens[1]	Haynes*	R Charlton[3]	
Flowers[1]	Douglas	Greaves	R Smith	Haynes*	R Charlton	
Flowers	Douglas	Greaves[1]	Hitchens[2]	Haynes*	R Charlton	
Flowers	Douglas	Greaves[1]	Hitchens	Haynes*	R Charlton	
Flowers	Douglas	Fantham	Pointer[1]	Viollet[1]	R Charlton[2]	

Versus	Venue	Result	1	2	3	4	5
Wales	A	1–1	R Springett	Armfield	Wilson	R Robson	Swan
Portugal	H	2–0	R Springett	Armfield	Wilson	R Robson	Swan
Northern Ireland	H	1–1	R Springett	Armfield	Wilson	R Robson	Swan
Austria	H	3–1	R Springett	Armfield	Wilson	R Robson	Swan
Scotland	A	0–2	R Springett	Armfield	Wilson	Anderson	Swan
Switzerland	H	3–1	R Springett	Armfield	Wilson	Anderson	Swan
Peru	A	4–0	R Springett	Armfield	Wilson	R Robson	Swan
Hungary	N	1–2	R Springett	Armfield	Wilson	Moore	Norman
Argentina	N	3–1	R Springett	Armfield	Wilson	Moore	Norman
Bulgaria	N	0–0	R Springett	Armfield	Wilson	Moore	Norman
Brazil	N	1–3	R Springett	Armfield	Wilson	Moore	Norman

1962–63

Versus	Venue	Result	1	2	3	4	5
France	H	1–1	R Springett	Armfield*	Wilson	Moore	Norman
Northern Ireland	A	3–1	R Springett	Armfield*	Wilson	Moore	Labone
Wales	H	4–0	R Springett	Armfield*	G Shaw	Moore	Labone
France	A	2–5	R Springett	Armfield*	Henry	Moore	Labone
Scotland	H	1–2	G Banks	Armfield*	G Byrne	Moore	Norman
Brazil	H	1–1	G Banks	Armfield*	Wilson	Milne	Norman
Czechoslovakia	A	4–2	G Banks	Shellito	Wilson	Milne	Norman
East Germany	A	2–1	G Banks	Armfield*	Wilson	Milne	Norman
Switzerland	A	8–1	R Springett	Armfield*	Wilson	Kay[1]	Moore

1963–64

Versus	Venue	Result	1	2	3	4	5
Wales	A	4–0	G Banks	Armfield*	Wilson	Milne	Norman
Rest of the World	H	2–1	G Banks	Armfield*	Wilson	Milne	Norman
Northern Ireland	H	8–3	G Banks	Armfield*	R Thomson	Milne	Norman
Scotland	A	0–1	G Banks	Armfield*	Wilson	Milne	Norman
Uruguay	H	2–1	G Banks	Cohen	Wilson	Milne	Norman
Portugal	A	4–3	G Banks	Cohen	Wilson	Milne	Norman
Republic of Ireland	A	3–1	Waiters	Cohen	Wilson	Milne	Flowers
USA	A	10–0	G Banks	Cohen	R Thomson	M Bailey	Norman
Brazil	A	1–5	Waiters	Cohen	Wilson	Milne	Norman
Portugal	N	1–1	G Banks	R Thomson	Wilson	Flowers	Norman
Argentina	N	0–1	G Banks	R Thomson	Wilson	Milne	Norman

1964–65

Versus	Venue	Result	1	2	3	4	5
Northern Ireland	A	4–3	G Banks	Cohen	R Thomson	Milne	Norman
Belgium	H	2–2	Waiters	Cohen	R Thomson	Milne	Norman
Wales	H	2–1	Waiters	Cohen	R Thomson	M Bailey	Flowers*
Holland	A	1–1	Waiters	Cohen	R Thomson	Mullery	Norman
Scotland	H	2–2	G Banks	Cohen	Wilson	Stiles	J Charlton
Hungary	H	1–0	G Banks	Cohen	Wilson	Stiles	J Charlton
Yugoslavia	A	1–1	G Banks	Cohen	Wilson	Stiles	J Charlton
West Germany	A	1–0	G Banks	Cohen	Wilson	Stiles	J Charlton
Sweden	A	2–1	G Banks	Cohen	Wilson	Flowers	J Charlton

1965–66

Versus	Venue	Result	1	2	3	4	5
Wales	A	0–0	R Springett	Cohen	Wilson	Stiles	J Charlton
Austria	H	2–3	R Springett	Cohen	Wilson	Stiles	J Charlton
Northern Ireland	H	2–1	G Banks	Cohen	Wilson	Stiles	J Charlton
Spain	A	2–0	G Banks	Cohen	Wilson	Stiles	J Charlton
Poland	H	1–1	G Banks	Cohen	Wilson	Stiles	J Charlton
West Germany	H	1–0	G Banks	Cohen	K Newton	Moore*	J Charlton
Scotland	A	4–3	G Banks	Cohen	K Newton	Stiles	J Charlton
Yugoslavia	H	2–0	G Banks	Armfield*	Wilson	Peters	J Charlton

6	7	8	9	10	11	Substitutes
Flowers	Connelly	Douglas[1]	Pointer	Haynes*	R Charlton	
Flowers	Connelly[1]	Douglas	Pointer[1]	Haynes*	R Charlton	
Flowers	Douglas	J Byrne	Crawford	Haynes*	R Charlton[1]	
Flowers[1]	Connelly	Hunt[1]	Crawford[1]	Haynes*	R Charlton	
Flowers	Douglas `	Greaves	R Smith	Haynes*	R Charlton	
Flowers[1]	Connelly[1]	Greaves	Hitchens[1]	Haynes*	R Charlton	
Flowers[1]	Douglas	Greaves[3]	Hitchens	Haynes*	R Charlton	
Flowers[1]	Douglas	Greaves	Hitchens	Haynes*	R Charlton	
Flowers[1]	Douglas	Greaves[1]	Peacock	Haynes*	R Charlton[1]	
Flowers	Douglas	Greaves	Peacock	Haynes*	R Charlton	
Flowers	Douglas	Greaves	Hitchens[1]	Haynes*	R Charlton	
Flowers[1]	Hellawell	Crowe	Charnley	Greaves	A Hinton	
Flowers	Hellawell	F Hill	Peacock	Greaves[1]	O'Grady[2]	
Flowers	Connelly[1]	F Hill	Peacock[2]	Greaves[1]	Tambling	
Flowers	Connelly	Tambling[1]	R Smith[1]	Greaves	R Charlton	
Flowers	Douglas[1]	Greaves	R Smith	Melia	R Charlton	
Moore	Douglas[1]	Greaves	R Smith	Eastham	R Charlton	
Moore*	Paine	Greaves[2]	R Smith[1]	Eastham	R Charlton[1]	
Moore	Paine	Hunt[1]	R Smith	Eastham	R Charlton[1]	
Flowers	Douglas[1]	Greaves	J Byrne[2]	Melia[1]	R Charlton[3]	
Moore	Paine	Greaves[1]	R Smith[2]	Eastham	R Charlton[1]	
Moore	Paine[1]	Greaves[1]	R Smith	Eastham	R Charlton	
Moore	Paine[3]	Greaves[4]	R Smith[1]	Eastham	R Charlton	
Moore	Paine	Hunt	J Byrne	Eastham	R Charlton	
Moore*	Paine	Greaves	J Byrne[2]	Eastham	R Charlton	
Moore*	P Thompson	Greaves	J Byrne[3]	Eastham	R Charlton[1]	
Moore*	P Thompson	Greaves[1]	J Byrne[1]	Eastham[1]	R Charlton	
Flowers*	Paine[2]	Hunt[4]	Pickering[3]	Eastham	P Thompson	R Charlton 10[1]
Moore*	P Thompson	Greaves[1]	J Byrne	Eastham	R Charlton	
Moore*	Paine	Greaves	J Byrne	Hunt[1]	P Thompson	
Moore*	P Thompson	Greaves*	J Byrne_	Eastham	R Charlton	
Moore*	Paine	Greaves[3]	Pickering[1]	R Charlton	P Thompson	
Moore*	P Thompson	Greaves	Pickering[1]	Venables	A Hinton	†
Young	P Thompson	Hunt	Wignall[2]	J Byrne	A Hinton	
Flowers*	P Thompson	Greaves[1]	Wignall	Venables	R Charlton	
Moore*	P Thompson	Greaves[1]	Bridges	J Byrne	R Charlton[1]	
Moore*	Paine	Greaves[1]	Bridges	Eastham	Connelly	
Moore*	Paine	Greaves	Bridges[1]	Ball	Connelly	
Moore*	Paine[1]	Ball	M Jones	Eastham	Temple	
Moore*	Paine	Ball[1]	M Jones	Eastham	Connelly[1]	
Moore*	Paine	Greaves	Peacock	R Charlton	Connelly	
Moore*	Paine	Greaves	Bridges	R Charlton[1]	Connelly[1]	
Moore*	P Thompson	Baker[1]	Peacock[1]	R Charlton	Connelly	
Moore*	Ball	Hunt[1]	Baker[1]	Eastham	R Charlton	Hunter 9
Moore*[1]	Ball	Hunt	Baker	Eastham	G Harris	
Hunter	Ball	Hunt	Stiles[1]	G Hurst	R Charlton	Wilson 3
Moore*	Ball	Hunt[2]	R Charlton[1]	G Hurst[1]	Connelly	
Hunter	Paine	Greaves[1]	R Charlton[1]	G Hurst	Tambling	

Versus	Venue	Result	1	2	3	4	5
Finland	A	3–0	G Banks	Armfield*	Wilson	Peters[1]	J Charlton[1]
Norway	A	6–1	R Springett	Cohen	G Byrne	Stiles	Flowers
Denmark	A	2–0	Bonetti	Cohen	Wilson	Stiles	J Charlton[1]
Poland	A	1–0	G Banks	Cohen	Wilson	Stiles	J Charlton
Uruguay	H	0–0	G Banks	Cohen	Wilson	Stiles	J Charlton
Mexico	H	2–0	G Banks	Cohen	Wilson	Stiles	J Charlton
France	H	2–0	G Banks	Cohen	Wilson	Stiles	J Charlton
Argentina	H	1–0	G Banks	Cohen	Wilson	Stiles	J Charlton
Portugal	H	2–1	G Banks	Cohen	Wilson	Stiles	J Charlton
West Germany	H	4–2	G Banks	Cohen	Wilson	Stiles	J Charlton
1966–67							
Northern Ireland	A	2–0	G Banks	Cohen	Wilson	Stiles	J Charlton
Czechoslovakia	H	0–0	G Banks	Cohen	Wilson	Stiles	J Charlton
Wales	H	5–1	G Banks	Cohen	Wilson	Stiles	J Charlton[1]
Scotland	H	2–3	G Banks	Cohen	Wilson	Stiles	J Charlton[1]
Spain	H	2–0	Bonetti	Cohen	K Newton	Mullery	Labone
Austria	A	1–0	Bonetti	K Newton	Wilson	Mullery	Labone
1967–68							
Wales	A	3–0	G Banks	Cohen	K Newton	Mullery	J Charlton
Northern Ireland	H	2–0	G Banks	Cohen	Wilson	Mullery	Sadler
USSR	H	2–2	G Banks	C Knowles	Wilson	Mullery	Sadler
Scotland	A	1–1	G Banks	K Newton	Wilson	Mullery	Labone
Spain	H	1–0	G Banks	C Knowles	Wilson	Mullery	J Charlton
Spain	A	2–1	Bonetti	K Newton	Wilson	Mullery	Labone
Sweden	H	3–1	Stepney	K Newton	C Knowles	Mullery	Labone
West Germany	A	0–1	G Banks	K Newton	C Knowles	Hunter	Labone
Yugoslavia	N	0–1	G Banks	K Newton	Wilson	Mullery	Labone
USSR	N	2–0	G Banks	T Wright	Wilson	Stiles	Labone
1968–69							
Romania	A	0–0	G Banks	T Wright	K Newton	Mullery	Labone
Bulgaria	H	1–1	West	K Newton	McNab	Mullery	Labone
Romania	H	1–1	G Banks	T Wright	McNab	Stiles	J Charlton[1]
France	H	5–0	G Banks	K Newton	Cooper	Mullery	J Charlton
Northern Ireland	A	3–1	G Banks	K Newton	McNab	Mullery	Labone
Wales	H	2–1	West	K Newton	Cooper	Moore*	J Charlton
Scotland	H	4–1	G Banks	K Newton	Cooper	Mullery	Labone
Mexico	A	0–0	West	K Newton	Cooper	Mullery	Labone
Uruguay	A	2–1	G Banks	T Wright	K Newton	Mullery	Labone
Brazil	A	1–2	G Banks	T Wright	K Newton	Mullery	Labone
1969–70							
Holland	A	1–0	Bonetti	T Wright	E Hughes	Mullery	J Charlton
Portugal	H	1–0	Bonetti	Reaney	E Hughes	Mullery	J Charlton[1]
Holland	H	0–0	G Banks	K Newton	Cooper	Peters	J Charlton
Belgium	A	3–1	G Banks	T Wright	Cooper	Moore*	Labone
Wales	A	1–1	G Banks	T Wright	E Hughes	Mullery	Labone
Northern Ireland	H	3–1	G Banks	K Newton	E Hughes	Mullery	Moore*
Scotland	A	0–0	G Banks	K Newton	E Hughes	Stiles	Labone
Colombia	A	4–0	G Banks	K Newton	Cooper	Mullery	Labone
Ecuador	A	2–0	G Banks	K Newton	Cooper	Mullery	Labone
Romania	N	1–0	G Banks	K Newton	Cooper	Mullery	Labone
Brazil	N	0–1	G Banks	T Wright	Cooper	Mullery	Labone
Czechoslovakia	N	1–0	G Banks	K Newton	Cooper	Mullery	J Charlton

6	7	8	9	10	11	*Substitutes*
Hunter	Callaghan	Hunt[1]	R Charlton	G Hurst	Ball	
Moore*[1]	Paine	Greaves[4]	R Charlton	Hunt	Connelly[1]	
Moore*	Ball	Greaves	G Hurst	Eastham[1]	Connelly	
Moore*	Ball	Greaves	R Charlton	Hunt[1]	Peters	
Moore*	Ball	Greaves	R Charlton	Hunt	Connelly	
Moore*	Paine	Greaves	R Charlton[1]	Hunt[1]	Peters	
Moore*	Callaghan	Greaves	R Charlton	Hunt[2]	Peters	
Moore*	Ball	G Hurst[1]	R Charlton	Hunt	Peters	
Moore*	Ball	G Hurst	R Charlton[2]	Hunt	Peters	
Moore*	Ball	G Hurst[3]	R Charlton	Hunt	Peters[1]	
Moore*	Ball	G Hurst	R Charlton	Hunt[1]	Peters[1]	
Moore*	Ball	G Hurst	R Charlton	Hunt	Peters	
Moore*	Ball	G Hurst[2]	R Charlton[1]	Hunt	Peters	†
Moore*	Ball	Greaves	R Charlton[1]	G Hurst[1]	Peters	
Moore*	Ball	Greaves[1]	G Hurst	Hunt[1]	Hollins	
Moore*	Ball[1]	Greaves	G Hurst	Hunt	Hunter	
Moore*	Ball[1]	Hunt	R Charlton[1]	G Hurst	Peters[1]	
Moore*	P Thompson	Hunt	R Charlton[1]	G Hurst[1]	Peters	
Moore*	Ball[1]	Hunt	R Charlton	G Hurst	Peters[1]	
Moore*	Ball	G Hurst	Summerbee	R Charlton	Peters[1]	
Moore*	Ball	Hunt	Summerbee	R Charlton[1]	Peters	
Moore*	Ball	Peters[1]	R Charlton	Hunt	Hunter[1]	
Moore*	Bell	Peters[1]	R Charlton[1]	Hunt[1]	Hunter	G Hurst 9
Moore*	Ball	Bell	Summerbee	G Hurst	P Thompson	
Moore*	Ball	Peters	R Charlton	Hunt	Hunter	
Moore*	Hunter	Hunt	R Charlton[1]	G Hurst[1]	Peters	
Moore*	Ball	Hunt	R Charlton	G Hurst	Peters	McNab 2
Moore*	F Lee	Bell	R Charlton	G Hurst[1]	Peters	Reaney 2
Hunter	Radford	Hunt	R Charlton*	G Hurst	Ball	
Moore*	F Lee[1]	Bell	G Hurst[3]	Peters	O'Grady[1]	
Moore*	Ball	F Lee[1]	R Charlton	G Hurst[1]	Peters[1]	
Hunter	F Lee[1]	Bell	Astle	R Charlton[1]	Ball	
Moore*	F Lee	Ball	R Charlton	G Hurst[2]	Peters[2]	
Moore*	F Lee	Ball	R Charlton	G Hurst	Peters	T Wright 2
Moore*	F Lee[1]	Bell	G Hurst[1]	Ball	Peters	
Moore*	Ball	Bell[1]	R Charlton	G Hurst	Peters	
Moore*	F Lee	Bell[1]	R Charlton	G Hurst	Peters	P Thompson 7
Moore*	F Lee	Bell	Astle	R Charlton	Ball	Peters 8
Hunter	F Lee	Bell	M Jones	R Charlton*	Storey-Moore	Mullery 7, G Hurst 9
E Hughes	F Lee	Ball[2]	Osgood	G Hurst[1]	Peters	
Moore*	F Lee[1]	Ball	R Charlton	G Hurst	Peters	
Stiles	Coates	Kidd	R Charlton[1]	G Hurst[1]	Peters[1]	Bell 2
Moore*	P Thompson	Ball	Astle	G Hurst	Peters	Mullery 7
Moore*	F Lee	Ball[1]	R Charlton[1]	G Hurst	Peters[2]	
Moore*	F Lee[1]	Ball	R Charlton	G Hurst	Peters	Kidd 7[1], Sadler 9
Moore*	F Lee	Ball	R Charlton	G Hurst[1]	Peters	T Wright 2, Osgood 7
Moore*	F Lee	Ball	R Charlton	G Hurst	Peters	Astle 7, Bell 9
Moore*	Bell	R Charlton	Astle	A Clarke[1]	Peters	Ball 8, Osgood 10

● 61

Versus	Venue	Result	1	2	3	4	5
West Germany	N	2–3	Bonetti	K Newton	Cooper	Mullery[1]	Labone

1970–71

Versus	Venue	Result	1	2	3	4	5
East Germany	H	3–1	Shilton	E Hughes	Cooper	Mullery	Sadler
Malta	A	1–0	G Banks	Reaney	E Hughes	Mullery*	McFarland
Greece	H	3–0	G Banks	Storey	E Hughes	Mullery	McFarland
Malta	H	5–0	G Banks	Lawler[1]	Cooper	Moore*	McFarland
Northern Ireland	A	1–0	G Banks	Madeley	Cooper	Storey	McFarland
Wales	H	0–0	Shilton	Lawler	Cooper	T Smith	Lloyd
Scotland	H	3–1	G Banks	Lawler	Cooper	Storey	McFarland

1971–72

Versus	Venue	Result	1	2	3	4	5
Switzerland	A	3–2	G Banks	Lawler	Cooper	Mullery	McFarland
Switzerland	H	1–1	Shilton	Madeley	Cooper	Storey	Lloyd
Greece	A	2–0	G Banks	Madeley	E Hughes	Bell	McFarland
West Germany	H	1–3	G Banks	Madeley	E Hughes	Bell	Moore*
West Germany	A	0–0	G Banks	Madeley	E Hughes	Storey	McFarland
Wales	A	3–0	G Banks	Madeley	E Hughes[1]	Storey	McFarland
Northern Ireland	H	0–1	Shilton	Todd	E Hughes	Storey	Lloyd
Scotland	A	1–0	G Banks	Madeley	E Hughes	Storey	McFarland

1972–73

Versus	Venue	Result	1	2	3	4	5
Yugoslavia	H	1–1	Shilton	M Mills	Lampard	Storey	Blockley
Wales	A	1–0	Clemence	Storey	E Hughes	Hunter	McFarland
Wales	H	1–1	Clemence	Storey	E Hughes	Hunter[1]	McFarland
Scotland	A	5–0	Shilton	Storey	E Hughes	Bell	Madeley
Northern Ireland	A	2–1	Shilton	Storey	Nish	Bell	McFarland
Wales	H	3–0	Shilton	Storey	E Hughes	Bell	McFarland
Scotland	H	1–0	Shilton	Storey	E Hughes	Bell	McFarland
Czechoslovakia	A	1–1	Shilton	Madeley	Storey	Bell	McFarland
Poland	A	0–2	Shilton	Madeley	E Hughes	Storey	McFarland
USSR	A	2–1	Shilton	Madeley	E Hughes	Storey	McFarland
Italy	A	0–2	Shilton	Madeley	E Hughes	Storey	McFarland

1973–74

Versus	Venue	Result	1	2	3	4	5
Austria	H	7–0	Shilton	Madeley	E Hughes	Bell[1]	McFarland
Poland	H	1–1	Shilton	Madeley	E Hughes	Bell	McFarland
Italy	H	0–1	Shilton	Madeley	E Hughes	Bell	McFarland
Portugal	A	0–0	Parkes	Nish	Pejic	Dobson	Watson
Wales	A	2–0	Shilton	Nish	Pejic	E Hughes*	McFarland
Northern Ireland	H	1–0	Shilton	Nish	Pejic	E Hughes*	McFarland
Scotland	A	0–2	Shilton	Nish	Pejic	E Hughes*	Hunter
Argentina	H	2–2	Shilton	E Hughes*	Lindsay	Todd	Watson
East Germany	A	1–1	Clemence	E Hughes*	Lindsay	Todd	Watson
Bulgaria	A	1–0	Clemence	E Hughes*	Todd	Watson	Lindsay
Yugoslavia	A	2–2	Clemence	E Hughes*	Lindsay	Todd	Watson

1974–75

Versus	Venue	Result	1	2	3	4	5
Czechoslovakia	H	3–0	Clemence	Madeley	E Hughes*	Dobson	Watson
Portugal	H	0–0	Clemence	Madeley	Watson	E Hughes*	Cooper
West Germany	H	2–0	Clemence	Whitworth	Gillard	Bell[1]	Watson
Cyprus	H	5–0	Shilton	Madeley	Watson	Todd	Beattie
Cyprus	A	1–0	Clemence	Whitworth	Beattie	Watson	Todd
Northern Ireland	A	0–0	Clemence	Whitworth	E Hughes	Bell	Watson
Wales	H	2–2	Clemence	Whitworth	Gillard	G Francis	Watson

6	7	8	9	10	11	Substitutes
Moore*	F Lee	Ball	R Charlton	G Hurst	Peters[1]	Bell 9, Hunter 11
Moore*	F Lee[1]	Ball	G Hurst	A Clarke[1]	Peters[1]	
Hunter	Ball	Chivers	Royle	Harvey	Peters[1]	
Moore*	F Lee[1]	Ball	Chivers[1]	G Hurst[1]	Peters	Coates 8
E Hughes	F Lee[1]	Coates	Chivers[2]	A Clarke[1]	Peters	Ball 11
Moore*	F Lee	Ball	Chivers	A Clarke[1]	Peters	
E Hughes	F Lee	Coates	G Hurst	Coates	Peters*	A Clarke 8
Moore*	F Lee	Ball	Chivers[2]	G Hurst	Peters[1]	A Clarke 7
Moore*	F Lee	Madeley	Chivers[1]	G Hurst[1]	Peters	†Radford 10
Moore*	Summerbee[1]	Ball	G Hurst	F Lee	E Hughes	Chivers 7, Marsh 10
Moore*	F Lee	Ball	Chivers[1]	G Hurst[1]	Peters	
Hunter	F Lee[1]	Ball	Chivers	G Hurst	Peters	Marsh 10
Moore*	Ball	Bell	Chivers	Marsh	Hunter	Summerbee 10, Peters 11
Moore*	Summerbee	Bell[1]	MacDonald	Marsh[1]	Hunter	
Hunter	Summerbee	Bell*	MacDonald	Marsh	Currie	Chivers 9, Peters 11
Moore*	Ball[1]	Bell	Chivers	Marsh	Hunter	MacDonald 10
Moore*	Ball	Channon	Royle[1]	Bell	Marsh	
Moore*	Keegan	Chivers	Marsh	Bell[1]	Ball	
Moore*	Keegan	Bell	Chivers	Marsh	Ball	
Moore*	Ball	Channon[1]	Chivers[1]	A Clarke[2]	Peters	†
Moore*	Ball	Channon	Chivers[2]	Richards	Peters	
Moore*	Ball	Channon[1]	Chivers[1]	A Clarke	Peters[1]	
Moore*	Ball	Channon	Chivers	A Clarke	Peters[1]	
Moore*	Ball	Channon	Chivers	A Clarke[1]	Peters	
Moore*	Ball	Bell	Chivers	A Clarke	Peters	
Moore*	Currie	Channon	Chivers[1]	A Clarke	Peters	† MacDonald 10,
Moore*	Currie	Channon	Chivers	A Clarke	Peters	Hunter 11, Summerbee 8
Hunter	Currie[1]	Channon[2]	Chivers[1]	A Clarke[2]	Peters*	
Hunter	Currie	Channon	Chivers	A Clarke[1]	Peters*	Hector 9
Moore*	Currie	Channon	Osgood	A Clarke	Peters	Hector 10
Todd	Bowles	Channon	MacDonald	Brooking	Peters*	Ball 9
Todd	Keegan[1]	Bell	Channon	Weller	Bowles[1]	
Todd	Keegan	Weller[1]	Channon	Bell	Bowles	Hunter 5, Worthington 11
Todd	Channon	Bell	Worthington	Weller	Peters	Watson 5, MacDonald 9
Bell	Keegan	Channon[1]	Worthington[1]	Weller	Brooking	
Dobson	Keegan	Channon[1]	Worthington	Bell	Brooking	
Dobson	Brooking	Bell	Keegan	Channon	Worthington[1]	
Dobson	Keegan[1]	Channon[1]	Worthington	Bell	Brooking	MacDonald 9
Hunter	Bell[2]	G Francis	Worthington	Channon[1]	Keegan	Brooking 4, Thomas 9
Brooking	G Francis	Bell	Thomas	Channon	A Clarke	Todd 5, Worthington 11
Todd	Ball*	MacDonald[1]	Channon	Hudson	Keegan	
Bell	Ball*	Hudson	Channon	MacDonald[5]	Keegan	Thomas 9
Bell	Thomas	Ball*	Channon	MacDonald	Keegan[1]	E Hughes 3, Tueart 11
Todd	Ball*	Viljoen	MacDonald	Keegan	Tueart	Channon 9
Todd	Ball*	Channon	Johnson[2]	Viljoen	Thomas	Little 8

Versus	Venue	Result	1	2	3	4	5
Scotland	H	5–1	Clemence	Whitworth	Beattie[1]	Bell[1]	Watson
1975–76							
Switzerland	A	2–1	Clemence	Whitworth	Todd	Watson	Beattie
Czechoslovakia	A	1–2	Clemence	Madeley	Gillard	G Francis*	McFarland
Portugal	A	1–1	Clemence	Whitworth	Beattie	G Francis*	Watson
Wales	A	2–1	Clemence	Cherry	M Mills	Neal	P Thompson
Wales	A	1–0	Clemence	Clement	M Mills	Towers	B Greenhoff
Northern Ireland	H	4–0	Clemence	Todd	M Mills	P Thompson	B Greenhoff
Scotland	A	1–2	Clemence	Todd	M Mills	P Thompson	McFarland
Brazil	N	0–1	Clemence	Todd	Doyle	P Thompson	Doyle
Italy	N	3–2	Rimmer	Clement	Neal	P Thompson[1]	Doyle
Finland	A	4–1	Clemence	Todd	M Mills	P Thompson	Madeley
1976–77							
Republic of Ireland	H	1–1	Clemence	Todd	Madeley	Cherry	McFarland
Finland	H	2–1	Clemence	Todd	Beattie	P Thompson	Greenhoff
Italy	A	0–2	Clemence	Clement	M Mills	B Greenhoff	McFarland
Holland	H	0–2	Clemence	Clement	Beattie	Doyle	Watson
Luxembourg	H	5–0	Clemence	Gidman	Cherry	Kennedy[1]	Watson
Northern Ireland	A	2–1	Shilton	Cherry	M Mills	Greenhoff	Watson
Wales	H	0–1	Shilton	Neal	M Mills	Greenhoff	Watson
Scotland	H	1–2	Clemence	Neal	M Mills	Greenhoff	Watson
Brazil	A	0–0	Clemence	Neal	Cherry	B Greenhoff	Watson
Argentina	A	1–1	Clemence	Neal	Cherry	B Greenhoff	Watson
Uruguay	A	0–0	Clemence	Neal	Cherry	B Greenhoff	Watson
1977–78							
Switzerland	H	0–0	Clemence	Neal	Cherry	McDermott	Watson
Luxembourg	A	2–0	Clemence	Cherry	Watson	E Hughes*	R Kennedy[1]
Italy	H	2–0	Clemence	Neal	Cherry	Wilkins	Watson
West Germany	A	1–2	Clemence	Neal	M Mills	Wilkins	Watson
Brazil	H	1–1	Corrigan	M Mills	Cherry	B Greenhoff	Watson
Wales	A	3–1	Shilton	M Mills*	Cherry	B Greenhoff	Watson
Northern Ireland	H	1–0	Clemence	Neal[1]	M Mills	Wilkins	Watson
Scotland	A	1–0	Clemence	Neal	M Mills	Currie	Watson
Hungary	H	4–1	Shilton	Neal[1]	M Mills	Wilkins	Watson
1978–79							
Denmark	A	4–3	Clemence	Neal[1]	M Mills	Wilkins	Watson
Republic of Ireland	A	1–1	Clemence	Neal	M Mills	Wilkins	Watson
Czechoslovakia	H	1–0	Shilton	Anderson	Cherry	P Thompson	Watson
Northern Ireland	H	4–0	Clemence	Neal	M Mills	Currie	Watson[1]
Northern Ireland	A	2–0	Clemence	Neal	M Mills*	P Thompson	Watson[1]
Wales	H	0–0	Corrigan	Cherry	Sansom	Wilkins	Watson
Scotland	H	3–1	Clemence	Neal	M Mills	P Thompson	Watson
Bulgaria	A	3–0	Clemence	Neal	M Mills	P Thompson	Watson[1]
Sweden	A	0–0	Shilton	Anderson	Cherry	McDermott	Watson
Austria	A	3–4	Shilton	Neal	M Mills	P Thompson	Watson
1979–80							
Denmark	H	1–0	Clemence	Neal	M Mills	P Thompson	Watson
Northern Ireland	A	5–1	Shilton	Neal	M Mills	P Thompson	Watson
Bulgaria	H	2–0	Clemence	Anderson	Sansom	P Thompson*	Watson[1]
Republic of Ireland	H	2–0	Clemence	Cherry	Sansom	P Thompson	Watson

6	7	8	9	10	11	*Substitutes*
Todd	Ball*	Channon	Johnson[1]	G Francis[2]	Keegan	Thomas 11
Bell	Currie	G Francis*	Channon[1]	Johnson	Keegan[1]	MacDonald 10
Todd	Keegan	Channon[1]	MacDonald	A Clarke	Bell	Watson 5, Thomas 8
Todd	Keegan	Channon[1]	MacDonald	Brooking	Madeley	A Clarke 11, Thomas 9
Doyle	Keegan*	Channon	Boyer	Brooking	Kennedy[1]	Clement 2, P Taylor 8[1]
P Thompson	Keegan	G Francis*	Pearson	Kennedy	P Taylor[1]	
R Kennedy	Keegan	G Francis*[1]	Pearson[1]	Channon[2]	P Taylor	Towers 11, Royle 7
R Kennedy	Keegan	G Francis*	Pearson	Channon[1]	P Taylor	Cherry 9, Doyle 5
G Francis*	Cherry	Brooking	Keegan	Pearson	Channon	
Towers	Wilkins	Brooking	Royle	Channon*[2]	Hill	Corrigan 1, M Mills 3
Cherry	Keegan[2]	Channon[1]	Pearson[1]	Brooking	G Francis*	
Greenhoff	Keegan*	Wilkins	Pearson[1]	Brooking	George	Hill 11
Wilkins	Keegan*	Channon	Royle[1]	Brooking	Tueart[1]	M Mills 10, Hill 11
E Hughes	Keegan*	Channon	Bowles	Cherry	Brooking	Beattie 2
Madeley	Keegan*	Greenhoff	T Francis	Bowles	Brooking	Todd 8, S Pearson 6
E Hughes	Keegan*[1]	Channon[2]	Royle	T Francis[1]	Hill	Mariner 9
Todd	Wilkins	Channon*[1]	Mariner	Brooking	Tueart[1]	Talbot 7
E Hughes	Keegan*	Channon	Pearson	Brooking	R Kennedy	Tueart 10
E Hughes*	T Francis	Channon[1]	Pearson	Talbot	R Kennedy	Cherry 4, Tueart 11
E Hughes*	Keegan*	T Francis	Pearson	Wilkins	Talbot	Channon 9, R Kennedy 10
E Hughes*	Keegan*	Channon	Pearson[1]	Wilkins	Talbot	R Kennedy 4
E Hughes	Keegan*	Channon	Pearson	Wilkins	Talbot	
E Hughes*	Keegan	Channon	T Francis	R Kennedy	Callaghan	Hill 8, Wilkins 11
Callaghan	McDermott	Wilkins	T Francis	Mariner[1]	G Hill	Whymark 7, Beattie 3
E Hughes*	Keegan[1]	Coppell	R Latchford	Brooking[1]	P Barnes	Pearson 9, T Francis 7
E Hughes*	Keegan	Coppell	S Pearson[1]	Brooking	P Barnes	T Francis 7
Currie	Keegan*[1]	Coppell	R Latchford	T Francis	P Barnes	
Wilkins	Coppell	T Francis	R Latchford[1]	Brooking	P Barnes[1]	Currie 3[1], Mariner 9
E Hughes*	Currie	Coppell	Pearson	Woodcock	B Greenhoff	
E Hughes*	Wilkins	Coppell[1]	Mariner	T Francis	P Barnes	B Greenhoff 6, Brooking 9
E Hughes*	Keegan	Coppell	T Francis[1]	Brooking	P Barnes[1]	B Greenhoff 5, Currie 8[1]
E Hughes*	Keegan[2]	Coppell	Latchford[1]	Brooking	P Barnes	
E Hughes*	Keegan	Coppell	Latchford[1]	Brooking	P Barnes	P Thompson 5, Woodcock 11
Wilkins	Keegan*	Coppell[1]	Woodcock	Currie	P Barnes	Latchford 9
E Hughes*	Keegan[1]	Coppell	Latchford[2]	Brooking	P Barnes	
Wilkins	Coppell[1]	Wilkins	Latchford	Currie	P Barnes	
E Hughes*	Keegan	Wilkins	Latchford	McDermott	Cunningham	Coppell 7, Brooking 4
Wilkins	Keegan*[1]	Coppell[1]	Latchford	Brooking	P Barnes[1]	
Wilkins	Keegan*[1]	Coppell	Latchford	Brooking	P Barnes[1]	T Francis 9, Woodcock 11
E Hughes*	Keegan	T Francis	T Francis	Woodcock	Cunningham	Wilkins 4, Brooking 8
Wilkins[1]	Keegan*[1]	Coppell[1]	Latchford	Brooking	P Barnes	Clemence 1, T Francis 9 Cunningham 11
Wilkins	Coppell	McDermott	Keegan*[1]	Brooking	P Barnes	
Wilkins	Keegan*	Coppell	T Francis[2]	Brooking	Woodcock[2]	† McDermott 10
Wilkins	Reeves	Hoddle[1]	T Francis	Kennedy	Woodcock	
Robson	Keegan*[2]	McDermott	Johnson	Woodcock	Cunningham	Coppell 9

Versus	Venue	Result	1	2	3	4	5
Spain	A	2–0	Shilton	Neal	M Mills	P Thompson	Watson
Argentina	H	3–1	Clemence	Neal	Sansom	P Thompson	Watson
Wales	A	1–4	Clemence	Neal	Cherry	P Thompson*	Lloyd
Northern Ireland	H	1–1	Corrigan	Cherry	Sansom	E Hughes	Watson
Scotland	A	2–0	Clemence	Cherry	Sansom	P Thompson*	Watson
Australia	A	2–1	Corrigan	Cherry*	Lampard	Talbot	Osman
Belgium	N	1–1	Clemence	Neal	Sansom	P Thompson	Watson
Italy	A	0–1	Shilton	Neal	Sansom	P Thompson	Watson
Spain	N	2–1	Clemence	Anderson	M Mills	P Thompson	Watson

1980–81

Versus	Venue	Result	1	2	3	4	5
Norway	H	4–0	Shilton	Anderson	Sansom	P Thompson*	Watson
Romania	A	1–2	Clemence	Neal	Sansom	P Thompson*	Watson
Switzerland	H	2–1	Shilton	Neal	Sansom	Robson	Watson
Spain	H	1–2	Clemence	Neal	Sansom	Robson	Butcher
Romania	H	0–0	Shilton	Anderson	Sansom	Robson	Watson*
Brazil	H	0–1	Clemence*	Neal	Sansom	Robson	Martin
Wales	H	0–0	Corrigan	Anderson	Sansom	Robson	Watson*
Scotland	H	0–1	Corrigan	Anderson	Sansom	Wilkins	Watson*
Switzerland	A	1–2	Clemence	M Mills	Sansom	Wilkins	Watson
Hungary	A	3–1	Clemence	Neal	M Mills	P Thompson	Watson

1981–82

Versus	Venue	Result	1	2	3	4	5
Norway	A	1–2	Clemence	Neal	M Mills	P Thompson	Osman
Hungary	H	1–0	Shilton	Neal	M Mills	P Thompson	Martin
Northern Ireland	H	4–0	Clemence	Anderson	Sansom	Wilkins[1]	Watson
Wales	A	1–0	Corrigan	Neal	Sansom	P Thompson*	Butcher
Holland	H	2–0	Shilton*	Neal	Sansom	P Thompson	Foster
Scotland	A	1–0	Shilton	M Mills	Sansom	P Thompson	Butcher
Iceland	A	1–1	Corrigan	Anderson	Neal*	Watson	Osman
Finland	A	4–1	Clemence	M Mills	Sansom	P Thompson	Martin
France	N	3–1	Shilton	M Mills*	Sansom	P Thompson	Butcher
Czechoslovakia	N	2–0	Shilton	M Mills*	Sansom	P Thompson	Butcher
Kuwait	N	1–0	Shilton	Neal	M Mills*	P Thompson	Foster
West Germany	N	0–0	Shilton	M Mills*	Sansom	P Thompson	Butcher
Spain	A	0–0	Shilton	M Mills*	Sansom	P Thompson	Butcher

1982–83

Versus	Venue	Result	1	2	3	4	5
Denmark	A	2–2	Shilton	Neal	Sansom	Wilkins*	Osman
West Germany	H	1–2	Shilton	Mabbutt	Sansom	P Thompson	Butcher
Greece	A	3–0	Shilton	Neal	Sansom	P Thompson	Martin
Luxembourg	H	9–0	Clemence	Neal[1]	Sansom	Robson*	Martin
Wales	H	2–1	Shilton*	Neal[1]	Statham	S Lee	Martin
Greece	H	0–0	Shilton*	Neal	Sansom	S Lee	Martin
Hungary	H	2–0	Shilton*	Neal	Sansom	S Lee	Martin
Northern Ireland	A	0–0	Shilton*	Neal	Sansom	Hoddle	Roberts
Scotland	H	2–0	Shilton	Neal	Sansom	S Lee	Roberts
Australia	A	0–0	Shilton*	Thomas	Statham	Williams	Osman
Australia	A	1–0	Shilton*	Neal	Statham	Barham	Osman
Australia	A	1–1	Shilton*	Neal	Pickering	S Lee	Osman

6	7	8	9	10	11	*Substitutes*
Wilkins	Keegan*	Coppell	T Francis[1]	R Kennedy	Woodcock[1]	E Hughes, 2 Cunningham 9
Wilkins	Keegan*[1]	Coppell	Johnson[2]	Woodcock	R Kennedy	Cherry 2 Birtles 9
						Brooking 11
R Kennedy	Coppell	Hoddle	Mariner[1]	Brooking	Barnes	Sansom 2, Wilkins 5
Wilkins	Reeves	Wilkins	Johnson[1]	Brooking	Devonshire	Mariner 7
Wilkins	Coppell[1]	McDermott	Johnson	Mariner	Brooking[1]	E Hughes 10
Butcher	Robson	Sunderland	Mariner[1]	Hoddle[1]	Armstrong	B Greenhoff 7, Ward 10
						Devonshire 11
Wilkins*	Keegan*	Coppell	Johnson	Woodcock	Brooking	McDermott 8, R Kennedy 9
Wilkins	Keegan*	Coppell	Birtles	R Kennedy	Woodcock	Mariner 9
Wilkins	McDermott	Hoddle	Keegan*	Woodcock[1]	Brooking[1]	Cherry 3, Mariner 8
Robson	Gates	McDermott[2]	Mariner[1]	Woodcock[1]	Rix	
Robson	Rix	McDermott	Birtles	Woodcock[1]	Gates	Cunningham 9, Coppell 11
M Mills*	Coppell	McDermott	Mariner[1]	Brooking	Woodcock	† Rix 10
Osman	Keegan*	T Francis	Mariner	Brooking	Hoddle[1]	P Barnes 8, Wilkins 10
Osman	Wilkins	Brooking	Coppell	T Francis	Woodcock	McDermott 11
Wilkins	Coppell	McDermott	Withe	Rix	P Barnes	
Wilkins	Coppell	Hoddle	Withe	Rix	P Barnes	Woodcock 9
Robson	Coppell	Hoddle	Withe	Rix	Woodcock	Martin 5, T Francis 11
Osman	Keegan*	Robson	Coppell	Mariner	T Francis	McDermott 11[1], P Barnes 5
Robson	Keegan*[1]	McDermott	Mariner	Brooking[2]	Coppell	Wilkins 10
Robson[1]	Keegan*	T Francis	Mariner	Hoddle	McDermott	Withe 9, P Barnes 10
Robson	Keegan*	Coppell	Mariner[1]	Brooking	McDermott	Morley 8
Foster	Keegan*[1]	Robson[1]	T Francis	Hoddle[1]	Morley	Regis 9, Woodcock 11
Robson	Wilkins	T Francis	Withe	Hoddle	Morley	McDermott 8, Regis 10
Robson	Wilkins	Devonshire	Mariner[1]	McDermott	Woodcock[1]	Rix 8, Barnes 9
Robson	Keegan*	Coppell	Mariner[1]	Brooking	Wilkins	McDermott 7, T Francis 9
McDermott	Hoddle	Devonshire	Withe	Regis	Morley	Perryman 8, Goddard 10[1]
Robson[2]	Keegan*	Coppell	Mariner[2]	Brooking	Wilkins	Rix 6, T Francis 8
						Woodcock 10
Robson[2]	Coppell	T Francis	Mariner[1]	Rix	Wilkins	Neal 3
Robson	Coppell	T Francis[1]	Mariner	Rix	Wilkins	† Hoddle 6
Hoddle	Coppell	T Francis[1]	Mariner	Rix	Wilkins	
Robson	Coppell	T Francis	Mariner	Rix	Wilkins	Woodcock 8
Robson	Rix	T Francis	Mariner	Woodcock	Wilkins	Brooking 7, Keegan 10
Butcher	Morley	Robson	Mariner	T Francis[2]	Rix	Hill 7
Wilkins*	R Hill	Regis	Mariner	Armstrong	Devonshire	Woodcock 8[1], Blissett 9
						Rix 10
Robson*	S Lee[1]	Mabbutt	Mariner	Woodcock[2]	Morley	
Butcher	Coppell[1]	S Lee	Woodcock[1]	Blissett[3]	Mabbutt	† Chamberlain 7[1], Hoddle 11[1]
Butcher[1]	Mabbutt	Blissett	Mariner	Cowans	Devonshire	
Butcher	Coppell	Mabbutt	T Francis	Woodcock	Devonshire	Blissett 10, Rix 11
Butcher	Mabbutt	T Francis[1]	Withe[1]	Blissett	Cowans	
Butcher	Mabbutt	T Francis	Withe	Blissett	Cowans	J Barnes 10
Butcher	Robson*[1]	T Francis	Withe	Hoddle	Cowans[1]	Mabbutt 7, Blissett 9
Butcher	Barham	Gregory	Blissett	T Francis	Cowans	J Barnes 3, Walsh 9
Butcher	Gregory	T Francis	Walsh[1]	Cowans	J Barnes	Williams 3
Butcher	Gregory	T Francis[1]	Walsh	Cowans	J Barnes	Spink 1, Thomas 2, Blissett 9

*captain   †own goal   *Small numerals goals scored*   *Numbers after sub player replaced*

Versus	Venue	Result	1	2	3	4	5
1983–84							
Denmark	H	0–1	Shilton	Neal	Sanson	S Lee	Osman
Hungary	A	3–0	Shilton	Gregory	Sansom	S Lee[1]	Martin
Luxembourg	A	4–0	Clemence	Duxbury	Sansom	S Lee	Martin
France	A	0–2	Shilton	Duxbury	Sansom	S Lee	Roberts
Northern Ireland	H	1–0	Shilton	Anderson	A Kennedy	S Lee	Roberts
Wales	A	0–1	Shilton	Duxbury	A Kennedy	S Lee	Martin
Scotland	A	1–1	Shilton	Duxbury	Sansom	Wilkins	Roberts
USSR	H	0–2	Shilton	Duxbury	Sansom	Wilkins	Roberts
Brazil	A	2–0	Shilton	Duxbury	Sansom	Wilkins	Watson
Uruguay	A	0–2	Shilton	Duxbury	Sansom	Wilkins	Watson
Chile	A	0–0	Shilton	Duxbury	Sansom	Wilkins	Watson
1984–85							
East Germany	H	1–0	Shilton	Duxbury	Sansom	Williams	Wright
Finland	H	5–0	Shilton	Duxbury	Sansom[1]	Williams	Wright
Turkey	A	8–0	Shilton	Anderson[1]	Sansom	Williams	Wright
Northern Ireland	A	1–0	Shilton	Anderson	Sansom	Steven	Martin
Republic of Ireland	H	2–1	Bailey	Anderson	Sansom	Steven[1]	Wright
Romania	A	0–0	Shilton	Anderson	Sansom	Steven	Wright
Finland	A	1–1	Shilton	Anderson	Sansom	Steven	Fenwick
Scotland	A	0–1	Shilton	Anderson	Sansom	Hoddle	Fenwick
Italy	N	1–2	Shilton	Stevens	Sansom	Steven	Wright
Mexico	A	0–1	Bailey	Anderson	Sansom	Hoddle	Fenwick
West Germany	N	3–0	Shilton	Stevens	Sansom	Hoddle	Wright
USA	A	5–0	Woods	Anderson	Sansom	Hoddle	Fenwick
1985–86							
Romania	H	1–1	Shilton	Stevens	Sansom	Reid	Wright
Turkey	H	5–0	Shilton	Stevens	Sansom	Hoddle	Wright
Northern Ireland	H	0–0	Shilton	GA Stevens	Sansom	Hoddle	Wright
Egypt	A	4–0	Shilton	Stevens	Sansom	Cowans[1]	Wright
Israel	A	2–1	Shilton	Stevens	Sansom	Hoddle	Martin
USSR	A	1–0	Shilton	Anderson	Sansom	Hoddle	Wright
Scotland	H	2–1	Shilton	Stevens	Sansom	Hoddle[1]	Watson
Mexico	N	3–0	Shilton	Anderson	Sansom	Hoddle	Fenwick
Canada	A	1–0	Shilton	Stevens	Sansom	Hoddle	Martin
Portugal	N	0–1	Shilton	Stevens	Sansom	Hoddle	Fenwick
Morocco	N	0–0	Shilton	Stevens	Sansom	Hoddle	Fenwick
Poland	N	3–0	Shilton*	Stevens	Sansom	Hoddle	Fenwick
Paraguay	N	3–0	Shilton*	Stevens	Sansom	Hoddle	Martin
Argentina	N	1–2	Shilton*	Stevens	Sansom	Hoddle	Fenwick
1986–87							
Sweden	A	0–1	Shilton*	Anderson	Sansom	Hoddle	Martin
Northern Ireland	H	3–0	Shilton	Anderson	Sansom	Hoddle	Watson
Yugoslavia	H	2–0	Woods	Anderson[1]	Sansom	Hoddle	Wright
Spain	A	4–2	Shilton	Anderson	Sansom	Hoddle	Adams
Northern Ireland	A	2–0	Shilton	Anderson	Sansom	Mabbutt	Wright
Turkey	A	0–0	Woods	Anderson	Sansom	Hoddle	Adams

6	7	8	9	10	11	Substitutes
Butcher	Wilkins*	Gregory	Mariner	T Francis	J Barnes	Blissett 4, Chamberlain 11
Butcher	Robson*	Hoddle[1]	Mariner[1]	Blissett	Mabbutt	Withe 10
Butcher[1]	Robson*[2]	Hoddle	Mariner[1]	Woodcock	Devonshire	J Barnes 10
Butcher	Robson*	Stein	Walsh	Hoddle	Williams	J Barnes 4, Woodcock 8
Butcher	Robson*	Wilkins	Woodcock[1]	T Francis	Rix	
Wright	Wilkins*	Gregory	Walsh	Woodcock	Armstrong	Fenwick 5, Blissett 11
Fenwick	Chamberlain	Robson*	Woodcock[1]	Blissett	J Barnes	Hunt 7, Lineker 9
Fenwick	Chamberlain	Robson*	T Francis	Blissett	J Barnes	Hateley 9, Hunt 11
Fenwick	Robson*	Chamberlain	Hateley[1]	Woodcock	J Barnes[1]	Allen 10
Fenwick	Robson*	Chamberlain	Hateley	Allen	J Barnes	Woodcock 10
Fenwick	Robson*	Chamberlain	Hateley	Allen	J Barnes	S Lee 8
Butcher	Robson*[1]	Wilkins	Mariner	Woodcock	J Barnes	Hateley 9, T Francis 10
Butcher	Robson*[1]	Wilkins	Hateley[2]	Woodcock[1]	J Barnes	GA Stevens 2, Chamberlain 7
Butcher	Robson*[3]	Wilkins	Withe	Woodcock[2]	J Barnes[2]	GA Stevens 4, Francis 10
Butcher	Steven	Wilkins*	Hateley[1]	Woodcock	J Barnes	T Francis 10
Butcher	Robson*	Wilkins	Hateley	Lineker[1]	Waddle	Hoddle 7, Davenport 9
Butcher	Robson*	Wilkins	Mariner	T Francis	J Barnes	Lineker 9, Waddle 11
Butcher	Robson*	Wilkins	Hateley[1]	T Francis	J Barnes	Waddle 4
Butcher	Robson*	Wilkins	Hateley	T Francis	J Barnes	Lineker 4, Waddle 11
Butcher	Robson*	Wilkins	Hateley[1]	T Francis	Waddle	Hoddle 4, Lineker 10 J Barnes 11
Watson	Robson*	Wilkins	Hateley	T Francis	J Barnes	K Dixon 4, Reid 8, Waddle 11
Butcher	Robson*[1]	Reid	K Dixon[2]	Lineker	Waddle	Bracewell 7, J Barnes 10
Butcher	Robson*	Bracewell	K Dixon[2]	Lineker[2]	Waddle	Watson 3, Steven 4[1] Reid 7, J Barnes 11
Fenwick	Robson*	Hoddle[1]	Hateley	Lineker	Waddle	Woodcock 10, J Barnes 11
Fenwick	Robson*[1]	Wilkins	Hateley	Lineker[3]	Waddle[1]	Steven 7, Woodcock 9
Fenwick	Bracewell	Wilkins*	K Dixon	Lineker	Waddle	
Fenwick	Steven[1]	Wilkins*	Hateley	Lineker	Wallace[1]	† Woods 1, Hill 7 Beardsley 10
Butcher	Robson*[2]	Wilkins	Dixon	Beardsley	Waddle	Woods 1, Woodcock 9 J Barnes 10
Butcher	Cowans	Wilkins*	Beardsley	Lineker	Waddle[1]	Hodge 7, Steven 11
Butcher[1]	Wilkins*	T Francis	Hateley	Hodge	Waddle	Reid 7, GA Stevens 10
Butcher	Robson*	Wilkins	Hateley[2]	Beardsley[1]	Waddle	GA Stevens 7, Steven 8 K Dixon 9, J Barnes 11
Butcher	Hodge	Wilkins*	Hateley[1]	Lineker	Waddle	Woods 1, Reid 8 Beardsley 10, J Barnes 11
Butcher	Robson*	Wilkins	Hateley	Lineker	Waddle	Hodge 7, Beardsley 11
Butcher	Robson*	Wilkins	Hateley	Lineker	Waddle	Hodge 7, GA Stevens 9
Butcher	Hodge	Reid	Beardsley	Lineker[3]	Steven	Waddle 9, K Dixon 10
Butcher	Hodge	Reid	Beardsley[1]	Lineker[2]	Steven	GA Stevens 8, Hateley 9
Butcher	Hodge	Reid	Beardsley	Lineker[1]	Steven	Waddle 8, J Barnes 11
Butcher	Steven	Wilkins	K Dixon	Hodge	J Barnes	Cottee 7, Waddle 11
Butcher	Robson*	Hodge	Beardsley	Lineker[2]	Waddle[1]	Cottee 9
Butcher*	Mabbutt[1]	Hodge	Beardsley	Lineker	Waddle	Wilkins 8, Steven 11
Butcher	Robson*	Hodge	Beardsley	Lineker[4]	Waddle	Woods 1, Steven 11
Butcher	Robson*[1]	Hodge	Beardsley	Lineker	Waddle[1]	Woods 1
Mabbutt	Robson*	Hodge	Allen	Lineker	Waddle	J Barnes 8, Hateley 9

Versus	Venue	Result	1	2	3	4	5
Brazil	H	1–1	Shilton	Stevens	Pearce	Reid	Adams
Scotland	A	0–0	Woods	Stevens	Pearce	Hoddle	Wright
1987–88							
West Germany	A	1–3	Shilton*	Anderson	Sansom	Hoddle	Adams
Turkey	H	8–0	Shilton	Stevens	Sansom	Steven	Adams
Yugoslavia	A	4–1	Shilton	Stevens	Sansom	Steven	Adams¹
Israel	A	0–0	Woods	Stevens	Pearce	Webb	Watson
Holland	H	2–2	Shilton	Stevens	Sansom	Steven	Adams¹
Hungary	A	0–0	Woods	Anderson	Pearce	Steven	Adams
Scotland	H	1–0	Shilton	Stevens	Sansom	Webb	Watson
Colombia	H	1–1	Shilton	Anderson	Sansom	McMahon	Wright
Switzerland	A	1–0	Shilton	Stevens	Sansom	Webb	Wright
Republic of Ireland	N	0–1	Shilton	Stevens	Sansom	Webb	Wright
Holland	N	1–3	Shilton	Stevens	Sansom	Hoddle	Wright
USSR	N	1–3	Woods	Stevens	Sansom	Hoddle	Watson
1988–89							
Denmark	H	1–0	Shilton	Stevens	Pearce	Rocastle	Adams
Sweden	H	0–0	Shilton	Stevens	Pearce	Webb	Adams
Saudi Arabia	A	1–1	Seaman	Sterland	Pearce	M Thomas	Adams¹
Greece	A	2–1	Shilton	Stevens	Pearce	Webb	Walker
Albania	A	2–0	Shilton	Stevens	Pearce	Webb	Walker
Albania	H	5–0	Shilton	Stevens	Pearce	Webb	Walker
Chile	H	0–0	Shilton	Parker	Pearce	Webb	Walker
Scotland	A	2–0	Shilton	Stevens	Pearce	Webb	Walker
Poland	H	3–0	Shilton	Stevens	Pearce	Webb¹	Walker
Denmark	A	1–1	Shilton	Parker	Pearce	Webb	Walker
1989–90							
Sweden	A	0–0	Shilton	Stevens	Pearce	Webb	Walker
Poland	A	0–0	Shilton	Stevens	Pearce	McMahon	Walker
Italy	H	0–0	Shilton	Stevens	Pearce	McMahon	Walker
Yugoslavia	H	2–1	Shilton	Parker	Pearce	M Thomas	Walker
Brazil	H	1–0	Shilton	Stevens	Pearce	McMahon	Walker
Czechoslovakia	H	4–2	Shilton	Dixon	Pearce¹	Steven	Walker
Denmark	H	1–0	Shilton	Stevens	Pearce	McMahon	Walker
Uruguay	H	1–2	Shilton	Parker	Pearce	Hodge	Walker
Tunisia	A	1–1	Shilton	Stevens	Pearce	Hodge	Walker
Republic of Ireland	N	1–1	Shilton	Stevens	Pearce	Gascoigne	Walker
Holland	N	0–0	Shilton	Parker	Pearce	Wright	Walker
Egypt	N	1–0	Shilton*	Parker	Pearce	Gascoigne	Walker
Belgium	N	1–0	Shilton	Parker	Pearce	Wright	Walker
Cameroon	N	3–2	Shilton	Parker	Pearce	Wright	Walker
West Germany	N	1–1	Shilton	Parker	Pearce	Wright	Walker

6	7	8	9	10	11	Substitutes
Butcher	Robson*	J Barnes	Beardsley	Lineker[1]	Waddle	Hateley 10
Butcher	Robson*	Hodge	Beardsley	Hateley	Waddle	
Mabbutt	Reid	J Barnes	Beardsley	Lineker[1]	Waddle	Pearce 3, Webb 4, Hateley 11
Butcher	Robson*[1]	Webb[1]	Beardsley[1]	Lineker[3]	J Barnes[2]	Hoddle 4, Regis 9
Butcher	Robson*[1]	Webb	Beardsley[1]	Lineker	J Barnes[1]	Reid 7, Hoddle 8
Wright	Allen	McMahon	Beardsley*	J Barnes	Waddle	Fenwick 6, Harford 7
Watson	Robson*	Webb	Beardsley	Lineker*[1]	J Barnes	Wright 6, Hoddle 8 Hateley 9
Pallister	Robson*	McMahon	Beardsley	Lineker	Waddle	Stevens 3, Hateley 9 Cottee 10, Hoddle 11
Adams	Robson*	Steven	Beardsley[1]	Lineker	J Barnes	Waddle 8
Adams	Robson*	Waddle	Beardsley	Lineker[1]	J Barnes	Hoddle 8, Hateley 9
Adams	Robson*	Steven	Beardsley	Lineker*	J Barnes	Woods 1, Watson 6 Reid 7, Waddle 8
Adams	Robson*	Waddle	Beardsley	Lineker	J Barnes	Hoddle 4, Hateley 9
Adams	Robson*	Steven	Beardsley	Lineker	J Barnes	Waddle 8, Hateley 9
Adams[1]	Robson*	Steven	McMahon	Lineker	J Barnes	Webb 9, Hateley 10
Butcher	Robson*	Webb[1]	Harford	Beardsley	Hodge	Woods 1, Walker 5 Cottee 9, Gascoigne 10
Butcher	Robson*	Beardsley	Waddle	Lineker	J Barnes	Walker 5, Cottee 11
Pallister	Robson*	Rocastle	Beardsley	Lineker	Waddle	Gascoigne 4, A Smith 9 Marwood 11
Butcher	Robson*[1]	Rocastle	A Smith	Lineker	J Barnes[1]	Beardsley 9
Butcher	Robson*[1]	Rocastle	Waddle	Lineker	J Barnes[1]	Beardsley 9, A Smith 10
Butcher	Robson*	Rocastle	Beardsley[2]	Lineker[1]	Waddle[1]	Parker 2, Gascoigne 8[1]
Butcher	Robson*	Gascoigne	Clough	Fashanu	Waddle	Cottee 10
Butcher	Robson*	Steven	Fashanu	Cottee	Waddle[1]	Bull 9[1], Gascoigne 10
Butcher	Robson*	Waddle	Beardsley	Lineker[1]	J Barnes[1]	Rocastle 8, A Smith 9
Butcher	Robson*	Rocastle	Beardsley	Lineker[1]	J Barnes	Seaman 1, McMahon 4 Bull 9, Waddle 11
Butcher*	Beardsley	McMahon	Waddle	Lineker	J Barnes	Gascoigne 4, Rocastle 11
Butcher	Robson*	Rocastle	Beardsley	Lineker	Waddle	
Butcher	Robson*	Waddle	Beardsley	Lineker	J Barnes	Beasant 1, Winterburn 3 Hodge 4 Phelan 7, Platt 9
Butcher	Robson*[2]	Rocastle	Bull	Lineker	Waddle	Beasant 1, Dorigo 3, Platt 4 McMahon 7, Hodge 8
Butcher*	Platt	Waddle	Beardsley	Lineker[1]	J Barnes	Woods 1, Gascoigne 9
Butcher	Robson*	Gascoigne[1]	Bull[2]	Lineker	Hodge	Seaman 1, Dorigo 3 Wright 5, McMahon 7
Butcher*	Hodge	Gascoigne	Waddle	Lineker[1]	J Barnes	Woods 1, Dorigo 3 Platt 4 Rocastle 9, Bull 10
Butcher	Robson*	Gascoigne	Waddle	Lineker	J Barnes[1]	Beardsley 4, Bull 10
Butcher	Robson*	Waddle	Gascoigne	Lineker	J Barnes	Beardsley 4, Wright 6 Platt 8, Bull 10[1]
Butcher	Waddle	Robson*	Beardsley	Lineker[1]	J Barnes	McMahon 9, Bull 10
Butcher	Robson*	Waddle	Gascoigne	Lineker	J Barnes	Platt 7, Bull 8
Wright[1]	McMahon	Waddle	Bull	Lineker	J Barnes	Platt 8, Beardsley 9
Butcher*	McMahon	Waddle	Gascoigne	Lineker	J Barnes	Platt 7[1], Bull 11
Butcher*	Platt[1]	Waddle	Gascoigne	Lineker[2]	J Barnes	Steven 6, Beardsley 11
Butcher*	Platt	Waddle	Gascoigne	Lineker[1]	Beardsley	Steven 6

* *captain* † *own goal* *Small numerals goals scored* *Numbers after sub player replaced*

Versus	Venue	Result	1	2	3	4	5
Italy	A	1–2	Shilton*	Stevens	Dorigo	Parker	Walker
1990–91							
Hungary	H	1–0	Woods	Dixon	Pearce	Parker	Walker
Poland	H	2–0	Woods	Dixon	Pearce	Parker	Walker
Republic of Ireland	A	1–1	Woods	Dixon	Pearce	Adams	Walker
Cameroon	H	2–0	Seaman	Dixon	Pearce	Steven	Walker
Republic of Ireland	H	1–1	Seaman	Dixon¹	Pearce	Adams	Walker
Turkey	A	1–0	Seaman	Dixon	Pearce	Wise¹	Walker
USSR	H	3–1	Woods	Stevens	Dorigo	Wise	Parker
Argentina	H	2–2	Seaman	Dixon	Pearce	Batty	Walker
Australia	A	1–0	Woods	Parker	Pearce	Batty	Walker
New Zealand	A	1–0	Woods	Parker	Pearce	Batty	Walker
New Zealand	A	2–0	Woods	Charles	Pearce*¹	Wise	Walker
Malaysia	A	4–2	Woods	Charles	Pearce	Batty	Walker
1991–92							
Germany	H	0–1	Woods	Dixon	Dorigo	Batty	Pallister
Turkey	H	1–0	Woods	Dixon	Pearce	Batty	Walker
Poland	A	1–1	Woods	Dixon	Pearce	Gray	Walker
France	H	2–0	Woods	R Jones	Pearce*	Keown	Walker
Czechoslovakia	A	2–2	Seaman	Keown¹	Pearce*	Rocastle	Walker
CIS	A	2–2	Woods	Stevens	Sinton	Palmer	Walker
Hungary	A	1–0	Martyn	Stevens	Dorigo	Curle	Walker
Brazil	H	1–1	Woods	Stevens	Dorigo	Palmer	Walker
Finland	A	2–1	Woods	Stevens	Pearce	Keown	Walker
Denmark	N	0–0	Woods	Curle	Pearce	Palmer	Walker
France	N	0–0	Woods	Batty	Pearce	Palmer	Walker
Sweden	A	1–2	Woods	Batty	Pearce	Keown	Walker
1992–93							
Spain	A	0–1	Woods	Dixon	Pearce*	Ince	Walker
Norway	H	1–1	Woods	Dixon	Pearce*	Batty	Walker
Turkey	H	4–0	Woods	Dixon	Pearce*¹	Palmer	Walker
San Marino	H	6–0	Woods	Dixon	Dorigo	Palmer¹	Walker
Turkey	A	2–0	Woods	Dixon	Sinton	Palmer	Walker
Holland	H	2–2	Woods	Dixon	Keown	Palmer	Walker
Poland	A	1–1	Woods	Bardsley	Dorigo	Palmer	Walker
Norway	A	0–2	Woods	Dixon	Pallister	Palmer	Walker
United States	A	0–2	Woods	Dixon	Dorigo	Palmer	Pallister
Brazil	N	1–1	Flowers	Barrett	Dorigo	Walker	Pallister
Germany	N	1–2	Martyn	Barrett	Sinton	Walker	Pallister
1993–94							
Poland	H	3–0	Seaman	Jones	Pearce*¹	Ince	Pallister
Holland	A	0–2	Seaman	Parker	Dorigo	Ince	Pallister
San Marino	A	7–1	Seaman	Dixon	Pearce*	Ince²	Pallister
Denmark	H	1–0	Seaman	Parker	Le Saux	Ince	Adams
Greece	H	5–0	Flowers	Jones	Le Saux	Richardson	Bould

6	7	8	9	10	11	Substitutes
Wright	Platt[1]	Steven	McMahon	Lineker	Beardsley	Waddle 6, Webb 9
Wright	Platt	Gascoigne	Bull	Lineker*[1]	J Barnes	Dorigo 3, Waddle 9
Wright	Platt	Gascoigne	Bull	Lineker*[1]	J Barnes	Beardsley 9[1], Waddle 10
Wright	Platt[1]	Cowans	Beardsley	Lineker*	McMahon	
Wright	Robson	Gascoigne	I Wright	Lineker*[2]	J Barnes	Pallister 7, Hodge 8
Wright	Robson	Platt	Beardsley	Lineker*	J Barnes	Sharpe 4, I Wright 10
Pallister	Platt	G Thomas	A Smith	Lineker*	J Barnes	Hodge 8
Wright*	Platt[2]	G Thomas	A Smith[1]	I Wright	J Barnes	Batty 4, Beardsley 10
Wright	Platt[1]	G Thomas	A Smith	Lineker*[1]	J Barnes	Clough 11
Wright	Platt	G Thomas	Clough	Lineker*	Hirst	† Wise 10, Salako 11
Barrett	Platt	G Thomas	Wise	Lineker*[1]	Walters	Deane 4, Salako 11
Wright	Platt	G Thomas	Deane	I Wright	Salako	Hirst 9[1]
Wright	Platt	G Thomas	Clough	Lineker*[4]	Salako	
Parker	Platt	Steven	A Smith	Lineker*	Salako	Stewart 8, Merson 11
Mabbutt	Robson	Platt	A Smith[1]	Lineker*	Waddle	
Mabbutt	Platt	G Thomas	Rocastle	Lineker*[1]	Sinton	A Smith 4, Daley 11
Wright	Webb	G Thomas	Clough	Shearer[1]	Hirst	Lineker 11[1]
Mabbutt	Platt	Merson[1]	Clough	Hateley	J Barnes	Dixon 4, Lineker 6 / Stewart 9, Dorigo 11
Keown	Platt	Steven[1]	Shearer	Lineker*[1]	Daley	Martyn 1, Curle 3 / Stewart 8, Clough 9
Keown	Webb[1]	Palmer	Merson	Lineker*	Daley	Seaman 1, Sinton 4, Batty 7 / A Smith 9, I Wright 10
Keown	Daley	Steven	Platt[1]	Lineker*	Sinton	Pearce 3, Merson 7, Webb 8 / Rocastle 11
Wright	Platt[2]	Steven	Webb	Lineker*	J Barnes	Palmer 2, Daley 8, Merson 11
Keown	Platt	Steven	A Smith	Lineker*	Merson	Daley 2, Webb 11
Keown	Platt	Steven	Shearer	Lineker*	Palmer	
Palmer	Platt[1]	Webb	Sinton	Lineker*	Daley	Merson 9, A Smith 10
Wright	White	Platt	Clough	Shearer	Sinton	Bardsley 2, Palmer 2 / Merson 7, Deane 11
Adams	Platt[1]	Gascoigne	Shearer	I Wright	Ince	Palmer 2, Merson 10
Adams	Platt	Gascoigne[2]	Shearer[1]	I Wright	Ince	
Adams	Platt*[4]	Gascoigne	Ferdinand[1]	J Barnes	Batty	
Adams	Platt*[1]	Gascoigne[1]	J Barnes	I Wright	Ince	Clough 2, Sharpe 10
Adams	Platt*[1]	Gascoigne	Ferdinand	J Barnes*[1]	Ince	Merson 8
Adams	Platt*	Gascoigne	Sheringham	J Barnes	Ince	I Wright 4[1], Clough 8
Adams	Platt*	Gascoigne	Ferdinand	Sheringham	Sharpe	Clough 5, I Wright 10
Batty	Ince*	Clough	Sharpe	Ferdinand	J Barnes	Walker 4, I Wright 10
Batty	Ince*	Clough	I Wright	Sinton	Sharpe	Platt 6[1], Palmer 7, Merson 8
Ince	Platt*[1]	Clough	Sharpe	J Barnes	Merson	Keown 5, I Wright 8 / Winterburn 9
Adams	Platt	Gascoigne[1]	Ferdinand[1]	Wright	Sharpe	
Adams	Platt*	Palmer	Shearer	Merson	Sharpe	Sinton 8, I Wright 10
Walker	Platt	Ripley	Ferdinand[1]	I Wright[4]	Sinton	
Pallister	Platt*[1]	Gascoigne	Shearer	Beardsley	Anderton	Batty 4, Le Tissier 8
Adams	Platt*[2]	Merson	Shearer[1]	Beardsley[1]	Anderton[1]	Pearce 2, I Wright 10 / Le Tissier 11

Versus	Venue	Result	1	2	3	4	5
Norway	H	0–0	Seaman	Jones	Le Saux	Ince	Bould
1994–95							
United States	H	2–0	Seaman	Jones	Le Saux	Venison	Adams
Romania	H	1–1	Seaman	Jones	Le Saux	Ince	Adams*
Nigeria	H	1–0	Flowers	Jones	Le Saux	Lee	Howey
Rep. of Ireland	A	0–1§	Seaman	Barton	Le Saux	Ince	Adams
Uruguay	H	0–0	Flowers	Jones	Le Saux	Venison	Adams
Japan	H	2–1	Flowers	Neville	Pearce	Batty	Scales
Sweden	H	3–3	Flowers	Barton	Le Saux	Barnes	Cooper
Brazil	H	1–3	Flowers	Neville	Pearce	Batty	Cooper
1995–96							
Colombia	H	0–0	Seaman	G. Neville	Le Saux	Redknapp	Adams*
Norway	A	0–0	Seaman	G. Neville	Pearce	Redknapp	Adams*
Switzerland	H	3–1	Seaman	G. Neville	Pearce¹	Redknapp	Adams*
Portugal	H	1–1	Seaman	G. Neville	Pearce	Wise	Adams*
Bulgaria	H	1–0	Seaman	G. Neville	Pearce*	Ince	Southgate
Croatia	H	0–0	Seaman	G. Neville	Pearce	Ince	Wright
Hungary	H	3–0	Seaman	G. Neville	Pearce	Ince	Wright
China	A	3–0	Flowers	G. Neville	P. Neville	Redknapp	Adams*
Switzerland	H	1–1	Seaman	G. Neville	Pearce	Ince	Adams*
Scotland	H	2–0	Seaman	G. Neville	Pearce	Ince	Adams*
Holland	H	4–1	Seaman	G. Neville	Pearce	Ince	Adams*
Spain	H	0–0¶	Seaman	G. Neville	Pearce	McManaman	Adams*
Germany	H	1–1‖	Seaman	McManaman	Pearce	Ince	Adams*

‡ *West Germany won 4–3 on penalties*
§ *Match abandoned after 27 minutes*
¶ *England won 4–2 on penalties*
‖ *Germany won 6–5 on penalties*

6	7	8	9	10	11	Substitutes
Adams	Platt*	Wise	Shearer	Beardsley	Anderton	Le Tissier 4, Wright 11
Pallister	Platt*	Barnes	Shearer[2]	Sheringham	Anderton	Ferdinand 9, Wright 10
Pallister	Lee[1]	Wright	Shearer	Barnes	Le Tissier	Pearce 2, Wise 7, Sheringham 8
Ruddock	Platt*[1]	Beardsley	Shearer	Barnes	Wise	McManaman 4, Le Tissier 8, Sheringham 9
Pallister	Platt*	Beardsley	Shearer	Le Tissier	Anderton	
Pallister	Platt*	Beardsley	Sheringham	Barnes	Anderton	McManaman 3, Barmby 8, Cole 9
Unsworth	Platt*[1]	Beardsley	Shearer	Collymore	Anderton[1]	McManaman 4, Gascoigne 8, Sheringham 10
Pallister	Platt*[1]	Beardsley	Shearer	Sheringham[1]	Anderton[1]	Gascoigne 4, Scales 6, Barmby 8
Scales	Platt*	Le Saux[1]	Shearer	Sheringham	Anderton	Gascoigne 4, Barton 6, Collymore 10
Howey	Barmby	Gascoigne	Shearer	McManaman	Wise	Lee 4, Barnes 8, Sheringham 9
Pallister	Barmby	Lee	Shearer	McManaman	Wise	Sheringham 7, Stone 11
Pallister	Lee	Gascoigne	Shearer	Sheringham[1]	McManaman	Stone 4[1]
Howey	Barmby	Gascoigne	Shearer	Ferdinand	Stone[1]	Le Saux 3, Southgate 4, McManaman 7, Beardsley 10
Howey	McManaman	Gascoigne	Ferdinand[1]	Sheringham	Stone	Lee 8, Fowler 9, Platt 10
McManaman	Platt*	Gascoigne	Fowler	Sheringham	Stone	
Lee	Platt*[1]	Wilcox	Ferdinand	Sheringham	Anderton[2]	Walker 1, Campbell 4, Southgate 5, Wise 7, Shearer 9
Southgate	Barmby[2]	Gascoigne[1]	Shearer	McManaman	Anderton	Walker 1, Ehiogu 5, Beardsley 7, Fowler 9, Stone 10
Southgate	McManaman	Gascoigne	Shearer[1]	Sheringham	Anderton	Stone 7, Platt 8, Barmby 10
Southgate	McManaman	Gascoigne[1]	Shearer[1]	Sheringham	Anderton	Redknapp 3, Campbell 3, Stone 4
Southgate	McManaman	Gascoigne	Shearer[2]	Sheringham[2]	Anderton	Platt 4, Fowler 9, Barmby 10
Southgate	Platt	Gascoigne	Shearer	Sheringham	Anderton	Barmby 4, Stone 10, Fowler 11
Southgate	Platt	Gascoigne	Shearer[1]	Sheringham	Anderton	

21 ● ENGLAND'S INTERNATIONAL MATCHES 1872–1996

WCQ	World Cup Qualifier
WCF	World Cup Finals
ECQ	European Championship Qualifier
ECF	European Championship Finals
RC	Rous Cup
BJT	Brazilian Jubilee Tournament
USBT	US Bicentennial Tournament
USC	US Cup

v Albania

| 1989 | 8/3 | Tirana | W | 2–0 | WCQ |
| 1989 | 26/4 | Wembley | W | 5–0 | WCQ |

P 2, W 2, D 0, L 0, F 7, A 0

v Argentina

1951	9/5	Wembley	W	2–1	
1953	17/5	Buenos Aires	D	0–0	*
1962	2/6	Rancagua	W	3–1	WCF
1964	6/6	Rio de Janeiro	L	0–1	BJT
1966	23/7	Wembley	W	1–0	WCF
1974	22/5	Wembley	D	2–2	
1977	12/6	Buenos Aires	D	1–1	
1980	13/5	Wembley	W	3–1	
1986	22/6	Mexico City	L	1–2	WCF
1991	25/5	Wembley	D	2–2	

P 10, W 4, D 4, L 2, F 15, A 11

Abandoned after 21 minutes

v Australia

1980	31/5	Sydney	W	2–1	
1983	12/6	Sydney	D	0–0	
1983	15/6	Brisbane	W	1–0	
1983	19/6	Melbourne	D	1–1	
1991	1/6	Sydney	W	1–0	

P 5, W 3, D 2, L 0, F 5, A 2

v Austria

1908	6/6	Vienna	W	6–1	
1908	8/6	Vienna	W	11–1	
1909	1/6	Vienna	W	8–1	
1930	14/5	Vienna	D	0–0	
1932	7/12	Chelsea	W	4–3	
1936	6/5	Vienna	L	1–2	
1951	28/11	Wembley	D	2–2	
1952	25/5	Vienna	W	3–2	
1958	15/6	Boras	D	2–2	WCF
1961	27/5	Vienna	L	1–3	
1962	4/4	Wembley	W	3–1	
1965	20/10	Wembley	L	2–3	
1967	27/5	Vienna	W	1–0	

| 1973 | 26/9 | Wembley | W | 7–0 | |
| 1979 | 13/6 | Vienna | L | 3–4 | |

P 15, W 8, D 3, L 4, F 54, A 25

v Belgium

1921	21/5	Brussels	W	2–0	
1923	19/3	Arsenal	W	6–1	
1923	1/11	Antwerp	D	2–2	
1924	8/12	West Bromwich	W	4–0	
1926	24/5	Antwerp	W	5–3	
1927	11/5	Brussels	W	9–1	
1928	19/5	Antwerp	W	3–1	
1929	11/5	Brussels	W	5–1	
1931	16/5	Brussels	W	4–1	
1936	9/5	Brussels	L	2–3	
1947	21/9	Brussels	W	5–2	
1950	18/5	Brussels	W	4–1	
1952	26/11	Wembley	W	5–0	
1954	17/6	Basle	D	4–4	WCE
1964	21/10	Wembley	D	2–2	
1970	25/2	Brussels	W	3–1	
1980	12/6	Turin	D	1–1	ECF
1990	26/6	Bologna	W	1–0	WCF

P 18, W 13, D 4, L 1, F 67, A 24

v Bohemia

| 1908 | 13/6 | Prague | W | 4–0 | |

P 1, W 1, D 0, L 0, F 4, A 0

v Brazil

1956	9/5	Wembley	W	4–2	
1958	11/6	Gothenburg	D	0–0	WCF
1959	13/5	Rio de Janeiro	L	0–2	
1962	10/6	Vina del Mar	L	1–3	WCF
1963	8/5	Wembley	D	1–1	
1964	30/5	Rio de Janeiro	L	1–5	BJT
1969	12/6	Rio de Janeiro	L	1–2	
1970	7/6	Guadalajara	L	0–1	WCF
1976	23/5	Los Angeles	L	0–1	USBT
1977	8/6	Rio de Janeiro	D	0–0	
1978	19/4	Wembley	D	1–1	
1981	12/5	Wembley	L	0–1	
1984	10/6	Rio de Janeiro	W	2–0	
1987	19/5	Wembley	D	1–1	RC
1990	28/3	Wembley	W	1–0	
1992	17/5	Wembley	D	1–1	
1993	13/6	Washington	D	1–1	USC
1995	11/6	Wembley	L	1–3	

P 18, W 3, D 7, L 8, F 16, A 25

v Bulgaria

1962	7/6	Rancagua	D	0–0	WCF
1968	11/12	Wembley	D	1–1	
1974	1/6	Sofia	W	1–0	
1979	6/6	Sofia	W	3–0	ECQ
1979	22/11	Wembley	W	2–0	ECQ
1996	27/3	Wembley	W	1–0	

P 6, W 4, D 2, L 0, F 8, A 1

v Cameroon

| 1990 | 1/7 | Naples | W | 3–2 | WCF |
| 1991 | 6/2 | Wembley | W | 2–0 | |

P 2, W 2, D 0, L 0, F 5, A 2

v Canada

| 1986 | 24/5 | Vancouver | W | 1–0 | |

P 1, W 1, D 0, L 0, F 1, A 0

v Chile

1950	25/6	Rio de Janeiro	W	2–0	WCF
1953	24/5	Santiago	W	2–1	
1984	17/6	Santiago	D	0–0	
1989	23/5	Wembley	D	0–0	RC

P 4, W 2, D 2, L 0, F 4, A 1

v China

| 1996 | 23/5 | Beijing | W | 3–0 | |

P 1, W 1, D 0, L 0, F 3, A 0

v CIS

| 1992 | 29/4 | Moscow | W | 2–2 | |

P 1, W 0, D 1, L 0, F 2, A 2

v Colombia

1970	20/5	Bogota	W	4–0	
1988	24/5	Wembley	D	1–1	RC
1995	6/9	Wembley	D	0–0	

P 3, W 1, D 2, L 0, F 5, A 1

v Croatia

| 1996 | 24/4 | Wembley | W | 0–0 | |

P 1, W 0, D 1, L 0, F 0, A 0

v Cyprus

| 1975 | 16/4 | Wembley | W | 5–0 | ECQ |
| 1975 | 11/5 | Limassol | W | 1–0 | ECQ |

P 2, W 2, D 0, L 0, F 6, A 0

v Czechoslovakia

| 1934 | 16/5 | Prague | L | 1–2 | |
| 1937 | 1/12 | Tottenham | W | 5–4 | |

1963	29/5	Bratislava	W	4–2	
1966	2/11	Wembley	D	0–0	
1970	11/6	Guadalajara	W	1–0	WCF
1973	27/5	Prague	D	1–1	
1974	30/10	Wembley	W	3–0	ECQ
1975	30/10	Bratislava	L	1–2	ECQ
1978	29/11	Wembley	W	1–0	
1982	20/6	Bilbao	W	2–0	WCF
1990	25/4	Wembley	W	4–2	
1992	25/3	Prague	D	2–2	

P 12, W 7, D 3, L 2, F 25, A 15

v Denmark

1948	26/9	Copenhagen	D	0–0	
1955	2/10	Copenhagen	W	5–1	
1956	5/12	Wolverhampton	W	5–2	WCQ
1957	15/5	Copenhagen	W	4–1	WCQ
1966	3/7	Copenhagen	W	2–0	
1978	20/9	Copenhagen	W	4–3	ECQ
1979	12/9	Wembley	W	1–0	ECQ
1982	22/9	Copenhagen	D	2–2	ECQ
1983	21/9	Wembley	L	0–1	ECQ
1988	14/9	Wembley	W	1–0	
1989	7/6	Copenhagen	D	1–1	
1990	15/5	Wembley	W	1–0	
1992	11/6	Malmö	D	0–0	ECF
1994	9/3	Wembley	W	1–0	

P 14, W 9, D 4, L 1, F 27, A 11

v Ecuador

| 1970 | 24/5 | Quito | W | 2–0 | |

P 1, W 1, D 0, L 0, F 2, A 0

v Egypt

| 1986 | 29/1 | Cairo | W | 4–0 | |
| 1990 | 21/6 | Cagliari | W | 1–0 | WCF |

P 2, W 2, D 0, L 0, F 5, A 0

v FIFA

| 1953 | 21/10 | Wembley | D | 4–4 | |

P 1, W 0, D 1, L 0, F 4, A 4

v Finland

1937	20/5	Helsinki	W	8–0	
1956	20/5	Helsinki	W	5–1	
1966	26/6	Helsinki	W	3–0	
1976	13/6	Helsinki	W	4–1	WCQ
1976	13/10	Wembley	W	2–1	WCQ
1982	3/6	Helsinki	W	4–1	
1984	17/10	Wembley	W	5–0	WCQ
1985	22/5	Helsinki	D	1–1	WCQ
1992	3/6	Helsinki	W	2–1	

P 9, W 8, D 1, L 0, F 34, A 6

v France

1923	10/5	Paris	W	4–1	
1924	17/5	Paris	W	3–1	
1925	21/5	Paris	W	3–2	
1927	26/5	Paris	W	6–0	
1928	17/5	Paris	W	5–1	
1929	9/5	Paris	W	4–1	
1931	14/5	Paris	L	2–5	
1933	6/12	Tottenham	W	4–1	
1938	26/5	Paris	W	4–2	
1947	3/5	Arsenal	W	3–0	
1949	22/5	Paris	W	3–1	
1951	3/10	Arsenal	D	2–2	
1955	15/5	Paris	L	0–1	
1957	27/11	Wembley	W	4–0	
1962	3/10	Sheffield	D	1–1	ECQ
1963	27/2	Paris	L	2–5	ECQ
1966	20/7	Wembley	W	2–0	WCF
1969	12/3	Wembley	W	5–0	
1982	16/6	Bilbao	W	3–1	WCF
1984	29/2	Paris	L	0–2	
1992	19/2	Wembley	W	2–0	
1992	14/6	Malmö	D	0–0	ECF

P 22, W 15, D 3, L 4, F 62, A 27

v East Germany

1963	2/6	Leipzig	W	2–1
1970	25/11	Wembley	W	3–1
1974	29/5	Leipzig	D	1–1
1984	12/9	Wembley	W	1–0

P 4, W 3, D 1, L 0, F 7, A 3

v West Germany

1930	10/5	Berlin	D	3–3	†
1935	4/12	Tottenham	W	3–0	†
1938	14/5	Berlin	W	6–3	†
1954	1/12	Wembley	W	3–1	
1956	26/5	Berlin	W	3–1	
1965	12/5	Nuremberg	W	1–0	
1966	23/2	Wembley	W	1–0	
1966	30/7	Wembley	W	4–2	WCF
1968	1/6	Hanover	L	0–1	
1970	14/6	Leon	L	2–3	WCF
1972	29/4	Wembley	L	1–3	ECQ
1972	13/5	Berlin	D	0–0	ECQ
1975	12/3	Wembley	W	2–0	
1978	22/2	Munich	L	1–2	
1982	29/6	Madrid	D	0–0	WCF
1982	13/10	Wembley	L	1–2	
1985	12/6	Mexico City	W	3–0	
1987	9/9	Düsseldorf	L	1–3	
1990	4/7	Turin	D	1–1	*WCF

P 19, W 9, D 4, L 6, F 36, A 25

* After extra time (England lost 3–4 on penalties)
† as Germany

v Germany

1991	11/9	Wembley	L	0–1	
1993	19/6	Detroit	L	1–2	USC
1996	26/6	Wembley	D	1–1	*ECF

P 3, W 0, D 1, L 2, F 2, A 4

* After extra time (England lost 5–6 on penalties)

v Greece

1971	21/4	Wembley	W	3–0	ECQ
1971	1/12	Athens	W	2–0	ECQ
1982	17/11	Salonika	W	3–0	ECQ
1983	30/3	Wembley	D	0–0	ECQ
1989	8/2	Athens	W	2–1	
1994	17/5	Wembley	W	5–0	

P 6, W 5, D 1, L 0, F 15, A 1

v Holland

1935	18/5	Amsterdam	W	1–0	
1946	27/11	Huddersfield	W	8–2	
1964	9/12	Amsterdam	D	1–1	
1969	5/11	Amsterdam	W	1–0	
1970	14/1	Wembley	D	0–0	
1977	9/2	Wembley	L	0–2	
1982	25/5	Wembley	W	2–0	
1988	23/3	Wembley	D	2–2	
1988	15/6	Düsseldorf	L	1–3	ECF
1990	16/6	Cagliari	D	0–0	WCF
1993	28/4	Wembley	D	2–2	WCQ
1993	13/10	Rotterdam	L	0–2	WCQ
1996	18/6	Wembley	W	4–1	ECF

P 13, W 5, D 5, L 3, F 22, A 15

v Hungary

1908	10/6	Budapest	W	7–0	
1909	29/5	Budapest	W	4–2	
1909	31/5	Budapest	W	8–2	
1934	10/5	Budapest	L	1–2	
1936	2/12	Arsenal	W	6–2	
1953	25/11	Wembley	L	3–6	
1954	23/5	Budapest	L	1–7	
1960	22/5	Budapest	L	0–2	
1962	31/5	Rancagua	L	1–2	WCF
1965	5/5	Wembley	W	1–0	
1978	24/5	Wembley	W	4–1	
1981	6/6	Budapest	W	3–1	WCQ
1981	18/11	Wembley	W	1–0	WCQ
1983	27/4	Wembley	W	2–0	ECQ
1983	12/10	Budapest	W	3–0	ECQ
1988	27/4	Budapest	D	0–0	
1990	12/9	Wembley	W	1–0	
1992	12/5	Budapest	W	1–0	
1996	18/5	Wembley	W	3–0	

P 19, W 13, D 1, L 5, F 50, A 27

v Iceland

1982	2/6	Reykjavik	D	1–1

P 1, W 0, D 1, L 0, F 1, A 1

v Ireland

1882	18/2	Belfast	W	13–0	
1883	24/2	Liverpool	W	7–0	
1884	23/2	Belfast	W	8–1	
1885	28/2	Manchester	W	4–0	
1886	13/3	Belfast	W	6–1	
1887	5/2	Sheffield	W	7–0	
1888	31/3	Belfast	W	5–1	
1889	2/3	Everton	W	6–1	
1890	15/3	Belfast	W	9–1	
1891	7/3	Wolverhampton	W	6–1	
1892	5/3	Belfast	W	2–0	
1893	25/2	Birmingham	W	6–1	
1894	3/3	Belfast	D	2–2	
1895	9/3	Derby	W	9–0	
1896	7/3	Belfast	W	2–0	
1897	20/2	Nottingham	W	6–0	
1898	5/3	Belfast	W	3–2	
1899	18/2	Sunderland	W	13–2	
1900	17/3	Dublin	W	2–0	
1901	9/3	Southampton	W	3–0	
1902	22/3	Belfast	W	1–0	
1903	14/2	Wolverhampton	W	4–0	
1904	12/3	Belfast	W	3–1	
1905	25/2	Middlesbrough	D	1–1	
1906	17/2	Belfast	W	5–0	
1907	16/2	Everton	W	1–0	
1908	15/2	Belfast	W	3–1	
1909	13/2	Bradford	W	4–0	
1910	12/2	Belfast	D	1–1	
1911	11/2	Derby	W	2–1	
1912	10/2	Dublin	W	6–1	
1913	15/2	Belfast	L	1–2	
1914	14/2	Middlesbrough	L	0–3	
1919	25/10	Belfast	D	1–1	
1920	23/10	Sunderland	W	2–0	
1921	22/10	Belfast	D	1–1	
1922	21/10	West Bromwich	W	2–0	
1923	20/10	Belfast	L	1–2	
1924	22/10	Everton	W	3–1	
1925	24/10	Belfast	D	0–0	
1926	20/10	Liverpool	D	3–3	
1927	22/10	Belfast	L	0–2	
1928	22/10	Everton	W	2–1	
1929	19/10	Belfast	W	3–0	
1930	20/10	Sheffield	W	5–1	
1931	17/10	Belfast	W	6–2	
1932	17/10	Blackpool	W	1–0	
1933	14/10	Belfast	W	3–0	
1935	6/2	Everton	W	2–1	
1935	19/10	Belfast	W	3–1	
1936	18/11	Stoke	W	3–1	
1937	23/10	Belfast	W	5–1	
1938	16/11	Manchester	W	7–0	

1946	28/9	Belfast	W	7–2	
1947	5/11	Everton	D	2–2	
1948	9/10	Belfast	W	6–2	
1949	16/11	Manchester	W	9–2	WCQ
1950	7/10	Belfast	W	4–1	
1951	14/11	Aston Villa	W	2–0	
1952	4/10	Belfast	D	2–2	
1953	11/11	Everton	W	3–1	WCQ
1954	2/10	Belfast	W	2–0	
1955	2/11	Wembley	W	3–0	
1956	6/10	Belfast	D	1–1	
1957	6/11	Wembley	L	2–3	
1958	4/10	Belfast	D	3–3	
1959	18/11	Wembley	W	2–1	
1960	8/10	Belfast	W	5–2	
1961	22/11	Wembley	D	1–1	
1962	20/10	Belfast	W	3–1	
1963	20/11	Wembley	W	8–3	
1964	3/10	Belfast	W	4–3	
1965	10/11	Wembley	W	2–1	
1966	20/10	Belfast	W	2–0	ECQ
1967	22/11	Wembley	W	2–0	ECQ
1969	3/5	Belfast	W	3–1	
1970	21/4	Wembley	W	3–1	
1971	15/5	Belfast	W	1–0	
1972	23/5	Wembley	L	0–1	
1973	12/5	Everton	W	2–1	
1974	15/5	Wembley	W	1–0	
1975	17/5	Belfast	D	0–0	
1976	11/5	Wembley	W	4–0	
1977	28/5	Belfast	W	2–1	
1978	16/5	Wembley	W	1–0	
1979	7/2	Wembley	W	4–0	ECQ
1979	19/5	Belfast	W	2–0	
1979	17/10	Belfast	W	5–1	ECQ
1980	20/5	Wembley	D	1–1	
1982	23/2	Wembley	W	4–0	
1983	28/5	Belfast	D	0–0	
1984	4/4	Wembley	W	1–0	
1985	27/2	Belfast	W	1–0	WCQ
1985	13/11	Wembley	D	0–0	WCQ
1986	15/10	Wembley	W	3–0	ECQ
1987	1/4	Belfast	W	2–0	ECQ

P 96, W 74, D 16, L 6, F 319, A 80

v Israel

1986	26/2	Tel Aviv	W	2–1
1988	17/2	Tel Aviv	D	0–0

P 2, W 1, D 1, L 0, F 2, A 1

v Italy

1933	13/5	Rome	D	1–1
1934	14/11	Arsenal	W	3–2
1939	13/5	Milan	D	2–2
1948	16/5	Turin	W	4–0
1949	30/11	Tottenham	W	2–0
1952	18/5	Florence	D	1–1
1959	6/5	Wembley	D	2–2

1961	24/5	Rome	W	3–2	
1973	14/6	Turin	L	0–2	
1973	14/11	Wembley	L	0–1	
1976	28/5	New York	W	3–2	USBT
1976	17/11	Rome	L	0–2	WCQ
1977	16/11	Wembley	W	2–0	WCQ
1980	15/6	Turin	L	0–1	ECF
1985	6/6	Mexico City	L	1–2	
1989	15/11	Wembley	D	0–0	
1990	7/7	Bari	L	1–2	WCF

P 17, W 6, D 5, L 6, F 25, A 22

v Japan

| 1995 | 3/6 | Wembley | W | 2–1 | |

P 1, W 1, D 0, L 0, F 2, A 1

v Kuwait

| 1982 | 25/6 | Bilbao | W | 1–0 | WCF |

P 1, W 1, D 0, L 0, F 1, A 0

v Luxembourg

1927	21/5	Luxembourg	W	5–2	
1960	19/10	Luxembourg	W	9–0	WCQ
1961	28/9	Arsenal	W	4–1	WCQ
1977	30/3	Wembley	W	5–0	WCQ
1977	12/10	Luxembourg	W	2–0	WCQ
1982	15/12	Wembley	W	9–0	ECQ
1983	16/11	Luxembourg	W	4–0	ECQ

P 7, W 7, D 0, L 0, F 38, A 3

v Malaysia

| 1991 | 12/6 | Kuala Lumpur | W | 4–2 | |

P 1, W 1, D 0, L 0, F 4, A 2

v Malta

| 1971 | 3/2 | Valletta | W | 1–0 | ECQ |
| 1971 | 12/5 | Wembley | W | 5–0 | ECQ |

P 2, W 2, D 0, L 0, F 6, A 0

v Mexico

1959	24/5	Mexico City	L	1–2	
1961	10/5	Wembley	W	8–0	
1966	16/7	Wembley	W	2–0	WCF
1969	1/6	Mexico City	D	0–0	
1985	9/6	Mexico City	L	0–1	
1986	17/5	Los Angeles	W	3–0	

P 6, W 3, D 1, L 2, F 14, A 3

v Morocco

| 1986 | 6/6 | Monterrey | D | 0–0 | WCF |

P 1, W 0, D 1, L 0, F 0, A 0

v New Zealand

| 1991 | 3/6 | Auckland | W | 1–0 | |
| 1991 | 8/6 | Wellington | W | 2–0 | |

P 2, W 2, D 0, L 0, F 3, A 0

v Nigeria

| 1994 | 16/11 | Wembley | W | 1–0 | |

P 1, W 1, D 0, L 0, F 1, A 0

v Northern Ireland (see Ireland)

v Norway

1937	14/5	Oslo	W	6–0	
1938	9/11	Newcastle	W	4–0	
1949	18/5	Oslo	W	4–1	
1966	29/6	Oslo	W	6–1	
1980	10/9	Wembley	W	4–0	WCQ
1981	9/9	Oslo	L	1–2	WCQ
1992	14/10	Wembley	D	1–1	WCQ
1993	2/6	Oslo	L	0–2	WCQ
1994	22/5	Wembley	D	0–0	
1995	11/10	Oslo	D	0–0	

P 10, W 5, D 3, L 2, F 26, A 7

v Paraguay

| 1986 | 18/6 | Mexico City | W | 3–0 | WCF |

P 1, W 1, D 0, L 0, F 3, A 0

v Peru

| 1959 | 17/5 | Lima | L | 1–4 | |
| 1962 | 20/5 | Lima | W | 4–0 | |

P 2, W 1, D 0, L 1, F 5, A 4

v Poland

1966	5/1	Everton	D	1–1	
1966	5/7	Chorzow	W	1–0	
1973	6/6	Chorzow	L	0–2	WCQ
1973	17/10	Wembley	D	1–1	WCQ
1986	11/6	Monterrey	W	3–0	WCF
1989	3/6	Wembley	W	3–0	WCQ
1989	11/10	Katowice	D	0–0	WCQ
1990	17/10	Wembley	W	2–0	ECQ
1991	13/11	Poznan	D	1–1	ECQ
1993	29/5	Katowice	D	1–1	WCQ
1993	8/9	Wembley	W	3–0	WCQ

P 11, W 5, D 5, L 1, F 16, A 6

v Portugal

1947	25/5	Lisbon	W	10–0	
1950	14/5	Lisbon	W	5–3	
1951	19/5	Everton	W	5–2	
1955	22/5	Oporto	L	1–3	
1958	7/5	Wembley	W	2–1	

1961	21/5	Lisbon	D	1–1	WCQ
1961	25/10	Wembley	W	2–0	WCQ
1964	17/5	Lisbon	W	4–3	
1964	4/6	São Paolo	D	1–1	BJT
1966	26/7	Wembley	W	2–1	WCF
1969	10/12	Wembley	W	1–0	
1974	3/4	Lisbon	D	0–0	
1974	20/11	Wembley	D	0–0	ECQ
1975	19/11	Lisbon	D	1–1	ECQ
1986	3/6	Monterrey	L	0–1	WCF
1995	12/12	Wembley	D	1–1	

P 16, W 8, D 6, L 2, F 36, A 18

v Republic of Ireland

1946	30/9	Dublin	W	1–0	
1949	21/9	Everton	L	0–2	
1957	8/5	Wembley	W	5–1	WCQ
1957	19/5	Dublin	D	1–1	WCQ
1964	24/5	Dublin	W	3–1	
1976	8/9	Wembley	D	1–1	
1978	25/10	Dublin	D	1–1	ECQ
1980	6/2	Wembley	W	2–0	ECQ
1985	26/3	Wembley	W	2–1	
1988	12/6	Stuttgart	L	0–1	ECF
1990	11/6	Cagliari	D	1–1	WCF
1990	14/11	Dublin	D	1–1	ECQ
1991	27/3	Wembley	D	1–1	ECQ

P 13, W 5, D 6, L 2, F 19, A 12

v Rest of Europe

1938	26/10	Arsenal	W	3–0	

P 1, W 1, D 0, L 0, F 3, A 0

v Rest of the World

1963	23/10	Wembley	W	2–1	

P 1, W 1, D 0, L 0, F 2, A 1

v Romania

1939	24/5	Bucharest	W	2–0	
1968	6/11	Bucharest	D	0–0	
1969	15/1	Wembley	D	1–1	
1970	2/6	Guadalajara	W	1–0	WCF
1980	15/10	Bucharest	L	1–2	WCQ
1981	29/4	Wembley	D	0–0	WCQ
1985	1/5	Bucharest	D	0–0	WCQ
1985	11/9	Wembley	D	1–1	WCQ
1994	12/10	Wembley	D	1–1	

P 9, W 2, D 6, L 1, F 7, A 5

v San Marino

1993	17/2	Wembley	W	6–0	WCQ
1993	17/11	Bologna	W	7–1	WCQ

P 2, W 2, D 0, L 0, F 13, A 1

v Saudi Arabia

1988	16/11	Riyadh	D	1–1

P 1, W 0, D 1, L 0, F 1, A 1

v Scotland

1872	30/11	Glasgow	D	0–0
1873	8/3	Kennington	W	4–2
1874	7/3	Glasgow	L	1–2
1875	6/3	Kennington	D	2–2
1876	4/3	Glasgow	L	0–3
1877	3/3	Kennington	L	1–3
1878	2/3	Glasgow	L	2–7
1879	5/4	Kennington	W	5–4
1880	13/3	Glasgow	L	4–5
1881	12/3	Kennington	L	1–6
1882	11/3	Glasgow	L	1–5
1883	10/3	Sheffield	L	2–3
1884	15/3	Glasgow	L	0–1
1885	21/3	Kennington	D	1–1
1886	31/3	Glasgow	D	1–1
1887	19/3	Blackburn	L	2–3
1888	17/3	Glasgow	W	5–0
1889	13/4	Kennington	L	2–3
1890	5/4	Glasgow	D	1–1
1891	6/4	Blackburn	W	2–1
1892	2/4	Glasgow	W	4–1
1893	1/4	Richmond	W	5–2
1894	7/4	Glasgow	D	2–2
1895	6/4	Everton	W	3–0
1896	4/4	Glasgow	L	1–2
1897	3/4	Crystal Palace	L	1–2
1898	2/4	Glasgow	W	3–1
1899	8/4	Birmingham	W	2–1
1900	7/4	Glasgow	L	1–4
1901	30/3	Crystal Palace	D	2–2
1902	3/3	Birmingham	D	2–2
1903	4/4	Sheffield	L	1–2
1904	9/4	Glasgow	W	1–0
1905	1/4	Crystal Palace	W	1–0
1906	7/4	Glasgow	L	1–2
1907	6/4	Newcastle	D	1–1
1908	4/4	Glasgow	D	1–1
1909	3/4	Crystal Palace	W	2–0
1910	2/4	Glasgow	L	0–2
1911	1/4	Everton	D	1–1
1912	23/3	Glasgow	D	1–1
1913	5/4	Chelsea	W	1–0
1914	14/4	Glasgow	L	1–3
1920	10/4	Sheffield	W	5–4
1921	9/4	Glasgow	L	0–3
1922	8/4	Aston Villa	L	0–1
1923	14/4	Glasgow	D	2–2
1924	12/4	Wembley	D	1–1
1925	4/4	Glasgow	L	0–2
1926	17/4	Manchester	L	0–1
1927	2/4	Glasgow	W	2–1
1928	31/3	Wembley	L	1–5
1929	13/4	Glasgow	L	0–1

1930	5/4	Wembley	W	5–2	
1931	28/3	Glasgow	L	0–2	
1932	9/4	Wembley	W	3–0	
1933	1/4	Glasgow	L	1–2	
1934	14/4	Wembley	W	3–0	
1935	6/4	Glasgow	L	0–2	
1936	4/4	Wembley	D	1–1	
1937	17/4	Glasgow	L	1–3	
1938	9/4	Wembley	L	0–1	
1939	15/4	Glasgow	W	2–1	
1947	12/4	Wembley	D	1–1	
1948	10/4	Glasgow	W	2–0	
1949	9/4	Wembley	L	1–3	
1950	15/4	Glasgow	W	1–0	WCQ
1951	14/4	Wembley	L	2–3	
1952	5/4	Glasgow	W	2–1	
1953	18/4	Wembley	D	2–2	
1954	3/4	Glasgow	W	4–2	WCQ
1955	2/4	Wembley	W	7–2	
1956	14/4	Glasgow	D	1–1	
1957	6/4	Wembley	W	2–1	
1958	19/4	Glasgow	W	4–0	
1959	11/4	Wembley	W	1–0	
1960	19/4	Glasgow	D	1–1	
1961	15/4	Wembley	W	9–3	
1962	14/4	Glasgow	L	0–2	
1963	6/4	Wembley	L	1–2	
1964	11/4	Glasgow	L	0–1	
1965	10/4	Wembley	D	2–2	
1966	2/4	Glasgow	W	4–3	
1967	15/4	Wembley	L	2–3	ECQ
1968	24/2	Glasgow	D	1–1	ECQ
1969	10/5	Wembley	W	4–1	
1970	25/4	Glasgow	D	0–0	
1971	22/5	Wembley	W	3–1	
1972	27/5	Glasgow	W	1–0	
1973	14/2	Glasgow	W	5–0	
1973	19/5	Wembley	W	1–0	
1974	18/5	Glasgow	L	0–2	
1975	24/5	Wembley	W	5–1	
1976	15/5	Glasgow	L	1–2	
1977	4/6	Wembley	L	1–2	
1978	20/5	Glasgow	W	1–0	
1979	26/5	Wembley	W	3–1	
1980	24/5	Glasgow	W	2–0	
1981	23/5	Wembley	L	0–1	
1982	29/5	Glasgow	W	1–0	
1983	1/6	Wembley	W	2–0	
1984	26/5	Glasgow	D	1–1	
1985	25/5	Glasgow	L	0–1	RC
1986	23/4	Wembley	W	2–1	RC
1987	23/5	Glasgow	D	0–0	RC
1988	21/5	Wembley	W	1–0	RC
1989	27/5	Glasgow	W	2–0	RC
1996	15/6	Wembley	W	2–0	ECF

P 108, W 44, D 24, L 40, F 190, A 168

v Spain

1929	15/5	Madrid	L	3–4	
1931	9/12	Arsenal	W	7–1	
1950	2/7	Rio de Janeiro	L	0–1	WCF
1955	18/5	Madrid	D	1–1	
1955	30/11	Wembley	W	4–1	
1960	15/5	Madrid	L	0–3	
1960	26/10	Wembley	W	4–2	
1965	8/12	Madrid	W	2–0	
1967	24/5	Wembley	W	2–0	
1968	3/4	Wembley	W	1–0	ECQ
1968	8/5	Madrid	W	2–1	ECQ
1980	26/3	Barcelona	W	2–0	
1980	18/6	Naples	W	2–1	ECF
1981	25/3	Wembley	L	1–2	
1982	5/7	Madrid	D	0–0	WCF
1987	18/2	Madrid	W	4–2	
1992	9/9	Santander	L	0–1	
1996	22/6	Wembley	D	0–0	*ECF

P 18, W 10, D 3, L 5, F 35, A 20

After extra time (England won 4–2 on penalties)

v Sweden

1923	21/5	Stockholm	W	4–2	
1923	24/5	Stockholm	W	3–1	
1937	17/5	Stockholm	W	4–0	
1947	19/11	Arsenal	W	4–2	
1949	13/5	Stockholm	L	1–3	
1956	16/5	Stockholm	D	0–0	
1959	28/10	Wembley	L	2–3	
1965	16/5	Gothenburg	W	2–1	
1968	22/5	Wembley	W	3–1	
1979	10/6	Stockholm	D	0–0	
1986	10/9	Stockholm	L	0–1	
1988	19/10	Wembley	D	0–0	WCQ
1989	6/9	Stockholm	D	0–0	WCQ
1992	17/6	Stockholm	L	1–2	ECF
1995	8/6	Leeds	D	3–3	

P 15, W 6, D 5, L 4, F 27, A 19

v Switzerland

1933	29/5	Berne	W	4–0	
1938	21/5	Zurich	L	1–2	
1947	18/5	Zurich	L	0–1	
1948	2/12	Arsenal	W	6–0	
1952	28/5	Zurich	W	3–0	
1954	20/6	Berne	W	2–0	WCF
1962	9/5	Wembley	W	3–1	
1963	5/6	Basle	W	8–1	
1971	13/10	Basle	W	3–2	ECQ
1971	10/11	Wembley	D	1–1	ECQ
1975	3/9	Basle	W	2–1	
1977	7/9	Wembley	D	0–0	
1980	19/11	Wembley	W	2–1	WCQ
1981	30/5	Basle	L	1–2	WCQ
1988	28/5	Lausanne	W	1–0	
1995	15/11	Wembley	W	3–1	
1996	8/6	Wembley	D	1–1	ECF

P 17, W 11, D 3, L 3, F 41, A 14

v Tunisia

1990	2/6	Tunis	D	1–1	

P 1, W 0, D 1, L 0, F 1, A 1

v Turkey

1984	14/11	Istanbul	W	8–0	WCQ
1985	16/10	Wembley	W	5–0	WCQ
1987	29/4	Izmir	D	0–0	ECQ
1987	14/10	Wembley	W	8–0	ECQ
1991	1/5	Izmir	W	1–0	ECQ
1991	16/10	Wembley	W	1–0	ECQ
1992	18/11	Wembley	W	4–0	WCQ
1993	31/3	Izmir	W	2–0	WCQ

P 8, W 7, D 1, L 0, F 29, A 0

v USA

1950	29/6	Belo Horizonte	L	0–1	WCF
1953	8/6	New York	W	6–3	
1959	28/5	Los Angeles	W	8–1	
1964	27/5	New York	W	10–0	
1985	16/6	Los Angeles	W	5–0	
1993	9/6	Boston	L	0–2	
1994	7/9	Wembley	W	2–0	

P 7, W 5, D 0, L 2, F 31, A 7

v USSR (see also CIS)

1958	18/5	Moscow	D	1–1	
1958	8/6	Gothenburg	D	2–2	WCF
1958	17/6	Gothenburg	L	0–1	WCF
1958	22/10	Wembley	W	5–0	
1967	6/12	Wembley	D	2–2	
1968	8/6	Rome	W	2–0	ECF
1973	10/6	Moscow	W	2–1	
1984	2/6	Wembley	L	0–2	
1986	26/3	Tbilisi	W	1–0	
1988	18/6	Frankfurt	L	1–3	ECF
1991	21/5	Wembley	W	3–1	

P 11, W 5, D 3, L 3, F 19, A 13

v Uruguay

1953	31/5	Montevideo	L	1–2	
1954	26/6	Basle	L	2–4	WCF
1964	6/5	Wembley	W	2–1	
1966	11/7	Wembley	D	0–0	WCF
1969	8/6	Montevideo	W	2–1	
1977	15/6	Montevideo	D	0–0	
1984	13/6	Montevideo	L	0–2	
1990	22/5	Wembley	L	1–2	
1995	29/3	Wembley	D	0–0	

P 9, W 2, D 3, L 4, F 8, A 12

v Wales

1879	18/1	Kennington	W	2–1	
1880	15/3	Wrexham	W	3–2	
1881	26/2	Blackburn	L	0–1	
1882	13/3	Wrexham	L	3–5	
1883	3/2	Kennington	W	5–0	
1884	17/3	Wrexham	W	4–0	
1885	14/3	Blackburn	D	1–1	
1886	29/3	Wrexham	W	3–1	
1887	26/2	Kennington	W	4–0	
1888	4/2	Crewe	W	5–1	
1889	23/2	Stoke	W	4–1	
1890	15/3	Wrexham	W	3–1	
1891	7/5	Sunderland	W	4–1	
1892	5/3	Wrexham	W	2–0	
1893	13/3	Stoke	W	6–0	
1894	12/3	Wrexham	W	5–1	
1895	18/3	Kennington	D	1–1	
1896	16/3	Cardiff	W	9–1	
1897	29/3	Sheffield	W	4–0	
1898	28/3	Wrexham	W	3–0	
1899	20/3	Bristol	W	4–0	
1900	26/3	Cardiff	D	1–1	
1901	18/3	Newcastle	W	6–0	
1902	3/3	Wrexham	D	0–0	
1903	2/3	Portsmouth	W	2–0	
1904	29/2	Wrexham	D	2–2	
1905	27/3	Liverpool	W	3–1	
1906	19/3	Cardiff	W	1–0	
1907	18/3	Fulham	D	1–1	
1908	16/3	Wrexham	W	7–1	
1909	15/3	Nottingham	W	2–0	
1910	14/3	Cardiff	W	1–0	
1911	13/3	Millwall	W	3–0	
1912	11/3	Wrexham	W	2–0	
1913	17/3	Bristol	W	4–3	
1914	16/3	Cardiff	W	2–0	
1920	15/3	Arsenal	L	1–2	
1921	14/3	Cardiff	D	0–0	
1922	13/3	Liverpool	W	1–0	
1923	5/3	Cardiff	D	2–2	
1924	3/3	Blackburn	L	1–2	
1925	28/2	Swansea	W	2–1	
1926	1/3	Crystal Palace	L	1–3	
1927	12/2	Wrexham	D	3–3	
1927	28/11	Burnley	L	1–2	
1928	17/11	Swansea	W	3–2	
1929	20/11	Chelsea	W	6–0	
1930	22/11	Wrexham	W	4–0	
1931	18/11	Liverpool	W	3–1	
1932	16/11	Wrexham	D	0–0	
1933	15/11	Newcastle	L	1–2	
1934	29/9	Cardiff	W	4–0	
1936	5/2	Wolverhampton	L	1–2	
1936	17/10	Cardiff	L	1–2	
1937	17/11	Middlesbrough	W	2–1	
1938	22/10	Cardiff	L	2–4	
1946	13/11	Manchester	W	3–0	
1947	18/10	Cardiff	W	3–0	
1948	10/11	Aston Villa	W	1–0	
1949	15/10	Cardiff	W	4–1	WCQ
1950	15/11	Sunderland	W	4–2	
1951	20/10	Cardiff	D	1–1	

Year	Date	Venue	Result	Score	Comp
1952	12/11	Wembley	W	5–2	
1953	10/10	Cardiff	W	4–1	WCQ
1954	10/11	Wembley	W	3–2	
1955	22/10	Cardiff	L	1–2	
1956	14/11	Wembley	W	3–1	
1957	19/10	Cardiff	W	4–0	
1958	26/11	Aston Villa	D	2–2	
1959	17/10	Cardiff	D	1–1	
1960	23/11	Wembley	W	5–1	
1961	14/10	Cardiff	D	1–1	
1962	21/11	Wembley	W	4–0	
1963	12/10	Cardiff	W	4–0	
1964	18/11	Wembley	W	2–1	
1965	2/10	Cardiff	D	0–0	
1966	16/11	Wembley	W	5–1	ECQ
1967	21/10	Cardiff	W	3–0	ECQ
1969	7/5	Wembley	W	2–1	
1970	18/4	Cardiff	D	1–1	
1971	19/5	Wembley	D	0–0	
1972	20/5	Cardiff	W	3–0	
1972	15/11	Cardiff	W	1–0	WCQ
1973	24/1	Wembley	D	1–1	WCQ
1973	15/5	Wembley	W	3–0	
1974	11/5	Cardiff	W	2–0	
1975	21/5	Wembley	D	2–2	
1976	24/3	Wrexham	W	2–1	
1976	8/5	Cardiff	W	1–0	
1977	31/5	Wembley	L	0–1	
1978	3/5	Cardiff	W	3–1	
1979	23/5	Wembley	D	0–0	
1980	17/5	Wrexham	L	1–4	
1981	20/5	Wembley	D	0–0	
1982	27/4	Cardiff	W	1–0	
1983	23/2	Wembley	W	2–1	
1984	2/5	Wrexham	L	0–1	

P 97 W 62, D 21, L 14, F 239, A 90

v Yugoslavia

Year	Date	Venue	Result	Score	Comp
1939	18/5	Belgrade	L	1–2	
1950	22/11	Highbury	D	2–2	
1954	16/5	Belgrade	L	0–1	
1956	28/11	Wembley	W	3–0	
1958	11/5	Belgrade	L	0–5	
1960	11/5	Wembley	D	3–3	
1965	9/5	Belgrade	D	1–1	
1966	4/5	Wembley	W	2–0	
1968	5/6	Florence	L	0–1	ECF
1972	11/10	Wembley	D	1–1	
1974	5/6	Belgrade	D	2–2	
1986	12/11	Wembley	W	2–0	ECQ
1987	11/11	Belgrade	W	4–1	ECQ
1989	13/12	Wembley	W	2–1	

P 14, W 5, D 5, L 4, F 23, A 20

22 ● SEMI-PROFESSIONAL INTERNATIONAL/FA REPRESENTATIVE MATCHES 1995–96

FA XI 0   Northern Premier League 2

14th November 1995, Accrington Stanley FC

FA XI: Collings (Altrincham), Bates (Runcorn), Prindiville (Halifax Town), Jones (Stalybridge Celtic), Dove and Haw (Southport), Terry (Altrincham), McDonald (Macclesfield Town), Midwood (Halifax Town), Carmody and Sharratt (Altrincham)

Subs: Butler (Northwich Victoria) for Carmody, Lyons (Macclesfield Town) for Midwood, Greygoose (Northwich Victoria) for Collings, Gamble (Southport) for Haw

Team Manager: John King (Altrincham)

FA XI 2   British Students 0

9th January 1996, Hednesford Town FC

FA XI: Steadman (Kidderminster Harriers), Bignot (Telford United), Collins (Hednesford Town), Deakin (Kidderminster Harriers), Simpson (Hednesford Town), Gaunt and Smith (Bromsgrove Rovers), Yates (Kidderminster Harriers), Hunt (Bromsgrove Rovers), Hughes (Kidderminster Harriers), O'Connor (Hednesford Town)

Subs: Carty (Hednesford Town) for Bignot, Goodwin (Telford United) for Steadman, Myers (Telford United) for Smith, Davies (Kidderminster Harriers) for Hunt, Street (Hednesford Town) for Hughes

Scorers: Carty, Street

Team Manager: Graham Allner (Kidderminster Harriers)

FA XI 1   Combined Services 0

16th January 1996, Mangotsfield United FC

FA XI: Pennock (Yeovil Town), Gill (Bath City), Engwell (Yeovil Town), Banks (Cheltenham Town), Freeman (Gloucester City), Wright (Cheltenham Town), Knight (Gloucester City), Chenoweth and Eaton (Cheltenham Town), Killick (Dorchester Town), Holmes (Gloucester City)

Subs: Francis (Yeovil Town) for Gill, Bowles (Cinderford Town) for Pennock, Dunphy (Cheltenham Town) for Banks, Howell (Cheltenham Town) for Eaton

Scorer: Holmes

Team Manager: Chris Robinson (Cheltenham Town)

England 4   Republic of Ireland (FAI National League) 0

27th February 1996, Kidderminster Harriers FC

England: Price (Macclesfield Town), Webb (Kidderminster Harriers), Ashby and Stott (Rushden & Diamonds), Smith (Stevenage Borough), Tucker (Woking), Venables and Hayles (Stevenage Borough), Alford (Kettering Town), Cramman (Gateshead), Hughes (Kidderminster Harriers)

Subs: Rose (Witton Albion) for Venables, Power (Macclesfield Town) for Alford, Kimmins (Hyde United) for Hayles

Scorers: Alford, Hayles, Kimmins, OG

Attendance: 1,034

Team Manager: Tony Jennings

England 3   Holland 1

2nd April 1996, Rushden & Diamonds FC

England: Price (Macclesfield Town), Webb (Kidderminster Harriers), Ashby and Stott (Rushden & Diamonds), Smith (Stevenage Borough), Brown (Woking), Endersby (Harrow Borough), Hayles (Stevenage Borough), Alford (Rushden & Diamonds), Rose (Witton Albion), Hughes (Kidderminster Harriers)

Subs: Kimmins (Hyde United) for Alford, Venables (Stevenage Borough) for Endersby, Power (Macclesfield Town) for Rose

Scorers: Stott, Alford, Hayles

Attendance: 1,660

Team Manager: Tony Jennings

23 ● FA CUP WINNERS 1872–1996

Final venues:

1872 & 1874–92	Kennington Oval	1895–1914	Crystal Palace
1873	Lillie Bridge, London	1915	Old Trafford, Manchester
1893	Fallowfield, Manchester	1920–22	Stamford Bridge, London
1894	Goodison Park, Liverpool	1923 to date	Wembley Stadium

Year	Winners		Runners-up	Result	
1872	Wanderers	v	Royal Engineers	1–0	
1873	Wanderers	v	Oxford University	2–0	
1874	Oxford University	v	Royal Engineers	2–0	
1875	Royal Engineers	v	Old Etonians	2–0	after 1–1 draw
1876	Wanderers	v	Old Etonians	3–0	after 0–0 draw
1877	Wanderers	v	Oxford University	2–0	after extra time
1878	Wanderers*	v	Royal Engineers	3–1	
1879	Old Etonians	v	Clapham Rovers	1–0	
1880	Clapham Rovers	v	Oxford University	1–0	
1881	Old Carthusians	v	Old Etonians	3–0	
1882	Old Etonians	v	Blackburn Rovers	1–0	
1883	Blackburn Olympic	v	Old Etonians	2–1	after extra time
1884	Blackburn Rovers	v	Queen's Park, Glasgow	2–1	
1885	Blackburn Rovers	v	Queen's Park, Glasgow	2–0	
1886	Blackburn Rovers†	v	West Bromwich Albion	2–0	after 0–0 draw
1887	Aston Villa	v	West Bromwich Albion	2–0	
1888	West Bromwich Albion	v	Preston North End	2–1	
1889	Preston North End	v	Wolverhampton Wanderers	3–0	
1890	Blackburn Rovers	v	Sheffield Wednesday	6–1	
1891	Blackburn Rovers	v	Notts County	3–1	
1892	West Bromwich Albion	v	Aston Villa	3–0	
1893	Wolverhampton Wanderers	v	Everton	1–0	
1894	Notts County	v	Bolton Wanderers	4–1	
1895	Aston Villa	v	West Bromwich Albion	1–0	
1896	Sheffield Wednesday	v	Wolverhampton Wanderers	2–1	
1897	Aston Villa	v	Everton	3–2	
1898	Nottingham Forest	v	Derby County	3–1	
1899	Sheffield United	v	Derby County	4–1	
1900	Bury	v	Southampton	4–0	
1901	Tottenham Hotspur	v	Sheffield United	3–1	after 2–2 draw
1902	Sheffield United	v	Southampton	2–1	after 1–1 draw
1903	Bury	v	Derby County	6–0	
1904	Manchester City	v	Bolton Wanderers	1–0	
1905	Aston Villa	v	Newcastle United	2–0	
1906	Everton	v	Newcastle United	1–0	
1907	Sheffield Wednesday	v	Everton	2–1	
1908	Wolverhampton Wanderers	v	Newcastle United	3–1	
1909	Manchester United	v	Bristol City	1–0	
1910	Newcastle United	v	Barnsley	2–0	after 1–1 draw
1911	Bradford City	v	Newcastle United	1–0	after 0–0 draw
1912	Barnsley	v	West Bromwich Albion	1–0	after 0–0 draw

* Won outright but restored to The Association
† A special trophy was awarded for third consecutive win

Year	Winners		Runners-up	Result	
1913	Aston Villa	v	Sunderland	1–0	
1914	Burnley	v	Liverpool	1–0	
1915	Sheffield United	v	Chelsea	3–0	
1920	Aston Villa	v	Huddersfield Town	1–0	after extra time
1921	Tottenham Hotspur	v	Wolverhampton Wanderers	1–0	
1922	Huddersfield Town	v	Preston North End	1–0	
1923	Bolton Wanderers	v	West Ham United	2–0	
1924	Newcastle United	v	Aston Villa	2–0	
1925	Sheffield United	v	Cardiff City	1–0	
1926	Bolton Wanderers	v	Manchester City	1–0	
1927	Cardiff City	v	Arsenal	1–0	
1928	Blackburn Rovers	v	Huddersfield Town	3–1	
1929	Bolton Wanderers	v	Portsmouth	2–0	
1930	Arsenal	v	Huddersfield Town	2–0	
1931	West Bromwich Albion	v	Birmingham City	2–1	
1932	Newcastle United	v	Arsenal	2–1	
1933	Everton	v	Manchester City	3–0	
1934	Manchester City	v	Portsmouth	2–1	
1935	Sheffield Wednesday	v	West Bromwich Albion	4–2	
1936	Arsenal	v	Sheffield United	1–0	
1937	Sunderland	v	Preston North End	3–1	
1938	Preston North End	v	Huddersfield Town	1–0	after extra time
1939	Portsmouth	v	Wolverhampton Wanderers	4–1	
1946	Derby County	v	Charlton Athletic	4–1	after extra time
1947	Charlton Athletic	v	Burnley	1–0	after extra time
1948	Manchester United	v	Blackpool	4–2	
1949	Wolverhampton Wanderers	v	Leicester City	3–1	
1950	Arsenal	v	Liverpool	2–0	
1951	Newcastle United	v	Blackpool	2–0	
1952	Newcastle United	v	Arsenal	1–0	
1953	Blackpool	v	Bolton Wanderers	4–3	
1954	West Bromwich Albion	v	Preston North End	3–2	
1955	Newcastle United	v	Manchester City	3–1	
1956	Manchester City	v	Birmingham City	3–1	
1957	Aston Villa	v	Manchester United	2–1	
1958	Bolton Wanderers	v	Manchester United	2–0	
1959	Nottingham Forest	v	Luton Town	2–1	
1960	Wolverhampton Wanderers	v	Blackburn Rovers	3–0	
1961	Tottenham Hotspur	v	Leicester City	2–0	
1962	Tottenham Hotspur	v	Burnley	3–1	
1963	Manchester United	v	Leicester City	3–1	
1964	West Ham United	v	Preston North End	3–2	
1965	Liverpool	v	Leeds United	2–1	after extra time
1966	Everton	v	Sheffield Wednesday	3–2	
1967	Tottenham Hotspur	v	Chelsea	2–1	
1968	West Bromwich Albion	v	Everton	1–0	after extra time
1969	Manchester City	v	Leicester City	1–0	
1970	Chelsea	v	Leeds United	2–1	after 2–2 draw both games extra time
1971	Arsenal	v	Liverpool	2–1	after extra time
1972	Leeds United	v	Arsenal	1–0	
1973	Sunderland	v	Leeds United	1–0	
1974	Liverpool	v	Newcastle United	3–0	
1975	West Ham United	v	Fulham	2–0	
1976	Southampton	v	Manchester United	1–0	
1977	Manchester United	v	Liverpool	2–1	
1978	Ipswich Town	v	Arsenal	1–0	

Year	Winners		Runners-up	Result	
1979	Arsenal	v	Manchester United	3–2	
1980	West Ham United	v	Arsenal	1–0	
1981	Tottenham Hotspur	v	Manchester City	3–2	after 1–1 draw after extra time
1982	Tottenham Hotspur	v	Queens Park Rangers	1–0	after 1–1 draw after extra time
1983	Manchester United	v	Brighton & Hove Albion	4–0	after 2–2 draw after extra time
1984	Everton	v	Watford	2–0	
1985	Manchester United	v	Everton	1–0	after extra time
1986	Liverpool	v	Everton	3–1	
1987	Coventry City	v	Tottenham Hotspur	3–2	after extra time
1988	Wimbledon	v	Liverpool	1–0	
1989	Liverpool	v	Everton	3–2	after extra time
1990	Manchester United	v	Crystal Palace	1–0	after 3–3 draw after extra time
1991	Tottenham Hotspur	v	Nottingham Forest	2–1	after extra time
1992	Liverpool	v	Sunderland	2–0	
1993	Arsenal	v	Sheffield Wednesday	2–1	after 1–1 draw both games extra time
1994	Manchester United	v	Chelsea	4–0	
1995	Everton	v	Manchester United	1–0	
1996	Manchester United	v	Liverpool	1–0	

Eric Cantona and United colleagues celebrate their Cup success.

24 ● FA CUP – FINAL TIE 1996
Sponsored by Littlewoods

Manchester United 1   Liverpool 0

History was made at the 115th FA Cup Final – Manchester United became the first club to win the League and Cup "double" twice. It was their second "double" success in three seasons and, for good measure, they were FA Cup winners for a record ninth time. The Frenchman Eric Cantona, whose season had only begun on 1 October – as a result of his contretemps at Selhurst Park – was United's captain at Wembley and also scored the goal that won the Cup.

Footballer of the Year Cantona, aka "The Magnificent Seven", had a quiet match by his standards – a flick here, a back-heel there – but made the most significant contribution with a little over five minutes to go of a far-from-classic final. David Beckham, scorer of the semi-final winner at Villa Park in March, chipped over a flag-kick from the right and Liverpool 'keeper James clambered over Wright and United's May in an attempt to palm the ball to safety. Instead it fell in front of Cantona, momentarily alone on the edge of the box. He adjusted his stride before crashing the ball right-footed through a host of Liverpool players on the line and into the net. The ebullient Frenchman raced towards his adoring fans, proudly showing them the United badge on his shirt.

Although it was Cantona who had fittingly had the last word, United's best performer on the day was arguably Roy Keane. Certainly the Republic of Ireland midfielder with the short fuse was later named man-of-the-match. Keane held a deep position alongside Nicky Butt and, with Beckham and Giggs tucking in further forward, United gained supremacy in midfield. Rarely could England men McManaman, Redknapp and Barnes have been so ineffective, the last-mentioned in his distinctive white boots.

James, perhaps an international goalkeeper of the future, looked huge and elastic in front of the Liverpool net. He made a blinding save from a Beckham screamer in the first half and a reflex stop from a fiercely-struck close-in Cantona effort in the second period was equally as impressive. Scales was adequate in defence but too many had off days. The much-acclaimed Fowler struggled to fashion a chance and Collymore's shots even cleared the ball-boys' heads. Ian Rush, already with a record five FA Cup Final goals to his name, came on for his last Liverpool appearance but achieved little in the 16 minutes allotted to him.

Manchester United: Schmeichel, Irwin, May, Pallister, Neville P., Beckham (Neville G.), Butt, Keane, Giggs, Cantona, Cole (Scholes).

Liverpool: James, McAteer, Scales, Wright, Babb, Jones (Thomas), McManaman, Redknapp, Barnes, Collymore (Rush), Fowler.

Referee: D. J. Gallagher (Oxfordshire)

Attendance: 79,007

Presentation: HRH The Duchess of Kent presented the Cup

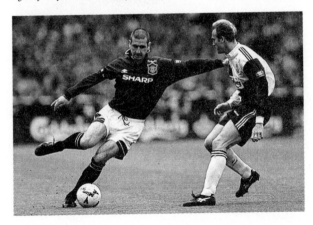

Match-winner Cantona is confronted by Liverpool's Scales.

25 ● FA CUP 1995–96
Sponsored by Littlewoods

Preliminary round – 26 August 1995

(Replays in italics)   *Results*   *Att*

Liversedge	v	Blackpool(Wren)Rovers	1–4	51
Guisborough Town	v	Gretna	1–0	100
Willington	v	Dunston Federation Brewery	0–0	42
Dunston Federation Brewery	*v*	*Willington*	*5–2*	*115*
Prudhoe Town	v	Consett	1–3	30
(at Consett FC)				
South Shields	v	Pickering Town	3–4	116
Netherfield	v	Evenwood Town	10–1	116
RTM Newcastle	v	Harrogate Railway	1–2	48
Brandon United	v	Chester-Le-Street Town	1–4	29
Seaham Red Star	v	Billingham Town	1–2	32
Esh Winning	v	Stockton	3–1	7
Workington	v	Hebburn	8–1	253
Alnwick Town	v	Glasshoughton Welfare	1–3	70
Whitley Bay	v	Easington Colliery	3–0	142
Tadcaster Albion	v	Bedlington Terriers	1–1	80
Bedlington Terriers	*v*	*Tadcaster Albion*	*3–0*	*127*
Ryhope CA	v	Morpeth Town	2–2	43
Morpeth Town	*v*	*Ryhope CA*	*3–1*	*79*
Shotton Comrades	v	Shildon	1–1	55
Shildon	*v*	*Shotton Comrades*	*2–1*	*84*
Washington	v	Garforth Town	1–0	56
(Washington removed from the Competition for playing a suspended player – Garforth Town re-instated)				
Darlington Cleveland Soc	v	Billingham Synthonia	0–3	9
Prescot Cables	v	Atherton Collieries	3–0	28
Chadderton	v	Eastwood Town	0–1	96
Lincoln United	v	Stocksbridge Park Steels	3–2	164
Burscough	v	Northallerton 1994	2–2	134
Northallerton 1994	*v*	*Burscough*	*1–2*	*115*
Eccleshill United	v	Atherton LR	3–2	37
Arnold Town	v	Maine Road	2–0	170
Glossop North End	v	Nantwich Town	1–2	176
Radcliffe Borough	v	Alfreton Town	3–2	118
Sheffield	v	Caernarfon Town		
(walkover for Sheffield – Caernarfon Town withdrawn)				
Belper Town	v	Worksop Town	2–3	261
North Ferriby United	v	Heanor Town	2–4	83
Maltby MW	v	Mossley	3–3	60
Mossley	*v*	*Maltby MW*	*4–0*	*136*
Leigh RMI	v	Flixton	2–0	60
Brigg Town	v	Clitheroe	1–1	68
Clitheroe	*v*	*Brigg Town*	*1–0*	*140*
Farsley Celtic	v	Oldham Town	2–2	103
Oldham Town	*v*	*Farsley Celtic*	*0–2*	*75*
Blidworth MW	v	Rossendale United	0–0	41
Rossendale United	*v*	*Blidworth MW*	*3–0*	*92*
St Helens Town	v	Bootle	1–2	112
Winterton Rangers	v	Darwen	2–0	32

			Results	Att
Denaby United	v	Hucknall Town	4–0	80
Trafford	v	Fleetwood	2–1	101
Crook Town	v	Kimberley Town	3–2	99
Ossett Town	v	Castleton Gabriels	3–2	47
Armthorpe Welfare	v	Bradford (Park Avenue)	1–1	85
Bradford (Park Avenue)	*v*	*Armthorpe Welfare*	*1–0*	*148*
Goole Town	v	Great Harwood Town	2–2	104
Great Harwood Town	*v*	*Goole Town*	*3–2*	*104*
(after abandoned tie 1–0, 50 mins due to floodlight failure)				
Ossett Albion	v	Hatfield Main	1–3	42
Immingham Town	v	Rossington Main	1–1	20
(at Rossington Main FC)				
Rossington Main	*v*	*Immingham Town*	*1–4*	*49*
Louth United	v	Harworth CI	4–0	26
Salford City	v	Newcastle Town	1–2	25
Pontefract Collieries	v	Oakham United	4–1	50
Hinckley Athletic	v	Ashton United	1–1	218
Ashton United	*v*	*Hinckley Athletic*	*1–3*	*170*
Thackley	v	Cheadle Town	5–2	100
Yorkshire Amateur	v	Borrowash Victoria	2–4	63
Bilston Town	v	Blakenall	0–0	131
Blakenall	*v*	*Bilston Town*	*2–1*	*103*
Redditch United	v	Bridgnorth Town	2–2	153
Bridgnorth Town	*v*	*Redditch United*	*1–4*	*101*
Desborough Town	v	Rocester	0–0	62
(at Rocester)				
Rocester	*v*	*Desborough Town*	*2–4*	*48*
Shifnal Town	v	Willenhall Town	0–0	86
Willenhall Town	*v*	*Shifnal Town*	*0–1*	*101*
West Midlands Police	v	Raunds Town	1–1	82
Raunds Town	*v*	*West Midlands Police*	*3–2*	*109*
Stourport Swifts	v	Armitage	0–1	53
Chasetown	v	Halesowen Harriers	2–1	82
Tamworth	v	Hinckley Town	3–1	514
Westfields	v	Corby Town	1–1	122
Corby Town	*v*	*Westfields*	*7–5*	*217*
Wellingborough Town	v	Bolehall Swifts	0–4	40
Shepshed Dynamo	v	Grantham Town	0–1	211
Stapenhill	v	Lye Town	1–2	32
Northampton Spencer	v	Cogenhoe United	2–2	44
Cogenhoe United	*v*	*Northampton Spencer*	*1–0*	*108*
Pelsall Villa	v	Dudley Town	1–1	142
Dudley Town	*v*	*Pelsall Villa*	*1–0*	*161*
Brierley Hill Town	v	Sandwell Borough	0–0	19
Sandwell Borough	*v*	*Brierley Hill Town*	*5–3*	*19*
Pershore Town	v	Evesham United	1–1	259
Evesham United	*v*	*Pershore Town*	*3–2*	*206*
Newport Pagnell Town	v	Boldmere St Michaels	0–2	25
Leicester United	v	Barwell	0–0	59
Barwell	*v*	*Leicester United*	*1–1*	*76*
Barwell	*v*	*Leicester United*	*3–4*	*79*
Wednesfield	v	Banbury United	2–2	38
Banbury United	*v*	*Wednesfield*	*0–3*	*110*
Oldbury United	v	Darlaston	4–0	69
Long Buckby	v	Stewarts & Lloyds	2–1	35
Knypersley Victoria	v	Stratford Town	0–3	47
(at Newcastle Town FC)				
Rothwell Town	v	Rushall Olympic	2–0	96

East Thurrock United	v	Tiptree United	1–1	54
Tiptree United	*v*	*East Thurrock United*	*6–2*	*91*
Gorleston	v	Diss Town	1–5	301
Halstead Town	v	Stamford	1–1	225
Stamford	*v*	*Halstead Town*	*3–3*	*170*
Stamford	*v*	*Halstead Town*	*1–2*	*264*
Wisbech Town	v	Tring Town	4–0	338
Eynesbury Rovers	v	Witham Town	4–1	70
Wroxham	v	Canvey Island	0–0	186
Canvey Island	*v*	*Wroxham*	*3–1*	*251*
Spalding United	v	Harwich & Parkeston	2–3	128
Kings Lynn	v	Wivenhoe Town	3–0	621
Newmarket Town	v	Boston Town	0–1	116
Basildon United	v	Saffron Walden Town	1–2	64
Aveley	v	Stowmarket Town	0–0	54
Stowmarket Town	*v*	*Aveley*	*3–4*	*119*
Great Yarmouth Town	v	Bourne Town	2–1	86
Burnham Ramblers	v	Holbeach United	1–3	74
Bury Town	v	Collier Row	1–2	214
March Town United	v	Fakenham Town	1–0	86
Leyton Pennant	v	Clacton Town	2–2	74
Clacton Town	*v*	*Leyton Pennant*	*0–4*	*92*
East Ham United	v	Sudbury Wanderers	0–7	100
Hertford Town	v	Ware	2–1	154
Cheshunt	v	Wealdstone	0–1	155
Tufnell Park	v	Potton United	1–0	21
Felixstowe Town	v	Burnham	1–1	85
Burnham	*v*	*Felixstowe Town*	*2–3*	*38*
Bedford Town	v	Edgware Town	1–4	413
Hillingdon Borough	v	Cornard United	2–0	58
Hornchurch	v	Bowers United	3–0	45
Biggleswade Town	v	Berkhamsted Town	0–4	42
(at Langford FC)				
Lowestoft Town	v	Chalfont St Peter	2–2	170
Chalfont St Peter	*v*	*Lowestoft Town*	*4–1*	*51*
Haverhill Rovers	v	Hampton	0–1	52
Uxbridge	v	Kempston Rovers	4–0	98
Brook House	v	Welwyn Garden City	0–0	
Welwyn Garden City	*v*	*Brook House*	*0–2*	*34*
Northwood	v	Ford United	3–2	102
Hadleigh United	v	Southall	1–0	63
Soham Town Rangers	v	Stotfold	1–1	115
Stotfold	*v*	*Soham Town Rangers*	*4–1*	*88*
Tilbury	v	Woodbridge Town	1–2	53
Brimsdown Rovers	v	Barton Rovers	0–2	32
Harefield United	v	Hoddesdon Town	0–1	18
Metropolitan Police	v	Viking Sports	7–0	70
Concord Rangers	v	Wootton Blue Cross	2–1	80
Clapton	v	Leighton Town	2–1	46
Flackwell Heath	v	Potters Bar Town	1–0	45
Barking	v	Royston Town	1–0	101
Bedfont	v	Langford	0–0	22
Langford	*v*	*Bedfont*	*1–1*	*75*
Bedfont	*v*	*Langford*	*0–4*	*53*
Hanwell Town	v	Wingate & Finchley	2–4	49
Harlow Town	v	Thamesmead Town	2–3	67
Milton Keynes	v	Leatherhead	0–4	50
Bracknell Town	v	Kingsbury Town	0–0	73

(Replays in italics)			*Results*	*Att*
Kingsbury Town	*v*	*Bracknell Town*	*0–0*	*63*
Kingsbury Town	*v*	*Bracknell Town*	*1–1*	*63*
Bracknell Town	*v*	*Kingsbury Town*	*3–2*	*98*
Three Bridges	v	Camberley Town	0–5	81
Corinthian-Casuals	v	Stamco	3–0	108
Lewes	v	Lancing	2–1	59
Dartford	v	Egham Town	3–1	123
(at Egham Town FC)				
Fisher	v	Merstham	0–0	91
Merstham	*v*	*Fisher*	*0–2*	*137*
Tonbridge	v	Croydon Athletic	3–1	487
Croydon	v	Dorking	5–2	51
Folkestone Invicta	v	Peacehaven & Telscombe	1–1	181
Peacehaven & Telscombe	*v*	*Folkestone Invicta*	*4–1*	*221*
Shoreham	v	Corinthian	4–2	81
Epsom & Ewell	v	Tooting & Mitcham United	0–4	148
Littlehampton Town	v	Southwick	1–1	96
(at Southwick FC)				
Southwick	*v*	*Littlehampton Town*	*1–0*	*160*
Chatham Town	v	Whyteleafe	3–1	116
Banstead Athletic	v	Burgess Hill Town	3–1	43
Bognor Regis Town	v	Whitehawk	4–3	227
Raynes Park Vale	v	Canterbury City	3–0	58
Redhill	v	Tunbridge Wells	3–1	121
Chipstead	v	Horsham	0–4	75
Wick	v	Portfield	3–2	148
Herne Bay	v	Horsham YMCA	1–1	144
Horsham YMCA	*v*	*Herne Bay*	*1–4*	*85*
Sheppey United	v	Arundel	2–0	72
Slade Green	v	Langney Sports	0–2	61
Whitstable Town	v	Hailsham Town	3–2	122
Crowborough Athletic	v	Godalming & Guildford	1–3	70
Bicester Town	v	Ringmer	0–1	88
(at Ringmer FC)				
Aldershot Town	v	Selsey	5–0	1644
Steyning Town	v	Cove	3–0	42
Newbury Town	v	Buckingham Town		
(walkover for Buckingham Town – Newbury Town removed from the Competition)				
Thatcham Town	v	Oakwood	2–1	79
Hungerford Town	v	Poole Town	5–0	99
Abingdon Town	v	Andover	3–2	136
Totton AFC	v	Fleet Town	3–1	107
Witney Town	v	BAT Sports	5–0	127
Thame United	v	Maidenhead United	4–0	161
Bournemouth	v	Wimborne Town	0–4	308
Westbury United	v	Basingstoke Town	2–2	209
(at Basingstoke Town FC)				
Basingstoke Town	*v*	*Westbury United*	*5–1*	*196*
Fareham Town	v	Weymouth	1–1	152
Weymouth	*v*	*Fareham Town*	*3–2*	*807*
Lymington AFC	v	Calne Town	0–2	50
(at Calne Town FC)				
Bemerton Heath Harlequins	v	Ryde	2–3	52
Brockenhurst	v	Swanage Town & Herston	0–0	49
Swanage Town & Herston	*v*	*Brockenhurst*	*1–1*	
Brockenhurst	*v*	*Swanage Town & Herston*	*1–0*	*65*
Melksham Town	v	Bridport	1–2	158
Welton Rovers	v	Odd Down	2–0	71

● 93

			Results	Att
Gosport Borough	v	Eastleigh	2–0	111
Chippenham Town	v	Paulton Rovers	0–0	118
Paulton Rovers	*v*	*Chippenham Town*	*1–1*	*104*
Chippenham Town	*v*	*Paulton Rovers*	*0–2*	*218*
Devizes Town	v	Bristol Manor Farm	1–1	58
Bristol Manor Farm	*v*	*Devizes Town*	*3–1*	*55*
Glastonbury	v	Tuffley Rovers	1–5	45
Clevedon Town	v	Mangotsfield United	1–5	407
Worcester City	v	Yate Town	1–2	595
Forest Green Rovers	v	Exmouth Town	4–0	114
Backwell United	v	Elmore	0–1	28
Saltash United	v	Torrington	3–2	62
Weston-Super-Mare	v	St Blazey	7–0	180
Barnstaple Town	v	Minehead	2–0	123
Falmouth Town	v	Frome Town	3–0	206

First round qualifying – 9 September 1995

Durham City	v	Blackpool(Wren)Rovers	1–1	237
Blackpool(Wren)Rovers	*v*	*Durham City*	*1–5*	*41*
Barrow	v	Consett	3–0	1029
Gateshead	v	Dunston Federation Brewery	3–2	492
Guisborough Town	v	Murton	1–0	120
Lancaster City	v	Pickering Town	2–1	208
Tow Law Town	v	Chester-le-Street Town	3–3	114
Chester-le-Street Town	*v*	*Tow Law Town*	*1–3*	*129*
Bishop Auckland	v	Harrogate Railway	2–1	156
Netherfield	v	Peterlee Newtown	2–4	128
Whitby Town	v	Billingham Town	0–1	125
Spennymoor United	v	Glasshoughton Welfare	1–0	247
Whitley Bay	v	Workington	1–2	277
Esh Winning	v	West Auckland Town	1–2	98
Harrogate Town	v	Bedlington Terriers	1–2	183
Blyth Spartans	v	Garforth Town	6–0	498
Billingham Synthonia	v	Shildon	3–1	95
Morpeth Town	v	Whickham	1–2	70
Frickley Athletic	v	Prescot Cables	0–0	179
Prescot Cables	*v*	*Frickley Athletic*	*2–2*	*17*
Prescot Cables	*v*	*Frickley Athletic*	*0–1*	*52*
(at St Helens Town FC)				
Northwich Victoria	v	Burscough	5–0	655
Eccleshill United	v	Lincoln United	2–3	73
Eastwood Town	v	Buxton	2–1	229
Gainsborough Trinity	v	Arnold Town	2–0	385
Morecambe	v	Sheffield	7–0	469
Worksop Town	v	Radcliffe Borough	4–0	357
Nantwich Town	v	Droylsden	3–0	84
Bamber Bridge	v	Heanor Town	4–1	453
Leek Town	v	Clitheroe	1–1	202
Clitheroe	*v*	*Leek Town*	*2–2*	*237*
Clitheroe	*v*	*Leek Town*	*0–0*	*258*
Leek Town	*v*	*Clitheroe*	*1–0*	*181*
Guiseley	v	Leigh RMI	3–0	484
Mossley	v	Hallam	1–0	176
Chorley	v	Farsley Celtic	2–2	251
Farsley Celtic	*v*	*Chorley*	*1–2*	*221*

			Results	Att
Hyde United	v	Winterton Rangers	6–0	240
(at Curzon Ashton FC)				
Denaby United	v	Bootle	3–0	114
Rossendale United	v	Colwyn Bay	1–4	102
Warrington Town	v	Trafford	2–2	87
Trafford	*v*	*Warrington Town*	*4–3*	*118*
Knowsley United	v	Bradford (Park Avenue)	0–0	74
(at Bootle FC)				
Bradford (Park Avenue)	*v*	*Knowsley United*	*3–2*	*158*
Accrington Stanley	v	Ossett Town	2–1	429
Crook Town	v	Curzon Ashton	1–1	118
Curzon Ashton	*v*	*Crook Town*	*2–1*	*108*
Matlock Town	v	Great Harwood Town	5–2	290
Marine	v	Lough United	4–0	259
Newcastle Town	v	Immingham Town	5–0	57
Hatfield Main	v	Ilkeston Town	0–2	185
Congleton Town	v	Pontefract Collieries	3–1	139
Winsford United	v	Borrowash Victoria	1–0	
Emley	v	Thackley	6–0	186
Hinckley Athletic	v	Kidsgrove Athletic	3–1	271
Halesowen Town	v	Blakenall	3–2	618
Telford United	v	Shifnal Town	4–0	837
Raunds Town	v	Desborough Town	3–0	112
Redditch United	v	Moor Green	1–3	210
Atherstone United	v	Armitage	2–2	258
Armitage	*v*	*Atherstone United*	*3–3*	*229*
Armitage	*v*	*Atherstone United*	*5–4*	*280*
Hednesford Town	v	Corby Town	3–1	732
Bolehall Swifts	v	Tamworth	0–1	803
Chasetown	v	Solihull Borough	1–3	126
Rushden & Diamonds	v	Grantham Town	4–1	1681
Gresley Rovers	v	Dudley Town	1–2	541
Sandwell Borough	v	Cogenhoe United	2–1	28
Lye Town	v	Eastwood Hanley	1–2	68
Stourbridge	v	Evesham United	2–2	141
Evesham United	*v*	*Stourbridge*	*3–0*	*154*
Paget Rangers	v	Wednesfield	1–0	51
VS Rugby	v	Leicester United	1–2	307
Boldmere St Michaels	v	Bedworth United	1–2	108
Racing Club Warwick	v	Oldbury United	1–0	108
Stafford Rangers	v	Rothwell Town	6–1	306
Burton Albion	v	Stratford Town	4–0	746
Long Buckby	v	Sutton Coldfield Town	2–1	82
Sudbury Town	v	Tiptree United	3–0	285
Boston United	v	Wisbech Town	1–2	983
Eynesbury Rovers	v	Halstead Town	7–1	150
Diss Town	v	Heybridge Swifts	0–2	406
Cambridge City	v	Canvey Island	2–3	268
Bishop's Stortford	v	Boston Town	2–2	352
Boston Town	*v*	*Bishop's Stortford*	*5–2*	*183*
Saffron Walden Town	v	Kings Lynn	0–2	268
Harwich & Parkeston	v	Braintree Town	0–1	269
Billericay Town	v	Aveley	2–0	304
Chelmsford City	v	Collier Row	1–0	991
March Town United	v	Holbeach United	0–3	102
Great Yarmouth Town	v	Mirrlees Blackstone	2–1	102
Arlesey Town	v	Leyton Pennant	3–0	156
Grays Athletic	v	Wealdstone	2–2	291

			Results	Att
Wealdstone	v	*Grays Athletic*	*4–3*	*209*
Tufnell Park	v	Hertford Town	2–2	
Hertford Town	v	*Tufnell Park*	*5–1*	*62*
Sudbury Wanderers	v	Watton United	3–1	42
Purfleet	v	Felixstowe Town	4–0	105
Dagenham & Redbridge	v	Hornchurch	4–0	539
Berkhamsted Town	v	Hillingdon Borough	3–2	75
Edgware Town	v	Chesham United	0–1	226
Boreham Wood	v	Chalfont St Peter	1–0	181
Stevenage Borough	v	Brook House	0–0	814
Brook House	v	*Stevenage Borough*	*1–5*	*167*
(at Yeading FC)				
Northwood	v	Uxbridge	0–5	143
Hampton	v	Staines Town	1–2	218
Romford	v	Hadleigh United	1–0	197
St Albans City	v	Barton Rovers	4–1	408
Hoddesdon Town	v	Woodbridge Town	0–2	50
Stotfold	v	Hemel Hempstead	2–1	60
Baldock Town	v	Metropolitan Police	2–1	176
Hendon	v	Flackwell Heath	8–0	156
Barking	v	Clapton	1–3	154
Concord Rangers	v	Hayes	0–3	150
Wembley	v	Langford	3–0	39
Harrow Borough	v	Leatherhead	2–1	198
Bracknell Town	v	Thamesmead Town	1–1	43
Thamesmead Town	v	*Bracknell Town*	*2–3*	*44*
Wingate & Finchley	v	Ruislip Manor	2–3	102
Walton & Hersham	v	Camberley Town	4–0	164
Farnborough Town	v	Dartford	1–0	602
Fisher	v	Lewes	7–0	161
Corinthian-Casuals	v	Margate	2–5	78
Ashford Town	v	Tonbridge	2–0	732
Chertsey Town	v	Shoreham	2–2	272
Shoreham	v	*Chertsey Town*	*1–3*	*206*
Tooting & Mitcham United	v	Peacehaven & Telscombe	0–0	197
Peacehaven & Telscombe	v	*Tooting & Mitcham Utd*	*0–1*	*251*
Croydon	v	Hastings Town	2–3	116
Dulwich Hamlet	v	Southwick	7–1	298
Dover Athletic	v	Bognor Regis Town	1–2	578
Raynes Park Vale	v	Banstead Athletic	1–2	58
Chatham Town	v	Ramsgate	1–1	131
Ramsgate	v	*Chatham Town*	*0–2*	*105*
Erith & Belvedere	v	Redhill	4–1	87
Bromley	v	Herne Bay	3–1	338
Welling United	v	Wick	2–0	547
Horsham	v	Sittingbourne	0–5	356
Carshalton Athletic	v	Sheppey United	3–1	274
Gravesend & Northfleet	v	Godalming & Guildford	7–0	443
Molesey	v	Whitstable Town	4–1	130
Langney Sports	v	Windsor & Eton	1–3	236
Wokingham Town	v	Ringmer	3–1	266
Worthing	v	Buckingham Town	1–1	293
Buckingham Town	v	*Worthing*	*0–0*	*100*
Worthing	v	*Buckingham Town*	*2–2*	*277*
Buckingham Town	v	*Worthing*	*6–1*	*100*
Thatcham Town	v	Steyning Town	5–1	91
Aldershot Town	v	Pagham	4–0	1614
Salisbury City	v	Hungerford Town	5–2	373

(Replays in italics)			Results	Att
Oxford City	v	Witney Town	1–1	376
Witney Town	*v*	*Oxford City*	*3–1*	*331*
Thame United	v	Totton AFC	1–1	180
Totton AFC	*v*	*Thame United*	*0–4*	*208*
Abingdon Town	v	Newport (IW)	2–3	168
Dorchester Town	v	Wimborne Town	2–2	764
Wimborne Town	*v*	*Dorchester Town*	*0–2*	*520*
Waterlooville	v	Calne Town	5–0	223
Ryde	v	Weymouth	1–1	180
Weymouth	*v*	*Ryde*	*2–1*	*609*
Basingstoke Town	v	Havant Town	2–1	212
Newport AFC	v	Brockenhurst	5–0	1011
Trowbridge Town	v	Gosport Borough	8–1	282
Paulton Rovers	v	Welton Rovers	1–1	117
Welton Rovers	*v*	*Paulton Rovers*	*2–1*	*173*
Bridport	v	Merthyr Tydfil	0–3	311
Gloucester City	v	Bristol Manor Farm	8–0	514
Cheltenham Town	v	Yate Town	5–0	659
Forest Green Rovers	v	Mangotsfield United	2–1	179
Tuffley Rovers	v	Cinderford Town	0–4	124
Bideford	v	Elmore	2–2	120
Elmore	*v*	*Bideford*	*2–6*	*75*
Tiverton Town	v	Barnstaple Town	9–0	448
Falmouth Town	v	Weston-Super-Mare	1–1	225
Weston–Super–Mare	*v*	*Falmouth Town*	*5–0*	*250*
Saltash United	v	Taunton Town	1–2	95

Second round qualifying – 23 September 1995

			Results	Att
Durham City	v	Guisborough Town	2–1	308
Gateshead	v	Barrow	2–2	721
Barrow	*v*	*Gateshead*	*1–0*	*1908*
Lancaster City	v	Peterlee Newtown	3–0	217
Bishop Auckland	v	Tow Law Town	2–1	311
Billingham Town	v	West Auckland Town	1–0	32
Workington	v	Spennymoor United	2–4	487
Bedlington Terriers	v	Whickham	1–0	132
Billingham Synthonia	v	Blyth Spartans	0–2	246
Frickley Athletic	v	Eastwood Town	2–4	201
Lincoln United	v	Northwich Victoria	1–4	354
Gainsborough Trinity	v	Nantwich Town	5–0	375
Worksop Town	v	Morecambe	2–3	529
Bamber Bridge	v	Mossley	0–2	583
Guiseley	v	Leek Town	4–0	507
Chorley	v	Colwyn Bay	1–2	234
Denaby United	v	Hyde United	1–2	185
Trafford	v	Curzon Ashton	1–2	108
Accrington Stanley	v	Bradford (Park Avenue)	1–2	553
Matlock Town	v	Ilkeston Town	1–2	759
Newcastle Town	v	Marine	0–1	313
Congleton Town	v	Hinckley Athletic	1–1	203
Hinckley Athletic	*v*	*Congleton Town*	*1–0*	*216*
Emley	v	Winsford United	1–1	252
Winsford United	*v*	*Emley*	*2–1*	*248*
Halesowen Town	v	Moor Green	1–0	620
Raunds Town	v	Telford United	1–2	225
Armitage	v	Solihull Borough	2–3	118

			Results	Att
Tamworth	v	Hednesford Town	1–2	1138
Rushden & Diamonds	v	Eastwood Hanley	1–0	1652
Sandwell Borough	v	Dudley Town	2–1	90
Evesham United	v	Bedworth United	2–0	223
Leicester United	v	Paget Rangers	3–2	53
Racing Club Warwick	v	Long Buckby	2–0	159
Burton Albion	v	Stafford Rangers	1–1	1014
Stafford Rangers	*v*	*Burton Albion*	*2–3*	*610*
Sudbury Town	v	Heybridge Swifts	2–1	502
Eynesbury Rovers	v	Wisbech Town	3–3	320
Wisbech Town	*v*	*Eynesbury Rovers*	*6–1*	*422*
Canvey Island	v	Braintree Town	2–0	301
Kings Lynn	v	Boston Town	5–1	1157
Billericay Town	v	Great Yarmouth Town	2–0	298
Holbeach United	v	Chelmsford City	0–0	350
Chelmsford City	*v*	*Holbeach United*	*3–1*	*858*
Arlesey Town	v	Sudbury Wanderers	1–2	157
Hertford Town	v	Wealdstone	1–0	262
Purfleet	v	Chesham United	3–1	220
Berkhamsted Town	v	Dagenham & Redbridge	1–2	292
Boreham Wood	v	Staines Town	0–1	264
Uxbridge	v	Stevenage Borough	0–1	460
Romford	v	Stotfold	4–1	188
Woodbridge Town	v	St Albans City	1–1	308
St Albans City	*v*	*Woodbridge Town*	*2–0*	*358*
Baldock Town	v	Hayes	0–1	390
Clapton	v	Hendon	2–3	150
Wembley	v	Ruislip Manor	3–0	118
Bracknell Town	v	Harrow Borough	2–1	122
Walton & Hersham	v	Margate	2–2	225
Margate	*v*	*Walton & Hersham*	*0–1*	*189*
Fisher	v	Farnborough Town	1–4	335
Ashford Town	v	Hastings Town	3–1	966
Tooting & Mitcham United	v	Chertsey Town	2–2	252
Chertsey Town	*v*	*Tooting & Mitcham United*	*1–2*	*327*
Dulwich Hamlet	v	Chatham Town	2–1	295
Banstead Athletic	v	Bognor Regis Town	0–3	174
Erith & Belvedere	v	Sittingbourne	2–2	247
Sittingbourne	*v*	*Erith & Belvedere*	*6–1*	*556*
Welling United	v	Bromley	2–2	722
Bromley	*v*	*Welling United*	*3–3*	*451*
Welling United	*v*	*Bromley*	*1–2*	*701*
Carshalton Athletic	v	Windsor & Eton	4–3	360
Molesey	v	Gravesend & Northfleet	0–6	295
Wokingham Town	v	Aldershot Town	1–2	1469
Thatcham Town	v	Buckingham Town	0–1	130
Salisbury City	v	Newport(IW)	1–3	412
Thame United	v	Witney Town	1–1	334
Witney Town	*v*	*Thame United*	*2–3*	*273*
Dorchester Town	v	Basingstoke Town	2–0	609
Weymouth	v	Waterlooville	1–0	754
Newport AFC	v	Merthyr Tydfil	3–3	1816
Merthyr Tydfil	*v*	*Newport AFC*	*1–2*	*887*
Welton Rovers	v	Trowbridge Town	1–2	374
Gloucester City	v	Cinderford Town	0–1	921
Forest Green Rovers	v	Cheltenham Town	3–0	544
Bideford	v	Taunton Town	4–3	170
Weston-Super-Mare	v	Tiverton Town	1–1	640
Tiverton Town	*v*	*Weston-Super-Mare*	*1–0*	*801*

Third round qualifying – 7 October 1995

			Results	Att
Barrow	v	Durham City	1–1	1413
Durham City	*v*	*Barrow*	*0–1*	*764*
Bishop Auckland	v	Lancaster City	0–1	298
Spennymoor United	v	Billingham Town	6–1	337
Blyth Spartans	v	Bedlington Terriers	3–1	648
Northwich Victoria	v	Eastwood Town	0–0	742
Eastwood Town	*v*	*Northwich Victoria*	*1–2*	*640*
Morecambe	v	Gainsborough Trinity	6–2	807
Guiseley	v	Mossley	6–1	608
Hyde United	v	Colwyn Bay	1–2	414
(at Curzon Ashton FC)				
Bradford (Park Avenue)	v	Curzon Ashton	2–1	202
Marine	v	Ilkeston Town	0–0	499
Ilkeston Town	*v*	*Marine*	*1–2*	*801*
Winsford United	v	Hinckley Athletic	3–2	236
Telford United	v	Halesowen Town	4–1	905
Hednesford Town	v	Solihull Borough	2–2	899
Solihull Borough	*v*	*Hednesford Town*	*1–2*	*421*
Sandwell Borough	v	Rushden & Diamonds	1–6	250
Leicester United	v	Evesham United	0–1	169
Burton Albion	v	Racing Club Warwick	2–0	867
Wisbech Town	v	Sudbury Town	1–0	705
Kings Lynn	v	Canvey Island	1–0	1737
(Kings Lynn removed from the Competition for playing a suspended player – Canvey Island re-instated)				
Chelmsford City	v	Billericay Town	1–1	2074
Billericay Town	*v*	*Chelmsford City*	*2–1*	*1704*
Hertford Town	v	Sudbury Wanderers	0–2	205
Dagenham & Redbridge	v	Purfleet	1–1	718
Purfleet	*v*	*Dagenham & Redbridge*	*2–1*	*683*
Stevenage Borough	v	Staines Town	·2–0	1176
St Albans City	v	Romford	3–1	648
Hendon	v	Hayes	0–3	376
Bracknell Town	v	Wembley	4–1	169
Farnborough Town	v	Walton & Hersham	3–2	761
Tooting & Mitcham United	v	Ashford Town	0–1	540
Bognor Regis Town	v	Dulwich Hamlet	4–2	788
Bromley	v	Sittingbourne	1–1	692
Sittingbourne	*v*	*Bromley*	*3–2*	*1030*
Gravesend & Northfleet	v	Carshalton Athletic	2–1	685
Buckingham Town	v	Aldershot Town	0–1	916
Thame United	v	Newport (IW)	1–1	308
Newport(IW)	*v*	*Thame United*	*3–1*	*863*
Weymouth	v	Dorchester Town	2–3	2527
Trowbridge Town	v	Newport AFC	2–0	623
Forest Green Rovers	v	Cinderford Town	1–1	335
Cinderford Town	*v*	*Forest Green Rovers*	*1–1*	*684*
Forest Green Rovers	*v*	*Cinderford Town*	*1–3*	*671*
Tiverton Town	v	Bideford	4–1	653

Fourth round qualifying – 21 October 1995

Blyth Spartans	v	Guiseley	2–0	775
Spennymoor United	v	Lancaster City	1–0	621
Marine	v	Bradford (Park Avenue)	2–0	626
Telford United	v	Southport	3–0	898
Winsford United	v	Barrow	0–3	714

			Results	Att
Macclesfield Town	v	Northwich Victoria	0–1	1707
Witton Albion	v	Morecambe	3–2	931
Stalybridge Celtic	v	Colwyn Bay	2–2	617
Colwyn Bay	*v*	*Stalybridge Celtic*	*3–0*	*613*
Runcorn	v	Halifax Town	2–1	901
Purfleet	v	Rushden & Diamonds	1–1	794
Rushden & Diamonds	*v*	*Purfleet*	*3–1*	*2850*
Canvey Island	v	Hednesford Town	2–0	537
Aylesbury United	v	Stevenage Borough	1–3	1480
Nuneaton Borough	v	Evesham United	6–1	1415
Billericay Town	v	Wisbech Town	1–1	1106
Wisbech Town	*v*	*Billericay Town*	*2–0*	*1220*
Hayes	v	Sudbury Wanderers	4–0	420
Burton Albion	v	Bracknell Town	3–1	1008
Hitchin Town	v	St Albans City	2–1	1147
Kettering Town	v	Bromsgrove Rovers	0–0	2427
Bromsgrove Rovers	*v*	*Kettering Town*	*2–2*	*1426*
Kettering Town	*v*	*Bromsgrove Rovers*	*1–2*	*2283*
Kingstonian	v	Trowbridge Town	3–1	781
Tiverton Town	v	Bognor Regis Town	1–4	1101
Farnborough Town	v	Yeovil Town	2–1	1409
Newport (IW)	v	Bashley	1–1	1061
Bashley	*v*	*Newport (IW)*	*2–3*	*558*
Yeading	v	Slough Town	0–2	473
Sutton United	v	Crawley Town	4–1	1637
Gravesend & Northfleet	v	Marlow	1–1	814
Marlow	*v*	*Gravesend & Northfleet*	*3–3*	*767*
Gravesend & Northfleet	*v*	*Marlow*	*4–0*	*1346*
Sittingbourne	v	Dorchester Town	1–2	1232
Ashford Town	v	Aldershot Town	2–0	2016
Cinderford Town	v	Bath City	3–2	723

First round proper – 11 November 1995

Hull City	v	Wrexham	0–0	3724
Wrexham	*v*	*Hull City*	*0–0*	*4250*
(Wrexham won on kicks from the penalty mark 3–1)				
Blackpool	v	Chester City	2–1	5004
Barrow	v	Nuneaton Borough	2–1	2869
Bradford City	v	Burton Albion	4–3	4920
Runcorn	v	Wigan Athletic	1–1	2844
Wigan Athletic	*v*	*Runcorn*	*4–2*	*3224*
Scarborough	v	Chesterfield	0–2	2354
Mansfield Town	v	Doncaster Rovers	4–2	3116
Northwich Victoria	v	Scunthorpe United	1–3	2685
Shrewsbury Town	v	Marine	11–2	2845
Carlisle United	v	Preston North End	1–2	7046
Telford United	v	Witton Albion	2–1	1277
York City	v	Notts County	0–1	4228
Bury	v	Blyth Spartans	0–2	3076
Altrincham	v	Crewe Alexandra	0–2	3062
Burnley	v	Walsall	1–3	6539
Hartlepool United	v	Darlington	2–4	3835
Rochdale	v	Rotherham United	5–3	3817
Stockport County	v	Lincoln City	5–0	3952
Spennymoor United	v	Colwyn Bay	0–1	824
Hereford United	v	Stevenage Borough	2–1	3210
Kingstonian	v	Wisbech Town	5–1	1396

			Results	Att
(Replays in italics)				
Canvey Island	v	Brighton & Hove Albion	2–2	3403
Brighton & Hove Albion	*v*	*Canvey Island*	*4–1*	*7008*
Wycombe Wanderers	v	Gillingham	1–1	5064
Gillingham	*v*	*Wycombe Wanderers*	*1–0*	*8592*
Rushden & Diamonds	v	Cardiff City	1–3	4212
Oxford United	v	Dorchester Town	9–1	3819
Kidderminster Harriers	v	Sutton United	2–2	2513
Sutton United	*v*	*Kidderminster Harriers*	*1–1*	*1804*
(Sutton United won on kicks from the penalty mark 3–2)				
Exeter City	v	Peterborough United	0–1	3783
Fulham	v	Swansea City	7–0	4798
Bournemouth AFC	v	Bristol City	0–0	5304
Bristol City	*v*	*Bournemouth AFC*	*0–1*	*5069*
Torquay United	v	Leyton Orient	1–0	2434
Barnet	v	Woking	2–2	3034
Woking	*v*	*Barnet*	*2–1*	*3546*
Gravesend & Northfleet	v	Colchester United	2–0	3112
Swindon Town	v	Cambridge United	4–1	7383
Hitchin Town	v	Bristol Rovers	2–1	3101
Newport (IW)	v	Enfield	1–1	1818
Enfield	*v*	*Newport (IW)*	*2–1*	*2034*
Bognor Regis Town	v	Ashford Town	1–1	2507
Ashford Town	*v*	*Bognor Regis Town*	*0–1*	*2542*
Slough Town	v	Plymouth Argyle	0–2	3030
Brentford	v	Farnborough Town	1–1	4711
Farnborough Town	*v*	*Brentford*	*0–4*	*3581*
Cinderford Town	v	Bromsgrove Rovers	2–1	1850
Northampton Town	v	Hayes	1–0	5389

Second round proper – 2 December 1995

Barrow	v	Wigan Athletic	0–4	3500
Stockport County	v	Blyth Spartans	2–0	5693
Telford United	v	Notts County	0–2	2831
Rochdale	v	Darlington	2–2	3732
Darlington	*v*	*Rochdale*	*0–1*	*4181*
Blackpool	v	Colwyn Bay	2–0	4581
Scunthorpe United	v	Shrewsbury Town	1–1	2718
Shrewsbury Town	*v*	*Scunthorpe United*	*2–1*	*3313*
Bradford City	v	Preston North End	2–1	7602
Crewe Alexandra	v	Mansfield Town	2–0	3691
Wrexham	v	Chesterfield	3–2	4918
Torquay United	v	Walsall	1–1	3552
Walsall	*v*	*Torquay United*	*8–4*	*3230*
Hereford United	v	Sutton United	2–0	2875
Fulham	v	Brighton & Hove Albion	0–0	8072
Brighton & Hove Albion	*v*	*Fulham*	*0–0*	*6209*
(Fulham won on kicks from the penalty mark 4–1)				
Oxford United	v	Northampton Town	2–0	6355
Gillingham	v	Hitchin Town	3–0	7251
Peterborough United	v	Bognor Regis Town	4–0	5004
Cinderford Town	v	Gravesend & Northfleet	1–1	2067
Gravesend & Northfleet	*v*	*Cinderford Town*	*3–0*	*2852*
Swindon Town	v	Cardiff City	2–0	8300
Enfield	v	Woking	1–1	3477

(Replays in italics)

			Results	Att
Woking	v	*Enfield*	*2–1*	2253
(at Wycombe Wanderers FC)				
Bournemouth AFC	v	Brentford	0–1	4451
Kingstonian	v	Plymouth Argyle	1–2	2961

Third round proper – 6 January 1996

Crewe Alexandra	v	West Bromwich Albion	4–3	5750
Reading	v	Gillingham	3–1	10324
Tranmere Rovers	v	Queens Park Rangers	0–2	10230
Norwich City	v	Brentford	1–2	10082
Leicester City	v	Manchester City	0–0	20640
Manchester City	*v*	*Leicester City*	*5–0*	*19980*
Gravesend & Northfleet	v	Aston Villa	0–3	26032
(at Aston Villa FC)				
Crystal Palace	v	Port Vale	0–0	10456
Port Vale	*v*	*Crystal Palace*	*4–3*	*6754*
Stoke City	v	Nottingham Forest	1–1	17947
Nottingham Forest	*v*	*Stoke City*	*2–0*	*17372*
Swindon Town	v	Woking	2–0	10322
Bradford City	v	Bolton Wanderers	0–3	10265
Huddersfield Town	v	Blackpool	2–1	12424
Plymouth Argyle	v	Coventry City	1–3	17721
Grimsby Town	v	Luton Town	7–1	5387
Southampton	v	Portsmouth	3–0	15236
Birmingham City	v	Wolverhampton Wanderers	1–1	21349
Wolverhampton Wanderers	*v*	*Birmingham City*	*2–1*	*28088*
Everton	v	Stockport County	2–2	28921
Stockport County	*v*	*Everton*	*2–3*	*11283*
Peterborough United	v	Wrexham	1–0	5983
Barnsley	v	Oldham Athletic	0–0	9751
Oldham Athletic	*v*	*Barnsley*	*2–1*	*6670*
West Ham United	v	Southend United	2–0	23284
Walsall	v	Wigan Athletic	1–0	5626
Millwall	v	Oxford United	3–3	7564
Oxford United	*v*	*Millwall*	*1–0*	*8035*
Manchester United	v	Sunderland	2–2	41563
Sunderland	*v*	*Manchester United*	*1–2*	*21378*
Liverpool	v	Rochdale	7–0	28126
Hereford United	v	Tottenham Hotspur	1–1	8806
Tottenham Hotspur	*v*	*Hereford United*	*5–1*	*31534*
Arsenal	v	Sheffield United	1–1	33453
Sheffield United	*v*	*Arsenal*	*1–0*	*22255*
Derby County	v	Leeds United	2–4	16155
Fulham	v	Shrewsbury Town	1–1	7265
Shrewsbury Town	*v*	*Fulham*	*2–1*	*7983*
Chelsea	v	Newcastle United	1–1	25151
Newcastle United	*v*	*Chelsea*	*2–2*	*36535*
(Chelsea won on kicks from the penalty mark 4–2)				
Ipswich Town	v	Blackburn Rovers	0–0	22146
Blackburn Rovers	*v*	*Ipswich Town*	*0–1*	*19606*
Charlton Athletic	v	Sheffield Wednesday	2–0	13815
Notts County	v	Middlesbrough	1–2	12621
Watford	v	Wimbledon	1–1	11187
Wimbledon	*v*	*Watford*	*1–0*	*5142*

Fourth round proper – 27 January 1996

Shrewsbury Town	v	Liverpool	0–4	7752
Charlton Athletic	v	Brentford	3–2	15000
Ipswich Town	v	Walsall	1–0	18489
Bolton Wanderers	v	Leeds United	0–1	16694
Queens Park Rangers	v	Chelsea	1–2	18542
Huddersfield Town	v	Peterborough Utd	2–0	11629
Coventry City	v	Manchester City	2–2	18709
Manchester City	*v*	*Coventry City*	*2–1*	*22419*
Middlesbrough	v	Wimbledon	0–0	28915
Wimbledon	*v*	*Middlesbrough*	*1–0*	*5220*
Reading	v	Manchester United	0–3	14780
Nottingham Forest	v	Oxford United	1–1	15050
Oxford United	*v*	*Nottingham Forest*	*0–3*	*8022*
Southampton	v	Crewe Alexandra	1–1	13736
Crewe Alexandra	*v*	*Southampton*	*2–3*	*5579*
Swindon Town	v	Oldham Athletic	1–0	9508
Everton	v	Port Vale	2–2	33168
Port Vale	*v*	*Everton*	*2–1*	*19197*
West Ham United	v	Grimsby Town	1–1	22020
Grimsby Town	*v*	*West Ham United*	*3–0*	*8382*
Sheffield United	v	Aston Villa	0–1	18749
Tottenham Hotspur	v	Wolverhampton Wanderers	1–1	32812
Wolverhampton Wanderers	*v*	*Tottenham Hotspur*	*0–2*	*27846*

Fifth round proper – 17 February 1996

Liverpool	v	Charlton Athletic	2–1	36818
Nottingham Forest	v	Tottenham Hotspur	2–2	18600
Tottenham Hotspur	*v*	*Nottingham Forest*	*1–1*	*31055*

(Nottingham Forest won on kicks from the penalty mark 3–1)
(first match abandoned 0–0, after 15 mins, due to snow)

Leeds United	v	Port Vale	0–0	18607
Port Vale	*v*	*Leeds United*	*1–2*	*14023*
Ipswich Town	v	Aston *Villa*	1–3	20748
Swindon Town	v	Southampton	1–1	15035
Southampton	*v*	*Swindon Town*	*2–0*	*13962*
Manchester United	v	Manchester City	2–1	42692
Huddersfield Town	v	Wimbledon	2–2	17307
Wimbledon	*v*	*Huddersfield Town*	*3–1*	*7015*
Grimsby Town	v	Chelsea	0–0	9648
Chelsea	*v*	*Grimsby Town*	*4–1*	*28545*

Sixth round proper – 9 March 1996

Leeds United	v	Liverpool	0–0	24632
Liverpool	*v*	*Leeds United*	*3–0*	*30812*
Nottingham Forest	v	Aston Villa	0–1	21067
Manchester United	v	Southampton	2–0	45446
Chelsea	v	Wimbledon	2–2	30805
Wimbledon	*v*	*Chelsea*	*1–3*	*21380*

Semi-finals – 31 March 1996

Aston Villa	v	Liverpool	0–3	39072
(at Manchester United FC)				
Chelsea	v	Manchester United	1–2	38421
(at Aston Villa FC)				

26 ● FA UMBRO TROPHY – FINAL TIE 1996

Macclesfield Town 3   Northwich Victoria 1

By common consent the pick of the year's Wembley finals, the climax to the 27th FA Trophy competition saw a spectacular game involving two Vauxhall Conference clubs from Cheshire. Macclesfield Town, Trophy winners in its inaugural season (1969–70) and managed by former Manchester United and Northern Ireland star Sammy McIlroy, withstood a furious second-half onslaught from Northwich Victoria to secure a 3–1 victory by the finish.

Macclesfield's giant goalkeeper Ryan Price had been forced to block with his legs a close-range effort from Northwich's Steve Walters, an ex-pupil at the FA National School at Lilleshall, before the "Silkmen" charged into a two-goal lead by the 28th minute. Full-back Mark Gardiner curled in an inch-perfect free-kick for Steve Payne to glance them in front with his head on 18 minutes; then unlucky Vics defender Burgess put through his own goal as he attempted to divert Marc Coates' left-wing cross away from the menacing Phil Power.

But Vics hit back with such a vengeance that they nearly scored twice in the next couple of minutes. Firstly a smart shot on the turn by Carwyn Williams was turned over the bar at full stretch by Price and, seconds later, Ian Cooke ran in unchallenged for a close-range header but struck the outside of the post with the goal at his mercy. Vics turned the screw even more in the second half as they strove to get back into the game. The lively Williams ran onto Walters' clever ball through the middle and took it on a stride before shooting confidently past Price on 53 minutes – and Vics had a real chance. Then Macclesfield winger Tony Hemmings, destined for the "man of the match" award, got to work.

With nine minutes to go he started a mazy run from near the halfway line that ended with a simple shot past Greygoose's left-hand and into the far corner. Vics had full-back Derek Ward red-carded for a second crunching tackle from behind on the mercurial Hemmings two minutes after the goal and by that time they knew the game was up. The match finished in Wagnerian wind and rain before Neil Howarth ascended the famous steps with his team to receive the Trophy from Mr Alan Hadfield, Managing Director of Umbro UK Limited.

Macclesfield Town: Price, Edey, Gardiner, Payne, Howarth, Sorvel, Lyons, Wood (Hulme), Coates, Power, Hemmings (Cavell).

Northwich Victoria: Greygoose, Ward, Duffy, Burgess (Simpson), Abel (Steele), Walters, Williams, Butler, Cooke, Humphreys, Vicary.

Referee: M. Reed (Birmingham FA)

Attendance: 8,672

Chief Guest: Mr. A. Hadfield

27 ● FA UMBRO TROPHY 1995–96

First round qualifying – 14 October 1995

(Replays in italics)

			Results	Att
Harrogate Town	v	Grantham Town	1–4	191
Farsley Celtic	v	Bedworth United	3–1	159
Droylsden	v	Matlock Town	0–3	173
Atherstone United	v	Lincoln United	2–1	278
Accrington Stanley	v	Bradford (Park Avenue)	2–2	415
Bradford (Park Avenue)	*v*	*Accrington Stanley*	*2–3*	*258*
Atherton LR	v	Chorley	1–2	298
Sutton Coldfield Town	v	Bilston Town	1–1	116
Bilston Town	*v*	*Sutton Coldfield Town*	*4–4*	*85*
Bilston Town	*v*	*Sutton Coldfield Town*	*2–1*	*154*
Racing Club Warwick	v	Warrington Town	1–0	130
Bridgnorth Town	v	Leigh RMI	1–1	90
Leigh RMI	*v*	*Bridgnorth Town*	*7–0*	*37*
Winsford United	v	Paget Rangers	1–1	183
Paget Rangers	*v*	*Winsford United*	*0–2*	*52*
Curzon Ashton	v	Worksop Town	4–3	113
Knowsley United	v	Moor Green	3–2	80
Alfreton Town	v	Congleton Town	5–0	202
Workington	v	Leicester United	1–1	286
Leicester United	*v*	*Workington*	*5–0*	*125*
Barrow	v	Hinckley Town	3–0	1119
Stourbridge	v	Frickley Athletic	1–2	126
Lancaster City	v	Solihull Borough	3–0	173
Fleetwood	v	Whitley Bay	2–1	119
Tamworth	v	Caernarfon Town		
(walkover for Tamworth – Caernarfon Town withdrawn)				
Radcliffe Borough	v	Redditch United	3–1	107
Erith & Belvedere	v	Basingstoke Town	0–6	112
Leyton Pennant	v	Fleet Town	0–1	66
Hastings Town	v	Havant Town	2–2	392
Havant Town	*v*	*Hastings Town*	*1–0*	*141*
Chertsey Town	v	Poole Town	9–0	328
Bury Town	v	Trowbridge Town	1–2	107
Buckingham Town	v	Braintree Town	1–1	65
Braintree Town	*v*	*Buckingham Town*	*1–0*	*102*
Carshalton Athletic	v	Dulwich Hamlet	1–1	499
Dulwich Hamlet	*v*	*Carshalton Athletic*	*1–1*	*293*
Dulwich Hamlet	*v*	*Carshalton Athletic*	*1–3*	*301*
Ruislip Manor	v	Cinderford Town	3–1	142
Barton Rovers	v	Crawley Town	1–3	331
Salisbury City	v	Fisher	2–0	319
Weston-Super-Mare	v	Bognor Regis Town	2–6	226
Yate Town	v	Witney Town	3–2	156
Ashford Town	v	Sudbury Town	0–2	569
Billericay Town	v	Wembley	0–4	261
Fareham Town	v	Maidenhead United	2–4	90
Barking	v	Baldock Town	0–0	136
Baldock Town	*v*	*Barking*	*3–2*	*136*
Forest Green Rovers	v	Sittingbourne	1–2	101
Abingdon Town	v	Bishop's Stortford	1–1	182

(Replays in italics)   *Results*   *Att*

Bishop's Stortford	v	Abingdon Town	*5–1*	*208*
Berkhamsted Town	v	Purfleet	1–2	98
Newport (IW)	v	Chesham United	1–3	462
Kings Lynn	v	Uxbridge	1–2	833
Staines Town	v	Wokingham Town	2–1	244
Weymouth	v	Tonbridge	4–0	714
Hendon	v	Waterlooville	2–2	179
Waterlooville	*v*	*Hendon*	*0–1*	*110*
Whyteleafe	v	Tooting & Mitcham United	1–2	161
Harrow Borough	v	Marlow	1–1	244
Marlow	*v*	*Harrow Borough*	*1–4*	*261*
Worthing	v	Thame United	1–1	400
Thame United	*v*	*Worthing*	*2–0*	*152*
Bashley	v	Margate	1–1	220
Margate	*v*	*Bashley*	*1–2*	*157*

Second round qualifying – 4 November 1995

Barrow	v	Winsford United	0–1	1222
Tamworth	v	Netherfield	3–1	409
Bilston Town	v	Leicester United	5–2	100
Alfreton Town	v	Dudley Town	2–2	260
Dudley Town	*v*	*Alfreton Town*	*2–0*	*183*
Great Harwood Town	v	Frickley Athletic	3–2	105
Atherstone United	v	Accrington Stanley	1–3	422
Radcliffe Borough	v	Fleetwood	2–0	136
Eastwood Town	v	Chorley	0–1	231
Grantham Town	v	Farsley Celtic	1–3	303
Leigh RMI	v	Matlock Town	0–2	90
Emley	v	Racing Club Warwick	2–1	225
Curzon Ashton	v	Lancaster City	1–1	221
Lancaster City	*v*	*Curzon Ashton*	*3–0*	*206*
Nuneaton Borough	v	Knowsley United	3–2	1017
Carshalton Athletic	v	Weymouth	5–1	379
Braintree Town	v	Harrow Borough	4–0	203
Chertsey Town	v	Chesham United	2–2	438
Chesham United	*v*	*Chertsey Town*	*2–3*	*397*
Staines Town	v	Havant Town	3–1	207
Walton & Hersham	v	Oxford City	0–0	193
Oxford City	*v*	*Walton & Hersham*	*5–2*	*196*
Trowbridge Town	v	Bishop's Stortford	1–0	361
Clevedon Town	v	Worcester City	0–4	420
Crawley Town	v	Bashley	0–1	609
Evesham United	v	Aldershot Town	0–2	465
Newport AFC	v	Fleet Town	2–1	679
Tooting & Mitcham United	v	Baldock Town	2–1	174
Basingstoke Town	v	Uxbridge	0–2	165
Purfleet	v	Corby Town	6–1	88
Wembley	v	Ruislip Manor	1–1	85
Ruislip Manor	*v*	*Wembley*	*1–2*	*145*
Bognor Regis Town	v	Sittingbourne	2–2	517
Sittingbourne	*v*	*Bognor Regis Town*	*1–2*	*674*
Hendon	v	Gravesend & Northfleet	3–0	291
Salisbury City	v	Sudbury Town	2–2	249
Sudbury Town	*v*	*Salisbury City*	*2–2*	*251*
Sudbury Town	*v*	*Salisbury City*	*3–2*	*249*
Yate Town	v	Heybridge Swifts	1–2	163
Maidenhead United	v	Thame United	0–5	93

Third round qualifying – 25 November 1995

Spennymoor United	v	Nuneaton Borough	0–2	486
Halesowen Town	v	Bilston Town	0–0	601
Bilston Town	*v*	*Halesowen Town*	*1–4*	*307*
Burton Albion	v	Bamber Bridge	3–3	964
Bamber Bridge	*v*	*Burton Albion*	*2–3*	*502*
Ashton United	v	Lancaster City	1–1	229
Lancaster City	*v*	*Ashton United*	*0–2*	*228*
Bishop Auckland	v	Witton Albion	0–0	222
Witton Albion	*v*	*Bishop Auckland*	*0–0*	*461*
Bishop Auckland	*v*	*Witton Albion*	*3–1*	*222*
Radcliffe Borough	v	Farsley Celtic	3–1	155
Emley	v	Great Harwood Town	3–1	224
Chorley	v	Winsford United	3–1	297
Stafford Rangers	v	Tamworth	1–1	647
Tamworth	*v*	*Stafford Rangers*	*0–3*	*741*
Matlock Town	v	Buxton	1–0	516
Blyth Spartans	v	Gretna	3–2	453
Dudley Town	v	VS Rugby	4–3	283
Accrington Stanley	v	Gresley Rovers	2–3	542
Leek Town	v	Boston United	0–0	370
Boston United	*v*	*Leek Town*	*2–0*	*819*
Ilkeston Town	v	Gainsborough Trinity	0–5	626
Chelmsford City	v	Yeading	2–1	828
Gloucester City	v	Aldershot Town	5–1	1041
Boreham Wood	v	Heybridge Swifts	3–0	204
Bromley	v	Oxford City	1–1	183
Oxford City	*v*	*Bromley*	*3–2*	*202*
Worcester City	v	Aylesbury United	3–0	863
Chertsey Town	v	Purfleet	0–1	366
Molesey	v	Staines Town	2–2	158
Staines Town	*v*	*Molesey*	*5–0*	*208*
Carshalton Athletic	v	Braintree Town	1–1	309
Braintree Town	*v*	*Carshalton Athletic*	*0–5*	*260*
St Albans City	v	Thame United	4–2	407
Sutton United	v	Trowbridge Town	0–1	612
Wembley	v	Bashley	2–0	116
Rothwell Town	v	Uxbridge	3–2	126
Dorchester Town	v	Hayes	2–3	515
Hitchin Town	v	Bognor Regis Town	1–2	394
Newport AFC	v	Grays Athletic	1–0	679
Cambridge City	v	Hendon	2–0	234
Sudbury Town	v	Tooting & Mitcham United	2–0	406

First round proper – 20 January 1996

Stalybridge Celtic	v	Gresley Rovers	1–1	638
Gresley Rovers	*v*	*Stalybridge Celtic*	*1–0*	*603*
Stafford Rangers	v	Guiseley	1–1	689
Guiseley	*v*	*Stafford Rangers*	*2–1*	*365*
Colwyn Bay	v	Altrincham	3–3	596
Altrincham	*v*	*Colwyn Bay*	*2–0*	*527*
Halifax Town	v	Southport	2–1	966
Ashton United	v	Blyth Spartans	1–3	244

			Results	*Att*
Dudley Town	v	Halesowen Town	4–2	769
Macclesfield Town	v	Runcorn	1–0	1401
Burton Albion	v	Telford United	3–1	950
Gainsborough Trinity	v	Nuneaton Borough	4–1	867
Morecambe	v	Emley	2–2	656
Emley	*v*	*Morecambe*	*3–1*	*412*
Hednesford Town	v	Northwich Victoria	1–1	935
Northwich Victoria	*v*	*Hednesford Town*	*2–0*	*636*
Kidderminster Harriers	v	Gateshead	0–0	1319
Gateshead	*v*	*Kidderminster Harriers*	*2–0*	
Marine	v	Hyde United	0–0	450
Hyde United	*v*	*Marine*	*0–0*	*416*
Hyde United	*v*	*Marine*	*3–0*	*374*
Boston United	v	Chorley	1–1	808
Chorley	*v*	*Boston United*	*2–1*	*294*
Bromsgrove Rovers	v	Bishop Auckland	1–0	999
Radcliffe Borough	v	Matlock Town	3–2	241
Oxford City	v	Merthyr Tydfil	1–2	352
Rothwell Town	v	Welling United	2–2	238
Welling United	*v*	*Rothwell Town*	*3–0*	*312*
Bognor Regis Town	v	Worcester City	1–0	524
Dover Athletic	v	Cheltenham Town	2–2	904
Cheltenham Town	*v*	*Dover Athletic*	*1–1*	*640*
Dover Athletic	*v*	*Cheltenham Town*	*1–0*	*598*
Chelmsford City	v	Newport AFC	0–1	1121
Bath City	v	Yeovil Town	1–1	2225
Yeovil Town	*v*	*Bath City*	*2–3*	*2731*
Gloucester City	v	Staines Town	5–0	748
Trowbridge Town	v	Sudbury Town	2–2	319
Sudbury Town	*v*	*Trowbridge Town*	*1–1*	*224*
Trowbridge Town	*v*	*Sudbury Town*	*1–1*	*327*
Sudbury Town	*v*	*Trowbridge Town*	*4–3*	*368*
Carshalton Athletic	v	Woking	3–1	1485
Farnborough Town	v	Slough Town	1–1	865
Slough Town	*v*	*Farnborough Town*	*4–3*	*742*
Rushden & Diamonds	v	Purfleet	0–1	1906
Kettering Town	v	St Albans City	1–1	1577
St Albans City	*v*	*Kettering Town*	*2–3*	*705*
Cambridge City	v	Boreham Wood	1–2	287
Hayes	v	Enfield	0–0	507
Enfield	*v*	*Hayes*	*2–2*	*436*
Enfield	*v*	*Hayes*	*2–2*	*398*
Hayes	*v*	*Enfield*	*2–0*	*369*
Stevenage Borough	v	Dagenham & Redbridge	3–2	1338
Wembley	v	Kingstonian	2–1	192

Second round proper – 10 February 1996

Hyde United	v	Welling United	4–1	680
Sudbury Town	v	Gloucester City	3–1	262
Guiseley	v	Altrincham	4–0	690
Emley	v	Gateshead	1–2	668
Dudley Town	v	Merthyr Tydfil	1–2	268
Bognor Regis Town	v	Radcliffe Borough	1–3	539
Boreham Wood	v	Dover Athletic	2–1	506
Slough Town	v	Kettering Town	1–2	1058
Chorley	v	Gainsborough Trinity	2–0	425

			Results	Att
Bath City	v	Hayes	2–0	699
Macclesfield Town	v	Purfleet	2–1	1003
Blyth Spartans	v	Gresley Rovers	1–2	626
Carshalton Athletic	v	Newport AFC	2–1	682
Stevenage Borough	v	Burton Albion	2–1	1362
Wembley	v	Northwich Victoria	0–2	268
Halifax Town	v	Bromsgrove Rovers	0–1	887

Third round proper – 2 March 1996

Guiseley	v	Gresley Rovers	1–2	790
Merthyr Tydfil	v	Northwich Victoria	1–1	528
Northwich Victoria	*v*	*Merthyr Tydfil*	*2–2*	*833*
Northwich Victoria	*v*	*Merthyr Tydfil*	*3–0*	*765*
Hyde United	v	Carshalton Athletic	3–2	854
Macclesfield Town	v	Sudbury Town	1–0	1140
Boreham Wood	v	Chorley	1–1	525
Chorley	*v*	*Boreham Wood*	*4–3*	*833*
Radcliffe Borough	v	Gateshead	1–2	716
Stevenage Borough	v	Kettering Town	3–0	2219
Bath City	v	Bromsgrove Rovers	1–1	1276
Bromsgrove Rovers	*v*	*Bath City*	*2–1*	*1133*

Fourth round proper – 23 March 1996

Hyde United	v	Stevenage Borough	3–2	2012
Gresley Rovers	v	Macclesfield Town	0–2	1724
Bromsgrove Rovers	v	Northwich Victoria	0–1	1807
Chorley	v	Gateshead	3–1	1136

Semi-finals

1st Leg – 13 April 1996

Hyde United	v	Northwich Victoria	1–2	2253
Macclesfield Town	v	Chorley	3–1	2260

2nd Leg – 20 April 1996

Northwich Victoria	v	Hyde United	1–0	2809
Chorley	v	Macclesfield Town	1–1	3048

Northwich Victoria won 3–1 on aggregate
Macclesfield Town won 4–2 on aggregate

Year	Venue	Winners		Runners-up	Result
1970	Wembley	Macclesfield Town	v	Telford United	2–0
1971	Wembley	Telford United	v	Hillingdon Borough	3–2
1972	Wembley	Stafford Rangers	v	Barnet	3–0
1973	Wembley	Scarborough	v	Wigan Athletic	2–1*
1974	Wembley	Morecambe	v	Dartford	2–1
1975	Wembley	Matlock Town	v	Scarborough	4–0
1976	Wembley	Scarborough	v	Stafford Rangers	3–2*
1977	Wembley	Scarborough	v	Dagenham	2–1
1978	Wembley	Altrincham	v	Leatherhead	3–1
1979	Wembley	Stafford Rangers	v	Kettering Town	2–0
1980	Wembley	Dagenham	v	Mossley	2–1
1981	Wembley	Bishop's Stortford	v	Sutton United	1–0
1982	Wembley	Enfield	v	Altrincham	1–0*
1983	Wembley	Telford United	v	Northwich Victoria	2–1
1984	Wembley	Northwich Victoria	v	Bangor City	1–1
	Stoke	Northwich Victoria	v	Bangor City	2–1
1985	Wembley	Wealdstone	v	Boston United	2–1
1986	Wembley	Altrincham	v	Runcorn	1–0
1987	Wembley	Kidderminster Harriers	v	Burton Albion	0–0
	West Bromwich	Kidderminster Harriers	v	Burton Albion	2–1
1988	Wembley	Enfield	v	Telford United	0–0
	West Bromwich	Enfield	v	Telford United	3–2
1989	Wembley	Telford United	v	Macclesfield Town	1–0*
1990	Wembley	Barrow	v	Leek Town	3–0
1991	Wembley	Wycombe Wanderers	v	Kidderminster Harriers	2–1
1992	Wembley	Colchester United	v	Witton Albion	3–1
1993	Wembley	Wycombe Wanderers	v	Runcorn	4–1
1994	Wembley	Woking	v	Runcorn	2–1
1995	Wembley	Woking	v	Kidderminster Harriers	2–1*
1996	Wembley	Macclesfield Town	v	Northwich Victoria	3–1

* *After extra time*

Macclesfield Town's
Oates and Hemmings
with the FA Umbro
Trophy.

29 ● FA CARLSBERG VASE – FINAL TIE 1996

Brigg Town 3   Clitheroe 0

Not many clubs have waited longer than Northern Counties East League club Brigg Town for the footballing spotlight to fall on them. More than a century of endeavour in the north Lincolnshire countryside had gone largely unnoticed –until now. One of the country's oldest clubs – formed in 1864 – has found fame at last by winning the 22nd FA Vase competition at Wembley Stadium.

Brigg Town manager Ralph Clayton praised the commitment of his team after revealing that a tortuous end-of-season run of 15 matches in 30 days had left him worried about being able to put out eleven fit players for the final. Two players concerning whom there had been pre-match doubts had wildly contrasting fortunes out on the famous Wembley pitch. Defender Neil Buckley was forced to leave the action on 19 minutes, having failed to recover from a knock a few minutes earlier when involved in a three-player collision near the touchline – but Carl Stead, 24 and a former trainee at Doncaster Rovers, scored a brace of goals and won the man-of-the-match award.

Brigg took the loss of Buckley in their stride, as David Mail – a Wembley winner with Blackburn Rovers in the Full Members' Cup in 1987 – slotted into his position and performed solidly throughout alongside Mark Greaves in the heart of the Brigg defence. There was evenness between the teams after the early exchanges but Brigg were on top from the moment Stead opening their account after 36 minutes.

Simon Roach, subjected to some rough approaches out on the right, wriggled free for once and crossed low into the box. The ball broke to Stead, in a similar position to Cantona's in another final about 24 hours earlier, and his crisp left-footed drive arrowed into the corner for 1–0.

Clitheroe, from the North West Counties League, were a well-beaten side by the end but may argue that the eventual outcome of the final turned on a penalty award for handball on 65 minutes, the result of an eagle-eyed spot by Barnsley referee Stephen Lodge. A nerveless Stead sent Nash the wrong way with the kick for a 2–0 advantage. The spring-heeled Roach then sealed Brigg's victory three minutes from time with a close-range effort that Clitheroe full-back Lampkin could only help into the net as he attempted to volley clear.

As a curtain-raiser to the Vase final, Grimethorpe Miners Welfare Club met Dawlish Town Sports and Social Club in the first-ever final of the Carlsberg Pub Cup. Dawlish won 4–2 on penalty-kicks after the match had finished goalless.

Brigg Town: Gawthorpe, Thompson, Rogers, Greaves (Clay), Buckley (Mail), Elston, Stead C., McLean, Stead N. (McNally), Flounders, Roach.

Clitheroe: Nash, Lampkin, Rowbotham (Otley), Baron, Westwell, Rouine, Butcher, Taylor (Smith G.), Grimshaw, Darbyshire, Hill (Dunn).

Referee: S. J. Lodge (Sheffield & Hallamshire)

Attendance: 7,340

Chief Guest: Mr. E. Dinesen, Chief Executive, Carlsberg-Tetley Brewing Limited

30 ● FA CARLSBERG VASE 1995–96

First round qualifying – 2 September 1995

(Replays in italics)

			Results	Att
Ponteland United	v	Billingham Town	4–3	39
Alnwick Town	v	Ryhope CA	1–1	46
Ryhope CA	*v*	*Alnwick*	*2–3*	*22*
Eppleton CW	v	Seaton Delaval Amateurs	2–2	
Seaton Delaval Amateurs	*v*	*Eppleton CW*	*2–2*	
Eppleton CW	*v*	*Seaton Del Amats*	*0–2*	*30*
Jarrow Roofing Boldon CA	v	Evenwood Town	2–3	
West Allotment Celtic	v	North Shields Athletic	1–0	66
Harrogate Railway	v	Shotton Comrades	0–0	65
Shotton Comrades	*v*	*Harrogate Railway*	*2–1*	*43*
Shirebrook Town	v	Cheadle Town	1–3	45
Salford City	v	Sheffield	2–1	45
Castleton Gabriels	v	Wythenshawe Amateur	2–3	57
Garforth Town	v	Nuthall	1–1	83
Nuthall	*v*	*Garforth Town*	*3–2*	*100*
Maghull	v	Denaby United	2–3	58
Priory (Eastwood)	v	Harworth CI		
(walkover for Harwarth CI – Priory (Eastwood) withdrawn)				
Grove United	v	Pontefract Collieries	3–3	19
Pontefract Collieries	*v*	*Grove United*	*0–1*	
Heswall	v	Sandiacre Town	2–1	37
Tetley Walker	v	South Normanton Athletic	1–4	41
Rossington Main	v	Louth United	2–3	
Maltby MW	v	Kimberley Town	4–2	53
Hallam	v	Selby Town	0–1	
(at Selby Town FC)				
Kidsgrove Athletic	v	Formby	4–1	83
Hall Road Rangers	v	Nettleham	0–3	
Glasshoughton Welfare	v	Atherton Collieries	0–0	38
Atherton Collieries	*v*	*Glasshoughton Welfare*	*3–3*	
Glasshoughton Welfare	*v*	*Atherton Collieries*	*0–2*	*54*
Liversedge	v	Daisy Hill	3–0	48
Blackpool(Wren)Rovers	v	Newcastle Town	0–2	37
Eccleshill United	v	Worsbro Bridge MW	3–0	30
Long Eaton United	v	Merseyside Police	1–2	70
Tadcaster Albion	v	Ossett Town	1–2	
Tividale	v	Stafford Town	0–3	70
Darlaston	v	Gedling Town	4–2	53
(match ordered to be replayed)				
Darlaston	*v*	*Gedling Town*	*3–2*	*93*
Cradley Town	v	Holwell Sports	1–0	90
(at Holwell Sports FC)				
Boldmere St Michaels	v	Knypersley Victoria	6–0	48
Wellingborough Town	v	Pegasus Juniors	6–0	30
Rushall Olympic	v	Highgate United	3–1	38
Shifnal Town	v	Northfield Town	5–1	79
Stourport Swifts	v	Brierley Hill Alliance	4–0	
Chasetown	v	Bloxwich Town	1–2	86

(Replays in italics)

			Results	Att
Rocester	v	Northampton Spencer	1–3	
Tiptree United	v	Sawbridgeworth Town	2–3	39
Cornard United	v	Witham Town	1–4	63
Norwich United	v	Stamford	2–5	42
Fakenham Town	v	Sudbury Wanderers	2–0	30
(at Watton United FC)				
March Town United	v	Hullbridge Sports	4–0	87
Downham Town	v	Southend Manor	2–3	50
(at Southend Manor FC)				
Haverhill Rovers	v	Harwich & Parkeston	1–3	
Brantham Athletic	v	Stowmarket Town		
(walkover for Stowmarket Town – Brantham Athletic withdrawn)				
Ford United	v	Tilbury	1–3	102
Kempston Rovers	v	Amersham Town	0–1	32
Milton Keynes	v	Edgware Town	1–2	50
Harlow Town	v	Beaconsfield Sycob	2–0	48
Hemel Hempstead	v	Stansted	1–3	45
Wealdstone	v	East Ham United	10–0	305
Hanwell Town	v	Bedford Town	1–2	69
Harpenden Town	v	Ware	1–4	41
Tottemhoe	v	Feltham	2–3	24
Romford	v	Tufnell Park	2–1	
Kingsbury Town	v	Rayners Lane	2–1	41
Clapton	v	Leverstock Green	4–2	45
Bedfont	v	Ramsgate	2–3	
Ashford Town (Middx)	v	Southwick	6–0	86
East Grinstead	v	Folkestone Invicta	1–4	58
Crowborough Athletic	v	Lancing	1–2	
Bracknell Town	v	Redhill	2–0	75
Horsham YMCA	v	Epsom & Ewell	2–1	120
Merstham	v	Chichester City	1–4	60
Burgess Hill Town	v	Oakwood	3–0	64
Saltdean United	v	Sidley United	2–0	72
Chipstead	v	Beckenham Town	3–1	64
Dartford	v	Steyning Town	2–2	275
(at Slade Green FC)				
Steyning Town	*v*	*Dartford*	*0–4*	*124*
EastbourneTown	v	Littlehampton Town	0–1	104
(at Littlehampton Town FC)				
Portfield	v	Broadbridge Heath	2–0	53
Furness	v	Sheppey United	1–1	80
Sheppey United	*v*	*Furness*	*0–3*	*75*
Langney Sports	v	Mile Oak	3–2	174
Newhaven	v	Canterbury City	1–3	70
Swindon Supermarine	v	Downton	2–1	70
Abingdon United	v	BAT Sports	3–0	32
Carterton Town	v	Swanage Town & Herston	2–0	
Bemerton Heath Harlequins	v	Kintbury Rangers	5–2	44
Didcot Town	v	Totton AFC	2–3	47
Sherborne Town	v	Portsmouth Royal Navy	5–3	
Brockenhurst	v	Ryde	0–4	47
Cowes Sports	v	Gosport Borough	1–2	103
Odd Down	v	Hallen	1–0	52
Crediton United	v	Glastonbury	1–3	
Chippenham Town	v	Clyst Rovers	2–0	105
St Blazey	v	DRG AFC	3–0	36
Shortwood United	v	Ilfracombe Town	4–0	60
Exmouth Town	v	Warminster Town	1–2	54

Fairford Town	v	Backwell United	2–3	45
Bridgwater Town	v	Larkhall Athletic	2–0	174

Second round qualifying – 30 September 1995

Easington Colliery	v	West Allotment Celtic	4–2	18
Alnwick Town	v	Esh Winning	1–2	44
Seaton Delaval Amateurs	v	Marske United	1–5	
Pickering Town	v	Washington	3–4	76
Evenwood Town	v	Crook Town	1–3	92
Ashington	v	Darlington Cleveland Social	3–0	
Penrith	v	Willington	0–1	79
Shotton Comrades	v	Morpeth Town	1–0	19
Annfield Plain	v	Norton & Stockton Ancients	2–1	
Benfield Park	v	Whickham	2–3	
Bedlington Terriers	v	Horden CW	5–1	89
Stockton	v	Ponteland United	0–1	32
Ferryhill Athletic	v	Yorkshire Amateur	0–1	28
Wythenshawe Amateur	v	Arnold Town	3–2	94
Oakham United	v	Blidworth MW	2–1	40
Flixton	v	Poulton Victoria	2–1	92
Darwen	v	Ossett Albion	0–3	104
Clitheroe	v	Immingham Town	4–0	154
Oldham Town	v	Prescot Cables	3–2	45
Liversedge	v	Newcastle Town	0–1	56
Denaby United	v	Ossett Town	0–1	
Nettleham	v	Louth United	1–1	30
Louth United	*v*	*Nettleham*	*0–1*	*38*
Merseyside Police	v	North Ferriby United	2–3	
Nantwich Town	v	Harworth CI	3–0	81
Selby Town	v	Armthorpe Welfare	2–0	52
Ashfield United	v	Heswall	5–1	66
Maltby MW	v	Nuthall	0–2	40
Salford City	v	Atherton Collieries	3–0	52
St Helens Town	v	Eccleshill United	4–0	99
Kidsgrove Athletic	v	Chadderton	3–0	96
Hatfield Main	v	Parkgate	7–1	84
Brigg Town	v	Rossendale United	9–0	78
Bootle	v	Grove United	2–1	65
Trafford	v	Staveley MW	4–2	89
Winterton Rangers	v	Rainworth MW	3–1	50
South Normanton Athletic	v	Hucknall Town	0–5	180
Heanor Town	v	Maine Road	2–2	
Maine Road	*v*	*Heanor Town*	*5–2*	*48*
Borrowash Victoria	v	Cheadle Town	1–4	43
Stapenhill	v	West Midlands Police	1–2	68
Sandwell Borough	v	Lye Town	0–3	39
Long Buckby	v	Stourport Swifts	4–1	47
Shepshed Dynamo	v	Kings Heath	4–0	169
Darlaston	v	Northampton Spencer	4–1	82
Barwell	v	Stratford Town	1–0	31
Blakenall	v	Desborough Town	1–0	61
Rushall Olympic	v	Upton Town	3–1	70
Cradley Town	v	Halesowen Harriers	2–3	145
Shifnal Town	v	Bolehall Swifts	1–1	107
Bolehall Swifts	*v*	*Shifnal Town*	*1–3*	*59*
Anstey Nomads	v	Radford	4–1	111

			Results	Att
Westfields	v	Brackley Town	0–2	61
Knowle	v	Pershore Town	2–3	36
Meir KA	v	Walsall Wood	0–5	61
Friar Lane OB	v	Oldbury United	0–1	98
Stafford Town	v	Willenhall Town	2–4	91
(at Willenhall Town FC)				
Stewarts & Lloyds	v	Boldmere St Michaels	1–3	32
Banbury United	v	Birstall United	2–2	133
Birstall United	*v*	*Banbury United*	*1–3*	
Newport Pagnell Town	v	Wellingborough Town	3–3	40
Wellingborough Town	*v*	*Newport Pagnell Town*	*3–0*	30
Bloxwich Town	v	Wednesfield	3–1	57
Cogenhoe United	v	Barrow Town	2–0	96
Lowestoft Town	v	Mildenhall Town	5–2	114
Watton United	v	Stowmarket Town	0–1	68
Ipswich Wanderers	v	Gorleston	0–3	91
Warboys Town	v	March Town United	2–0	129
Long Sutton Athletic	v	Brightlingsea United		
(walkover for Brightlingsea United – Long Sutton Athletic removed from the Competition)				
Felixstowe Town	v	Harwich & Parkeston	1–2	135
Maldon Town	v	Burnham Ramblers	3–1	77
Saffron Walden Town	v	Swaffham Town	1–2	101
Histon	v	Fakenham Town	1–3	40
Woodbridge Town	v	Chatteris Town	5–0	85
Soham Town Rangers	v	Ely City	1–4	240
Bourne Town	v	Great Yarmouth Town	2–1	120
Holbeach United	v	Sawbridgeworth Town	1–4	148
Southend Manor	v	Newmarket Town	0–2	50
Stamford	v	St Neots Town	0–1	105
Great Wakering Rovers	v	Clacton Town	1–2	101
Wroxham	v	Somersham Town	7–3	73
Eynesbury Rovers	v	Mirrlees Blackstone	2–2	80
Mirrlees Blackstone	*v*	*Eynesbury Rovers*	*2–1*	67
Witham Town	v	Spalding United	1–1	59
Spalding United	*v*	*Witham Town*	*2–1*	112
Hertford Town	v	Eton Manor	3–1	70
Kingsbury Town	v	Northwood	0–1	60
Wootton Blue Cross	v	Hillingdon Borough	4–3	50
Brentwood	v	Welwyn Garden City	1–1	55
Welwyn Garden City	*v*	*Brentwood*	*0–1*	
Harlow Town	v	East Thurrock United	5–4	52
Cockfosters	v	Edgware Town	1–2	120
Tilbury	v	Waltham Abbey	2–1	45
Hampton	v	Viking Sports	3–0	88
Brimsdown Rovers	v	Romford	0–4	
Langford	v	London Colney	3–2	52
Shillington	v	Clapton	2–4	60
Bedford Town	v	Brook House	1–0	248
Concord Rangers	v	Potters Bar Town	2–0	49
Potton United	v	Aveley	1–2	110
Greenwich Borough	v	Chalfont St Peter	0–1	65
Letchworth	v	Leighton Town		
(walkover for Leighton Town – Letchworth removed from the Competition)				
Flackwell Heath	v	Hornchurch	1–0	102
Wealdstone	v	St Margaretsbury	1–1	241
St Margaretsbury	*v*	*Wealdstone*	*0–2*	
Cheshunt	v	Stansted	1–0	44
Eton Wick	v	Stotfold	2–6	35

● 115

			Results	Att
Feltham	v	Biggleswade Town	2–3	28
Ware	v	Bowers United	3–0	70
Southall	v	Royston Town	1–3	
(at Royston Town FC)				
Amersham Town	v	Hoddesdon Town	0–0	30
Hoddesdon Town	*v*	*Amersham Town*	*4–0*	*40*
Tring Town	v	Wingate & Finchley	2–4	
Barkingside	v	Harefield United	2–1	40
Horsham	v	Crockenhill	3–0	141
Dartford	v	Furness	1–3	408
Ash United	v	Shoreham	0–6	37
West Wickham	v	Eastbourne United	2–0	69
Lancing	v	Corinthian	2–3	81
Windsor & Eton	v	Folkestone Invicta	2–2	149
Folkestone Invicta	*v*	*Windsor & Eton*	*4–5*	*141*
Ramsgate	v	Hassocks	1–2	90
Pagham	v	Arundel	4–3	81
Thamesmead Town	v	Chipstead	1–0	36
Ringmer	v	Whitstable Town	2–3	144
Worthing United	v	Littlehampton Town	1–4	68
Chichester City	v	Canterbury City	1–0	50
Herne Bay	v	Cray Wanderers	1–0	112
Slade Green	v	Leatherhead	5–1	68
Cove	v	Wick	0–2	
Chatham Town	v	Camberley Town	5–2	86
Godalming & Guildford	v	Three Bridges	1–0	
Horsham YMCA	v	Faversham Town	0–0	42
Faversham Town	*v*	*Horsham YMCA*	*3–4*	*38*
Croydon Athletic	v	Bracknell Town	0–0	33
Bracknell Town	*v*	*Croydon Athletic*	*4–3*	
Hailsham Town	v	Portfield	4–0	130
Saltdean United	v	Corinthian-Casuals	3–2	245
Burgess Hill Town	v	Selsey	3–1	96
Cranleigh	v	Egham Town	3–1	99
Ashford Town (Middx)	v	Raynes Park Vale	2–1	48
Deal Town	v	Langney Sports	2–1	156
Netheme	v	Lewes	3–1	41
Bicester Town	v	Ryde	1–1	55
Ryde	*v*	*Bicester Town*	*3–1*	*70*
Totton AFC	v	Milton United	2–1	88
Gosport Borough	v	Calne Town	3–1	56
Lymington AFC	v	Carterton Town	1–0	112
Hungerford Town	v	Wantage Town	3–1	108
Swindon Supermarine	v	Thatcham Town	2–1	62
First Tower United	v	Bournemouth	1–2	50
Sandhurst Town	v	Peppard	2–3	53
Andover	v	Abingdon United	3–1	171
Petersfield Town	v	North Leigh	0–1	50
Westbury United	v	Bemerton Heath Harlequins	0–1	105
Sherborne Town	v	Christchurch	3–1	39
St Blazey	v	Chippenham Town	0–3	65
Endsleigh	v	Bridgwater Town	0–1	
Minehead	v	Warminster Town	0–1	39
Almondsbury Town	v	Devizes Town	1–2	61
Chard Town	v	Dawlish Town	2–0	56
Shortwood United	v	Tuffley Rovers	3–1	77
Cirencester Town	v	Old Georgians	1–5	47
Backwell United	v	Bristol Manor Farm	3–0	72

			Results	Att
Frome Town	v	Torpoint Athletic	1–2	92
Porthleven	v	Keynsham Town	0–0	64
Keynsham Town	*v*	*Porthleven*	*4–2*	*85*
Bishop Sutton	v	Welton Rovers	2–2	78
Welton Rovers	*v*	*Bishop Sutton*	*0–1*	*71*
Newquay	v	Bridport	0–3	133
Brislington	v	Torrington	0–2	72
Truro City	v	Cadbury Heath	6–2	151
Odd Down	v	Glastonbury	2–0	25
Wellington Town	v	Liskeard Athletic	2–4	65
Harrow Hill	v	Bideford	3–4	47
Melksham Town	v	Saltash United	0–1	65

First round proper – 28 October 1995

			Results	Att
Flixton	v	Glossop North End	3–0	130
Crook Town	v	Ashfield United	2–0	133
Oakham United	v	Washington	3–2	45
Eastwood Hanley	v	Shotton Comrades	2–0	82
Bedlington Terriers	v	Kidsgrove Athletic	4–0	110
Ponteland United	v	Thackley	2–5	76
Hatfield Main	v	Selby Town	0–2	82
Esh Winning	v	Winterton Rangers	2–5	86
Easington Colliery	v	Wythenshawe Amateur	2–1	58
Whickham	v	Marske United	3–2	50
Newcastle Town	v	Burscough	3–1	119
Ashington	v	North Ferriby United	0–3	152
Brigg Town	v	Stocksbridge Park Steels	2–1	79
Oldham Town	v	Annfield Plain	6–1	
Ossett Town	v	Willington	7–3	64
Yorkshire Amateur	v	Cheadle Town	2–0	40
Trafford	v	St Helens Town	2–1	74
Brandon United	v	Ossett Albion	0–2	46
Salford City	v	Nuthall	0–1	34
Clitheroe	v	Bootle	5–1	
Nettleham	v	Nantwich Town	2–0	59
South Shields	v	Maine Road	1–6	192
Hinckley Athletic	v	Wellingborough Town	3–2	
Pelsall Villa	v	Halesowen Harriers	3–1	104
Anstey Nomads	v	Oldbury United	2–1	115
Oadby Town	v	Boldmere St Michaels	2–5	88
West Midlands Police	v	Pershore Town	3–4	36
Bloxwich Town	v	St Andrews	1–0	64
Rushall Olympic	v	Cogenhoe United	2–1	
Boston Town	v	Shepshed Dynamo	2–6	109
Blakenall	v	Lye Town	1–4	84
Brackley Town	v	Banbury United	3–0	220
Barwell	v	Dunkirk	1–1	43
Dunkirk	*v*	*Barwell*	*0–2*	
Hucknall Town	v	Shifnal Town	2–1	
Darlaston	v	Walsall Wood	1–1	102
Walsall Wood	*v*	*Darlaston*	*0–1*	
Willenhall Town	v	Long Buckby	1–0	87
Harlow Town	v	Barkingside	2–1	52
Wroxham	v	Lowestoft Town	2–0	131
Brightlingsea United	v	Newmarket Town	0–1	84
Clapton	v	Leighton Town	1–2	58

			Results	Att
Edgware Town	v	Wingate & Finchley	4–1	206
Northwood	v	Stotfold	3–0	114
St Neots Town	v	Tilbury	1–4	150
Harwich & Parkeston	v	Warboys Town	2–0	231
Sawbridgeworth Town	v	Concord Rangers	1–0	55
Chalfont St Peter	v	Maldon Town	3–1	88
Royston Town	v	Cheshunt	1–2	79
Hadleigh United	v	Mirrlees Blackstone	4–2	77
Bourne Town	v	Bedford Town	0–1	221
Langford	v	Hoddesdon Town	3–1	90
Wealdstone	v	Hampton	0–3	333
Wootton Blue Cross	v	Flackwell Heath	2–2	64
Flackwell Heath	*v*	*Wootton Blue Cross*	*1–2*	*68*
Romford	v	Fakenham Town	2–4	241
Halstead Town	v	Wisbech Town	1–2	401
Swaffham Town	v	Brentwood	2–3	158
Gorleston	v	Biggleswade Town	4–0	173
Collier Row	v	Clacton Town	8–1	114
Spalding United	v	Ely City	1–3	131
Ware	v	Basildon United	4–2	100
Stowmarket Town	v	Woodbridge Town	2–2	209
Woodbridge Town	*v*	*Stowmarket Town*	*2–1*	
Aveley	v	Hertford Town	2–1	97
Thamesmead Town	v	Ashford Town (Middx)	1–0	71
Slade Green	v	Saltdean United	5–1	95
Burgess Hill Town	v	Bournemouth	2–1	117
Shoreham	v	Gosport Borough	1–0	131
Lymington AFC	v	Croydon	3–0	147
Cranleigh	v	Peppard	3–2	102
Banstead Athletic	v	Chatham Town	1–0	63
Andover	v	Furness	1–4	203
Corinthian	v	Totton AFC	2–1	48
Whitehawk	v	Littlehampton Town	5–1	95
Whitstable Town	v	Ryde	4–0	210
Netherne	v	Bracknell Town	3–4	50
Stamco	v	Godalming & Guildford	1–2	
Chichester City	v	Deal Town	2–0	80
Horsham YMCA	v	Wick	1–3	94
Pagham	v	Windsor & Eton	1–2	135
Horsham	v	Hassocks	6–3	217
West Wickham	v	Herne Bay	0–3	96
Tunbridge Wells	v	Hungerford Town	1–6	155
Eastleigh	v	Hailsham Town	2–1	131
Peacehaven & Telscombe	v	North Leigh	4–0	187
Falmouth Town	v	Liskeard Athletic	3–0	
Paulton Rovers	v	Shortwood United	2–0	167
Backwell United	v	Bridport	1–2	85
Mangotsfield United	v	Truro City	3–0	185
Swindon Supermarine	v	Keynsham Town	1–2	67
Bideford	v	Tiverton Town	2–1	465
Chard Town	v	Saltash United	2–1	
Elmore	v	Chippenham Town	1–4	52
Devizes Town	v	Bemerton Heath Harlequins	0–3	66
Torpoint Athletic	v	Odd Down	3–1	80
Warminster Town	v	Barnstaple Town	3–2	130
Wimborne Town	v	Old Georgians	2–1	185
Bridgwater Town	v	Bishop Sutton	1–2	197
Torrington	v	Sherborne Town	3–0	81

Second round proper – 18 November 1995

			Results	Att
Guisborough Town	v	Crook Town	1–1	107
Crook Town	*v*	*Guisborough Town*	*1–2*	*140*
Yorkshire Amateur	v	West Auckland Town	1–1	57
West Auckland Town	*v*	*Yorkshire Amateur*	*2–1*	
Winterton Rangers	v	Northallerton	1–0	70
Brigg Town	v	Tow Law Town	3–0	128
Selby Town	v	Billingham Synthonia	3–2	158
Shildon	v	Mossley	1–2	116
Hebburn	v	Ossett Albion	2–1	53
Chester-le-Street Town	v	Whickham	5–1	
North Ferriby United	v	Oldham Town	7–0	107
Durham City	v	Whitby Town	4–1	254
Clitheroe	v	RTM Newcastle	2–1	170
Seaham Red Star	v	Peterlee Newtown	2–1	40
Dunston FB	v	Cammell Laird	2–0	96
Prudhoe Town	v	Goole Town	2–0	48
Easington Colliery	v	Ossett Town	2–1	31
Murton	v	Consett	2–1	46
Thackley	v	Bedlington Terriers	0–1	80
Nettleham	v	Pershore Town	1–4	81
Anstey Nomads	v	Shepshed Dynamo	4–1	300
Armitage	v	Rushall Olympic	0–2	77
Nuthall	v	Boldmere St Michaels	1–3	50
Oakham United	v	Lye Town	1–4	45
Raunds Town	v	Hinckley Athletic	2–2	210
Hinckley Athletic	*v*	*Raunds Town*	*0–3*	*355*
Willenhall Town	v	Newcastle Town	3–1	107
Flixton	v	Hucknall Town	5–1	118
Belper Town	v	Bloxwich Town	3–1	250
Trafford	v	Darlaston	3–0	112
Maine Road	v	Eastwood Hanley	1–4	66
Pelsall Villa	v	Barwell	2–4	110
Northwood	v	Ely City	2–1	146
Hampton	v	Ware	5–2	128
Brackley Town	v	Aveley	2–3	100
Diss Town	v	Herne Bay	2–0	429
Burgess Hill Town	v	Wootton Blue Cross	3–2	110
Collier Row	v	Woodbridge Town	5–4	164
Cheshunt	v	Bedford Town	2–3	
Wisbech Town	v	Wivenhoe Town	2–3	538
Slade Green	v	Newmarket Town	2–0	86
Arlesey Town	v	Thamesmead Town	1–2	477
Metropolitan Police	v	Canvey Island	1–3	
Furness	v	Sawbridgeworth Town	0–0	
Sawbridgeworth Town	*v*	*Furness*	*1–1*	*60*
Sawbridgeworth Town	*v*	*Furness*	*1–2*	*118*
Harwich & Parkeston	v	Tilbury	2–3	192
Langford	v	Whitstable Town	0–1	155
Wroxham	v	Brentwood	1–2	115
Whitehawk	v	Corinthian	3–1	89
Burnham	v	Windsor & Eton	0–4	176
Gorleston	v	Fakenham Town	3–2	216
Peacehaven & Telscombe	v	Harlow Town	2–0	214
Hadleigh United	v	Edgware Town	0–2	104
Leighton Town	v	Chalfont St Peter	1–1	149
Chalfont St Peter	*v*	*Leighton Town*	*2–0*	*85*

			Results	Att
Keynsham Town	v	Chard Town	0–1	129
Lymington AFC	v	Warminster Town	2–0	170
Paulton Rovers	v	Bideford	2–0	182
Bridport	v	Bemerton Heath Harlequins	2–0	190
Horsham	v	Falmouth Town	0–2	302
Torpoint Athletic	v	Eastleigh	1–0	127
Shoreham	v	Chichester City	1–2	83
Dorking	v	Bishop Sutton	2–2	56
Bishop Sutton	*v*	*Dorking*	*2–0*	*81*
Godalming & Guildford	v	Mangotsfield United	2–5	215
Wimborne Town	v	Torrington	1–2	
Cranleigh	v	Banstead Athletic	0–2	
Wick	v	Chippenham Town	0–1	180
Taunton Town	v	Bracknell Town	3–3	377
Bracknell Town	*v*	*Taunton Town*	*1–2*	*103*

Third round proper – 9 December 1995

Winterton Rangers	v	Flixton	0–4	104
Rushall Olympic	v	Bedlington Terriers	0–4	100
Brigg Town	v	Guisborough Town	2–0	82
Hebburn	v	Durham City	0–4	65
Seaham Red Star	v	Belper Town	1–2	130
Prudhoe Town	v	Dunston FB	1–2	
North Ferriby United	v	Eastwood Hanley	4–2	109
Chester-le-Street Town	v	Lye Town	1–3	145
Easington Colliery	v	Anstey Nomads	2–3	65
Boldmere St Michaels	v	Trafford	0–2	83
Barwell	v	Mossley	3–1	130
Murton	v	Selby Town	3–5	
Clitheroe	v	West Auckland Town	6–0	210
Thamesmead Town	v	Brentwood	3–1	71
Willenhall Town	v	Chalfont St Peter	2–1	122
Whitstable Town	v	Peacehaven & Telscombe	0–1	295
Tilbury	v	Aveley	2–4	158
Slade Green	v	Diss Town	0–2	298
Northwood	v	Gorleston	0–1	158
Wivenhoe Town	v	Edgware Town	3–1	113
Raunds Town	v	Furness	1–1*	196
Furness	*v*	*Raunds Town*	*1–1*	
Furness	*v*	*Raunds Town*	*2–5*	*210*
(at Raunds Town FC)				
Canvey Island	v	Bedford Town	2–0	511
Hampton	v	Collier Row	0–1	242
Taunton Town	v	Chippenham Town	4–0	408
Bridport	v	Windsor & Eton	2–4	205
Lymington AFC	v	Bishop Sutton	4–0	177
Whitehawk	v	Banstead Athletic	0–2	108
Burgess Hill Town	v	Pershore Town	2–1	195
Torpoint Athletic	v	Chard Town	4–2	111
Paulton Rovers	v	Falmouth Town	2–0	275
Torrington	v	Chichester City	1–2	157
Hungerford Town	v	Mangotsfield United	0–0	175
Mangotsfield United	*v*	*Hungerford Town*	*5–1*	*186*

* abandoned after 105 minutes due to frozen pitch

Fourth round proper – 13 January 1996

North Ferriby United	v	Anstey Nomads	2–3	204
Lye Town	v	Barwell	0–2	310
Clitheroe	v	Willenhall Town	3–0	451
Trafford	v	Selby Town	0–0	151
Selby Town	*v*	*Trafford*	*1–1*	*320*
Selby Town	*v*	*Trafford*	*0–3*	*550*
Flixton	v	Dunston Federation Brewery	2–0	180
Durham City	v	Belper Town	2–3	570
Brigg Town	v	Bedlington Terriers	2–1	169
Burgess Hill Town	v	Collier Row	0–1	365
Windsor & Eton	v	Peacehaven & Telscombe	0–1	278
Diss Town	v	Banstead Athletic	1–2	682
Chichester City	v	Thamesmead Town	1–3	235
Wivenhoe Town	v	Aveley	4–0	301
Paulton Rovers	v	Mangotsfield United	0–3	360
Canvey Island	v	Gorleston	1–0	604
Raunds Town	v	Taunton Town	4–1	290
Lymington AFC	v	Torpoint Athletic	1–3	333

Fifth round proper – 3 February 1996

Raunds Town	v	Torpoint Athletic	2–0	296
Wivenhoe Town	v	Mangotsfield United	2–2	543
Mangotsfield United	*v*	*Wivenhoe Town*	*3–0*	*446*
Banstead Athletic	v	Peacehaven & Telscombe	2–3	252
Collier Row	v	Anstey Nomads	6–0	448
Brigg Town	v	Trafford	1–0	320
Flixton	v	Barwell	3–1	328
Thamesmead Town	v	Canvey Island	1–2	811
(at Slade Green FC)				
Belper Town	v	Clitheroe	0–3	754

Sixth round proper – 24 February 1996

Brigg Town	v	Collier Row	2–0	566
Mangotsfield United	v	Raunds Town	2–2	725
Raunds Town	*v*	*Mangotsfield United*	*0–1*	*638*
Clitheroe	v	Peacehaven & Telscombe	1–0	850
Flixton	v	Canvey Island	3–0	860

Semi-finals

First Leg – 16 March 1996

Brigg Town	v	Flixton	0–0	1128
Mangotsfield United	v	Clitheroe	1–0	837

Second Leg – 23 March 1996

Flixton	v	Brigg Town	0–1	1540
Clitheroe	v	Mangotsfield United	2–0	2000

Brigg Town won 1–0 on aggregate
Clitheroe won 2–1 on aggregate

31 ● FA VASE WINNERS 1975–1996

Year	Venue	Winners		Runners-up	Result
1975	Wembley	Hoddesdon Town	v	Epsom & Ewell	2–1
1976	Wembley	Billericay Town	v	Stamford	1–0*
1977	Wembley	Billericay Town	v	Sheffield	1–1*
	Nottingham	Billericay Town	v	Sheffield	2–1
1978	Wembley	Blue Star	v	Barton Rovers	2–1
1979	Wembley	Billericay Town	v	Almondsbury Greenway	4–1
1980	Wembley	Stamford	v	Guisborough Town	2–0
1981	Wembley	Whickham	v	Willenhall Town	3–2*
1982	Wembley	Forest Green Rovers	v	Rainworth Miners' Welfare	3–0
1983	Wembley	VS Rugby	v	Halesowen Town	1–0
1984	Wembley	Stansted	v	Stamford	3–2
1985	Wembley	Halesowen Town	v	Fleetwood Town	3–1
1986	Wembley	Halesowen Town	v	Southall	3–0
1987	Wembley	St Helens Town	v	Warrington Town	3–2
1988	Wembley	Colne Dynamoes	v	Emley	1–0*
1989	Wembley	Tamworth	v	Sudbury Town	1–1*
	Peterborough	Tamworth	v	Sudbury Town	3–0
1990	Wembley	Yeading	v	Bridlington Town	0–0*
	Leeds	Yeading	v	Bridlington Town	1–0
1991	Wembley	Guiseley	v	Gresley Rovers	4–4*
	Sheffield	Guiseley	v	Gresley Rovers	3–1
1992	Wembley	Wimborne Town	v	Guiseley	5–3
1993	Wembley	Bridlington Town	v	Tiverton Town	1–0
1994	Wembley	Diss Town	v	Taunton Town	2–1*
1995	Wembley	Arlesey Town	v	Oxford City	2–1
1996	Wembley	Brigg Town	v	Clitheroe	3–0

* *After extra time*

Clitheroe's Andrew Taylor resists a Brigg tackle.

32 ● FA YOUTH CUP WINNERS 1953–1996

The FA Youth Cup Final is played on a two–leg basis but the 1978 final between Crystal Palace and Aston Villa was a single match. The only final which needed a replay was the 1983 contest between Norwich and Everton.

Year	Winners		Runners–up	Result
1953	Manchester United	v	Wolverhampton Wanderers	9–3
1954	Manchester United	v	Wolverhampton Wanderers	5–4
1955	Manchester United	v	West Bromwich Albion	7–1
1956	Manchester United	v	Chesterfield	4–3
1957	Manchester United	v	West Ham United	8–2
1958	Wolverhampton Wanderers	v	Chelsea	7–6
1959	Blackburn Rovers	v	West Ham United	2–1
1960	Chelsea	v	Preston North End	5–2
1961	Chelsea	v	Everton	5–3
1962	Newcastle United	v	Wolverhampton Wanderers	2–1
1963	West Ham United	v	Liverpool	6–5
1964	Manchester United	v	Swindon Town	5–2
1965	Everton	v	Arsenal	3–2
1966	Arsenal	v	Sunderland	5–3
1967	Sunderland	v	Birmingham City	2–0
1968	Burnley	v	Coventry City	3–2
1969	Sunderland	v	West Bromwich Albion	6–3
1970	Tottenham Hotspur	v	Coventry City	4–3
1971	Arsenal	v	Cardiff City	2–0
1972	Aston Villa	v	Liverpool	5–2
1973	Ipswich Town	v	Bristol City	4–1
1974	Tottenham Hotspur	v	Huddersfield Town	2–1
1975	Ipswich Town	v	West Ham United	5–1
1976	West Bromwich Albion	v	Wolverhampton Wanderers	5–0
1977	Crystal Palace	v	Everton	1–0
1978	Crystal Palace	v	Aston Villa	1–0
1979	Millwall	v	Manchester City	2–0
1980	Aston Villa	v	Manchester City	3–2
1981	West Ham United	v	Tottenham Hotspur	2–1
1982	Watford	v	Manchester United	7–6
1983	Norwich City	v	Everton	6–5*
1984	Everton	v	Stoke City	4–2
1985	Newcastle United	v	Watford	4–1
1986	Manchester City	v	Manchester United	3–1
1987	Coventry City	v	Charlton Athletic	2–1
1988	Arsenal	v	Doncaster Rovers	6–1
1989	Watford	v	Manchester City	2–1
1990	Tottenham Hotspur	v	Middlesbrough	3–2
1991	Millwall	v	Sheffield Wednesday	3–0
1992	Manchester United	v	Crystal Palace	6–3
1993	Leeds United	v	Manchester United	4–1
1994	Arsenal	v	Millwall	5–3
1995	Manchester United	v	Tottenham Hotspur	2–2†
1996	Liverpool	v	West Ham United	4–1

* *aggregate score after replay*
† *won on penalty-kicks*

33 ● FA COUNTY YOUTH CUP WINNERS 1945–1996

From 1945 to 1969 the FA County Youth Cup final was played over two legs. Since 1970 it has been a one-match final and only twice (in 1988 and 1990) has a replay been required.

Year	Winners		Runners-up	Result
1945	Staffordshire	v	Wiltshire	3–2
1946	Berks & Bucks	v	Durham	4–3
1947	Durham	v	Essex	4–2
1948	Essex	v	Liverpool	5–3
1949	Liverpool	v	Middlesex	4–3
1950	Essex	v	Middlesex	4–3
1951	Middlesex	v	Leicestershire & Rutland	3–1
1952	Sussex	v	Liverpool	3–1
1953	Sheffield & Hallam	v	Hampshire	5–3
1954	Liverpool	v	Gloucestershire	4–1
1955	Bedfordshire	v	Sheffield & Hallam	2–0
1956	Middlesex	v	Staffordshire	3–2
1957	Hampshire	v	Cheshire	4–3
1958	Staffordshire	v	London	8–0
1959	Birmingham	v	London	7–5
1960	London	v	Birmingham	6–4
1961	Lancashire	v	Nottinghamshire	6–3
1962	Middlesex	v	Nottinghamshire	3–2
1963	Durham	v	Essex	3–2
1964	Sheffield & Hallam	v	Birmingham	1–0
1965	Northumberland	v	Middlesex	7–4
1966	Leics & Rutland	v	London	6–5
1967	Northamptonshire	v	Hertfordshire	5–4
1968	North Riding	v	Devon	7–4
1969	Northumberland	v	Sussex	1–0
1970	Hertfordshire	v	Cheshire	2–1
1971	Lancashire	v	Gloucestershire	2–0
1972	Middlesex	v	Liverpool	2–0
1973	Hertfordshire	v	Northumberland	3–0
1974	Nottinghamshire	v	London	2–0
1975	Durham	v	Bedfordshire	2–1
1976	Northamptonshire	v	Surrey	7–1
1977	Liverpool	v	Surrey	3–0
1978	Liverpool	v	Kent	3–1
1979	Hertfordshire	v	Liverpool	4–1
1980	Liverpool	v	Lancashire	2–0
1981	Lancashire	v	East Riding	3–1
1982	Devon	v	Kent	3–2*
1983	London	v	Gloucestershire	3–0
1984	Cheshire	v	Manchester	2–1
1985	East Riding	v	Middlesex	2–1
1986	Hertfordshire	v	Manchester	4–0
1987	North Riding	v	Gloucestershire	3–1
1988	East Riding	v	Middlesex	1–1
	East Riding	*v*	*Middlesex*	*5–3*
1989	Liverpool	v	Hertfordshire	2–1

Year	Winners		Runners-up	Result
1990	Staffordshire	v	Hampshire	1–1
	Staffordshire	*v*	*Hampshire*	*2–1*
1991	Lancashire	v	Surrey	6–0
1992	Nottinghamshire	v	Surrey	1–0
1993	Durham	v	Liverpool	4–0
1994	West Riding	v	Sussex	3–1
1995	Liverpool	v	Essex	3–2
1996	Durham	v	Gloucestershire	1–0

* *after extra time*

Extra preliminary round

(Replays in italics)   *Results*

Guisborough Town	v	Hartlepool United	0–2
Shotton Comrades	v	Carlisle United	0–3
Marine	v	Rochdale	0–0
Rochdale	*v*	*Marine*	*0–1*
Stalybridge Celtic	v	Southport	0–4
Leigh RMI	v	Huddersfield Town	0–9
Stockport County	v	Chorley	3–0
Hinckley Athletic	v	Chesterfield	2–1
Hinckley Town	v	Mansfield Town	
(walkover for Mansfield Town – Hinckley Town withdrawn)			
Bilston Town	v	Lye Town	1–1
Lye Town	*v*	*Bilston*	*1–2*
Brierley Hill Town	v	Pelsall Villa	4–1
Rushden & Diamonds	v	Raunds Town	1–1
Raunds Town	*v*	*Rushden & Diamonds*	*1–5*
Saffron Walden Town	v	Bury Town	
(walkover for Bury Town – Saffron Walden Town withdrawn)			
Wivenhoe Town	v	March Town United	10–0
Potters Bar Town	v	Berkhamsted Town	2–1
St Albans City	v	Bedford Town	4–3
Southend Manor	v	Collier Row	1–1
Collier Row	*v*	*Southend Manor*	*4–2*
Brook House	v	Clapton	5–1
Hayes	v	Enfield	0–1
Staines Town	v	Newport Pagnell Town	4–1
Hillingdon Borough	v	Hampton	7–1
Tonbridge	v	Faversham Town	4–0
Ashford Town	v	Thamesmead Town	0–3
Tooting & Mitcham United	v	Stamco	3–1
Whitehawk	v	Bromley	1–2
Horsham YMCA	v	Crawley Town	1–2
Oakwood	v	Lewes	4–2
Wokingham Town	v	Woking	0–1
Walton & Hersham	v	Chipstead	6–1
Romsey Town	v	Camberley Town	3–2
(at Camberley Town FC)			
Havant Town	v	Bognor Regis Town	0–2
Abingdon Town	v	Aldershot Town	3–0
Maidenhead United	v	Flackwell Heath	5–0
Mangotsfield United	v	Forest Green Rovers	2–4
Weston-Super-Mare	v	Cheltenham Town	2–0

Preliminary round

Hartlepool United	v	Harrogate Town	8–0
Morecambe	v	Lancaster City	1–1
Lancaster City	*v*	*Morecambe*	*3–0*
Darlington	v	Scarborough	2–1
Darwen	v	Carlisle United	1–0
Marine	v	Bolton Wanderers	1–2
Chester City	v	Wigan Athletic	4–0

Chadderton	v	Warrington Town	1–1
Warrington Town	*v*	*Chadderton*	*2–2*
(Chadderton Town won on kicks from the penalty mark 5–3)			
Trafford	v	Southport	0–1
Huddersfield Town	v	Bury	4–0
Immingham Town	v	Farsley Celtic	3–1
Port Vale	v	Northwich Victoria	6–1
Hall Road Rangers	v	Stockport County	2–2
Stockport County	*v*	*Hall Road Rangers*	*0–2*
Hinckley Athletic	v	Lincoln City	1–1
Lincoln City	*v*	*Hinckley Athletic*	*4–0*
Bedworth United	v	Leicester United	
(walkover for Bedworth United – Leicester United withdrawn)			
Worksop Town	v	Birstall United	2–3
Burton Albion	v	Mansfield	0–9
Bilston Town	v	Nuneaton Borough	1–4
Redditch United	v	Stourport Swifts	2–2
Stourport Swifts	*v*	*Redditch Utd*	*0–1*
Stratford Town	v	Chasetown	1–0
VS Rugby	v	Brierley Hill Town	3–2
Rushden & Diamonds	v	Corby Town	3–0
Bromsgrove Rovers	v	Banbury United	0–0
Banbury United	*v*	*Bromsgrove Rovers*	*3–0*
Kidderminster Harriers	v	Kettering Town	1–3
Worcester City	v	Daventry Town	3–2
Bury Town	v	Wisbech Town	1–2
Hitchin Town	v	Royston Town	5–1
Braintree Town	v	Stevenage Borough	0–1
Bishop's Stortford	v	Wivenhoe Town	2–5
Potters Bar Town	v	Hemel Hempstead	5–1
Hornchurch	v	Cheshunt	2–0
Barnet	v	Wingate & Finchley	7–0
Hoddesdon Town	v	St Albans City	1–2
Collier Row	v	Basildon United	0–3
Concord Rangers	v	Waltham Abbey	
(walkover for Waltham Abbey – Concord Rangers withdrawn)			
Billericay Town	v	Tilbury	0–1
Wembley	v	Canvey Island	3–0
Brook House	v	Harefield United	1–6
Northwood	v	Kingsbury Town	7–0
Eton Manor	v	Leyton Pennant	3–4
(at Barkingside FC)			
Viking Sports	v	Enfield	0–0
Enfield	*v*	*Viking Sports*	*9–0*
Staines Town	v	Uxbridge	0–2
Bedfont	v	Beaconsfield SYCOB	1–2
Ruislip Manor	v	Windsor & Eton	1–3
Bracknell Town	v	Hillingdon Borough	3–0
Tonbridge	v	Dover Athletic	3–1
Sittingbourne	v	Herne Bay	3–0
Hastings Town	v	Chatham Town	2–0
Gillingham	v	Thamesmead Town	9–1
Tooting & Mitcham United	v	Dartford	3–3
Dartford	*v*	*Tooting & Mitcham Utd*	*1–2*
Redhill	v	Whyteleafe	2–1
Three Bridges	v	Whitstable Town	0–3
Sutton United	v	Bromley	6–0
Crawley Town	v	Banstead Athletic	1–3

Shoreham	v	Ringmer	9–0
Carshalton Athletic	v	Peacehaven & Telscombe	4–0
Southwick	v	Oakwood	6–1
Woking	v	Raynes Park Vale	4–0
Croydon	v	Leatherhead	0–1
Kingstonian	v	Merstham	2–1
Corinthian-Casuals	v	Walton & Hersham	2–5

(Walton & Hersham removed from the Competition for playing a suspended player –
Corinthian Casuals re-instated)

| Romsey Town | v | Farnborough Town | 1–4 |

(at Farnborough Town FC)

Weymouth	v	Bashley	2–1
Waterlooville	v	Eastleigh	1–2
Bridport	v	Bognor Regis Town	0–2
Abingdon Town	v	Marlow	4–2
Thame United	v	Slough Town	1–6
Thatcham Town	v	Maidenhead United	0–3
Forest Green Rovers	v	Chippenham Town	3–0
Bristol Rovers	v	Oxford City	5–0
Gloucester City	v	Yate Town	6–1
Hereford United	v	Weston-Super-Mare	5–1

First round qualifying

Darwen	v	Darlington	3–3
Darlington	*v*	*Darwen*	*5–0*
Lancaster City	v	Hartlepool United	0–6
Southport	v	Chadderton	3–0
Chester City	v	Bolton Wanderers	1–2
Hall Road Rangers	v	Port Vale	0–0
Port Vale	*v*	*Hall Road Rangers*	*2–1*
Immingham Town	v	Huddersfield Town	1–9

(at Huddersfield Town FC)

Mansfield Town	v	Birstall United	6–2
Bedworth United	v	Lincoln City	2–0
VS Rugby	v	Stratford Town	0–3
Redditch United	v	Nuneaton Borough	0–2
Worcester City	v	Kettering Town	1–5
Banbury United	v	Rushden & Diamonds	1–2
Wivenhoe Town	v	Stevenage Borough	2–0
Hitchin Town	v	Wisbech Town	7–1
St Albans City	v	Barnet	0–4
Hornchurch	v	Potters Bar Town	2–4
Wembley	v	Tilbury	4–3
Waltham Abbey	v	Basildon United	0–3
Enfield	v	Leyton Pennant	6–0
Northwood	v	Harefield United	1–9
Bracknell Town	v	Windsor & Eton	3–4
Beaconsfield SYCOB	v	Uxbridge	2–5
Gillingham	v	Hastings Town	7–0

(at Hastings Town FC)

Sittingbourne	v	Tonbridge	6–0
Sutton United	v	Whitstable Town	4–0
Redhill	v	Tooting & Mitcham United	0–4
Southwick	v	Carshalton Athletic	2–4
Shoreham	v	Banstead Athletic	2–4

Corinthian Casuals	v	Kingstonian	2–2
Kingstonian	*v*	*Corinthinan Casuals*	*3–1*
Leatherhead	v	Woking	1–2
Bognor Regis Town	v	Eastleigh	3–3
Eastleigh	*v*	*Bognor Regis Town*	*1–0*
Weymouth	v	Farnborough Town	1–6
Maidenhead United	v	Basingstoke Town	2–2
Basingstoke Town	*v*	*Maidenhead United*	*1–2*
Slough Town	v	Abingdon Town	5–1
Hereford United	v	Gloucester City	6–0
Bristol Rovers	v	Forest Green Rovers	1–2
(at Yate Town)			

Second round qualifying

Darlington	v	Hartlepool United	2–2
Hartlepool United	*v*	*Darlington*	*1–1*
(Hartlepool won on kicks from the penalty mark 3–1)			
Southport	v	Bolton Wanderers	3–2
Port Vale	v	Huddersfield Town	1–1
Huddersfield Town	*v*	*Port Vale*	*5–0*
Mansfield Town	v	Bedworth United	2–1
Stratford Town	v	Nuneaton Borough	0–1
Kettering Town	v	Rushden & Diamonds	0–7
Wivenhoe Town	v	Hitchin Town	3–2
Barnet	v	Potters Bar Town	5–0
Wembley	v	Basildon United	1–2
Enfield	v	Harefield United	2–2
Harefield United	*v*	*Enfield*	*1–3*
Windsor & Eton	v	Uxbridge	2–4
Gillingham	v	Sittingbourne	2–1
Sutton United	v	Tooting & Mitcham United	4–1
Carshalton Athletic	v	Banstead Athletic	2–4
Kingstonian	v	Woking	0–5
Eastleigh	v	Farnborough Town	3–1
Maidenhead United	v	Slough Town	0–3
Hereford United	v	Forest Green Rovers	4–2

First round proper

				Att
Rotherham United	v	Hartlepool United	1–0	
Southport	v	Burnley	1–2	232
Tranmere Rovers	v	Wrexham	2–2	455
Wrexham	*v*	*Tranmere Rovers*	*1–3*	*272*
Newcastle United	v	Blackpool	3–1	255
(at Gateshead FC)				
Grimsby Town	v	Oldham Athletic	3–4	254
Derby County	v	Scunthorpe United	3–1	120
Preston North End	v	Huddersfield Town	1–1	242
Huddersfield Town	*v*	*Preston North End*	*2–1*	*368*
Everton	v	Notts County	1–0	403
Blackburn Rovers	v	Sheffield Wednesday	2–0	1198
Doncaster Rovers	v	Hull City	1–0	119
Leeds United	v	Barnsley	3–1	892
Basildon United	v	Chelsea	2–2	258
Chelsea	*v*	*Basildon United*	*0–1*	

			Results	Att
Boreham Wood	v	Enfield	0–3	141
Wivenhoe Town	v	Northampton Town	0–1	212
Wycombe Wanderers	v	Watford	2–2	267
Watford	*v*	*Wycombe Wanderers*	*3–1*	
Shrewsbury Town	v	Cambridge United	3–0	104
Wolverhampton Wanderers	v	Birmingham City	5–6	294
Leicester City	v	Nuneaton Borough	10–0	
Walsall	v	Mansfield Town	1–1	130
Mansfield Town	*v*	*Walsall*	*0–1*	*105*
Barnet	v	Leighton Town	7–1	
Boldmere St Michaels	v	Rushden & Diamonds	4–1	
Cambridge City	v	Luton Town	1–9	
Colchester United	v	Peterborough United	2–4	125
Bournemouth AFC	v	Swansea City	1–2	
Torquay United	v	Welling United	2–0	140
Southampton	v	Oxford United	1–1	324
Oxford United	*v*	*Southampton*	*1–2*	*136*
Woking	v	Croydon Athletic	5–1	151
Sutton United	v	Eastleigh	1–2	93
Reading	v	Cardiff City	0–2	96
Slough Town	v	Hereford United	2–4	131
Gillingham	v	Fulham	1–0	144
Dulwich Hamlet	v	Exeter City	0–0	88
Exeter City	*v*	*Dulwich Hamlet*	*3–2*	*110*
Uxbridge	v	Banstead Athletic	1–2	106
Plymouth Argyle	v	Charlton Athletic	1–4	

(tie awarded to Plymouth Argyle – Charlton Athletic played an ineligible player)

Second round proper

Manchester City	v	Huddersfield Town	3–0	158
Leeds United	v	Middlesbrough	0–1	
Everton	v	Tranmere Rovers	1–3	687
Oldham Athletic	v	York City	3–2	134
Sheffield United	v	Newcastle United	2–1	244
Sunderland	v	Crewe Alexandra	4–0	
Manchester United	v	Rotherham United	3–1	1222
Derby County	v	Doncaster Rovers	3–5	85
Burnley	v	Stoke City	1–0	610
Liverpool	v	Bradford City	4–2	381
Blackburn Rovers	v	Nottingham Forest	5–1	862
Ipswich Town	v	Walsall	0–0	160
Walsall	*v*	*Ipswich Town*	*0–1*	*126*
Peterborough United	v	Norwich City	1–1	427
Norwich City	*v*	*Peterborough United*	*2–1*	*241*
Barnet	v	Watford	0–4	311
Birmingham City	v	Basildon United	5–0	88
Tottenham Hotspur	v	Shrewsbury Town	4–1	73
West Ham United	v	Aston Villa	3–0	456
Leyton Orient	v	Enfield	0–2	95
Leicester City	v	Luton Town	1–2	175
Northampton Town	v	West Bromwich Albion	0–1	
Coventry City	v	Arsenal	1–2	288
Boldmere St Michaels	v	Southend United	2–1	117
Wimbledon	v	Brighton & Hove Albion	1–0	115
Gillingham	v	Woking	1–3	113
Brentford	v	Exeter City	4–0	93

Swindon Town	v	Crystal Palace	0–2	187
Plymouth Argyle	v	Eastleigh	1–1	177
Eastleigh	*v*	*Plymouth Argyle*	*1–3*	*129*
Torquay United	v	Hereford United	0–1	183
Swansea City	v	Portsmouth	0–0	
Portsmouth	*v*	*Swansea City*	*3–1*	*97*
Millwall	v	Southampton	3–2	
Queens Park Rangers	v	Cardiff City	1–0	247
Bristol City	v	Banstead Athletic	2–1	190

Third round proper

Norwich City	v	Burnley	2–1	322
Liverpool	v	Luton Town	5–0	643
Boldmere St Michaels	v	Manchester City	0–3	1095
West Bromwich Albion	v	Sheffield United	1–2	
Blackburn Rovers	v	Tranmere Rovers	0–2	1800
Doncaster Rovers	v	Oldham Athletic	0–5	234
Sunderland	v	Manchester United	1–4	
Ipswich Town	v	Middlesbrough	2–0	
Queens Park Rangers	v	Brentford	2–0	
Crystal Palace	v	Bristol City	7–0	104
Portsmouth	v	Watford	1–2	81
Hereford United	v	Enfield	1–1	
Enfield	*v*	*Hereford United*	*0–2*	
Plymouth Argyle	v	Tottenham Hotspur	2–1	
(at Saltash United FC)				
Woking	v	West Ham United	0–3	742
Arsenal	v	Wimbledon	3–4	422
Millwall	v	Birmingham City	5–2	168

Fourth round proper

Plymouth Argyle	v	Crystal Palace	0–2	1301
Hereford United	v	Manchester City	1–2	
Oldham Athletic	v	Millwall	2–0	282
Liverpool	v	Sheffield United	3–2	562
Manchester United	v	Norwich City	1–0	2545
Queens Park Rangers	v	West Ham United	1–4	534
Wimbledon	v	Ipswich Town	2–2	
(first match abandoned after 55 mins, 0–0)				
Ipswich Town	*v*	*Wimbledon*	*1–2*	*350*
Tranmere Rovers	v	Watford	1–1	543
Watford	*v*	*Tranmere Rovers*	*4–1*	*378*

Fifth round proper

Liverpool	v	Manchester United	3–2	4433
Oldham Athletic	v	West Ham United	1–2	920
Crystal Palace	v	Watford	2–0	314
Manchester City	v	Wimbledon	1–3	974

Semi-finals

1st Leg

Liverpool	v	Crystal Palace	4–2	1406
West Ham United	v	Wimbledon	2–1	6179

2nd Leg

Crystal Palace	v	Liverpool	3–3	1818
Wimbledon	v	West Ham United	2–3	2010

Liverpool won 7–5 on aggregate
West Ham United won 5–3 on aggregate

Final

1st Leg – 30 April 1996

West Ham United	v	Liverpool	0–2	15386

2nd Leg – 17 May 1996

Liverpool	v	West Ham United	2–1	20600

Liverpool won 4–1 on aggregate

35 ● FA COUNTY YOUTH CUP 1995–96

First round

(Replays in italics)

Cumberland	v	Lincolnshire	2–1
Nottinghamshire	v	Lancashire	1–3
Westmorland	v	East Riding	2–4
Sheffield & Hallamshire	v	Birmingham	1–3
Cambridgeshire	v	Herefordshire	1–1
Herefordshire	*v*	*Cambridgeshire*	*3–2*
Northamptonshire	v	Staffordshire	2–1
Berks & Bucks	v	London	2–0
Huntingdonshire	v	Oxfordshire	0–2
Sussex	v	Army	3–0
Kent	v	Bedfordshire	1–4
Gloucestershire	v	Dorset	1–0
Devon	v	Wiltshire	3–2

20 Counties receiving byes to the Second round

Cornwall	Essex	Liverpool	North Riding	Surrey
Cheshire	Hampshire	Manchester	Norfolk	Suffolk
Derbyshire	Hertfordshire	Middlesex	Somerset & Avon (South)	West Riding
Durham	Leicestershire & Rutland	Northumberland	Shropshire	Worcestershire

Second round

Northumberland	v	West Riding	4–0
Liverpool	v	Manchester	6–0
Cumberland	v	Durham	0–4
Lancashire	v	Shropshire	4–1
East Riding	v	Cheshire	2–2
Cheshire	*v*	*East Riding*	*1–0*
Birmingham	v	North Riding	4–1
Herefordshire	v	Derbyshire	4–2
Northamptonshire	v	Worcestershire	1–1
Worcestershire	*v*	*Northamptonshire*	*0–1*
Berks & Bucks	v	Leicestershire & Rutland	5–0
Essex	v	Norfolk	6–2
Oxfordshire	v	Surrey	1–2
Sussex	v	Hertfordshire	3–3
Hertfordshire	*v*	*Sussex*	*1–2*
Bedfordshire	v	Suffolk	2–1
Gloucestershire	v	Middlesex	2–2 (abandoned)
Middlesex	*v*	*Gloucestershire*	*0–4*
Devon	v	Hampshire	2–1
Cornwall	v	Somerset	1–2

Third round

Durham	v	Herefordshire	3–1
Cheshire	v	Northumberland	3–3

(Replays in italics)

Results

Northumberland	v	*Cheshire*	*0–2*
Liverpool	v	Lancashire	2–1
Birmingham	v	Northamptonshire	3–2
Surrey	v	Devon	2–1
Bedfordshire	v	Berks & Bucks	1–2
Essex	v	Sussex	5–1
Gloucestershire	v	Somerset	1–1
Somerset	v	*Gloucestershire*	*1–4*

Fourth round

Durham	v	Berks & Bucks	3–0
Birmingham	v	Essex	4–3
Surrey	v	Liverpool	3–2
Gloucestershire	v	Cheshire	2–1

Semi-finals

Durham	v	Surrey	2–1
Gloucestershire	v	Birmingham	7–0

Final – 27 April 1996

Gloucestershire	v	Durham	0–1
(at Cheltenham Town FC)			

36 ● YOUTH INTERNATIONAL MATCHES 1995–96

Date	Venue				Result	

Under-18

Date	Venue				Result	
16.11.95	Rushden	England	v	Latvia	2–0	*
18.11.95	Kettering	England	v	Sweden	6–2	*
28.2.96	Meaux	France	v	England	1–1	
19.3.96	Motherwell	Scotland	v	England	0–3	*
23.4.96	Yeovil	England	v	Scotland	3–0	*

* UEFA Championship – Qualifying Competition

Under-16

Date	Venue				Result	
23.10.95	Osteras	Belgium	v	England	0–1	*
27.10.95	Osteras	Sweden	v	England	0–5	*
3.2.96	Lilleshall	England	v	Denmark	4–0	
20.2.96	Lilleshall	England	v	Rep. of Ireland	2–1	
9.3.96	Menorca	Spain	v	England	2–0	
29.4.96	Gmund	Slovakia	v	England	0–2	†
1.5.96	Schrems	Turkey	v	England	1–2	†
3.5.96	Retz	Israel	v	England	2–1	†
6.5.96	Baden	Greece	v	England	1–0	†

* UEFA Championship – Qualifying Competition
† UEFA Championship – Finals

Under-18

	Latvia	Sweden	France	Scotland	Scotland
D. Lucas (Preston North End)	1	1		1	1
J. Curtis (Manchester United)	2	2	2	5	5
J. Crowe (Arsenal)	3	3	3	3	3
D. Thompson (Liverpool)	4	4			
R. Wallwork (Manchester United)	5	5	5	2	2
M. Broomes (Blackburn Rovers)	6	6			
P. Shepherd (Leeds United)	7	7	7	4	4
S. Clemence (Tottenham Hotspur)	8	8	8	8	11
M. Branch (Everton)	9	9	9	9	9
E. Heskey (Leicester City)	10	10		10	10
N. Quashie (Queens Park Rangers)	11				
A. Ducros (Coventry City)	4*		10	9*	10*
L. Piper (Wimbledon)	7*	11	11	11	
P. Brayson (Newcastle United)	11*		9*		
J. Dungey (Plymouth Argyle)			1		
J. Blunt (Leeds United)			4		8
M. Jackson (Leeds United)			6	6	6
R. Ferdinand (West Ham United)			5*		
J. Cassidy (Liverpool)			7*	6*	
P. Barrett (Newcastle United)				7	7
F. Lampard (West Ham United)					11*

Under-16

	Belgium	Sweden	Denmark	Rep. of Ireland	Spain	Slovakia	Turkey	Israel	Greece
G. Stewart (Blackburn Rovers)	1	1	1		1	1	1	1	1
R. Cooper (Nottm Forest)	2	2	2		2	2	2	2	2
M. Ball (Everton)	3	3	3	11	11	3	3	3	3
S. Haslam (Sheffield Wednesday)	4	4	4	2	4	4	4	4	4
W. Brown (Man United)	5	5	5*	9	5	5	5	5	5
J. Day (Arsenal)	6	6	6	6*	7*	6	6	6	6
A. Quinn (Sheffield Wednesday)	7	7	7		7	7	7	7	7
K. Lunt (Crewe Alexandra)	8	8	8*		6	8	8	8	8
M. Jones (Aston Villa)	9	9	9		10	9	9		9
M. Owen (Liverpool)	10	10	10			10	10	9	10
D. Way (Norwich City)	11		11	7*		11	11		11
C. Woodcock (Newcastle United)	11*	11	8						
M. Stevenson (Notts County)		7*							
R. Hulbert (Everton)		10*		6					
A. Fenton (Man City)		11*		5	3			11	7*
K. Owen (Queens Park Rangers)			5	4	4*				
J. Bray (Wolverhampton Wanderers)			1*		1*				
S. Gerrard (Liverpool)			2*	8	8		2*		
M. Goodlad (Nottm Forest)				1					
N. Fenton (Manchester City)				3					
W. Purser (Queens Park Rangers)				7	3*				
P. Jevons (Everton)				10	9		9*	10	11*
J. Harley (Chelsea)				8*					
B. Marshall (Notts County)					8*		11*		6*

substitute

38 ● EUROPEAN UNDER-16 CHAMPIONSHIP FINALS

AUSTRIA – 29th April to 11th May 1996

First Stage

Date	Venue					Result

Group A

Date	Venue					Result
29.4.96	St Polten	Rep. of Ireland	v	Austria		1–0
29.4.96	Siemdorf	Portugal	v	Poland		3–0
1.5.96	Herzogenburg	Austria	v	Poland		0–0
1.5.96	Atzenbrugg	Rep. of Ireland	v	Portugal		0–2
3.5.96	Wurmla	Poland	v	Rep. of Ireland		0–1
3.5.96	Ziersdorf	Austria	v	Portugal		2–2

Portugal and Republic of Ireland qualified for quarter-finals

Group B

29.4.96	Bad Voslau	Romania	v	Ukraine		0–1
29.4.96	Neunkirchen	Greece	v	Germany		2–1
1.5.96	Scheiblingkirchen	Romania	v	Greece		0–1
1.5.96	Kirchschlag	Ukraine	v	Germany		1–6
3.5.96	Gloggnitz	Germany	v	Romania		4–1
3.5.96	Kottingbrunn	Ukraine	v	Greece		1–1

Greece and Germany qualified for quarter-finals

Group C

29.4.96	Scheibbs	France	v	Croatia		2–0
29.4.96	Pochlam	Spain	v	Switzerland		4–1
1.5.96	Gottsdorf	France	v	Spain		3–0
1.5.96	Ardagger	Croatia	v	Switzerland		2–1
3.5.96	Purgstall	Switzerland	v	France		0–1
3.5.96	Ybbs	Croatia	v	Spain		1–0

France and Croatia qualified for quarter-finals

Group D

29.4.96	Gmund	England	v	Slovakia		2–0
29.4.96	Horn	Turkey	v	Israel		3–0
1.5.96	Schrems	England	v	Turkey		2–1
1.5.96	Zellerndorf	Slovakia	v	Israel		0–2
3.5.96	Retz	Israel	v	England		2–1
3.5.96	Zwettl	Slovakia	v	Turkey		2–1

Israel and England qualified for quarter-finals

Quarter-Finals

6.5.96	Krems	Portugal	v	Croatia	5–1
6.5.96	Amstetten	France	v	Rep. of Ireland	0–0*
6.5.96	Baden	Greece	v	England	1–0
6.5.96	Stockerau	Israel	v	Germany	3–2

Semi-Finals

8.5.96	Tulln	Portugal	v	Greece	3–0
8.5.96	Wiener Neustadt	France	v	Israel	1–0

Third/Fourth Place

11.5.96	Wien	Greece	v	Israel	2–3

Final

11.5.96	Wien	Portugal	v	France	1–0

* France won on penalty-kicks.

The England Under-16 squad in Sweden.

39 ● YOUTH INTERNATIONAL MATCHES 1947-1996

WYC = World Youth Championship
IYT = International Youth Tournament
* Qualifying Competition
† Professionals
§ Abandoned

v Algeria

†1984	22/4	Cannes	W	3–0	

v Argentina

†1981	5/10	Sydney	D	1–1	WYC

v Australia

†1981	8/10	Sydney	D	1–1	WYC
†1993	20/3	Sydney	W	2–1	WYC

v Austria

1949	19/4	Zeist	W	4–2	IYT
1952	17/4	Barcelona	D	5–5	IYT
1957	16/4	Barcelona	L	0–3	IYT
1958	4/3	Highbury	W	3–2	
1958	1/6	Graz	W	4–3	
1960	20/4	Vienna	L	0–1	IYT
†1964	1/4	Rotterdam	W	2–1	IYT
†1980	6/9	Pazin	L	0–1	
†1981	29/5	Bonn	W	7–0	IYT
†1981	3/9	Umag	W	3–0	
†1984	6/9	Izola	D	2–2	

v Belgium

1948	16/4	West Ham	W	3–1	IYT
1951	22/3	Cannes	D	1–1	IYT
1953	31/3	Brussels	W	2–0	IYT
§1956	7/11	Brussels	W	3–2	
1957	13/11	Sheffield	W	2–0	
†1965	15/4	Ludwigshafen	W	3–0	IYT
1969	11/3	West Ham	W	1–0	IYT*
†1969	26/3	Waregem	W	2–0	IYT
1972	13/5	Palma	D	0–0	IYT*
†1973	4/6	Viareggio	D	0–0	IYT
†1977	19/5	Lokeren	W	1–0	IYT
†1979	17/1	Brussels	W	4–0	
†1980	8/9	Labia	W	6–1	
†1983	13/4	Birmingham	D	1–1	
†1988	20/5	Chatel	D	0–0	
†1990	24/7	Nyiregyhaza	D	1–1	IYT
†1990	16/10	Sunderland	D	0–0	IYT*
†1991	16/10	Eernegem	L	0–1	IYT*

v Brazil

†1986	29/3	Cannes	D	0–0	
†1986	13/5	Peking	L	1–2	
†1987	2/6	Niteroi	L	0–2	

v Bulgaria

1956	28/3	Salgotarjan	L	1–2	IYT
1960	16/4	Graz	L	0–1	IYT
1962	24/4	Ploesti	D	0–0	IYT
†1968	7/4	Nimes	D	0–0	IYT
†1969	26/3	Waregem	W	2–0	IYT
†1972	13/5	Palma	D	0–0	IYT
†1979	31/5	Vienna	L	0–1	IYT

v Cameroon

†1981	3/10	Sydney	W	2–0	WYC
†1985	1/6	Toulon	W	1–0	

v China

†1983	31/3	Cannes	W	5–1	
†1985	26/8	Baku	L	0–2	WYC
†1986	5/5	Peking	W	1–0	

v Czechoslovakia

1955	7/4	Lucca	L	0–1	IYT
†1966	21/5	Rijeka	L	2–3	IYT
1969	20/5	Leipzig	W	3–1	IYT
1979	24/5	Bischofshofen	W	3–0	IYT
†1979	8/9	Pula	L	1–2	
†1982	11/4	Cannes	L	0–1	
†1983	20/5	Highbury	D	1–1	IYT
†1989	26/4	Bystrica	L	0–1	IYT*
†1989	14/11	Portsmouth	W	1–0	IYT*
†1990	25/4	Wembley	D	1–1	

v Denmark

†1955	1/10	Plymouth	W	9–2	
1956	20/5	Esbjerg	W	2–1	
†1979	31/10	Esbjerg	W	3–1	IYT*
1980	26/3	Coventry	W	4–0	IYT*
†1982	15/7	Stjordal	W	5–2	
†1983	16/7	Holbeck	L	0–1	
†1987	16/2	Manchester	W	2–1	
†1990	28/3	Wembley	D	0–0	
†1991	6/2	Oxford	L	1–5	
†1993	30/3	Stoke	W	4–2	
†1993	7/7	Nykobing	W	5–0	
†1995	22/2	Walsall	L	5–6	

v Egypt

†1981	11/10	Sydney	W	4–2	WYC
†1992	13/10	Bournemouth	W	2–1	

v Finland

†1975	19/5	Berne	D	1–1	IYT

v France

1957	24/3	Fontainebleau	W	1–0	
1958	22/3	Eastbourne	L	0–1	
†1966	23/5	Rijeka	L	1–2	IYT
†1967	11/5	Istanbul	W	2–0	IYT
†1968	25/1	Paris	L	0–1	
1978	8/2	C Palace	W	3–1	IYT*
1978	1/3	Paris	D	0–0	IYT*
†1979	2/6	Vienna	D	0–0	IYT
†1982	12/4	Cannes	L	0–1	
†1983	2/4	Cannes	L	0–2	
1984	1/3	Watford	W	4–0	
†1984	23/4	Cannes	L	1–2	
†1985	7/6	Toulon	L	1–3	
†1986	31/3	Cannes	L	1–2	
†1986	11/5	Peking	D	1–1	
†1988	22/5	Monthey	L	1–2	
†1988	15/11	Bradford	D	1–1	IYT*
†1989	11/10	Martigues	D	0–0	IYT*
†1990	22/5	Wembley	L	1–3	
†1992	7/10	Boulogne	L	0–2	
1993	18/7	Stoke	W	2–0	IYT
†1993	27/10	Besançon	L	0–2	IYT*
†1993	16/11	Yeovil	D	3–3	IYT*
†1994	6/9	Reading	L	2–3	
†1996	28/2	Meaux	D	1–1	

v East Germany

1958	7/4	Neunkirchen	W	1–0	IYT
1959	8/3	Zwickau	L	3–4	
1960	2/4	Portsmouth	D	1–1	
†1965	25/4	Essen	L	2–3	IYT
†1969	22/5	Magdeburg	L	0–4	IYT
†1973	10/6	Florence	W	3–2	IYT
†1984	25/5	Moscow	D	1–1	IYT
†1988	21/5	Monthey	W	1–0	

v West Germany

1953	4/4	Boom	W	3–1	IYT
1954	15/4	Gelsenkirchen	D	2–2	IYT
1956	1/4	Sztalinvaros	W	2–1	IYT
1957	31/3	Oberhausen	W	4–1	
1958	12/3	Bolton	L	1–2	
1961	12/3	Flensberg	L	0–2	
†1962	31/3	Northampton	W	1–0	
†1967	14/2	Mönchengladbach	W	1–0	
†1972	22/5	Barcelona	W	2–0	IYT
†1975	25/1	Las Palmas	W	4–2	
†1976	14/11	Monte Carlo	D	1–1	
†1979	28/5	Salzburg	W	2–0	IYT
†1979	1/9	Pula	D	1–1	
†1983	5/9	Pazin	W	2–0	

v Ghana

1993	17/3	Sydney	L	1–2	WYC

v Greece

1957	18/4	Barcelona	L	2–3	IYT
1959	2/4	Dimitrovo	W	4–0	IYT
†1977	23/5	Beveren	D	1–1	IYT
†1983	28/6	Puspokladany	W	1–0	
†1988	26/10	Tranmere	W	5–0	IYT*
†1989	8/3	Xanthi	W	5–0	IYT*

v Holland

1948	17/4	Tottenham	W	3–2	IYT
1951	26/3	Cannes	W	2–1	IYT
†1954	21/11	Arnhem	L	2–3	
†1955	5/11	Norwich	W	3–1	
1957	2/3	Brentford	D	5–5	
1957	14/4	Barcelona	L	1–2	IYT
1957	2/10	Amsterdam	W	3–2	
1961	9/3	Utrecht	L	0–1	
†1962	31/1	Brighton	W	4–0	
†1962	22/4	Ploesti	L	0–3	IYT
†1963	13/4	Wimbledon	W	5–0	IYT
1968	9/4	Nimes	W	1–0	IYT
†1974	13/2	West Brom	D	1–1	IYT*
†1974	27/2	The Hague	W	1–0	IYT*
†1980	23/5	Halle	W	1–0	IYT*
†1982	9/4	Cannes	W	1–0	
†1985	7/4	Cannes	L	1–3	
†1987	1/8	Wembley	W	3–1	
†1993	20/7	Walsall	W	4–1	IYT

v Hungary

1954	11/4	Düsseldorf	L	1–3	IYT
1956	31/3	Tatabanya	L	2–4	IYT
1956	23/10	Tottenham	W	2–1	
†1956	25/10	Sunderland	W	2–1	
†1965	21/4	Wuppertal	W	5–0	IYT
†1975	16/5	Olten	W	3–1	IYT
†1977	16/10	Las Palmas	W	3–0	IYT
†1979	5/9	Pula	W	2–0	
†1980	11/9	Pula	L	1–2	
†1981	7/9	Porec	W	4–0	
†1983	29/7	Debrecen	L	1–2	
†1983	3/9	Umag	W	3–2	
†1986	30/3	Cannes	W	2–0	
†1995	29/3	Budapest	W	1–0	IYT*
†1995	25/4	Walsall	L	0–2	IYT*

v Iceland

†1973	31/5	Viareggio	W	2–0	IYT
†1977	21/5	Turnhout	D	0–0	IYT
†1983	7/9	Reykjavik	W	3–0	IYT*
1983	19/9	Blackburn	W	4–0	IYT*
1983	12/10	Reykjavik	W	3–0	
†1983	1/11	Crystal Palace	W	3–0	

†1984	16/10	Manchester	W	5–3	IYT*
†1985	11/9	Reykjavik	W	5–0	IYT*
†1990	12/9	Reykjavik	W	3–2	IYT*
†1991	12/9	Crystal Palace	W	2–1	IYT*

v Israel

†1962	20/5	Tel Aviv	W	3–1	
†1962	22/5	Haifa	L	1–2	

v Italy

1958	13/4	Luxembourg	L	0–1	IYT
1959	25/3	Sofia	L	1–3	IYT
1961	4/4	Braga	L	2–3	IYT
†1965	23/4	Marl-Huels	W	3–1	IYT
†1966	25/5	Rijeka	D	1–1	IYT
†1967	5/5	Izmir	W	1–0	IYT
†1973	14/2	Cava Dei Tirreni	L	0–1	
†1973	14/3	Highbury	W	1–0	
†1973	7/6	Viareggio	W	1–0	IYT
†1978	19/11	Monte Carlo	L	1–2	
†1979	28/2	Rome	W	1–0	IYT*
†1979	4/4	Birmingham	W	2–0	IYT*
†1983	22/5	Watford	D	1–1	IYT
†1984	20/4	Cannes	W	1–0	
†1985	5/4	Cannes	D	2–2	

v Latvia

†1994	17/11	Reading	D	0–0	IYT*
†1995	16/11	Rushden	W	2–0	IYT*

v Luxembourg

1950	25/5	Vienna	L	1–2	IYT
1954	17/4	Bad Neuenahr	L	0–2	IYT
1957	2/2	West Ham	W	7–1	
1957	17/11	Luxembourg	W	3–0	
1958	9/4	Esch sur Alzette	W	5–0	IYT
†1984	29/5	Moscow	W	2–0	IYT

v Malta

†1969	18/5	Wolfen	W	6–0	IYT
†1979	26/5	Salzburg	W	3–0	IYT

v Mexico

†1984	18/4	Cannes	W	4–0	
†1985	5/6	Toulon	W	2–0	
†1985	29/8	Baku	L	0–1	WYC
†1991	27/3	Port of Spain	L	1–3	
†1993	14/3	Melbourne	D	0–0	WYC

v Northern Ireland

1948	15/5	Belfast	D	2–2	
1949	18/4	Haarlem	D	3–3	IYT
1949	14/5	Hull	W	4–2	
1950	6/5	Belfast	L	0–1	
1951	5/5	Liverpool	W	5–2	
1952	19/4	Belfast	L	0–2	
1953	11/4	Wolverhampton	D	0–0	
1954	10/4	Bruehl	W	5–0	IYT
1954	8/5	Newtownards	D	2–2	
1955	14/5	Watford	W	3–0	
1956	12/5	Belfast	D	0–1	
1957	11/5	Leyton	W	6–2	
1958	10/5	Bangor	L	2–4	
1959	9/5	Liverpool	W	5–0	
1960	14/5	Belfast	W	5–2	
1961	13/5	Manchester	W	2–0	
1962	12/5	Londonderry	L	1–2	
†1963	23/4	Wembley	W	4–0	IYT
1963	11/5	Oldham	D	1–1	
1964	25/1	Belfast	W	3–1	
1965	22/1	Birkenhead	L	2–3	
1966	26/2	Belfast	W	4–0	
1967	25/2	Stockport	W	3–0	
1968	23/2	Belfast	L	0–2	
1969	28/2	Birkenhead	L	0–2	
1970	28/2	Lurgan	L	1–3	
1971	6/3	Blackpool	D	1–1	IYT
1972	11/3	Chester	D	1–1	
1972	17/5	Sabadell	W	4–0	IYT
1973	24/3	Wellington	W	3–0	
1974	19/4	Birkenhead	L	1–2	
†1975	13/5	Kriens	W	3–0	IYT
†1980	16/5	Arnstadt	W	1–0	IYT
†1981	11/2	Walsall	W	1–0	IYT*
†1981	11/3	Belfast	W	3–0	IYT*

v Norway

†1982	13/7	Levanger	L	1–4	
†1983	14/7	Korsor	W	1–0	
1992	24/7	Amberg	D	1–1	
†1994	24/7	Larvik	D	3–3	
†1994	26/7	Vikersund	W	3–2	

v Paraguay

†1985	24/8	Baku	D	2–2	WYC

v Poland

1960	18/4	Graz	W	4–2	IYT
†1964	26/3	Breda	D	1–1	IYT
†1971	26/5	Presov	D	0–0	IYT
†1972	20/5	Valencia	W	1–0	IYT
†1975	21/1	Las Palmas	D	1–1	
1978	9/5	Chorzow	L	0–2	IYT
†1979	3/9	Porec	L	0–1	
†1980	25/5	Leipzig	W	2–1	IYT
†1982	17/7	Steinkver	W	3–2	
†1983	12/7	Stagelse	W	1–0	
†1990	15/5	Wembley	W	3–0	
†1992	20/7	Regensburg	W	6–1	IYT

v Portugal

1954	18/4	Bonn	L	0–2	IYT
1961	2/4	Lisbon	L	0–4	IYT
†1964	3/4	The Hague	W	4–0	IYT
†1971	30/5	Prague	W	3–0	IYT

†1978	13/11	Monte Carlo	W	2–0	
†1980	18/5	Rosslau	D	1–1	IYT
†1982	7/4	Cannes	W	3–0	
†1992	22/7	Schweinfurt	D	1–1	IYT

v Qatar

†1981	14/10	Sydney	L	1–2	WYC
†1983	4/4	Cannes	D	1–1	

v Republic of Ireland

1953	5/4	Leuven	W	2–0	IYT
†1964	30/3	Middleburg	W	6–0	IYT
†1968	7/2	Dublin	D	0–0	IYT*
†1968	28/2	Portsmouth	W	4–1	IYT*
†1970	14/1	Dublin	W	4–1	IYT*
†1970	4/2	Luton	W	10–0	IYT*
†1975	9/5	Brunnen	W	1–0	IYT
†1985	26/2	Dublin	L	0–1	IYT*
†1986	25/2	Leeds	W	2–0	IYT*
†1988	17/2	Stoke	W	2–0	
†1988	20/9	Dublin	W	2–0	
†1993	24/8	Port Vale	D	2–2	

v Romania

1957	15/10	Tottenham	W	4–2	
1958	11/4	Luxembourg	W	1–0	IYT
1959	31/3	Pazardijc	L	1–2	IYT
†1963	15/4	Highbury	W	3–0	IYT
†1981	17/10	Adelaide	L	0–1	WYC
†1993	7/9	Port Vale	D	1–1	IYT*
†1993	13/10	Bucharest	D	1–1	IYT*

v Saar

1954	13/4	Dortmund	D	1–0	IYT
1955	9/4	Prato	W	3–1	IYT

v Scotland

1947	25/10	Doncaster	W	4–2	
1948	30/10	Aberdeen	L	1–3	
1949	21/4	Utrecht	L	0–1	IYT
1950	4/2	Carlisle	W	7–1	
1951	3/2	Kilmarnock	W	6–1	
1952	15/3	Sunderland	W	3–1	
1953	7/2	Glasgow	W	4–3	
1954	6/2	Middlesbrough	W	2–1	
1955	5/3	Kilmarnock	L	3–4	
1956	3/3	Preston	D	2–2	
1957	9/3	Aberdeen	W	3–1	
1958	1/3	Hull	W	2–0	
1959	28/2	Aberdeen	D	1–1	
1960	27/2	Newcastle	D	1–1	
1961	25/2	Elgin	W	3–2	
1962	24/2	Peterborough	W	4–2	
†1963	19/4	White City	W	1–0	IYT
1963	18/5	Dumfries	W	3–1	

1964	22/2	Middlesbrough	D	1–1	
1965	27/2	Inverness	L	1–2	
1966	5/2	Hereford	W	5–3	
1967	4/2	Aberdeen	L	0–1	
†1967	1/3	Southampton	W	1–0	IYT*
†1967	15/3	Dundee	D	0–0	IYT*
1968	3/2	Walsall	L	0–5	
1969	1/2	Stranraer	D	1–1	
1970	31/1	Derby	L	1–2	
1971	30/1	Greenock	L	1–2	
1972	29/1	Bournemouth	W	2–0	
1973	20/1	Kilmarnock	W	3–2	
1974	26/1	Brighton	D	2–2	
†1981	27/5	Aachen	L	0–1	IYT
†1982	23/2	Glasgow	L	0–1	IYT*
†1982	23/3	Coventry	D	2–2	IYT*
†1983	15/5	Birmingham	W	4–2	IYT
1983	5/10	Middlesbrough	W	3–1	IYT
1983	19/10	Motherwell	W	4–0	
†1984	27/11	Fulham	L	0–1	IYT*
1985	8/4	Cannes	W	1–0	IYT*
†1986	25/3	Aberdeen	L	1–4	IYT*
†1996	19/3	Motherwell	W	3–0	IYT*
†1996	23/4	Yeovil	W	3–0	IYT*

v Slovenia

†1994	13/11	High Wycombe	W	3–0	IYT*

v South Korea

†1993	7/3	Melbourne	D	1–1	WYC

v Spain

1952	15/4	Barcelona	L	1–4	IYT
1957	26/9	Birmingham	D	4–4	
1958	5/4	Saarbrücken	D	2–2	IYT
†1958	8/10	Madrid	W	4–2	
1961	30/3	Lisbon	D	0–0	IYT
†1964	27/2	Murcia	W	2–1	
†1964	5/4	Amsterdam	W	4–0	IYT
†1965	17/4	Heilbronn	D	0–0	IYT
1966	30/3	Swindon	W	3–0	
†1967	7/5	Manisa	W	2–1	IYT
†1971	31/3	Pamplona	L	2–3	
†1971	20/4	Luton	D	1–1	
†1972	9/2	Alicante	D	0–0	
†1972	15/3	Sheffield	W	4–1	IYT*
†1975	25/2	Bristol	D	1–1	IYT*
†1975	18/3	Madrid	W	1–0	IYT*
†1976	12/11	Monte Carlo	W	3–0	
†1978	7/5	Bukowas	W	1–0	IYT
†1978	17/11	Monte Carlo	D	1–1	
†1981	25/5	Siegen	L	1–2	IYT
†1983	13/5	Stoke	W	1–0	IYT
†1990	29/7	Gyula	L	0–1	IYT
†1991	25/5	Wembley	D	1–1	
†1991	15/6	Faro	L	0–1	WYC
†1993	17/2	Alicante	D	1–1	
†1993	22/7	Walsall	W	5–1	IYT

v Sweden

†1971	24/5	Poprad	W	1–0	IYT
†1981	5/9	Pazin	W	3–2	
†1984	10/9	Rovinj	D	1–1	
†1986	10/11	West Brom	D	3–3	
†1995	18/11	Kettering	W	6–2	IYT*

v Switzerland

1950	26/5	Stockerau	W	2–1	IYT
1951	27/3	Nice	W	3–1	IYT
1952	13/4	Barcelona	W	4–0	IYT
1955	11/4	Florence	D	0–0	IYT
1956	11/3	Schaffhausen	W	2–0	
1956	13/10	Brighton	D	2–2	
1958	26/5	Zurich	W	3–0	
†1960	8/10	Leyton	W	4–3	
1962	22/11	Coventry	W	1–0	
†1963	21/3	Bienne	W	7–1	
†1973	2/6	Forte Dei Marmi	W	2–0	IYT
†1975	11/5	Buochs	W	4–0	IYT
†1980	4/9	Rovinj	W	3–0	
†1982	6/9	Porec	W	2–0	
†1983	26/7	Hajduboszormeny	W	4–0	
†1983	1/9	Porec	W	4–2	
†1988	19/5	Sion	W	2–0	
†1992	17/11	Port Vale	W	7–2	

v Syria

†1991	18/6	Faro	D	3–3	WYC

v Thailand

†1986	7/5	Peking	L	1–2	

v Trinidad & Tobago

†1991	25/3	Port of Spain	W	4–0	

v Turkey

1959	29/3	Dimitrovo	D	1–1	IYT
†1978	5/5	Wodzislaw	D	1–1	IYT
†1992	17/11	High Wycombe	W	2–1	
†1993	11/3	Melbourne	W	1–0	WYC
†1993	25/7	Nottingham	W	1–0	IYT

v Uruguay

†1977	9/10	Las Palmas	D	1–1	
†1987	10/6	Montevideo	D	2–2	
†1991	20/6	Faro	D	0–0	WYC

v USA

†1993	9/3	Melbourne	W	1–0	WYC

v USSR

†1963	17/4	Tottenham	W	2–0	IYT
†1967	13/5	Istanbul	L	0–1	IYT
†1968	11/4	Nimes	D	1–1	IYT
†1971	28/5	Prague	D	1–1	IYT
†1978	10/10	Las Palmas	W	1–0	
†1982	4/9	Umag	W	1–0	
†1983	29/3	Cannes	D	0–0	
†1983	17/5	Aston Villa	L	0–2	IYT
1984	3/5	Ludwigsburg	L	0–2	
†1984	27/5	Moscow	D	1–1	IYT
†1984	8/9	Porec	W	1–0	
†1985	3/4	Cannes	W	2–1	
†1985	3/6	Toulon	L	0–2	
†1990	26/7	Debrecen	L	1–3	IYT

v Wales

1948	28/2	High Wycombe	W	4–3	
1948	15/4	London	W	4–0	
1949	26/2	Swansea	D	0–0	
1950	25/2	Worcester	W	1–0	
1951	17/2	Wrexham	D	1–1	
1952	23/2	Plymouth	W	6–0	
1953	21/2	Swansea	W	4–2	
1954	20/2	Derby	W	2–1	
1955	19/2	Milford Haven	W	7–2	
1956	18/2	Shrewsbury	W	5–1	
1957	9/2	Cardiff	W	7–1	
1958	15/2	Reading	W	8–2	
1959	14/2	Portmadoc	W	3–0	
1960	19/3	Canterbury	D	1–1	
1961	18/3	Newtown	W	4–0	
1962	17/3	Swindon	W	4–0	
1963	16/3	Haverfordwest	W	1–0	
1964	14/3	Leeds	W	2–1	
1965	20/3	Newport	D	2–2	
1966	19/3	Northampton	W	4–1	
1967	18/3	Cwmbran	D	3–3	
1968	16/3	Watford	L	2–3	
1969	15/3	Haverfordwest	W	3–1	
†1970	25/2	Newport	D	0–0	IYT*
†1970	18/3	Leyton	L	1–2	
1970	20/4	Reading	D	0–0	
1971	20/2	Aberystwyth	L	1–2	
1972	19/2	Swindon	W	4–0	
1973	24/2	Portmadoc	W	4–1	
†1974	9/1	West Brom	W	1–0	IYT*
1974	2/3	Shrewsbury	W	2–1	
†1974	13/3	Cardiff	L	0–1	IYT*
†1976	11/2	Cardiff	W	1–0	IYT*
†1976	3/3	Manchester	L	2–3	IYT*
†1977	9/3	West Brom	W	1–0	IYT*
†1977	23/3	Cardiff	D	1–1	IYT*
†1991	30/4	Wrexham	W	1–0	IYT*
†1991	22/5	Yeovil	W	3–0	IYT*

v Yugoslavia

1953	2/4	Liège	D	1–1	IYT
1958	4/2	Chelsea	D	2–2	
1962	20/4	Ploesti	L	0–5	IYT
†1967	9/5	Izmir	D	1–1	IYT
†1971	22/5	Bardejor	W	1–0	IYT
†1972	17/5	Barcelona	W	1–0	IYT
†1976	16/11	Monte Carlo	L	0–3	

1978	15/11	Monte Carlo	D	1–1		†1983	25/7	Debrecen	D	4–4
†1980	20/5	Altenberg	W	2–0	IYT	†1983	8/9	Pula	D	2–2
†1981	10/9	Pula	W	5–0		1984	5/5	Boblingen	W	1–0
†1982	9/9	Pula	W	1–0		†1984	12/9	Buje	L	1–4

40 ● FA PREMIER LEAGUE AND FOOTBALL LEAGUE CHAMPIONS 1888–1996

FA Premier League Champions 1992–96

Season	Winners	Pts	Max	Season	Winners	Pts	Max
1992–93	Manchester United	84	126	1994–95	Blackburn Rovers	89	126
1993–94	Manchester United	92	126	1995–96	Manchester United	82	114

Football League Champions 1888–1992

First Division 1888–1992

Season	Winners	Pts	Max	Season	Winners	Pts	Max
1888–89	Preston North End	40	44	1926–27	Newcastle United	56	84
1889–90	Preston North End	33	44	1927–28	Everton	53	84
1890–91	Everton	29	44	1928–29	Sheffield Wednesday	52	84
1891–92	Sunderland	42	52	1929–30	Sheffield Wednesday	60	84
1892–93	Sunderland	48	60	1930–31	Arsenal	66	84
1893–94	Aston Villa	44	60	1931–32	Everton	56	84
1894–95	Sunderland	47	60	1932–33	Arsenal	58	84
1895–96	Aston Villa	45	60	1933–34	Arsenal	59	84
1896–97	Aston Villa	47	60	1934–35	Arsenal	58	84
1897–98	Sheffield United	42	60	1935–36	Sunderland	56	84
1898–99	Aston Villa	45	68	1936–37	Manchester City	57	84
1899–1900	Aston Villa	50	68	1937–38	Arsenal	52	84
1900–01	Liverpool	45	68	1938–39	Everton	59	84
1901–02	Sunderland	44	68	1946–47	Liverpool	57	84
1902–03	Sheffield Wednesday	42	68	1947–48	Arsenal	59	84
1903–04	Sheffield Wednesday	47	68	1948–49	Portsmouth	58	84
1904–05	Newcastle United	48	68	1949–50*	Portsmouth	53	84
1905–06	Liverpool	51	76	1950–51	Tottenham Hotspur	60	84
1906–07	Newcastle United	51	76	1951–52	Manchester United	57	84
1907–08	Manchester United	52	76	1952–53*	Arsenal	54	84
1908–09	Newcastle United	53	76	1953–54	Wolverhampton Wanderers	57	84
1909–10	Aston Villa	53	76	1954–55	Chelsea	52	84
1910–11	Manchester United	52	76	1955–56	Manchester United	60	84
1911–12	Blackburn Rovers	49	76	1956–57	Manchester United	64	84
1912–13	Sunderland	54	76	1957–58	Wolverhampton Wanderers	64	84
1913–14	Blackburn Rovers	51	76	1958–59	Wolverhampton Wanderers	61	84
1914–15	Everton	46	76	1959–60	Burnley	55	84
1919–20	West Bromwich Albion	60	84	1960–61	Tottenham Hotspur	66	84
1920–21	Burnley	59	84	1961–62	Ipswich Town	56	84
1921–22	Liverpool	57	84	1962–63	Everton	61	84
1922–23	Liverpool	60	84	1963–64	Liverpool	57	84
1923–24*	Huddersfield Town	57	84	1964–65*	Manchester United	61	84
1924–25	Huddersfield Town	58	84	1965–66	Liverpool	61	84
1925–26	Huddersfield Town	57	84	1966–67	Manchester United	60	84

* Won on goal average/difference   No competition 1915–19 and 1939–46

Season	Winners	Pts	Max	Season	Winners	Pts	Max
1967–68	Manchester City	58	84	1980–81	Aston Villa	60	84
1968–69	Leeds United	67	84	1981–82	Liverpool	87	126
1969–70	Everton	66	84	1982–83	Liverpool	82	126
1970–71	Arsenal	65	84	1983–84	Liverpool	80	126
1971–72	Derby County	53	84	1984–85	Everton	90	126
1972–73	Liverpool	60	84	1985–86	Liverpool	88	126
1973–74	Leeds United	62	84	1986–87	Everton	86	126
1974–75	Derby County	58	84	1987–88	Liverpool	90	120
1975–76	Liverpool	60	84	1988–89*	Arsenal	76	114
1976–77	Liverpool	57	84	1989–90	Liverpool	79	114
1977–78	Nottingham Forest	64	84	1990–91	Arsenal	83	114
1978–79	Liverpool	68	84	1991–92	Leeds United	82	126
1979–80	Liverpool	60	84				

Football League Champions 1892–1996

First Division 1992–1996 (Second Division 1892–1992)

Season	Winners	Pts	Max	Season	Winners	Pts	Max
1892–93	Small Heath	36	44	1933–34	Grimsby Town	59	76
1893–94	Liverpool	50	56	1934–35	Brentford	61	76
1894–95	Bury	48	60	1935–36	Manchester United	56	76
1895–96*	Liverpool	46	60	1936–37	Leicester City	56	76
1896–97	Notts County	42	60	1937–38	Aston Villa	57	76
1897–98	Burnley	48	60	1938–39	Blackburn Rovers	55	84
1898–99	Manchester City	52	68	1946–47	Manchester City	62	84
1899–1900	Sheffield Wednesday	54	68	1947–48	Birmingham City	59	84
1900–01	Grimsby Town	49	68	1948–49	Fulham	57	84
1901–02	West Bromwich Albion	55	68	1949–50	Tottenham Hotspur	61	84
1902–03	Manchester City	54	68	1950–51	Preston North End	57	84
1903–04	Preston North End	50	68	1951–52	Sheffield Wednesday	53	84
1904–05	Liverpool	58	68	1952–53	Sheffield United	60	84
1905–06	Bristol City	66	76	1953–54*	Leicester City	56	84
1906–07	Nottingham Forest	60	76	1954–55*	Birmingham City	54	84
1907–08	Bradford City	54	76	1955–56	Sheffield Wednesday	55	84
1908–09	Bolton Wanderers	52	76	1956–57	Leicester City	61	84
1909–10	Manchester City	54	76	1957–58	West Ham United	57	84
1910–11	West Bromwich Albion	53	76	1958–59	Sheffield Wednesday	62	84
1911–12	Derby County	54	76	1959–60	Aston Villa	59	84
1912–13	Preston North End	53	76	1960–61	Ipswich Town	59	84
1913–14	Notts County	53	76	1961–62	Liverpool	62	84
1914–15	Derby County	53	76	1962–63	Stoke City	53	84
1919–20	Tottenham Hotspur	70	76	1963–64	Leeds United	63	84
1920–21	Birmingham	58	76	1964–65	Newcastle United	57	84
1921–22	Nottingham Forest	56	76	1965–66	Manchester City	59	84
1922–23	Notts County	53	76	1966–67	Coventry City	59	84
1923–24	Leeds United	54	76	1967–68	Ipswich Town	59	84
1924–25	Leicester City	59	76	1968–69	Derby County	63	84
1925–26	Sheffield Wednesday	60	76	1969–70	Huddersfield Town	60	84
1926–27	Middlesbrough	62	76	1970–71	Leicester City	59	84
1927–28	Manchester City	59	76	1971–72	Norwich City	57	84
1928–29	Middlesbrough	55	76	1972–73	Burnley	62	84
1929–30	Blackpool	58	76	1973–74	Middlesbrough	65	84
1930–31	Everton	61	76	1974–75	Manchester United	61	84
1931–32	Wolverhampton Wanderers	56	76	1975–76	Sunderland	56	84
1932–33	Stoke City	56	76	1976–77	Wolverhampton Wanderers	57	84

* *Won on goal average/difference   No competition 1915–19 and 1939–46*

Season	Winners	Pts	Max	Season	Winners	Pts	Max
1977–78	Bolton Wanderers	58	84	1987–88	Millwall	82	132
1978–79	Crystal Palace	57	84	1988–89	Chelsea	99	138
1979–80	Leicester City	55	84	1989–90	Leeds United	85	138
1980–81	West Ham United	66	84	1990–91	Oldham Athletic	88	138
1981–82	Luton Town	88	126	1991–92	Ipswich Town	84	138
1982–83	Queens Park Rangers	85	126	1992–93	Newcastle United	96	138
1983–84*	Chelsea	88	126	1993–94	Crystal Palace	90	138
1984–85	Oxford United	84	126	1994–95	Middlesbrough	82	138
1985–86	Norwich City	84	126	1995–96	Sunderland	83	138
1986–87	Derby County	84	126				

Third Division (S) 1920–1958

Season	Winners	Pts	Max	Season	Winners	Pts	Max
1920–21	Crystal Palace	59	84	1936–37	Luton Town	58	84
1921–22*	Southampton	61	84	1937–38	Millwall	56	84
1922–23	Bristol City	59	84	1938–39	Newport County	55	84
1923–24	Portsmouth	59	84	1946–47	Cardiff City	66	84
1924–25	Swansea Town	57	84	1947–48	Queens Park Rangers	61	84
1925–26	Reading	57	84	1948–49	Swansea Town	62	84
1926–27	Bristol City	62	84	1949–50	Notts County	58	84
1927–28	Millwall	65	84	1950–51	Nottingham Forest	70	92
1928–29*	Charlton Athletic	54	84	1951–52	Plymouth Argyle	66	92
1929–30	Plymouth Argyle	68	84	1952–53	Bristol Rovers	64	92
1930–31	Notts County	59	84	1953–54	Ipswich Town	64	92
1931–32	Fulham	57	84	1954–55	Bristol City	70	92
1932–33	Brentford	62	84	1955–56	Leyton Orient	66	92
1933–34	Norwich City	61	84	1956–57*	Ipswich Town	59	92
1934–35	Charlton Athletic	61	84	1957–58	Brighton and Hove Albion	60	92
1935–36	Coventry City	57	84				

Third Division (N) 1921–1958

Season	Winners	Pts	Max	Season	Winners	Pts	Max
1921–22	Stockport County	56	76	1936–37	Stockport County	60	84
1922–23	Nelson	51	76	1937–38	Tranmere Rovers	56	84
1923–24	Wolverhampton Wanderers	63	84	1938–39	Barnsley	67	84
1924–25	Darlington	58	84	1946–47	Doncaster Rovers	72	84
1925–26	Grimsby Town	61	84	1947–48	Lincoln City	60	84
1926–27	Stoke City	63	84	1948–49	Hull City	65	84
1927–28	Bradford	63	84	1949–50	Doncaster Rovers	55	84
1928–29	Bradford City	63	84	1950–51	Rotherham United	71	92
1929–30	Port Vale	67	84	1951–52	Lincoln City	69	92
1930–31	Chesterfield	58	84	1952–53	Oldham Athletic	59	92
1931–32*	Lincoln City	57	80	1953–54	Port Vale	69	92
1932–33	Hull City	59	84	1954–55	Barnsley	65	92
1933–34	Barnsley	62	84	1955–56	Grimsby Town	68	92
1934–35	Doncaster Rovers	57	84	1956–57	Derby County	63	92
1935–36	Chesterfield	60	84	1957–58	Scunthorpe United	66	92

Second Division 1992–1996 (Third Division 1958–1992)

Season	Winners	Pts	Max	Season	Winners	Pts	Max
1958–59	Plymouth Argyle	62	92	1966–67	Queens Park Rangers	67	92
1959–60	Southampton	61	92	1967–68	Oxford United	57	92
1960–61	Bury	68	92	1968–69*	Watford	64	92
1961–62	Portsmouth	65	92	1969–70	Orient	62	92
1962–63	Northampton Town	62	92	1970–71	Preston North End	61	92
1963–64*	Coventry City	60	92	1971–72	Aston Villa	70	92
1964–65	Carlisle United	60	92	1972–73	Bolton Wanderers	61	92
1965–66	Hull City	69	92				

Won on goal average/difference   No competition 1915–19 and 1939–46

Season	Winners	Pts	Max	Season	Winners	Pts	Max
1973–74	Oldham Athletic	62	92	1985–86	Reading	94	138
1974–75	Blackburn Rovers	60	92	1986–87	AFC Bournemouth	97	138
1975–76	Hereford United	63	92	1987–88	Sunderland	93	138
1976–77	Mansfield Town	64	92	1988–89	Wolverhampton Wanderers	92	138
1977–78	Wrexham	61	92	1989–90	Bristol Rovers	93	138
1978–79	Shrewsbury Town	61	92	1990–91	Cambridge United	86	138
1979–80	Grimsby Town	62	92	1991–92	Brentford	82	138
1980–81	Rotherham United	61	92	1992–93	Stoke City	93	138
1981–82*	Burnley	80	138	1993–94	Reading	89	138
1982–83	Portsmouth	91	138	1994–95	Birmingham City	89	138
1983–84	Oxford United	95	138	1995–96	Swindon Town	92	138
1984–85	Bradford City	94	138				

Third Division 1992–1996 (Fourth Division 1958–1992)

Season	Winners	Pts	Max	Season	Winners	Pts	Max
1958–59	Port Vale	64	92	1977–78	Watford	71	92
1959–60	Walsall	65	92	1978–79	Reading	65	92
1960–61	Peterborough United	66	92	1979–80	Huddersfield Town	66	92
1961–62	Millwall	56	88	1980–81	Southend United	67	92
1962–63	Brentford	62	92	1981–82	Sheffield United	96	138
1963–64*	Gillingham	60	92	1982–83	Wimbledon	98	138
1964–65	Brighton and Hove Albion	63	92	1983–84	York City	101	138
1965–66	Doncaster Rovers	59	92	1984–85	Chesterfield	91	138
1966–67	Stockport County	64	92	1985–86	Swindon Town	102	138
1967–68	Luton Town	66	92	1986–87	Northampton Town	99	138
1968–69	Doncaster Rovers	59	92	1987–88	Wolverhampton Wanderers	90	138
1969–70	Chesterfield	64	92	1988–89	Rotherham United	82	138
1970–71	Notts County	69	92	1989–90	Exeter City	89	138
1971–72	Grimsby Town	63	92	1990–91	Darlington	83	138
1972–73	Southport	62	92	1991–92	Burnley	83	126
1973–74	Peterborough United	65	92	1992–93	Cardiff City	83	126
1974–75	Mansfield Town	68	92	1993–94	Shrewsbury Town	79	126
1975–76	Lincoln City	74	92	1994–95	Carlisle United	91	126
1976–77	Cambridge United	65	92	1995–96	Preston North End	86	138

* Won on goal average/difference   No competition 1939–46

United's Keane and Bruce turn to celebrate Scholes' goal in the "derby" with City in October.

41 ● REVIEW OF THE LEAGUE SEASON 1995–96

Alex Ferguson's Manchester United secured their third FA Carling Premiership title in four years on the last day of the season (5 May) at the Riverside Stadium. A 3–0 victory against Bryan Robson's Middlesbrough – with goals by David May, Ryan Giggs and substitute Andy Cole – finally put paid to Newcastle United's gutsy challenge for the championship. Following their 1–1 home draw with Tottenham on the same day, Newcastle finished four points adrift – a sad end to a season in which they had once enjoyed a 12-point advantage at the top of the table.

While "double" winners United could plan for a UEFA Champions' League campaign that might take them to Milan or Madrid, Manchester City had to set their sights considerably lower after being relegated from the Premiership. City went down after their 2–2 home draw with Cup finalists Liverpool on the last day, finishing behind Coventry City and Southampton on goal difference. QPR and Bolton Wanderers had known their fate earlier.

Four Premiership sides had started that day with a chance of claiming the remaining UEFA Cup place, the other two spots having already gone to Newcastle (League runners-up) and Aston Villa (Coca-Cola Cup winners). Three hopeful teams – Blackburn, Everton and Tottenham – jockeyed for position before Arsenal, with late goals from David Platt and Dutchman Dennis Bergkamp, defeated doomed Bolton at Highbury to qualify.

Sunderland, under a much more "cheerful" Peter Reid, were promoted back into the top flight after a five-year absence, and they were joined by Derby County. Jim Smith's team clinched the second automatic promotion place after a tense match during the season's penultimate weekend against nearest challengers Crystal Palace (2–1). For their part, Palace had stormed through from 16th in Division 1 in February to a Wembley play-off final in May.

Ipswich Town, with play-off aspirations, and Millwall, fighting to avoid the drop, collided at Portman Road on the last day and a goalless scoreline did neither of them any favours: Leicester City's triumph at Watford denied Ipswich (and relegated Watford) and Portsmouth's precious win at Huddersfield sent Millwall down. The shell-shocked Londoners had spent most of the season in the top half.

Steve McMahon's Swindon Town were easily the best team in Division 2, topping the table by nine points, and Oxford United followed them up. United boss Denis Smith celebrated the fourth promotion of

his managerial career and his team's confident late run brought them thirteen wins and three draws from their final seventeen games. Promotion was confirmed on the last day as a spell of three goals in seven minutes helped to a 4–0 home win against Peterborough.

The situation at the other end of the table became complicated after the penultimate weekend's fixture between Brighton & Hove Albion (already relegated) and York City (in serious danger thereof) was abandoned at the Goldstone due to crowd disorder. With the match continuing to be relevant to the relegation issue, it was ultimately replayed on 9 May and York's 3–1 victory was enough to save them and send Carlisle down.

Gillingham, under former player Tony Pulis, were hard to beat in Division 3 – particularly at home where they conceded just six goals throughout the campaign – but Preston North End pipped them for the Championship by three points. There were big crowds on the last day at Deepdale (18,700), Priestfield Stadium (10,421) and Home Park (11,526 saw Plymouth Argyle reach the play-offs). The League's bottom club were Torquay United, eleven points adrift of Scarborough.

Endsleigh League Play-Offs

Division 1

Semi-Finals
Charlton Athletic v Crystal Palace 1–2, 0–1

Leicester City v Stoke City 0–0, 1–0

Final
Crystal Palace v Leicester City 1–2 (*at Wembley*)

Division 2

Semi-Finals
Bradford City v Blackpool 0–2, 3–0

Crewe Alexandra v Notts County 2–2, 0–1

Final
Bradford City v Notts County 2–0 (*at Wembley*)

Division 3

Semi-Finals
Colchester United v Plymouth Argyle 1–0, 1–3

Hereford United v Darlington 1–2, 1–2

Final
Darlington v Plymouth Argyle 0–1 (*at Wembley*)

42 ● FINAL LEAGUE TABLES 1995–96

FA Carling Premiership

			HOME					AWAY					
		P	*W*	*D*	*L*	*F*	*A*	*W*	*D*	*L*	*F*	*A*	*Pts*	*GD*
1	Manchester United	38	15	4	0	36	9	10	3	6	37	26	82	+38
2	Newcastle United	38	17	1	1	38	9	7	5	7	28	28	78	+29
3	Liverpool	38	14	4	1	46	13	6	7	6	24	21	71	+36
4	Aston Villa	38	11	5	3	32	15	7	4	8	20	20	63	+17
5	Arsenal	38	10	7	2	30	16	7	5	7	19	16	63	+17
6	Everton	38	10	5	4	35	19	7	5	7	29	25	61	+20
7	Blackburn Rovers	38	14	2	3	44	19	4	5	10	17	28	61	+14
8	Tottenham Hotspur	38	9	5	5	26	19	7	8	4	24	19	61	+12
9	Nottingham Forest	38	11	6	2	29	17	4	7	8	21	37	58	−4
10	West Ham United	38	9	5	5	25	21	5	4	10	18	31	51	−9
11	Chelsea	38	7	7	5	30	22	5	7	7	16	22	50	+2
12	Middlesbrough	38	8	3	8	27	27	3	7	9	8	23	43	−15
13	Leeds United	38	8	3	8	21	21	4	4	11	19	36	43	−17
14	Wimbledon	38	5	6	8	27	33	5	5	9	28	37	41	−15
15	Sheffield Wednesday	38	7	5	7	30	31	3	5	11	18	30	40	−13
16	Coventry City	38	6	7	6	21	23	2	7	10	21	37	38	−18
17	Southampton	38	7	7	5	21	18	2	4	13	13	34	38	−18
18	Manchester City	38	7	7	5	21	19	2	4	13	12	39	38	−25
19	Queens Park Rangers	38	6	5	8	25	26	3	1	15	13	31	33	−19
20	Bolton Wanderers	38	5	4	10	16	31	3	1	15	23	40	29	−32

Endsleigh Insurance League First Division

		P	W	D	L	F	A	W	D	L	F	A	Pts	Gls
				HOME						*AWAY*				
1	Sunderland	46	13	8	2	32	10	9	9	5	27	23	83	59
2	Derby County	46	14	8	1	48	22	7	8	8	23	29	79	71
3	Crystal Palace	46	9	9	5	34	22	11	6	6	33	26	75	67
4	Stoke City	46	13	6	4	32	15	7	7	9	28	34	73	60
5	Leicester City	46	9	7	7	32	29	10	7	6	34	31	71	66*
6	Charlton Athletic	46	8	11	4	28	23	9	9	5	29	22	71	57
7	Ipswich Town	46	13	5	5	45	30	6	7	10	34	39	69	79
8	Huddersfield Town	46	14	4	5	42	23	3	8	12	19	35	63	61
9	Sheffield United	46	9	7	7	29	25	7	7	9	28	29	62	57
10	Barnsley	46	9	10	4	34	28	5	8	10	26	38	60	60
11	West Bromwich Albion	46	11	5	7	34	29	5	7	11	26	39	60	60
12	Port Vale	46	10	5	8	30	29	5	10	8	29	37	60	59
13	Tranmere Rovers	46	9	9	5	42	29	5	8	10	22	31	59	64
14	Southend United	46	11	8	4	30	22	4	6	13	22	39	59	52
15	Birmingham City	46	11	7	5	37	23	4	6	13	24	41	58	61
16	Norwich City	46	7	9	7	26	24	7	6	10	33	31	57	59
17	Grimsby Town	46	8	10	5	27	25	6	4	13	28	44	56	55
18	Oldham Athletic	46	10	7	6	33	20	4	7	12	21	30	56	54
19	Reading	46	8	7	8	28	30	5	10	8	26	33	56	54
20	Wolverhampton Wanderers	46	8	9	6	34	28	5	7	11	22	34	55	56
21	Portsmouth	46	8	6	9	34	32	5	7	11	27	37	52	61
22	Millwall	46	7	6	10	23	28	6	7	10	20	35	52	43
23	Watford	46	7	8	8	40	33	3	10	10	22	37	48	62
24	Luton Town	46	7	6	10	30	34	4	6	13	10	30	45	40

* *promoted via the play-offs*

Endsleigh Insurance League Second Division

				HOME					AWAY					
		P	W	D	L	F	A	W	D	L	F	A	Pts	Gls
1	Swindon Town	46	12	10	1	37	16	13	7	3	34	18	92	71
2	Oxford United	46	17	4	2	52	14	7	7	9	24	25	83	76
3	Blackpool	46	14	5	4	41	20	9	8	6	26	20	82	67
4	Notts County	46	14	6	3	42	21	7	9	7	21	18	78	63
5	Crewe Alexandra	46	13	3	7	40	24	9	4	10	37	36	73	77
6	Bradford City	46	15	4	4	41	25	7	3	13	30	44	73	71*
7	Chesterfield	46	14	6	3	39	21	6	6	11	17	30	72	56
8	Wrexham	46	12	6	5	51	27	6	10	7	25	28	70	76
9	Stockport County	46	8	9	6	30	20	11	4	8	31	27	70	61
10	Bristol Rovers	46	12	4	7	29	28	8	6	9	28	32	70	57
11	Walsall	46	12	7	4	38	20	7	5	11	22	25	69	60
12	Wycombe Wanderers	46	9	8	6	36	26	6	7	10	27	33	60	63
13	Bristol City	46	10	6	7	28	22	5	9	9	27	38	60	55
14	Bournemouth	46	12	5	6	33	25	4	5	14	18	45	58	51
15	Brentford	46	12	6	5	24	15	3	7	13	19	34	58	43
16	Rotherham United	46	11	7	5	31	20	3	7	13	23	42	56	54
17	Burnley	46	9	8	6	35	28	5	5	13	21	40	55	56
18	Shrewsbury Town	46	7	8	8	32	29	6	6	11	26	41	53	58
19	Peterborough United	46	9	6	8	40	27	4	7	12	19	39	52	59
20	York City	46	8	6	9	28	29	5	7	11	30	44	52	58
21	Carlisle United	46	11	6	6	35	20	1	7	15	22	52	49	57
22	Swansea City	46	8	8	7	27	29	3	6	14	16	50	47	43
23	Brighton & Hove Albion	46	6	7	10	25	31	4	3	16	21	38	40	46
24	Hull City	46	4	8	11	26	37	1	8	14	10	41	31	36

promoted via the play-offs

Endsleigh Insurance League Third Division

		P	W	D	L	F	A	W	D	L	F	A	Pts	Gls
				HOME						*AWAY*				
1	Preston North End	46	11	8	4	44	22	12	9	2	34	16	86	78
2	Gillingham	46	16	6	1	33	6	6	11	6	16	14	83	49
3	Bury	46	11	6	6	33	21	11	7	5	33	27	79	66
4	Plymouth Argyle	46	14	5	4	41	20	8	7	8	27	29	78	68*
5	Darlington	46	10	6	7	30	21	10	12	1	30	21	78	60
6	Hereford United	46	13	5	5	40	22	7	9	7	25	25	74	65
7	Colchester United	46	13	7	3	37	22	5	11	7	24	29	72	61
8	Chester City	46	11	9	3	45	22	7	7	9	27	31	70	72
9	Barnet	46	13	6	4	40	19	5	10	8	25	26	70	65
10	Wigan Athletic	46	15	3	5	36	21	5	7	11	26	35	70	62
11	Northampton Town	46	9	10	4	32	22	9	3	11	19	22	67	51
12	Scunthorpe United	46	8	8	7	36	30	7	7	9	31	31	60	67
13	Doncaster Rovers	46	11	6	6	25	19	5	5	13	24	41	59	49
14	Exeter City	46	9	9	5	25	22	4	9	10	21	31	57	46
15	Rochdale	46	7	8	8	32	33	7	5	11	25	28	55	57
16	Cambridge United	46	8	8	7	34	30	6	4	13	27	41	54	61
17	Fulham	46	10	9	4	39	26	2	8	13	18	37	53	57
18	Lincoln City	46	8	7	8	32	26	5	7	11	25	47	53	57
19	Mansfield Town	46	6	10	7	25	29	5	10	8	29	35	53	54
20	Hartlepool United	46	8	9	6	30	24	4	4	15	17	43	49	47
21	Leyton Orient	46	11	4	8	29	22	1	7	15	15	41	47	44
22	Cardiff City	46	8	6	9	24	22	3	6	14	17	42	45	41
23	Scarborough	46	5	11	7	22	28	3	5	15	17	41	40	39
24	Torquay United	46	4	9	10	17	36	1	5	17	13	48	29	30

promoted via the play-offs

FA CARLING PREMIERSHIP

Home \ Away	Arsenal	Aston Villa	Blackburn Rovers	Bolton Wanderers	Chelsea	Coventry City	Everton	Leeds United	Liverpool	Manchester City	Manchester United	Middlesbrough	Newcastle United	Nottingham Forest	Queens Park Rangers	Sheffield Wednesday	Southampton	Tottenham Hotspur	West Ham United	Wimbledon
Arsenal	•	2–0	0–0	2–1	1–1	1–1	1–2	2–1	0–0	3–1	1–0	1–1	2–0	1–1	3–0	4–2	4–2	0–0	1–0	1–3
Aston Villa	1–1	•	2–0	1–0	0–1	4–1	1–0	3–0	0–2	0–1	3–1	0–0	1–1	1–1	4–2	3–2	3–0	2–1	1–1	2–0
Blackburn Rovers	1–1	1–1	•	3–1	3–0	5–1	0–3	1–0	2–3	2–0	1–2	1–0	2–1	7–0	1–0	3–0	2–1	2–1	4–2	3–2
Bolton Wanderers	1–0	0–2	2–1	•	2–1	1–2	1–1	0–2	0–1	1–1	0–6	1–1	1–3	1–0	1–0	2–1	0–1	2–3	0–3	1–0
Chelsea	1–0	2–2	2–3	3–2	•	2–2	0–0	4–1	2–2	1–1	1–4	5–0	1–0	1–1	1–0	0–0	3–0	0–0	1–2	1–2
Coventry City	0–0	0–3	5–0	3–2	1–0	•	2–1	0–0	1–0	2–1	0–4	4–0	0–1	1–1	1–0	0–1	1–1	2–3	2–2	3–3
Everton	0–2	1–0	0–0	3–0	1–1	2–2	•	2–0	1–0	2–0	2–3	4–0	1–3	3–0	2–0	2–2	2–0	1–1	3–0	2–4
Leeds United	0–3	2–0	0–0	0–1	1–0	3–1	2–2	•	1–0	0–1	3–1	0–1	0–1	1–3	1–3	2–0	1–0	1–3	2–0	1–1
Liverpool	3–1	1–0	3–0	5–2	0–1	0–0	1–2	5–0	•	0–0	2–2	1–0	4–3	4–2	1–0	1–0	1–1	0–0	2–2	2–2
Manchester City	0–1	0–0	1–1	1–1	1–1	1–1	0–2	0–1	2–2	•	2–3	0–1	3–3	3–0	1–0	1–0	2–1	1–1	4–2	3–0
Manchester United	1–0	1–1	1–1	3–0	1–1	2–1	2–0	1–0	2–2	1–0	•	2–0	2–0	1–1	2–1	2–0	4–1	1–0	3–0	3–1
Middlesbrough	2–3	0–2	2–0	1–4	2–0	2–1	1–0	1–1	2–1	4–1	0–3	•	1–2	3–1	1–0	3–1	0–0	0–1	4–2	1–2
Newcastle United	2–0	1–1	1–0	2–1	1–0	0–0	3–2	2–1	1–0	3–1	0–1	1–0	•	1–1	3–0	1–0	1–0	1–1	3–0	6–1
Nottingham Forest	0–1	1–0	1–5	3–2	0–0	1–1	3–1	1–2	1–2	3–0	1–1	1–1	1–1	•	1–1	0–3	1–0	2–1	1–1	4–1
Queens Park Rangers	1–1	1–0	0–1	4–2	1–2	1–1	2–5	6–2	1–1	1–1	1–1	1–1	2–3	1–3	•	1–0	3–0	2–3	3–0	0–3
Sheffield Wednesday	1–0	1–1	2–1	1–0	0–0	4–3	2–2	1–1	1–3	1–0	0–0	0–1	0–2	3–4	1–3	•	2–2	1–3	3–0	2–1
Southampton	0–0	2–0	1–0	1–0	3–0	1–0	0–0	1–0	1–3	1–0	3–1	2–1	1–0	3–4	3–0	2–2	•	0–0	0–0	0–0
Tottenham Hotspur	2–1	0–1	2–3	1–1	1–1	3–1	2–1	2–1	0–0	1–1	4–1	2–1	1–1	1–0	1–0	1–1	1–0	•	0–1	3–1
West Ham United	0–1	1–4	1–1	1–0	1–3	3–2	2–1	1–2	0–0	4–2	2–4	2–0	2–0	1–0	1–0	1–1	2–1	1–1	•	1–1
Wimbledon	0–3	3–3	1–1	3–2	1–1	0–2	2–3	2–4	1–0	3–0	2–4	0–0	3–3	1–0	2–1	2–2	1–2	0–1	0–1	•

ENDSLEIGH INSURANCE LEAGUE FIRST DIVISION

Home \ Away	Barnsley	Birmingham City	Charlton Athletic	Crystal Palace	Derby County	Grimsby Town	Huddersfield Town	Ipswich Town	Leicester City	Luton Town	Millwall	Norwich City	Oldham Athletic	Port Vale	Portsmouth	Reading	Sheffield United	Southend United	Stoke City	Sunderland	Tranmere Rovers	Watford	West Bromwich Albion	Wolverhampton Wanderers
Barnsley	•	0-5	1-1	4-3	4-1	3-1	3-0	2-2	2-2	1-3	0-1	3-1	0-1	3-0	0-0	0-0	1-0	0-0	3-1	0-1	2-1	2-1	1-1	1-0
Birmingham City	0-0	•	3-4	3-2	1-1	2-1	4-2	3-1	2-0	0-0	1-1	1-1	4-0	0-1	0-1	1-2	1-1	2-0	1-1	0-2	1-0	1-0	1-1	2-0
Charlton Athletic	1-1	3-1	•	1-1	0-0	3-0	2-1	0-2	1-5	1-0	0-0	1-1	1-1	3-1	1-0	2-1	2-0	1-1	2-1	1-1	0-0	2-1	4-1	1-1
Crystal Palace	4-3	3-2	0-0	•	0-0	0-2	2-1	1-1	2-3	2-3	1-2	2-0	1-1	2-2	2-1	0-2	2-3	1-1	0-0	0-1	2-1	4-0	1-0	3-2
Derby County	4-1	1-1	0-0	0-0	•	1-1	1-1	3-1	0-1	1-1	1-2	2-2	2-2	0-0	3-2	3-0	0-2	1-0	3-1	3-1	6-2	1-0	3-0	0-0
Grimsby Town	3-1	2-1	1-2	1-1	1-1	•	3-2	2-1	2-2	0-0	1-2	2-2	1-1	1-0	2-1	0-0	2-1	1-1	1-0	0-4	1-1	1-0	1-0	3-0
Huddersfield Town	3-0	4-2	2-2	2-1	1-1	1-1	•	1-1	2-1	2-1	3-0	3-2	0-0	0-2	0-1	3-1	0-0	3-1	1-1	1-1	1-0	4-2	4-1	2-1
Ipswich Town	2-2	2-0	2-2	0-1	0-1	3-1	2-1	•	3-1	0-2	1-0	2-1	2-1	5-1	3-2	1-2	1-1	3-1	4-1	3-0	0-1	0-1	2-1	1-2
Leicester City	2-2	2-0	1-5	1-0	4-2	3-1	1-0	4-2	•	4-1	2-1	3-2	2-1	2-3	4-2	1-1	1-3	1-2	2-3	0-2	3-2	2-0	1-2	1-0
Luton Town	1-3	0-0	1-0	2-3	0-1	0-0	0-1	0-1	0-1	•	1-0	2-1	0-1	2-1	1-0	0-1	3-1	1-0	1-1	1-2	2-2	1-2	2-1	0-1
Millwall	0-1	1-1	0-2	1-0	1-2	3-0	3-0	2-1	2-1	1-0	•	2-1	1-1	3-2	2-2	1-2	1-2	2-0	2-0	2-2	1-1	1-2	2-1	2-3
Norwich City	3-1	1-1	0-1	1-0	1-1	2-2	3-2	2-1	1-3	2-0	2-2	•	1-1	2-1	2-0	1-1	0-3	2-1	2-3	1-2	1-2	0-0	2-2	0-0
Oldham Athletic	0-1	4-0	1-3	3-1	0-1	2-1	0-0	2-1	2-1	1-0	2-0	2-0	•	2-1	1-3	3-3	2-0	2-1	2-0	1-2	0-2	4-2	1-2	2-2
Port Vale	3-0	0-1	2-1	1-2	5-1	1-0	1-0	1-1	2-1	5-1	0-1	1-0	1-3	•	0-2	3-2	2-2	1-1	3-3	2-2	1-0	2-0	3-1	3-0
Portsmouth	0-0	0-1	2-3	2-3	1-1	4-0	2-1	0-1	1-1	4-0	1-2	1-0	2-1	1-2	•	0-0	0-1	2-1	1-0	1-1	0-2	0-0	0-2	2-1
Reading	0-0	0-0	0-2	0-2	3-2	1-1	3-1	1-4	1-1	3-1	2-2	0-3	2-0	2-2	0-1	•	0-0	0-0	0-0	0-0	1-0	1-1	3-1	2-1
Sheffield United	1-0	1-1	2-3	2-3	0-2	2-2	0-2	2-2	1-3	1-0	2-0	2-1	1-1	1-1	4-1	0-0	•	3-0	2-4	0-0	0-2	1-1	1-2	2-1
Southend United	0-0	3-1	1-1	1-1	0-0	0-0	0-0	2-1	2-1	2-0	1-0	1-1	2-1	1-1	2-1	0-0	3-0	•	0-0	1-0	1-1	2-0	2-1	2-0
Stoke City	2-0	1-0	1-2	1-1	1-1	2-4	1-1	3-1	1-1	5-0	6-0	1-1	0-1	0-1	2-1	1-1	2-4	0-0	•	0-0	0-0	2-0	2-1	2-3
Sunderland	2-1	3-0	0-0	3-0	3-0	1-0	3-2	1-0	1-0	1-0	2-2	0-1	1-0	0-0	1-2	2-2	1-0	1-0	0-0	•	0-0	1-1	0-0	2-0
Tranmere Rovers	1-3	2-2	0-0	5-1	0-1	0-0	5-2	5-2	1-2	1-0	0-1	0-2	1-0	5-2	1-2	2-1	0-2	2-2	3-0	2-0	•	2-3	2-2	2-2
Watford	2-3	1-1	1-2	6-3	3-2	0-1	0-1	2-3	2-0	1-0	0-1	1-4	1-0	1-1	2-2	4-2	1-1	3-1	3-0	3-3	3-0	•	1-1	1-1
West Bromwich Albion	2-1	1-0	1-0	2-3	3-1	3-1	2-1	0-2	3-1	0-2	1-1	2-2	1-0	0-1	2-2	2-0	1-2	2-1	0-1	0-1	1-1	4-4	•	0-0
Wolverhampton Wanderers	2-2	3-2	0-2	3-0	3-0	2-1	2-0	2-2	2-3	0-0	3-1	0-0	2-2	0-1	2-1	2-1	2-1	2-0	2-3	3-0	2-1	1-1	1-1	•

	Blackpool	Bournemouth	Bradford City	Brentford	Brighton & Hove Albion	Bristol City	Bristol Rovers	Burnley	Carlisle United	Chesterfield	Crewe Alexandra	Hull City	Notts County	Oxford United	Peterborough United	Rotherham United	Shrewsbury Town	Stockport County	Swansea City	Swindon Town	Walsall	Wrexham	Wycombe Wanderers	York City
Blackpool	●	2-1	4-1	1-0	2-1	3-0	3-0	3-1	3-1	0-0	2-1	1-1	1-0	1-1	2-1	1-2	2-1	0-1	4-0	1-1	1-2	2-0	1-1	1-3
Bournemouth	1-0	●	3-1	1-0	3-1	1-1	2-1	0-2	2-0	2-0	1-1	2-0	0-2	0-1	3-0	2-1	0-2	2-3	3-1	0-0	0-0	1-1	2-3	2-2
Bradford City	2-1	1-0	●	2-1	1-3	3-0	2-3	2-2	3-1	2-1	2-1	1-1	1-0	0-1	2-1	2-1	3-1	0-1	5-1	1-1	1-0	2-0	0-4	2-2
Brentford	1-2	2-0	2-1	●	0-1	2-2	0-0	1-0	1-1	1-2	2-1	1-1	1-0	1-0	3-1	1-1	0-2	0-1	0-0	1-1	1-0	2-1	1-2	2-0
Brighton & Hove Albion	1-2	2-0	2-1	0-1	●	0-2	2-0	1-0	1-3	0-2	2-2	4-0	1-0	1-2	1-2	1-1	2-2	1-1	0-2	1-3	0-3	2-2	1-2	2-0
Bristol City	1-1	3-0	2-1	0-0	0-1	●	0-2	1-0	1-3	2-1	3-2	4-0	4-0	0-2	1-2	4-3	3-1	0-1	1-0	0-0	0-2	3-1	1-0	2-0
Bristol Rovers	1-1	0-2	1-2	2-0	1-0	2-4	●	1-0	1-1	1-1	3-2	2-1	0-3	2-0	1-1	1-0	2-1	1-3	2-2	0-0	2-0	1-2	2-1	1-0
Burnley	1-1	4-0	1-0	1-0	1-0	2-4	0-1	●	2-0	2-2	0-1	2-1	3-4	0-2	2-1	1-0	2-1	4-3	3-0	0-0	2-0	2-2	1-1	3-3
Carlisle United	1-0	3-0	3-0	2-2	1-0	1-1	2-0	4-2	●	1-1	1-2	2-1	1-0	0-2	1-1	3-0	2-1	0-1	3-2	1-3	1-1	2-2	4-2	2-0
Chesterfield	1-0	3-0	2-2	2-2	1-0	2-1	2-1	4-2	2-1	●	1-2	0-0	1-0	1-0	1-1	3-0	1-0	1-2	4-1	1-3	1-1	1-2	3-1	1-1
Crewe Alexandra	1-2	2-0	1-2	3-1	3-1	4-2	1-2	3-1	2-1	3-0	●	1-0	2-2	1-2	2-0	2-1	3-0	0-1	4-1	0-2	1-0	1-2	2-0	1-1
Hull City	2-1	1-1	2-3	0-1	0-0	2-3	1-3	3-0	2-5	0-0	1-2	●	0-0	0-0	2-3	1-1	2-3	1-1	5-1	1-3	2-1	0-0	4-2	0-3
Notts County	1-1	1-1	0-2	4-0	2-1	2-0	4-2	5-0	3-1	4-1	0-1	1-0	●	1-1	4-0	1-1	6-0	2-1	5-1	3-0	2-1	2-2	4-2	2-2
Oxford United	1-0	4-5	0-2	1-0	1-1	2-0	1-1	5-0	4-0	1-0	1-1	2-0	0-1	●	5-1	1-0	2-2	1-1	1-1	0-2	2-3	0-0	0-1	2-0
Peterborough United	0-0	1-0	3-1	1-0	3-1	2-3	0-1	0-2	6-1	0-1	3-1	3-1	0-1	4-0	●	1-0	2-2	0-3	2-1	0-2	1-0	0-1	3-0	2-2
Rotherham United	2-1	1-0	3-1	1-2	2-1	4-1	2-2	3-1	1-1	0-1	2-1	1-0	2-0	2-0	1-1	●	0-2	0-2	2-0	1-2	2-1	2-2	0-0	2-1
Shrewsbury Town	0-2	1-2	3-1	2-1	2-1	4-1	1-1	3-0	1-1	0-1	1-1	0-0	1-0	2-0	1-1	3-1	●	0-1	1-1	1-1	1-1	2-2	1-1	3-0
Stockport County	1-1	3-1	1-1	1-2	3-1	1-0	0-0	2-4	2-1	0-1	1-1	0-0	2-0	4-2	0-0	3-1	0-2	●	2-0	1-2	2-1	1-1	2-1	0-1
Swansea City	0-2	0-2	2-0	2-1	3-1	2-2	2-2	0-0	1-1	1-1	1-1	3-0	1-0	1-1	0-0	0-0	0-2	0-3	●	0-1	2-1	1-0	1-1	3-0
Swindon Town	1-1	5-0	2-1	0-1	1-1	0-0	3-2	3-1	3-2	3-0	2-3	5-0	0-0	2-1	1-0	7-0	3-0	0-2	4-1	●	0-1	1-2	4-2	2-0
Walsall	1-1	1-5	2-1	0-1	1-1	2-1	1-1	3-1	2-1	3-0	2-3	3-0	0-0	2-1	1-0	0-7	3-0	2-3	4-1	0-1	●	3-0	1-0	2-3
Wrexham	0-1	1-2	5-2	2-2	0-2	0-0	3-2	1-1	4-0	1-1	1-1	2-2	1-1	2-1	1-1	2-2	1-2	1-1	1-0	4-3	3-0	●	1-0	2-1
Wycombe Wanderers	0-1	1-2	2-5	0-2	3-1	1-1	0-1	1-1	4-0	1-0	2-3	0-0	2-2	3-0	1-1	7-0	2-0	2-3	0-1	1-2	3-0	1-1	●	2-1
York City	0-1	3-1	0-3	2-2	3-1	0-1	0-1	1-1	1-1	0-1	2-3	0-1	1-3	1-0	3-1	2-2	1-2	2-2	0-0	2-0	1-0	1-0	2-1	●

ENDSLEIGH INSURANCE LEAGUE THIRD DIVISION

	Wigan Athletic	Torquay United	Scunthorpe United	Scarborough	Rochdale	Preston North End	Plymouth Argyle	Northampton Town	Mansfield Town	Lincoln City	Leyton Orient	Hereford United	Hartlepool United	Gillingham	Fulham	Exeter City	Doncaster Rovers	Darlington	Colchester United	Chester City	Cardiff City	Cambridge United	Bury	Barnet
Barnet	0-0	4-0	1-0	0-0	0-4	1-0	1-2	2-0	0-0	3-1	3-0	1-3	5-1	0-2	3-0	3-2	1-1	1-1	1-1	1-1	1-0	2-0	0-0	•
Bury	5-0	1-0	3-0	0-2	1-1	0-0	0-5	0-1	0-2	7-1	2-1	2-0	0-3	1-0	3-0	0-0	4-1	0-0	0-0	1-1	3-0	1-2	•	0-0
Cambridge United	2-1	1-1	1-2	4-1	2-1	2-1	2-3	0-1	0-2	2-1	2-0	2-2	0-1	0-0	0-0	1-1	2-2	0-1	3-1	1-1	4-2	•	2-4	1-1
Cardiff City	2-1	0-0	0-1	2-1	1-0	0-1	0-1	1-0	3-1	1-1	0-0	3-2	2-0	2-0	1-4	0-1	3-2	0-2	1-2	0-0	•	4-2	1-1	1-1
Chester City	3-0	4-1	3-0	5-0	1-2	1-1	3-1	1-0	3-1	5-1	0-0	2-1	2-0	1-1	2-1	2-2	0-3	4-1	1-1	•	0-0	0-0	0-1	0-2
Colchester United	0-0	1-0	2-0	1-1	1-1	2-2	2-1	1-2	1-3	1-1	2-0	1-0	4-1	1-1	1-1	1-0	1-2	1-1	•	1-1	1-1	2-1	1-0	3-2
Darlington	1-0	1-2	0-0	1-2	0-1	2-2	0-0	1-2	1-1	3-2	4-1	1-0	1-0	1-0	1-1	2-0	1-2	•	2-2	1-1	1-1	1-0	1-1	1-1
Doncaster Rovers	1-2	2-1	2-0	1-0	0-3	0-1	1-0	1-1	2-2	1-1	2-2	0-0	1-0	0-1	0-2	2-1	•	1-2	3-2	1-0	1-1	1-1	4-0	1-0
Exeter City	2-1	1-0	1-0	1-1	2-0	2-2	2-0	2-1	4-2	1-2	2-1	0-2	2-0	0-0	2-0	•	2-0	0-1	2-2	2-1	2-0	2-0	0-1	1-1
Fulham	2-1	0-0	1-3	1-0	1-0	1-1	2-1	1-3	2-0	2-0	1-1	1-1	0-0	1-1	•	2-0	2-1	1-1	1-0	1-0	4-2	3-1	1-1	1-0
Gillingham	0-4	2-0	0-0	1-1	1-1	0-2	4-0	0-0	0-1	3-0	4-1	0-1	2-0	•	1-0	1-0	3-1	0-1	2-1	3-1	1-0	1-1	3-0	1-0
Hartlepool United	1-0	2-2	2-0	0-0	2-0	0-1	2-2	2-1	1-0	1-0	3-2	0-1	•	0-0	1-0	0-0	0-1	1-0	1-1	2-1	2-1	5-2	1-2	0-0
Hereford United	2-1	2-1	3-0	1-0	1-1	0-2	3-0	1-0	2-1	0-1	3-2	•	4-1	0-0	1-0	2-2	1-0	0-2	1-1	1-0	1-3	3-1	3-4	3-3
Leyton Orient	1-2	1-0	0-2	3-1	1-2	0-0	0-0	2-0	3-3	1-2	•	0-1	4-1	0-1	4-0	0-3	3-1	2-2	0-2	0-0	4-1	1-3	0-2	1-2
Lincoln City	2-2	5-0	1-1	2-0	2-2	0-0	0-1	2-1	6-0	•	1-0	1-2	1-0	1-1	1-0	1-1	4-0	2-2	0-0	0-0	1-0	2-1	2-2	3-3
Mansfield Town	1-1	1-1	2-0	2-0	2-1	3-3	1-1	0-0	•	1-1	0-0	1-1	0-3	1-0	2-2	0-0	3-3	0-1	1-2	3-4	1-1	2-1	1-1	2-1
Northampton Town	0-1	4-3	1-2	2-0	2-1	1-0	1-0	•	1-1	3-0	1-2	2-2	0-0	0-1	3-0	1-1	3-1	1-1	2-1	1-0	1-1	3-0	4-1	0-2
Plymouth Argyle	1-0	1-0	1-3	5-1	1-2	0-2	•	1-0	1-1	1-2	1-1	0-1	3-0	1-1	1-1	2-2	1-1	3-3	1-1	4-2	0-0	0-3	1-0	1-1
Preston North End	0-0	0-0	2-2	1-2	0-2	•	2-2	1-0	1-1	3-3	1-1	0-0	3-0	0-0	1-1	3-0	2-0	0-1	2-0	1-3	3-2	1-1	0-0	0-1
Rochdale	2-1	3-0	1-2	0-2	•	0-3	1-1	1-2	1-1	0-0	3-0	2-2	4-0	0-2	2-2	2-0	0-2	1-2	0-0	0-0	1-2	3-1	1-1	0-4
Scarborough	1-1	2-1	1-4	•	1-3	1-2	0-2	2-1	1-1	2-3	4-0	0-1	2-1	1-1	3-1	4-2	2-2	1-2	0-0	1-0	1-0	2-0	0-2	1-1
Scunthorpe United	0-2	1-0	•	3-3	1-3	1-2	2-2	0-0	2-6	0-2	2-1	2-1	0-1	0-0	2-1	4-0	1-2	1-1	2-3	1-0	1-1	1-2	1-2	2-0
Torquay United	0-1	•	1-8	0-0	1-2	0-4	1-1	3-0	3-0	1-1	2-1	1-0	1-0	2-1	1-1	0-2	1-2	1-0	2-0	2-1	0-0	0-3	0-2	1-1
Wigan Athletic	•	3-0	2-1	2-0	1-2	0-1	0-2	0-1	1-1	1-1	1-0	2-1	2-1	1-1	2-2	1-1	1-0	1-0	0-0	2-0	3-1	3-1	1-2	1-0

Two-legged finals until 1966, all finals after 1966 played at Wembley

Year	Winners		Runners-up	Result
1961	Aston Villa	v	Rotherham United	3–2 (0–2, 3–0 after extra time)
1962	Norwich City	v	Rochdale	4–0 (3–0, 1–0)
1963	Birmingham City	v	Aston Villa	3–1 (3–1, 0–0)
1964	Leicester City	v	Stoke City	4–3 (1–1, 3–2)
1965	Chelsea	v	Leicester City	3–2 (3–2, 0–0)
1966	West Bromwich Albion	v	West Ham United	5–3 (1–2, 4–1)
1967	Queens Park Rangers	v	West Bromwich Albion	3–2
1968	Leeds United	v	Arsenal	1–0
1969	Swindon Town	v	Arsenal	3–1 after extra time
1970	Manchester City	v	West Bromwich Albion	2–1 after extra time
1971	Tottenham Hotspur	v	Aston Villa	2–0
1972	Stoke City	v	Chelsea	2–1
1973	Tottenham Hotspur	v	Norwich City	1–0
1974	Wolverhampton Wanderers	v	Manchester City	2–1
1975	Aston Villa	v	Norwich City	1–0
1976	Manchester City	v	Newcastle United	2–1
1977	Aston Villa	v	Everton	0–0
	Aston Villa	v	Everton	1–1 after extra time replay at Hillsborough
	Aston Villa	v	Everton	3–2 after extra time; 2nd replay at Old Trafford
1978	Nottingham Forest	v	Liverpool	0–0 after extra time
	Nottingham Forest	v	Liverpool	1–0 replay at Old Trafford
1979	Nottingham Forest	v	Southampton	3–2
1980	Wolverhampton Wanderers	v	Nottingham Forest	1–0
1981	Liverpool	v	West Ham United	1–1 after extra time
	Liverpool	v	West Ham United	2–1 replay at Villa Park

as Milk Cup

Year	Winners		Runners-up	Result
1982	Liverpool	v	Tottenham Hotspur	3–1 after extra time
1983	Liverpool	v	Manchester United	2–1 after extra time
1984	Liverpool	v	Everton	0–0 after extra time
	Liverpool	v	Everton	1–0 replay at Maine Road
1985	Norwich City	v	Sunderland	1–0
1986	Oxford United	v	Queens Park Rangers	3–0

as Littlewoods Cup

Year	Winners		Runners-up	Result
1987	Arsenal	v	Liverpool	2–1
1988	Luton Town	v	Arsenal	3–2
1989	Nottingham Forest	v	Luton Town	3–1
1990	Nottingham Forest	v	Oldham Athletic	1–0

as Rumbelows Cup

Year	Winners		Runners-up	Result
1991	Sheffield Wednesday	v	Manchester United	1–0
1992	Manchester United	v	Nottingham Forest	1–0

as Coca-Cola Cup

Year	Winners		Runners-up	Result
1993	Arsenal	v	Sheffield Wednesday	2–1
1994	Aston Villa	v	Manchester United	3–1
1995	Liverpool	v	Bolton Wanderers	2–1
1996	Aston Villa	v	Leeds United	3–0

45 ● COCA-COLA CUP 1995–96

First Round (Two Legs)

Barnet	0;0	v	Charlton Athletic	0;2
Birmingham City	1;2	v	Plymouth Argyle	0;1
Bradford City	2;3	v	Blackpool	1;2
Cambridge United	2;0	v	Swindon Town	1;2
Chester City	4;3	v	Wigan Athletic	1;1
Crewe Alexandra	4;1	v	Darlington	0;1
Chesterfield	0;1	v	Bury	1;2
Colchester United	2;1	v	Bristol City	1;2*
Doncaster Rovers	1;0	v	Shrewsbury Town	1;0†
Fulham	3;2	v	Brighton & Hove Albion	0;0
Gillingham	1;2	v	Bristol Rovers	1;4
Hereford United	0;2	v	Oxford United	2;3
Huddersfield Town	1;3	v	Port Vale	2;1
Hull City	1;4	v	Carlisle United	2;2
Luton Town	1;1	v	AFC Bournemouth	1;2
Mansfield Town	0;1	v	Burnley	1;3
Notts County	2;2	v	Lincoln City	0;0
Portsmouth	0;0	v	Cardiff City	2;1
Preston North End	1;2	v	Sunderland	1;3
Rochdale	2;1	v	York City	1;5
Scarborough	1;0	v	Hartlepool United	0;1*
Scunthorpe United	4;0	v	Rotherham United	1;5
Stockport County	1;2	v	Wrexham	0;2
Swansea City	4;0	v	Peterborough United	1;3†
Torquay United	0;1†	v	Exeter City	0;1
Walsall	2;2	v	Brentford	2;3
West Bromwich Albion	1;4	v	Northampton Town	1;2
Wycombe Wanderers	3;0	v	Leyton Orient	0;2

Second Round (Two Legs)

Aston Villa	6;1	v	Peterborough United	0;1
Birmingham City	3;1	v	Grimsby Town	1;1
Blackburn Rovers	3;1	v	Swindon Town	2;1
Bolton Wanderers	1;3	v	Brentford	0;2
Bradford City	3;2	v	Nottingham Forest	2;2
Bristol City	0;1	v	Newcastle United	5;3
Bristol Rovers	0;0	v	West Ham United	1;3
Cardiff City	0;1	v	Southampton	3;2
Coventry City	2;1	v	Hull City	0;0
Crewe Alexandra	2;2	v	Sheffield Wednesday	2;5
Hartlepool United	0;0	v	Arsenal	3;5
Huddersfield Town	2;0	v	Barnsley	0;4
Leeds United	0;3	v	Notts County	0;2
Leicester City	2;2	v	Burnley	0;0
Liverpool	2;1	v	Sunderland	0;0
Manchester United	0;3	v	York City	3;1
Middlesbrough	2;1	v	Rotherham United	1;0
Millwall	0;4	v	Everton	0;2
Norwich City	6;3	v	Torquay United	1;2
Oxford United	1;1	v	Queens Park Rangers	1;2
Reading	1;4	v	West Bromwich Albion	1;2

Sheffield United	2;2	v	Bury	1;4
Shrewsbury Town	1;1	v	Derby County	3;1
Southend United	2;0	v	Crystal Palace	2;2
Stockport County	1;2	v	Ipswich Town	1;1
Stoke City	0;1	v	Chelsea	0;0
Tottenham Hotspur	4;3	v	Chester City	0;1
Tranmere Rovers	1;3	v	Oldham Athletic	0;1
Watford	1;1*	v	AFC Bournemouth	1;1
Wimbledon	4;3	v	Charlton Athletic	5;3
Wolverhampton Wanderers	2;5	v	Fulham	0;1
Wycombe Wanderers	0;0	v	Manchester City	0;4

Third Round (replays in italics)

Aston Villa	v	Stockport County	2–0
Barnsley	v	Arsenal	0–3
Birmingham City	v	Tranmere Rovers	1–1
Tranmere Rovers	*v*	*Birmingham City*	*1–3*
Crystal Palace	v	Middlesbrough	2–2
Middlesbrough	*v*	*Crystal Palace*	*2–0*
Coventry City	v	Tottenham Hotspur	3–2
Derby County	v	Leeds United	0–1
Leicester City	v	Bolton Wanderers	2–3
Liverpool	v	Manchester City	4–0
Millwall	v	Sheffield Wednesday	0–2
Norwich City	v	Bradford City	0–0
Bradford City	*v*	*Norwich City*	*3–5*
Queens Park Rangers	v	York City	3–1
Reading	v	Bury	2–1
Southampton	v	West Ham United	2–1
Stoke City	v	Newcastle United	0–4
Watford	v	Blackburn Rovers	1–2
Wolverhampton Wanderers	v	Charlton Athletic	2–1

Fourth Round (replays in italic)

Arsenal	v	Sheffield Wednesday	2–1
Aston Villa	v	Queens Park Rangers	1–0
Leeds United	v	Blackburn Rovers	2–1
Liverpool	v	Newcastle United	0–1
Middlesbrough	v	Birmingham City	0–0
Birmingham City	*v*	*Middlesbrough*	*2–0*
Norwich City	v	Bolton Wanderers	0–0
Bolton Wanderers	*v*	*Norwich City*	*0–0**
Reading	v	Southampton	2–1
Wolverhampton Wanderers	v	Coventry City	2–1

Fifth Round (replay in italic)

Arsenal	v	Newcastle United	2–0
Aston Villa	v	Wolverhampton Wanderers	1–0
Leeds United	v	Reading	2–1
Norwich City	v	Birmingham City	1–1
Birmingham City	*v*	*Norwich City*	*2–1*

Semi-Finals (Two Legs)

Arsenal	2;0	v	Aston Villa	2;0†
Leeds United	2;3	v	Birmingham City	1;0

Final

Aston Villa	v	Leeds United	3–0

* won on penalty-kicks
† won on away goals

46 ● UK LIVING WOMEN'S FA CUP – FINAL TIE 1996

Croydon 1   Liverpool 1 (a.e.t., Croydon won 3–2 on penalty-kicks)

Despite losing their player-manager Debbie Bampton after just nine minutes with a calf injury, Croydon dug in to hold Liverpool over two hours at Millwall FC and then lift the Cup after an exciting penalty shootout.

Croydon were formed in 1991 under the name of Bromley Borough WFC with the support of Bromley Borough Council Leisure Services. Bromley were WFA Cup semi-finalists in 1993, losing 2–0 to Arsenal, and a year later became part of the ICIS League side Croydon FC, changing their name accordingly.

In the Women's World Cup last summer Croydon had provided six members of the England squad, including captain Debbie Bampton whose Cup Final appearance in the New Den was so cruelly cut short. Another World Cup performer, Liverpool's Karen Burke, was a driving force in midfield who ran with the ball to link up well with the attack. She pushed a pass out to McQuiggan on the left and surged into the box to meet the return ball and hit it firmly past the diving Cooper's right hand for the opening goal on 23 minutes.

Croydon could easily have wilted in the circumstances but came back strongly to equalise before the break. Their captain, Hope Powell, shot high into the net over the head of Liverpool 'keeper Rachael Brown – making history as the youngest Cup finalist at 15 – after Tina Mapes had worked the ball over to her out on the right in the 38th minute.

Both sides were evenly matched thereafter and the two goalkeepers – Brown particularly showing a maturity beyond her years – were solid right to the end. Liverpool's Clare Taylor thumped the ball against the underside of the bar after a second-half corner-kick had eluded three Croydon players at the near post and Burke, already with one goal to her name on the day and two in last year's Final, shot straight at Cooper with the best chance to avoid penalties.

Burke and Powell were successful with their kicks, then three in a row were missed. Brenda Sempare and Mapes scored with ease, either side of a successful effort from Liverpool substitute Leanne Duffy. Another Liverpool miss left Croydon shootout winners by 3–2.

Croydon: Cooper, Dines (Mulligan), Osborne (McGloin), Powell, Smith D., Saunders, Mapes, Bampton (Cottier), Sempare, Davis, Proctor.

Liverpool: Brown, Taylor L., Griffiths (Formston), Taylor C., Thomas, Hayward, Burke, Easton (Duffy), Harper, Handley, McQuiggan (Holland).

Referee: S. Mathieson (Cheshire)
Attendance: 2,122
Guest of Honour: Lady Millichip

Croydon's Kerry Davis
puts in a brave challenge
on Jodie Handley.

47 ● UK LIVING WOMEN'S FA CUP 1995–96

Preliminary round – 10 September 1995

(Replays in italics)   *Results*

Hull City	v	Blackburn Rangers	4–2
Blackpool Wren Rovers	v	Scunthorpe Ironesses	0–4
Manchester Rangers	v	Winsford United	
(walkover for Winsford United – Manchester Rangers withdrawn)			
Deans	v	Runcorn	0–4
Royal Strikers	v	Lowestoft Town	
(walkover for Lowestoft Town – Royal Strikers withdrawn)			
West Ham	v	Great Wakering Rovers	5–0
Dulwich Hamlet	v	Hackney	8–1
Drayton Wanderers	v	Chelsea	0–4
Chesham United	v	Thames Valley	2–5
Sherborne	v	Tuffley Athletic	12–0
Hereford United	v	Cable-Tel (Newport)	1–5

First round – 17 September 1995

Preston Rangers	v	Hull City	3–2
Amble Town	v	Cleveland	7–0
Sheffield & Hallam	v	Haslingden	4–1
Sunderland	v	Leeds United	2–1
Darlington Spraire	v	Newcastle	3–13
Accrington Stanley	v	Doncaster Rovers	1–2
Brighouse	v	Wakefield	3–5
Kirklees	v	Barnsley	4–4
Barnsley	*v*	*Kirklees*	*1–0*
Lincoln United	v	Kilnhurst	0–4
Scunthorpe Ironesses	v	Bradford City	1–1
Bradford City	*v*	*Scunthorpe Ironesses*	*5–1*
Rochdale	v	Wigan	4–1
Manchester Belle Vue	v	Newsham PH	10–1
Radcliffe Borough	v	Chester City	12–0
Manchester United	v	Vernon-Carus	7–0
Leek Town	v	Bangor City	2–3
Blackburn Rovers	v	Derby County	4–2
Winsford United	v	Whalley Rangers	1–5
Highfield Rangers	v	Calverton MW	4–2
Nettleham	v	Wrexham	1–2
Warrington	v	Chesterfield	1–2
Manchester City	v	Oldham Athletic	0–1
Newcastle Town	v	Stockport County	4–5
Liverpool Feds	v	Rainworth MW	4–3
Stockport	v	Runcorn	10–1
Milton Keynes Athletic	v	Dunstable	1–1
Dunstable	*v*	*Milton Keynes Athletic*	*3–0*
Rugby	v	Coventry City	0–12
Bedford Bells	v	Lowestoft Town	4–1

Cambridge City	v	Birmingham City	2–4
Rea Valley Rovers	v	Cambridge United	1–4
Tamworth	v	Leicester City	1–2
Leighton Linslade	v	Atherstone	

(walkover for Leighton Linslade – Atherstone failed to fulfil the tie)

Canary Racers	v	Pye	4–0
Chelsea	v	Hassocks	8–0
Watford	v	Fulham	1–4
Collier Row	v	Abbey Rangers	4–2
Tottenham Hotspur	v	Winchester & Ealing	9–0
Charlton	v	Whitehawk	2–5
Dulwich Hamlet	v	Surbiton Town	2–1
Colchester	v	Romford	3–2
Mill Hill United	v	Redbridge Wanderers	6–0
Crowbrough Athletic	v	Barnet	2–3
Enfield	v	Sutton United	2–0
Palace Eagles	v	West Ham	1–0
Sittingbourne	v	Newham	0–7

(tie abandoned after 86 mins, tie awarded to Newham)

Edenbridge Town	v	Colchester Royals	3–4
Clacton	v	Crystal Palace	

(walkover for Clacton – Crystal Palace failed to fulfil the tie)

Gillingham	v	Harlow Town	3–7
St Georges	v	Teynham Gunners	5–0
Thames Valley	v	Sturminster Newton	

(walkover for Thames Valley – Sturminster Newton withdrawn)

AFC Bournemouth	v	Bow Brickhill	3–0
Leatherhead	v	Aylesbury United	4–1
Gosport Borough	v	Thame United	2–5
Binfield	v	Portsmouth	3–0
Reading Royals	v	Farnborough Town	1–2
Bracknell Town	v	Slough Town	6–2
Winchester City	v	Camberley Town	0–9
Denham United	v	Newbury	3–1
Cable–Tel (Newport)	v	Plymouth Pilgrims	1–5
Elmore Eagles	v	Frome	0–7
Inter Cardiff	v	Clevedon	15–0
Newton Abbot	v	Barry	1–3
Swindon Town	v	Cardiff Institute	

(walkover for Swindon Town – Cardiff Institute withdrawn)

Clevedon United	v	Swindon Town Spitfires	0–6
Brislington	v	Sherborne	2–8
Truro City	v	Yate Town	1–0
Cheltenham YMCA	v	Freeway	12–1
Exeter Rangers	v	Worcester City	2–8

Second round – 15 October 1995

Doncaster Rovers	v	Middlesbrough	0–3
Kilnhurst	v	Barnsley	5–1
RTM Newcastle Kestrels	v	Newcastle	0–1
Bronte	v	Preston Rangers	3–2
Amble Town	v	Huddersfield Town	1–5
Sheffield Wednesday	v	Sheffield Hallam United	6–0
Sunderland	v	Wakefield	0–2
Wrexham	v	Manchester United	1–3

Radcliffe Borough	v	Bangor City Girls	1–4
Leicester City	v	Oldham Athletic	1–5
Whalley Range	v	Highfield Rangers	0–4
Coventry City	v	Chesterfield	2–1
Garswood/St Helens	v	Bradford City	3–0
Liverpool Feds	v	Birmingham City	7–5
Dunstable	v	Blackburn Rovers	2–4
Stockport County	v	Stockport	2–1
Rochdale	v	Tranmere Rovers	0–9
Notts County	v	Manchester Belle Vue	1–3
Mill Hill United	v	Colchester Royals	4–2
Colchester	v	Langford	3–7
Camberley Town	v	Dulwich Hamlet	1–7
Denham United	v	Leighton Linslade	14–0
Barnet	v	St Georges	4–3
Brentford	v	Leyton Orient	2–3
Palace Eagles	v	Leatherhead	3–1
Cambridge United	v	Newham	0–1
Tottenham Hotspur	v	Enfield	5–4
Whitehawk	v	Wimbledon	1–0
Town & County	v	Chelsea	3–4
Bedford Bells	v	Collier Row	3–1
Clacton	v	Brighton & Hove Albion	1–5
Canary Racers	v	Harlow Town	6–0
Berkhamsted	v	Fulham	5–0
Ipswich Town	v	Three Bridges	3–1
Plymouth Pilgrims	v	Swindon Town	3–0
AFC Bournemouth	v	Thame United	0–2
Sherborne	v	Worcester City	18–0
Bracknell Town	v	Binfield	1–7
Swindon Town Spitfires	v	Farnborough Town	3–1
Bristol City	v	Southampton Saints	2–3
Truro City	v	Oxford United	0–1
Frome	v	Thames Valley	3–0
Cheltenham YMCA	v	Barry	2–2
Barry	*v*	*Cheltenham YMCA*	*2–1*
Inter Cardiff	v	Kidderminster Harriers	2–1

Third round – 12 November 1995

Oldham Athletic	v	Liverpool Feds	1–0
Bangor City Girls	v	Huddersfield Town	1–6
Bronte	v	Stockport County	1–3
Blackburn Rovers	v	Manchester United	1–3
Middlesbrough	v	Manchester Belle Vue	2–1
Newcastle	v	Wakefield	2–1
Coventry City	v	Sheffield Wednesday	0–2
Kilnhurst	v	Highfield Rangers	2–4
Tranmere Rovers	v	Garswood/St Helens	2–3
Leyton Orient	v	Langford	2–3
Ipswich Town	v	Denham United	7–3
Canary Racers	v	Mill Hill United	2–1
Bedford Bells	v	Berkhamsted Town	0–6
Chelsea	v	Palace Eagles	3–1
Brighton & Hove Albion	v	Dulwich Hamlet	6–0
Barnet	v	Whitehawk	0–4
Newham	v	Tottenham Hotspur	0–6

Oxford United	v	Thame United	3–0
Swindon Town Spitfires	v	Southampton Saints	2–3
Plymouth Pilgrims	v	Barry	1–1
Barry	*v*	*Plymouth Pilgrims*	*4–3*
Inter Cardiff	v	Sherborne	3–0
Frome	v	Binfield	1–4

Fourth round – 3 December 1995

Oxford United	v	Everton	3–6
Millwall Lionesses	v	Langford	5–0
Arsenal	v	Manchester United	10–0
Binfield	v	Doncaster Belles	0–9
Chelsea	v	Newcastle	0–0
Newcastle	*v*	*Chelsea*	*3–0*
Huddersfield Town	v	Berkhamsted Town	2–1
Liverpool	v	Garswood/St Helens	3–0
Oldham Athletic	v	Croydon	2–4
Ilkeston Town Rangers	v	Highfield Rangers	5–0
Southampton Saints	v	Whitehawk	1–2
Tottenham Hotspur	v	Villa Aztecs	3–4
Stockport County	v	Wembley	0–9
Sheffield Wednesday	v	Middlesbrough	2–3
Brighton & Hove Albion	v	Ipswich Town	0–1
Inter Cardiff	v	Wolverhampton Wanderers	1–0
Canary Racers	v	Barry	2–2
Barry	*v*	*Canary Racers*	*1–4*

Fifth round – 21 January 1996

Liverpool	v	Middlesbrough	7–1
Croydon	v	Inter Cardiff	2–0
Canary Racers	v	Ipswich Town	1–3
Ilkeston Town	v	Millwall Lionesses	2–0
Arsenal	v	Wembley	2–1
Whitehawk	v	Newcastle	1–0
Huddersfield Town	v	Everton	5–5
Everton	*v*	*Huddersfield Town*	*1–2*
Villa Aztecs	v	Doncaster Belles	1–5

Sixth round – 18 February 1996

Ilkeston Town	v	Arsenal	1–2
Huddersfield Town	v	Liverpool	0–9
Whitehawk	v	Ipswich Town	2–2
Ipswich Town	*v*	*Whitehawk*	*2–1*
Croydon	v	Doncaster Belles	1–0

Semi-Finals – 24 March 1996

Liverpool	v	Arsenal	0–0
(Liverpool won 5–4 on kicks from the penalty mark)			
(at Runcorn FC)			
Croydon	v	Ipswich Town	5–0
(at Dulwich Hamlet FC)			

Final – 28 April 1996

Croydon	v	Liverpool	1–1
(Croydon won on kicks from the penalty mark 3–2)			
(at Millwall FC)			

48 ● FA WOMEN'S PREMIER LEAGUE – FINAL TABLES 1995–96

National Division

	P	W	D	L	F	A	GD	Pts	
Croydon	18	13	5	0	58	17	+41	44	
Doncaster Belles	18	14	2	2	57	19	+38	44	
Arsenal	18	11	4	3	54	12	+42	37	
Everton	18	10	1	7	44	40	+4	31	
Liverpool	18	9	2	7	36	27	+9	29	
Wembley	18	7	5	6	43	21	+22	26	
Millwall Lionesses	18	5	3	10	20	32	−12	18	Villa Aztecs and
Ilkeston Town	18	4	3	11	21	46	−25	15	Wolverhampton Wanderers
Villa Aztecs	18	4	1	13	22	51	−29	13	relegated to Northern
Wolverhampton Wanderers	18	0	0	18	8	98	−90	0	Division

Northern Division

	P	W	D	L	F	A	GD	Pts	
Tranmere Rovers	16	14	2	0	73	11	+62	44	Tranmere Rovers promoted
Huddersfield Town	16	12	3	1	60	23	+37	39	to National Division
Garswood/St Helens	16	9	4	3	51	23	+28	31	
Sheffield Wednesday	16	9	3	4	41	22	+19	30	
Langford	16	6	2	8	27	44	−17	17*	
RTM Newcastle Kestrels	16	3	4	9	21	43	−22	13	
Notts County	16	4	1	11	18	43	−25	13	
Kidderminster Harriers	16	4	1	11	27	53	−26	13	Bradford City promoted to
Bronte	16	0	2	14	11	67	−56	2	Northern Division

* Langford deducted 3 points

Southern Division

	P	W	D	L	F	A	GD	Pts	
Southampton Saints	18	13	2	3	52	21	+31	41	Southampton Saints
Berkhamsted Town	18	13	1	4	42	26	+16	40	promoted to National
Wimbledon	18	12	1	5	53	36	+17	37	Division
Three Bridges	18	11	1	6	47	24	+23	34	
Ipswich Town	18	8	1	9	36	35	+1	25	Langford transferred to
Brighton & Hove Albion	18	5	4	9	35	47	−12	19	Southern Division
Town & County	18	6	1	11	27	48	−21	19	
Leyton Orient	18	5	2	11	33	45	−12	16*	
Oxford United	18	4	4	10	24	46	−22	16	Whitehawk promoted to
Brentford	18	3	3	12	29	50	−21	12	Southern Division

* Leyton Orient deducted 1 point

Brentford relegated

FA Women's Premier League Cup Final: Wembley Ladies 2 Doncaster Belles 2 (Wembley won 5–3 on penalties).

	Italy	Croatia	Portugal	Italy	Croatia	Portugal
P. Cope (Millwall Lionesses)	1	1	1	1	1	1
T. Mapes (Croydon)	2		8*	3*		8
K. Davis (Croydon)	3	3	10	10	10	10
K. Burke (Everton & Liverpool)	4	4	7		7	7
B. Easton (Liverpool)	5	5	3	3		
G. Coultard (Doncaster Belles)	6	6	6	6	6	6
M. Spacey (Arsenal)	7					
D. Bampton (Croydon)	8	8	8	8	8	
K. Farley (Hammarby)	9	9	9			
H. Powell (Croydon)	10	10	4	4	9	
K. Smith (Wembley)	11	11	11	11	11	11
K. Walker (Doncaster Belles)	2*	7		9		
K. Pealling (Arsenal)	10*					
C. Harwood (Wembley)		2		5*		
M. Marley (Everton)		2*	5	5	5	5
G. Borman (Doncaster Belles)		9*				
T. Proctor (Croydon)		10*		7		
C. Lacey (West Ham United)			1*			
S. Williams (Arsenal)			2	2	3	2
M. Catterall (Garswood/St. Helens)			10*		2	
V. Exley (Doncaster Belles)				10*	9*	9*
M. Phillip (Millwall Lionesses)					4	4
C. Wheatley (Arsenal)					2*	
K. Few (Arsenal)						3
M. Harper (Liverpool)						9
K. Jerray-Silver (Wembley)						3*
D. Smith (Croydon)						8*

* *substitute*

WOMEN'S INTERNATIONAL MATCHES 1995–96

Date	Venue	Match	Result
1.11.95	Sunderland	England v Italy	1–1
19.11.95	Charlton	England v Croatia	5–0
11.2.96	Benavente	Portugal v England	0–5
16.3.96	Calabria	Italy v England	2–1
18.4.96	Osijek	Croatia v England	0–2
19.5.96	Brentford	England v Portugal	3–0

All matches in the UEFA Championship for Women

Qualifying Group 3 – Final Table

	P	W	D	L	F	A	Pts
Italy	6	4	2	0	16	3	14
ENGLAND	6	4	1	1	17	3	13
Portugal	6	2	0	4	4	14	6
Croatia	6	0	1	5	0	17	1

England, as runners-up, now play Spain in a two-legged play-off in September for a place in the finals.

Year	Venue	Winners		Runners-up	Result
1965		London	v	Staffordshire	6–2†
1966	Dudley	Unique United	v	Aldridge Fabrications	1–0
1967	Hendon	Carlton United	v	Stoke Works	2–0
1968	Cambridge	Drovers	v	Brook United	2–0
1969	Romford	Leigh Park	v	Loke United	3–1
1970	Corby	Vention United	v	Unique United	1–0
1971	Leamington	Beacontree Rovers	v	Saltley United	2–0
1972	Dudley	Newton Unity	v	Springfield Colts	4–0
1973	Spennymoor	Carlton United	v	Wear Valley	2–1*
1974	Birmingham	Newton Unity	v	Brentford East	3–0
1975	High Wycombe	Fareham Town Centipedes	v	Players Athletic Engineers	1–0
1976	Spennymoor	Brandon United	v	Evergreen	2–1
1977	Spennymoor	Langley Park RH	v	Newton Unity	2–0
1978	Nuneaton	Arras	v	Lion Rangers	2–2
	Bishop's Stortford	Arras	v	Lion Rangers	2–1
1979	Southport	Lobster	v	Carlton United	3–2
1980	Letchworth	Fantail	v	Twin Foxes	1–0
1981	Birkenhead	Fantail	v	Mackintosh	1–0
1982	Hitchin	Dingle Rail	v	Twin Foxes	2–1
1983	Walthamstow	Eagle	v	Lee Chapel North	2–1
1984	Runcorn	Lee Chapel North	v	Eagle	1–1
	Dagenham	Lee Chapel North	v	Eagle	4–3*
1985	Norwich	Hobbies	v	Avenue	1–1
	Birkenhead	Hobbies	v	Avenue	2–2
	Nuneaton	Hobbies	v	Avenue	2–1
1986	Birkenhead	Avenue	v	Glenn Sports	1–0
1987	Birmingham	Lodge Cottrell	v	Avenue	1–0*
1988	Newcastle	Nexday	v	Sunderland Humb Plains	2–0
1989	Stockport	Almithak	v	East Levenshulme	3–1
1990	West Bromwich	Humbledon Plains Farm	v	Marston Sports	2–1
1991	Wigan	Nicosia	v	Ouzavich	3–2*
1992	Reading	Theale	v	Marston Sports	3–2
1993	Chester	Seymour	v	Bedfont Sunday	1–0
1994	Woking	Ranelagh Sports	v	Hartlepool Lion Hotel	2–0
1995	Hull	St Joseph's (Luton)	v	B&A Scaffolding	2–1
1996	Northampton	St Joseph's (Luton)	v	Croxteth & Gilmoss RBL	2–1

* after extra time
† two legs

51 ● FA SUNDAY CUP 1995–96

First round – 29 October 1995

Mitre	v	Stockton Roseworth Social	
(walkover for Stockton Roseworth Social – Mitre withdrawn)			
A3	v	Etnaward	
(walkover for A3 – Etnaward withdrawn)			
Albion Sports	v	Nenthead	3–0
Townley	v	Northwood	3–3
Northwood	*v*	*Townley*	*4–2*
Mode Force Boulevard	v	Boundary	3–2
Lobster	v	Eden Vale	0–4
Baildon Athletic	v	Seaton Sluice SC	2–5
Bolton Woods	v	Dock	1–1
Dock	*v*	*Bolton Woods*	*1–1*
(Dock won on kicks from the penalty mark 3–2)			
Manfast	v	Sandon	0–1
Littlewoods Athletic	v	Clubmoor Nalgo	1–2
SDV	v	The Tiger	3–5
East Bowling Unity	v	Hartlepool Staincliffe Hotel	0–2
BRNESC	v	Nicosia	2–3
Dudley & Weetslade	v	Britannia	2–1
Croxteth & Gilmoss RBL	v	Fiddlers	4–1
Caldway	v	Almithak	3–2
Stanley Road	v	Walford Maritime	2–1
Salerno	v	Hartlepool Rovers	8–1
Waterloo Social Club Blyth	v	Queens Park AFC	
(walkover for Queens Park – Waterloo Social Club Blyth withdrawn)			
Grosvenor Park	v	Courage	1–1
Courage	*v*	*Grosvenor Park*	*1–2*
Leicester City Bus	v	Sawston Keys	1–4
Willen	v	BRSC Aidan	1–0
Erdington Cosmos Swan	v	Evesham WMC	8–1
Altone Steels	v	Marston Sports	1–6
Park Inn	v	Hemel Hempstead Social	5–0
Girton Eagles	v	Slade Celtic	0–2
Hanham Sunday	v	Celtic SC (Luton)	0–1
Hundred Acre	v	Sun Kislingbury	
(walkover for Hundred Acre – Sun Kislingbury withdrawn)			
Clifton Albion	v	Brookvale Athletic	1–1
Brookvale Athletic	*v*	*Clifton Albion*	*4–0*
Birmingham Celtic	v	Ouzavich	1–2
St Clements Hospital	v	Watford Labour	2–1
Sandwell	v	Olympic Star	2–1
Dereham Hobbies	v	Roofwork	0–1
Poringland Wanderers	v	St Joseph's (South Oxhey)	2–1
Coach & Horses	v	Belstone	1–0
Melton Youth Old Boys	v	Heathfield	2–2
Heathfield	*v*	*Melton Youth Old Boys*	*2–0*
Pitsea	v	Continental	3–1
Holderness United	v	Bedfont Sunday	1–0
Morden Nomads	v	St Joseph's (Bristol)	2–2
St Joseph's (Bristol)	*v*	*Morden Nomads*	*0–0*
(Morden Nomads won on kicks from the penalty mark 4–3)			

(Replays in italics)

Reading Borough	v	Fryerns Community	0–4
Leavesden Sports & Social	v	Charlton Royal 89	6–1
Inter Royalle	v	Forest Athletic	1–2
Park Royals	v	Oakwood Sports	1–0

(at Oakwood Sports)

British Rail SA	v	Caversham Park	

(walkover for Caversham Park – British Rail SA withdrawn)

Northfield Rangers	v	Cherry Tree (Warley)	0–3
Cavaliers	v	Hallen United	0–1
Ford Basildon	v	South Croydon	9–0
Merton Admiral	v	Oxford Road Social	

(walkover for Oxford Road Social – Merton Admiral withdrawn)

Second round – 19 November 1995

Park Inn	v	Hartlepool Lion Hotel	1–1
Hartlepool Lion Hotel	*v*	*Park Inn*	*2–1*
Seaton Sluice SC	v	Caldway	5–1
Stanley Road	v	Newfield	5–1
Lodge Cottrell	v	Brookvale Athletic	2–1
Dudley & Weetslade	v	Eden Vale	4–1
Sandon	v	Clubmoor Nalgo	0–1
Croxteth & Gilmoss RBL	v	A3	3–0
Stockton Roseworth Social	v	Dock	4–0
Oakenshaw	v	Salerno	0–2
Allerton	v	Northwood	5–1
Hartlepool Staincliffe Hotel	v	Shankhouse United	0–2
Mode Force Boulevard	v	The Tiger	1–2
Humbledon Plains Farm	v	Nicosia	1–3
Seymour	v	Marston Sports	1–2
Lion Hotel	v	Queens Park AFC	0–0
Queens Park AFC	*v*	*Lion Hotel*	*2–1*
Albion Sports	v	Sandwell	4–2
Microgen Breakspear	v	Slade Celtic	0–3
Hundred Acre	v	Erdington Cosmos Swan	2–0
Berner United	v	Cherry Tree (Warley)	2–2
Cherry Tree (Warley)	*v*	*Berner United*	*1–2*
Hammer	v	Roofwork	3–0
Heathfield	v	Coach & Horses	4–0
Poringland Wanderers	v	Sawston Keys	1–3
Grosvenor Park	v	Fryerns Community	4–1
Caversham Park	v	Ouzavich	0–2
Park Royals	v	Oxford Road Social	2–1
Lebeq Tavern	v	Pitsea	3–1
Morden Nomads	v	St Clements Hospital	0–1
Hallen United	v	Capel Plough	0–2
Willen	v	Theale (Sunday)	3–2
Ford Basildon	v	Leavesden Sports & Social	6–2
Forest Athletic	v	Holderness United	3–0
Celtic SC (Luton)	v	St Josephs (Luton)	0–0
St Joseph's (Luton)	*v*	*Celtic SC (Luton)*	*6–2*

bye: Sheerness Steel United

● 171

Third round – 10 December 1995

Queens Park AFC	v	Stanley Road	2–1
Nicosia	v	Lodge Cottrell	3–1
Marston Sports	v	Seaton Sluice SC	6–2
Shankhouse United	v	Dudley & Weetslade	0–7
Stockton Roseworth Social	v	Allerton	2–1
Croxteth & Gilmoss RBL	v	Albion Sports	5–1
The Tiger	v	Hartlepool Lion Hotel	1–3
Salerno	v	Clubmoor Nalgo	1–0
Forest Athletic	v	Berner United	1–0
Willen	v	Hammer	2–0
Ford Basildon	v	Hundred Acre	2–1
St Clements Hospital	v	Heathfield	3–0
Ouzavich	v	Lebeq Tavern	2–2
Lebeq Tavern	*v*	*Ouzavich*	*5–1*
Grosvenor Park	v	St Joseph's (Luton)	2–4
Capel Plough	v	Slade Celtic	4–1
Park Royals	v	Sawston Keys	4–1

Fourth round – 14 January 1996

Croxteth & Gilmoss RBL	v	Stockton Roseworth Social	3–0
Nicosia	v	Marston Sports	1–0
Hartlepool Lion Hotel	v	Dudley & Weetslade	2–1
Salerno	v	Queens Park AFC	1–0
Lebeq Tavern	v	St Josephs (Luton)	1–2
Forest Athletic	v	Park Royals	1–6
Ford Basildon	v	Willen	0–3
St Clements Hospital	v	Capel Plough	1–0

Fifth round – 11 February 1996

Hartlepool Lion Hotel	v	Croxteth & Gilmoss RBL	0–4
Salerno	v	Nicosia	1–0
Park Royals	v	St Josephs (Luton)	1–2
St Clements Hospital	v	Willen	1–2

Semi-Finals – 17 March 1996

Croxteth & Gilmoss RBL *(at Southport FC)*	v	Salerno	4–3
St Josephs (Luton) *(at Leighton Town FC)*	v	Willen	2–0

Final – 5 May 1996

St Josephs (Luton) *(at Northampton Town FC)*	v	Croxteth & Gilmoss RBL	2–1

52 ● FA CHARITY SHIELD WINNERS
1908–1995

Year	Winners		Runners–up	Result
1908	Manchester United	v	Queens Park Rangers	1–1
	Manchester United	*v*	*Queens Park Rangers*	4–0
1909	Newcastle United	v	Northampton Town	2–0
1910	Brighton and Hove Albion	v	Aston Villa	1–0
1911	Manchester United	v	Swindon Town	8–4
1912	Blackburn Rovers	v	Queens Park Rangers	2–1
1913	Professionals	v	Amateurs	7–2
1914–18		not played		
1920	West Bromwich Albion	v	Tottenham Hotspur	2–0
1921	Tottenham Hotspur	v	Burnley	2–0
1922	Huddersfield Town	v	Liverpool	1–0
1923	Professionals	v	Amateurs	2–0
1924	Professionals	v	Amateurs	3–1
1925	Amateurs	v	Professionals	6–1
1926	Amateurs	v	Professionals	6–3
1927	Cardiff City	v	Corinthians	2–1
1928	Everton	v	Blackburn Rovers	2–1
1929	Professionals	v	Amateurs	3–0
1930	Arsenal	v	Sheffield Wednesday	2–1
1931	Arsenal	v	West Bromwich Albion	1–0
1932	Everton	v	Newcastle United	5–3
1933	Arsenal	v	Everton	3–0
1934	Arsenal	v	Manchester City	4–0
1935	Sheffield Wednesday	v	Arsenal	1–0
1936	Sunderland	v	Arsenal	2–1
1937	Manchester City	v	Sunderland	2–0
1938	Arsenal	v	Preston North End	2–1
1939–47		not played		
1948	Arsenal	v	Manchester United	4–3
1949	Portsmouth	v	Wolverhampton Wanderers	1–1*
1950	World Cup Team	v	Canadian Touring Team	4–2
1951	Tottenham Hotspur	v	Newcastle United	2–1
1952	Manchester United	v	Newcastle United	4–2
1953	Arsenal	v	Blackpool	3–1
1954	Wolverhampton Wanderers	v	West Bromwich Albion	4–4*
1955	Chelsea	v	Newcastle United	3–0
1956	Manchester United	v	Manchester City	1–0
1957	Manchester United	v	Aston Villa	4–0
1958	Bolton Wanderers	v	Wolverhampton Wanderers	4–1
1959	Wolverhampton Wanderers	v	Nottingham Forest	3–1
1960	Burnley	v	Wolverhampton Wanderers	2–2*
1961	Tottenham Hotspur	v	FA XI	3–2
1962	Tottenham Hotspur	v	Ipswich Town	5–1
1963	Everton	v	Manchester United	4–0
1964	Liverpool	v	West Ham United	2–2*
1965	Manchester United	v	Liverpool	2–2*
1966	Liverpool	v	Everton	1–0
1967	Manchester United	v	Tottenham Hotspur	3–3*
1968	Manchester City	v	West Bromwich Albion	6–1
1969	Leeds United	v	Manchester City	2–1

Year	Winners		Runners−up	Result
1970	Everton	v	Chelsea	2−1
1971	Leicester City	v	Liverpool	1−0
1972	Manchester City	v	Aston Villa	1−0
1973	Burnley	v	Manchester City	1−0
1974	Liverpool	v	Leeds United	1−1†
1975	Derby County	v	West Ham United	2−0
1976	Liverpool	v	Southampton	1−0
1977	Liverpool	v	Manchester United	0−0*
1978	Nottingham Forest	v	Ipswich Town	5−0
1979	Liverpool	v	Arsenal	3−1
1980	Liverpool	v	West Ham United	1−0
1981	Aston Villa	v	Tottenham Hotspur	2−2*
1982	Liverpool	v	Tottenham Hotspur	1−0
1983	Manchester United	v	Liverpool	2−0
1984	Everton	v	Liverpool	1−0
1985	Everton	v	Manchester United	2−0
1986	Everton	v	Liverpool	1−1*
1987	Everton	v	Coventry City	1−0
1988	Liverpool	v	Wimbledon	2−1
1989	Liverpool	v	Arsenal	1−0
1990	Liverpool	v	Manchester United	1−1*
1991	Arsenal	v	Tottenham Hotspur	0−0*
1992	Leeds United	v	Liverpool	4−3
1993	Manchester United	v	Arsenal	1−1†
1994	Manchester United	v	Blackburn Rovers	2−0
1995	Everton	v	Blackburn Rovers	1−0

* *each club retained Shield for six months*   † *won on penalty-kicks*

53 ● THE FOOTBALL ASSOCIATION FIXTURE PROGRAMME 1996–97

WC World Cup qualifying competition.   * closing date of rounds

August 1996

7	Wednesday	Euro Competitions Preliminary Round – 1st Leg
10	Saturday	Official Start of Season
11	Sunday	Littlewoods FA Charity Shield
17	Saturday	Commencement of FA Premier League and Football League
21	Wednesday	Euro Competitions Preliminary Round – 2nd Leg
		FL Coca-Cola Cup 1st Round – 1st Leg
26	Monday	Bank Holiday
28	Wednesday	FL Coca-Cola Cup 1st Round – 2nd Leg
31	Saturday	FA Cup Sponsored by Littlewoods Preliminary Round
		Austria v Scotland (WC)
		Wales v San Marino (WC)
		Liechtenstein v Republic of Ireland (WC)
		Northern Ireland v Ukraine (WC)

September 1996

1	Sunday	Moldova v England (WC)
4	Wednesday	International
7	Saturday	FA Carlsberg Vase 1st Round Qualifying
		FA Youth Cup Extra Preliminary Round*
8	Sunday	UK Living Women's FA Cup Preliminary Round
11	Wednesday	Euro Competitions 1st Round – 1st Leg
14	Saturday	FA Cup Sponsored by Littlewoods 1st Round Qualifying
18	Wednesday	FL Coca-Cola Cup 2nd Round – 1st Leg
21	Saturday	FA Youth Cup Preliminary Round*
25	Wednesday	Euro Competitions 1st Round – 2nd Leg
28	Saturday	FA Cup Sponsored by Littlewoods 2nd Round Qualifying
29	Sunday	UK Living Women's FA Cup 1st Round

October 1996

2	Wednesday	FL Coca-Cola Cup 2nd Round – Second Leg
5	Saturday	FA Carlsberg Vase 2nd Round Qualifying
		Latvia v Scotland (WC)
		Wales v Holland (WC)
		Northern Ireland v Armenia (WC)
9	Wednesday	England v Poland (WC)
		Estonia v Scotland (WC)
		Republic of Ireland v Macedonia (WC)
12	Saturday	FA Cup Sponsored by Littlewoods 3rd Round Qualifying
		FA Youth Cup 1st Round Qualifying Round*
		FA County Youth Cup 1st Round*
16	Wednesday	Euro Competitions 2nd Round – 1st Leg
19	Saturday	FA Umbro Trophy 1st Round Qualifying
23	Wednesday	FL Coca-Cola Cup 3rd Round
26	Saturday	FA Cup Sponsored by Littlewoods 4th Round Qualifying
27	Sunday	FA Sunday Cup 1st Round
30	Wednesday	Euro Competitions 2nd Round – 2nd Leg

November 1996

2	Saturday	FA Carlsberg Vase 1st Round Proper
		FA Youth Cup 2nd Round Qualifying*
3	Sunday	UK Living Women's FA Cup 1st Round
6	Wednesday	FL Coca-Cola Cup 3rd Round Replays
9	Saturday	FA Umbro Trophy 2nd Round Qualifying
		Georgia v England (WC)
		Holland v Wales (WC)
		Germany v Northern Ireland (WC)
10	Sunday	Scotland v Sweden (WC)
		Republic of Ireland v Iceland (WC)
16	Saturday	FA Cup Sponsored by Littlewoods 1st Round Proper
20	Wednesday	Euro Competitions 3rd Round – 1st Leg
23	Saturday	FA Carlsberg Vase 2nd Round Proper
		FA Youth Cup 1st Round Proper*
		FA County Youth Cup 2nd Round*
24	Sunday	FA Sunday Cup 2nd Round
27	Wednesday	FA Cup Sponsored by Littlewoods 1st Round Proper Replays
		FL Coca-Cola Cup 4th Round
30	Saturday	FA Umbro Trophy 3rd Round Qualifying

December 1996

1	Sunday	UK Living Women's FA Cup 3rd Round
4	Wednesday	Euro Competitions 3rd Round – 2nd Leg
7	Saturday	FA Cup Sponsored by Littlewoods 2nd Round Proper
14	Saturday	FA Carlsberg Vase 3rd Round Proper
		Wales v Turkey (WC) (*prov*)
		Northern Ireland v Albania (WC)
		FA Youth Cup 2nd Round Proper*
15	Sunday	FA Sunday Cup 3rd Round
		Wales v Turkey (WC) (*prov*)
18	Wednesday	FA Cup Sponsored by Littlewoods 2nd Round Proper Replays
		FL Coca-Cola Cup 4th Round Replays

January 1997

4	Saturday	FA Cup Sponsored by Littlewoods 3rd Round Proper
5	Sunday	UK Living Women's FA Cup 4th Round
8	Wednesday	FL Coca-Cola Cup 5th Round
11	Saturday	FA Carlsberg Vase 4th Round Proper
		FA Youth Cup 3rd Round Proper*
		FA County Youth Cup 3rd Round*
12	Sunday	FA Sunday Cup 4th Round
15	Wednesday	FA Cup Sponsored by Littlewoods 3rd Round Proper Replays
18	Saturday	FA Umbro Trophy 1st Round Proper
22	Wednesday	FL Coca-Cola Cup 5th Round Replays
25	Saturday	FA Cup Sponsored by Littlewoods 4th Round Proper

February 1997

1	Saturday	FA Carlsberg Vase 5th Round Proper
2	Sunday	UK Living Women's FA Cup 5th Round
5	Wednesday	FA Cup Sponsored by Littlewoods 4th Round Proper Replays
8	Saturday	FA Umbro Trophy 2nd Round Proper
9	Sunday	FA Sunday Cup 5th Round
12	Wednesday	England v Italy (WC)
15	Saturday	FA Cup Sponsored by Littlewoods 5th Round Proper
		FA Youth Cup 4th Round Proper*

		FA County Youth Cup 4th Round*
19	Wednesday	FL Coca-Cola Cup Semi-Final 1st Leg
22	Saturday	FA Carlsberg Vase 6th Round Proper
23	Sunday	FL Coca-Cola Cup Semi-Final 1st Leg
26	Wednesday	FA Cup Sponsored by Littlewoods 5th Round Proper Replays

March 1997

1	Saturday	FA Umbro Trophy 3rd Round Proper
2	Sunday	UK Living Women's FA Cup 6th Round
5	Wednesday	Euro Competitions Quarter-Final 1st Leg
8	Saturday	FA Cup Sponsored by Littlewoods 6th Round Proper
		FA Youth Cup 5th Round Proper*
12	Wednesday	FL Coca-Cola Cup Semi-Final 2nd Leg
15	Saturday	FA Carlsberg Vase Semi-Final 1st Leg
		FA County Youth Cup Semi-Finals*
16	Sunday	FL Coca-Cola Cup Semi-Final 2nd Leg
		FA Sunday Cup Semi-Final
19	Wednesday	Euro Competitions Quarter-Final 2nd Leg
		FA Cup Sponsored by Littlewoods 6th Round Proper Replays
22	Saturday	FA Umbro Trophy 4th Round Proper
		FA Carlsberg Vase Semi-Final 2nd Leg
29	Saturday	Scotland v Estonia (WC)
		Wales v Belgium (WC)
		Northern Ireland v Portugal (WC)
30	Sunday	UK Living Women's FA Cup Semi-Finals

April 1997

2	Wednesday	Scotland v Austria (WC)
		Macedonia v Republic of Ireland (WC)
		Ukraine v Northern Ireland (WC)
5	Saturday	FA Umbro Trophy Semi-Final 1st Leg
		FA Youth Cup Semi-Final*
6	Sunday	FL Coca-Cola Cup Final
9	Wednesday	Euro Competitions Semi-Final 1st Leg
12	Saturday	FA Umbro Trophy Semi-Final 2nd Leg
13	Sunday	FA Cup Sponsored by Littlewoods Semi-Final
16	Wednesday	FA Cup Sponsored by Littlewoods Semi-Final Replays (*prov*)
23	Wednesday	Euro Competitions Semi-Final 2nd Leg
		FA Cup Sponsored by Littlewoods Semi-Final Replays (*prov*)
26	Saturday	FA County Youth Final (*fixed date*)
27	Sunday	FA Sunday Cup Final
30	Wednesday	England v Georgia (WC)
		Sweden v Scotland (WC)
		Romania v Republic of Ireland (WC)
		Armenia v Northern Ireland (WC)

May 1997

3	Saturday	Final matches in Football League
4	Sunday	UK Living Women's FA Cup Final
7	Wednesday	UEFA Cup Final 1st Leg
10	Saturday	Final matches in FA Premier League
		FA Carlsberg Vase Final
		FA Youth Cup Final*
11	Sunday	FL Play-off Semi-Final 1st Leg
14	Wednesday	European Cup Winners' Cup Final
		FL Play-off Semi-Final 2nd Leg
17	Saturday	FA Cup Sponsored by Littlewoods Final

18	Sunday	FA Umbro Trophy Final
21	Wednesday	UEFA Cup Final 2nd Leg
22	Thursday	FA Cup Sponsored by Littlewoods Final Replay
24	Saturday	FL Play-Off Final Division 3
25	Sunday	FL Play-Off Final Divison 2
26	Monday	FL Play-Off Final Division 1
28	Wednesday	European Champions' Cup Final
31	Saturday	Poland v England (WC)

June 1997

| 7 | Saturday | Republic of Ireland v Liechtenstein (WC) |
| 8 | Sunday | Belarus v Scotland (WC) |

54 ● LEAGUE FIXTURES 1996–97

Friday, 16 August 1996

Nationwide Football League Division 1

Manchester City v Ipswich Town ....

Saturday, 17 August 1996

FA Carling Premiership

Arsenal v West Ham United ....
Blackburn Rovers v Tottenham Hotspur ....
Coventry City v Nottingham Forest ....
Derby County v Leeds United ....
Everton v Newcastle United ....
Middlesbrough v Liverpool ....
Sheffield Wednesday v Aston Villa ....
Sunderland v Leicester City ....
Wimbledon v Manchester United ....

Nationwide Football League Division 1

Bradford City v Portsmouth ....
Grimsby Town v Wolverhampton Wanderers .....
Huddersfield Town v Charlton Athletic ....
Norwich City v Swindon Town ....
Oldham Athletic v Stoke City ....
Port Vale v Bolton Wanderers ....
Queens Park Rangers v Oxford United ....
Reading v Sheffield United ....
Southend United v Tranmere Rovers ....
West Bromwich Albion v Barnsley ....

Nationwide Football League Division 2

A.F.C. Bournemouth v Watford ....
Blackpool v Chesterfield ....
Bristol Rovers v Peterborough United ....
Bury v Brentford ....
Crewe Alexandra v Stockport County ....
Gillingham v Bristol City ....
Luton Town v Burnley ....
Millwall v Wrexham ....
Notts County v Preston North End ....
Plymouth Argyle v York City ....
Walsall v Rotherham United ....

Nationwide Football League Division 3

Brighton & Hove Albion v Chester City ....
Cambridge United v Barnet ....
Colchester United v Hartlepool United ....
Doncaster Rovers v Carlisle United ....
Fulham v Hereford United ....
Hull City v Darlington ....
Leyton Orient v Scunthorpe United ....
Mansfield Town v Exeter City ....
Scarborough v Cardiff City ....
Swansea City v Rochdale ....
Torquay United v Lincoln City ....
Wigan Athletic v Northampton Town ....

Sunday, 18 August 1996

FA Carling Premiership

Southampton v Chelsea ....

Nationwide Football League Division 1

Birmingham City v Crystal Palace ....

Nationwide Football League Division 2

Shrewsbury Town v Wycombe Wanderers ....

Monday, 19 August 1996

FA Carling Premiership

Liverpool v Arsenal ....

Tuesday, 20 August 1996

FA Carling Premiership

Leeds United v Sheffield Wednesday ....

Nationwide Football League Division 1

Bolton Wanderers v Manchester City ....

Wednesday, 21 August 1996

FA Carling Premiership

Aston Villa v Blackburn Rovers ....
Chelsea v Middlesbrough ....
Leicester City v Southampton ....
Manchester United v Everton ....
Newcastle United v Wimbledon ....
Nottingham Forest v Sunderland ....
Tottenham Hotspur v Derby County ....
West Ham United v Coventry City ....

Friday, 23 August 1996

Nationwide Football League Division 1

Portsmouth v Queens Park Rangers ....
Tranmere Rovers v Grimsby Town ....

Saturday, 24 August 1996

FA Carling Premiership

Aston Villa v Derby County ....
Chelsea v Coventry City ....
Leicester City v Arsenal ....
Liverpool v Sunderland ....
Newcastle United v Sheffield Wednesday ....
Nottingham Forest v Middlesbrough ....
Tottenham Hotspur v Everton ....
West Ham United v Southampton ....

● 179

Nationwide Football League Division 1

Bolton Wanderers v Norwich City ....
Charlton Athletic v West Bromwich Albion ....
Crystal Palace v Oldham Athletic ....
Ipswich Town v Reading ....
Oxford United v Southend United ....
Sheffield United v Birmingham City ....
Stoke City v Manchester City ....
Swindon Town v Port Vale ....
Wolverhampton Wanderers v Bradford City ......

Nationwide Football League Division 2

Brentford v Luton Town ....
Bristol City v Blackpool ....
Burnley v Walsall ....
Chesterfield v Bury ....
Peterborough United v Crewe Alexandra ....
Preston North End v Bristol Rovers ....
Rotherham United v Shrewsbury Town ....
Stockport County v Notts County ....
Watford v Millwall ....
Wrexham v Plymouth Argyle ....
Wycombe Wanderers v Gillingham ....
York City v A.F.C. Bournemouth ....

Nationwide Football League Division 3

Barnet v Wigan Athletic ....
Cardiff City v Brighton and Hove Albion ....
Carlisle United v Hull City ....
Chester City v Cambridge United ....
Darlington v Swansea City ....
Exeter City v Scarborough ....
Hartlepool United v Fulham ....
Hereford United v Doncaster Rovers ....
Lincoln City v Leyton Orient ....
Northampton Town v Mansfield Town ....
Rochdale v Colchester United ....
Scunthorpe United v Torquay United ....

Sunday, 25 August 1996

FA Carling Premiership

Manchester United v Blackburn Rovers ....

Nationwide Football League Division 1

Barnsley v Huddersfield Town ....

Monday, 26 August 1996

FA Carling Premiership

Leeds United v Wimbledon ....

Tuesday, 27 August 1996

Nationwide Football League Division 1

Charlton Athletic v Birmingham City ....
Crystal Palace v West Bromwich Albion ....
Ipswich Town v Grimsby Town ....
Oxford United v Norwich City ....

Portsmouth v Southend United ....
Sheffield United v Huddersfield Town ....
Tranmere Rovers v Port Vale ....

Nationwide Football League Division 2

Brentford v Gillingham ....
Bristol City v Luton Town ....
Burnley v Shrewsbury Town ....
Chesterfield v Walsall ....
Peterborough United v Notts County ....
Preston North End v Crewe Alexandra ....
Rotherham United v Blackpool ....
Stockport County v A.F.C. Bournemouth ....
Watford v Plymouth Argyle ....
Wrexham v Bristol Rovers ....
Wycombe Wanderers v Bury ....
York City v Millwall ....

Nationwide Football League Division 3

Barnet v Brighton and Hove Albion ....
Cardiff City v Wigan Athletic ....
Carlisle United v Leyton Orient ....
Chester City v Swansea City ....
Darlington v Colchester United ....
Exeter City v Doncaster Rovers ....
Hartlepool United v Mansfield Town ....
Hereford United v Hull City ....
Lincoln City v Cambridge United ....
Northampton Town v Torquay United ....
Rochdale v Fulham ....
Scunthorpe United v Scarborough ....

Wednesday, 28 August 1996

Nationwide Football League Division 1

Barnsley v Reading ....
Stoke City v Bradford City ....
Swindon Town v Oldham Athletic ....
Wolverhampton Wanderers v Queens Park Rangers

Friday, 30 August 1996

Nationwide Football League Division 1

West Bromwich Albion v Sheffield United ....

Nationwide Football League Division 3

Swansea City v Lincoln City ....

Saturday, 31 August 1996

Nationwide Football League Division 1

Birmingham City v Barnsley ....
Bradford City v Tranmere Rovers ....
Grimsby Town v Portsmouth ....
Huddersfield Town v Crystal Palace ....
Manchester City v Charlton Athletic ....
Norwich City v Wolverhampton Wanderers ....
Oldham Athletic v Ipswich Town ....
Port Vale v Oxford United ....
Reading v Stoke City ....
Southend United v Swindon Town ....

Nationwide Football League Division 2

A.F.C. Bournemouth v Peterborough United .....
Blackpool v Wycombe Wanderers ....
Bristol Rovers v Stockport County ....
Bury v Bristol City ....
Crewe Alexandra v Watford ....
Gillingham v Chesterfield ....
Luton Town v Rotherham United ....
Millwall v Burnley ....
Notts County v York City ....
Plymouth Argyle v Preston North End ....
Shrewsbury Town v Brentford ....
Walsall v Wrexham ....

Nationwide Football League Division 3

Brighton and Hove Albion v Scunthorpe United.
Cambridge United v Cardiff City ....
Colchester United v Hereford United ....
Doncaster Rovers v Darlington ....
Fulham v Carlisle United ....
Hull City v Barnet ....
Leyton Orient v Hartlepool United ....
Mansfield Town v Rochdale ....
Scarborough v Northampton Town ....
Torquay United v Exeter City ....
Wigan Athletic v Chester City ....

Sunday, 1 September 1996

Nationwide Football League Division 1

Queens Park Rangers v Bolton Wanderers ....

Monday, 2 September 1996

FA Carling Premiership

Sheffield Wednesday v Leicester City ....

Tuesday, 3 September 1996

FA Carling Premiership

Wimbledon v Tottenham Hotspur ....

Wednesday, 4 September 1996

FA Carling Premiership

Arsenal v Chelsea ....
Blackburn Rovers v Leeds United ....
Coventry City v Liverpool ....
Derby County v Manchester United ....
Everton v Aston Villa ....
Middlesbrough v West Ham United ....
Southampton v Nottingham Forest ....
Sunderland v Newcastle United ....

Friday, 6 September 1996

Nationwide Football League Division 1

Wolverhampton Wanderers v Charlton Athletic .

Saturday, 7 September 1996

FA Carling Premiership

Aston Villa v Arsenal ....
Leeds United v Manchester United ....
Liverpool v Southampton ....
Middlesbrough v Coventry City ....
Nottingham Forest v Leicester City ....
Sheffield Wednesday v Chelsea ....
Tottenham Hotspur v Newcastle United ....
Wimbledon v Everton ....

Nationwide Football League Division 1

Bradford City v Norwich City ....
Grimsby Town v Swindon Town ....
Ipswich Town v Huddersfield Town ....
Manchester City v Barnsley ....
Oldham Athletic v Sheffield United ....
Portsmouth v Port Vale ....
Queens Park Rangers v West Bromwich Albion .
Southend United v Bolton Wanderers ....
Stoke City v Crystal Palace ....
Tranmere Rovers v Birmingham City ....

Nationwide Football League Division 2

A.F.C. Bournemouth v Crewe Alexandra ....
Blackpool v Walsall ....
Bristol City v Preston North End ....
Bury v Rotherham United ....
Chesterfield v Brentford ....
Gillingham v Burnley ....
Millwall v Bristol Rovers ....
Plymouth Argyle v Notts County ....
Watford v Stockport County ....
Wrexham v Peterborough United ....
Wycombe Wanderers v Luton Town ....
York City v Shrewsbury Town ....

Nationwide Football League Division 3

Barnet v Northampton Town ....
Brighton and Hove Albion v Scarborough ....
Cambridge United v Torquay United ....
Cardiff City v Exeter City ....
Carlisle United v Swansea City ....
Chester City v Lincoln City ....
Doncaster Rovers v Mansfield Town ....
Fulham v Colchester United ....
Hereford United v Hartlepool United ....
Hull City v Rochdale ....
Leyton Orient v Darlington ....
Wigan Athletic v Scunthorpe United ....

Sunday, 8 September 1996

FA Carling Premiership

Sunderland v West Ham United ....

Nationwide Football League Division 1

Reading v Oxford United ....

Monday, 9 September 1996

FA Carling Premiership

Blackburn Rovers v Derby County ....

Tuesday, 10 September 1996

Nationwide Football League Division 1

Barnsley v Stoke City ....
Birmingham City v Oldham Athletic ....
Bolton Wanderers v Grimsby Town ....
Charlton Athletic v Southend United ....
Crystal Palace v Ipswich Town ....
Huddersfield Town v Tranmere Rovers ....
Oxford United v Wolverhampton Wanderers .....
Port Vale v Manchester City ....
Sheffield United v Bradford City ....
West Bromwich Albion v Reading ....

Nationwide Football League Division 2

Brentford v Plymouth Argyle ....
Bristol Rovers v A.F.C. Bournemouth ....
Burnley v Blackpool ....
Crewe Alexandra v Bury ....
Luton Town v Gillingham ....
Notts County v Watford ....
Peterborough United v Millwall ....
Preston North End v York City ....
Rotherham United v Chesterfield ....
Shrewsbury Town v Bristol City ....
Stockport County v Wrexham ....
Walsall v Wycombe Wanderers ....

Nationwide Football League Division 3

Colchester United v Brighton and Hove Albion .
Darlington v Wigan Athletic ....
Exeter City v Fulham ....
Hartlepool United v Carlisle United ....
Lincoln City v Hull City ....
Mansfield Town v Barnet ....
Northampton Town v Leyton Orient ....
Rochdale v Chester City ....
Scarborough v Doncaster Rovers ....
Scunthorpe United v Cambridge United ....
Swansea City v Hereford United ....
Torquay United v Cardiff City ....

Wednesday, 11 September 1996

Nationwide Football League Division 1

Norwich City v Queens Park Rangers ....
Swindon Town v Portsmouth ....

Friday, 13 September 1996

Nationwide Football League Division 1

Huddersfield Town v Oldham Athletic ....

Saturday, 14 September 1996

FA Carling Premiership

Coventry City v Leeds United ....
Derby County v Sunderland ....
Everton v Middlesbrough ....
Manchester United v Nottingham Forest ....
Newcastle United v Blackburn Rovers ....
Southampton v Tottenham Hotspur ....
West Ham United v Wimbledon ....

Nationwide Football League Division 1

Barnsley v Queens Park Rangers ....
Birmingham City v Stoke City ....
Bolton Wanderers v Portsmouth ....
Charlton Athletic v Reading ....
Crystal Palace v Manchester City ....
Norwich City v Southend United ....
Oxford United v Bradford City ....
Port Vale v Grimsby Town ....
Sheffield United v Ipswich Town ....
Swindon Town v Tranmere Rovers ....

Nationwide Football League Division 2

Brentford v Blackpool ....
Bristol Rovers v Watford ....
Burnley v Wycombe Wanderers ....
Crewe Alexandra v Wrexham ....
Luton Town v Chesterfield ....
Notts County v Millwall ....
Peterborough United v York City ....
Preston North End v A.F.C. Bournemouth ....
Rotherham United v Bristol City ....
Shrewsbury Town v Bury ....
Stockport County v Plymouth Argyle ....
Walsall v Gillingham ....

Nationwide Football League Division 3

Colchester United v Hull City ....
Darlington v Hereford United ....
Exeter City v Brighton and Hove Albion ....
Hartlepool United v Wigan Athletic ....
Lincoln City v Barnet ....
Mansfield Town v Leyton Orient ....
Northampton Town v Cambridge United ....
Rochdale v Doncaster Rovers ....
Scarborough v Carlisle United ....
Scunthorpe United v Cardiff City ....
Swansea City v Fulham ....
Torquay United v Chester City ....

Sunday, 15 September 1996

FA Carling Premiership

Chelsea v Aston Villa ....
Leicester City v Liverpool ....

Nationwide Football League Division 1

West Bromwich v Wolverhampton
   Albion   Wanderers ....

Monday, 16 September 1996

FA Carling Premiership

Arsenal v Sheffield Wednesday ....

Friday, 20 September 1996

Nationwide Football League Division 1

Ipswich Town v Charlton Athletic ....

Saturday, 21 September 1996

FA Carling Premiership

Aston Villa v Manchester United ....
Blackburn Rovers v Everton ....
Leeds United v Newcastle United ....
Liverpool v Chelsea ....
Middlesbrough v Arsenal ....
Nottingham Forest v West Ham United ....
Sheffield Wednesday v Derby County ....
Sunderland v Coventry City ....

Nationwide Football League Division 1

Bradford City v Bolton Wanderers ....
Grimsby Town v Oxford United ....
Manchester City v Birmingham City ....
Oldham Athletic v Barnsley ....
Portsmouth v Norwich City ....
Queens Park Rangers v Swindon Town ....
Reading Crystal Palace ....
Southend United v Port Vale ....
Tranmere Rovers v West Bromwich Albion ....
Wolverhampton Wanderers v Sheffield United ..

Nationwide Football League Division 2

A.F.C. Bournemouth v Notts County ....
Blackpool v Shrewsbury Town ....
Bristol City v Walsall ....
Bury v Luton Town ....
Chesterfield v Burnley ....
Gillingham v Rotherham United ....
Millwall v Crewe Alexandra ....
Plymouth Argyle v Bristol Rovers ....
Watford v Peterborough United ....
Wrexham v Preston North End ....
Wycombe Wanderers v Brentford ....
York City v Stockport County ....

Nationwide Football League Division 3

Barnet v Exeter City ....
Brighton and Hove Albion v Torquay United .....
Cambridge United v Scarborough ....
Cardiff City v Northampton Town ....
Carlisle United v Darlington ....
Chester City v Scunthorpe United ....
Doncaster Rovers v Swansea City ....
Fulham v Mansfield Town ....
Hereford United v Rochdale ....
Hull City v Hartlepool United ....
Leyton Orient v Colchester United ....
Wigan Athletic v Lincoln City ....

Sunday, 22 September 1996

FA Carling Premiership

Tottenham Hotspur v Leicester City ....

Nationwide Football League Division 1

Stoke City v Huddersfield Town ....

Monday, 23 September 1996

FA Carling Premiership

Wimbledon v Southampton ....

Friday, 27 September 1996

Nationwide Football League Division 1

Swindon Town v Wolverhampton Wanderers ....

Saturday, 28 September 1996

FA Carling Premiership

Arsenal v Sunderland ....
Chelsea v Nottingham Forest ....
Coventry City v Blackburn Rovers ....
Derby Country v Wimbledon ....
Everton v Sheffield Wednesday ....
Leicester City v Leeds United ....
Southampton v Middlesbrough ....

Nationwide Football League Division 1

Barnsley v Grimsby Town ....
Birmingham City v Queens Park Rangers ....
Bolton Wanderers v Stoke City ....
Charlton Athletic v Oldham Athletic ....
Crystal Palace v Southend United ....
Huddersfield Town v Reading ....
Norwich City v Tranmere Rovers ....
Oxford United v Portsmouth ....
Sheffield United v Manchester City ....
West Bromwich Albion v Ipswich Town ....

Nationwide Football League Division 2

Brentford v York City ....
Bristol Rovers v Chesterfield ....
Burnley v Bristol City ....
Crewe Alexandra v Plymouth Argyle ....
Luton Town v Blackpool ....
Notts County v Wrexham ....
Peterborough United v Wycombe Wanderers .....
Preston North End v Millwall ....
Rotherham United v A.F.C. Bournemouth ....
Shrewsbury Town v Watford ....
Stockport County v Gillingham ....
Walsall v Bury ....

Nationwide Football League Division 3

Colchester United v Doncaster Rovers ....
Darlington v Fulham ....
Exeter City v Cambridge United ....

Hartlepool United v Chester City ....
Lincoln City v Cardiff City ....
Mansfield Town v Hereford United ....
Northampton Town v Brighton and Hove Albion.
Rochdale v Leyton Orient ....
Scarborough v Wigan Athletic ....
Scunthorpe United v Barnet ....
Swansea City v Hull City ....
Torquay United v Carlisle United ....

Sunday, 29 September 1996

FA Carling Premiership

Manchester United v Tottenham Hotspur ....
West Ham United v Liverpool ....

Nationwide Football League Division 1

Port Vale v Bradford City ....

Monday, 30 September 1996

FA Carling Premiership

Newcastle United v Aston Villa ....

Tuesday, 1 October 1996

Nationwide Football League Division 1

Bradford City v Swindon Town ....
Grimsby Town v Norwich City ....
Ipswich Town v Barnsley ....
Oldham Athletic v West Bromwich Albion ....
Portsmouth v Crystal Palace ....
Reading v Birmingham City ....
Southend United v Sheffield United ....
Stoke City v Charlton Athletic ....
Tranmere Rovers v Oxford United ....

Nationwide Football League Division 2

A.F.C. Bournemouth v Walsall ....
Bristol City v Brentford ....
Bury v Burnley ....
Chesterfield v Shrewsbury Town ....
Crewe Alexandra v Blackpool ....
Gillingham v Notts County ....
Plymouth Argyle v Peterborough United ....
Watford v Preston North End ....
Wrexham v Luton Town ....
Wycombe Wanderers v Rotherham United ....
York City v Bristol Rovers ....

Nationwide Football League Division 3

Barnet v Scarborough ....
Brighton and Hove Albion v Lincoln City ....
Cambridge United v Darlington ....
Cardiff City v Rochdale ....
Carlisle United v Colchester United ....
Chester City v Northampton Town ....
Doncaster Rovers v Hartlepool United ....
Fulham v Torquay United ....

Hereford United v Scunthorpe United ....
Hull City v Mansfield Town ....
Leyton Orient v Swansea City ....
Wigan Athletic v Exeter City ....

Wednesday, 2 October 1996

Nationwide Football League Division 1

Queens Park Rangers v Port Vale ....
Wolverhampton Wanderers v Bolton Wanderers .

Nationwide Football League Division 2

Millwall v Stockport County ....

Friday, 4 October 1996

Nationwide Football League Division 1

Stoke City v Norwich City ....

Nationwide Football League Division 2

Wrexham v Shrewsbury Town ....

Nationwide Football League Division 3

Swansea City v Colchester United ....

Saturday, 5 October 1996

Nationwide Football League Division 1

Bradford City v Southend United ....
Charlton Athletic v Barnsley ....
Grimsby Town v Queens Park Rangers ....
Huddersfield Town v Birmingham City ....
Ipswich Town v Swindon Town ....
Manchester City v West Bromwich Albion ....
Oldham Athletic v Port Vale ....
Oxford United v Bolton Wanderers ....
Tranmere Rovers v Portsmouth ....
Wolverhampton Wanderers v Reading ....

Nationwide Football League Division 2

Brentford v Rotherham United ....
Bristol Rovers v Crewe Alexandra ....
Burnley v Stockport County ....
Bury v Blackpool ....
Chesterfield v Bristol City ....
Gillingham v A.F.C. Bournemouth ....
Luton Town v Walsall ....
Plymouth Argyle v Millwall ....
Preston North End v Peterborough United ....
Wycombe Wanderers v Notts County ....
York City v Watford ....

Nationwide Football League Division 3

Barnet v Torquay United ....
Cambridge United v Hartlepool United ....
Carlisle United v Mansfield Town ....
Chester City v Cardiff City ....
Darlington v Rochdale ....
Doncaster Rovers v Leyton Orient ....

Hereford United v Scarborough ....
Hull City v Scunthorpe United ....
Lincoln City v Exeter City ....
Northampton Town v Fulham ....
Wigan Athletic v Brighton and Hove Albion ......

Sunday, 6 October 1996

Nationwide Football League Division 1

Crystal Palace v Sheffield United ....

Friday, 11 October 1996

Nationwide Football League Division 1

Norwich City v Ipswich Town ....

Nationwide Football League Division 2

Bristol City v York City ....

Saturday, 12 October 1996

FA Carling Premiership

Blackburn Rovers v Arsenal ....
Derby County v Newcastle United ....
Everton v West Ham United ....
Leeds United v Nottingham Forest ....
Leicester City v Chelsea ....
Manchester United v Liverpool ....
Tottenham Hotspur v Aston Villa ....
Wimbledon v Sheffield Wednesday ....

Nationwide Football League Division 1

Barnsley v Crystal Palace ....
Birmingham City v Bradford City ....
Bolton Wanderers v Oldham Athletic ....
Port Vale v Stoke City ....
Portsmouth v Charlton Athletic ....
Queens Park Rangers v Manchester City ....
Reading v Grimsby Town ....
Sheffield United v Tranmere Rovers ....
Swindon Town v Oxford United ....
West Bromwich Albion v Huddersfield Town ...

Nationwide Football League Division 2

A.F.C. Bournemouth v Wycombe Wanderers ....
Blackpool v Gillingham ....
Crewe Alexandra v Brentford ....
Millwall v Chesterfield ....
Notts County v Bristol Rovers ....
Peterborough United v Bury ....
Rotherham United v Burnley ....
Shrewsbury Town v Luton Town ....
Stockport County v Preston North End ....
Walsall v Plymouth Argyle ....
Watford v Wrexham ....

Nationwide Football League Division 3

Brighton and Hove Albion v Cambridge United
Cardiff City v Barnet ....
Colchester United v Wigan Athletic ....

Exeter City v Northampton Town ....
Fulham v Doncaster Rovers ....
Hartlepool United v Darlington ....
Leyton Orient v Hull City ....
Mansfield Town v Swansea City ....
Rochdale v Carlisle United ....
Scarborough v Chester City ....
Scunthorpe United v Lincoln City ....
Torquay United v Hereford United ....

Sunday, 13 October 1996

FA Carling Premiership

Coventry City v Southampton ....

Nationwide Football League Division 1

Southend United v Wolverhampton Wanderers .

Monday, 14 October 1996

FA Carling Premiership

Sunderland v Middlesbrough ....

Tuesday, 15 October 1996

Nationwide Football League Division 1

Barnsley v Oxford United ....
Birmingham City v Ipswich Town ....
Bolton Wanderers v Tranmere Rovers ....
Port Vale v Crystal Palace ....
Portsmouth v Wolverhampton Wanderers ....
Reading v Manchester City ....
Sheffield United v Charlton Athletic ....
Southend United v Grimsby Town ....

Nationwide Football League Division 2

A.F.C. Bournemouth v Plymouth Argyle ....
Blackpool v Wrexham ....
Bristol City v Wycombe Wanderers ....
Crewe Alexandra v York City ....
Notts County v Chesterfield ....
Peterborough United v Brentford ....
Rotherham United v Bristol Rovers ....
Shrewsbury Town v Gillingham ....
Stockport County v Luton Town ....
Walsall v Preston North End ....
Watford v Burnley ....

Nationwide Football League Division 3

Brighton and Hove Albion v Hereford United ...
Cardiff City v Darlington ....
Colchester United v Barnet ....
Exeter City v Carlisle United ....
Fulham v Cambridge United ....
Hartlepool United v Swansea City ....
Leyton Orient v Chester City ....
Mansfield Town v Wigan Athletic ....
Rochdale v Lincoln City ....
Scarborough v Hull City ....
Scunthorpe United v Northampton Town ....
Torquay United v Doncaster Rovers ....

Wednesday, 16 October 1996

Nationwide Football League Division 1

Norwich City v Oldham Athletic ....
Queens Park Rangers v Bradford City ....
Swindon Town v Huddersfield Town ....
West Bromwich Albion v Stoke City ....

Nationwide Football League Division 2

Millwall v Bury ....

Friday, 18 October 1996

Nationwide Football League Division 1

Oxford United v Birmingham City ....

Saturday, 19 October 1996

FA Carling Premiership

Arsenal v Coventry City ....
Aston Villa v Leeds United ....
Chelsea v Wimbledon ....
Middlesbrough v Tottenham Hotspur ....
Nottingham Forest v Derby County ....
Sheffield Wednesday v Blackburn Rovers ....
Southampton v Sunderland ....
West Ham United v Leicester City ....

Nationwide Football League Division 1

Bradford City v Barnsley ....
Charlton Athletic v Bolton Wanderers ....
Crystal Palace v Swindon Town ....
Grimsby Town v West Bromwich Albion ....
Huddersfield Town v Southend United ....
Ipswich Town v Portsmouth ....
Manchester City v Norwich City ....
Oldham Athletic v Reading ....
Stoke City v Sheffield United ....
Wolverhampton Wanderers v Port Vale ....

Nationwide Football League Division 2

Brentford v Walsall ....
Bristol Rovers v Blackpool ....
Burnley v Notts County ....
Bury v Watford ....
Chesterfield v Crewe Alexandra ....
Gillingham v Millwall ....
Luton Town v Peterborough United ....
Plymouth Argyle v Bristol City ....
Preston North End v Shrewsbury Town ....
Wrexham v A.F.C. Bournemouth ....
Wycombe Wanderers v Stockport County ....
York City v Rotherham United ....

Nationwide Football League Division 3

Barnet v Hartlepool United ....
Cambridge United v Rochdale ....
Carlisle United v Cardiff City ....
Chester City v Exeter City ....
Darlington v Mansfield Town ....

Doncaster Rovers v Brighton and Hove Albion ..
Hereford United v Leyton Orient ....
Hull City v Fulham ....
Lincoln City v Scarborough ....
Northampton Town v Colchester United ....
Swansea City v Scunthorpe United ....
Wigan Athletic v Torquay United ....

Sunday, 20 October 1996

FA Carling Premiership

Liverpool v Everton ....
Newcastle United v Manchester United ....

Nationwide Football League Division 1

Tranmere Rovers v Queens Park Rangers ....

Friday, 25 October 1996

Nationwide Football League Division 1

Barnsley v Bolton Wanderers ....

Nationwide Football League Division 3

Cambridge United v Doncaster Rovers ....

Saturday, 26 October 1996

FA Carling Premiership

Arsenal v Leeds United ....
Chelsea v Tottenham Hotspur ....
Coventry v Sheffield Wednesday ....
Leicester City v Newcastle United ....
Middlesbrough v Wimbledon ....
Southampton v Manchester United ....
Sunderland v Aston Villa ....
West Ham United v Blackburn Rovers ....

Nationwide Football League Division 1

Birmingham City v Norwich City ....
Charlton Athletic v Oxford United ....
Crystal Palace v Grimsby Town ....
Huddersfield Town v Port Vale ....
Ipswich Town v Tranmere Rovers ....
Oldham Athletic v Southend United ....
Reading v Swindon Town ....
Sheffield United v Queens Park Rangers ....
Stoke City v Portsmouth ....
West Bromwich Albion v Bradford City ....

Nationwide Football League Division 2

Blackpool v Watford ....
Brentford v Millwall ....
Bristol City v Notts County ....
Burnley v Plymouth Argyle ....
Bury v Bristol Rovers ....
Chesterfield v York City ....
Gillingham v Preston North End ....
Luton Town v A.F.C. Bournemouth ....
Rotherham United v Peterborough United ....

Shrewsbury Town v Crewe Alexandra ....
Walsall v Stockport County ....
Wycombe Wanderers v Wrexham ....

Nationwide Football League Division 3

Barnet v Carlisle United ....
Brighton and Hove Albion v Fulham ....
Cardiff City v Leyton Orient ....
Chester City v Hereford United ....
Exeter City v Hartlepool United ....
Lincoln City v Colchester United ....
Northampton Town v Darlington ....
Scarborough v Mansfield Town ....
Scunthorpe United v Rochdale ....
Torquay United v Swansea City ....
Wigan Athletic v Hull City ....

Sunday, 27 October 1996

FA Carling Premiership

Liverpool v Derby County ....

Nationwide Football League Division 1

Manchester City v Wolverhampton Wanderers ..

Monday, 28 October 1996

FA Carling Premiership

Nottingham Forest v Everton ....

Tuesday, 29 October 1996

Nationwide Football League Division 1

Bolton Wanderers v Reading ....
Bradford City v Crystal Palace ....
Grimsby Town v Oldham Athletic ....
Oxford United v Stoke City ....
Port Vale v Barnsley ....
Portsmouth v Birmingham City ....
Southend United v Manchester City ....
Tranmere Rovers v Charlton Athletic ....

Nationwide Football League Division 2

A.F.C. Bournemouth v Bristol City ....
Bristol Rovers v Brentford ....
Crewe Alexandra v Rotherham United ....
Notts County v Walsall ....
Peterborough United v Shrewsbury Town ....
Plymouth Argyle v Gillingham ....
Preston North End v Burnley ....
Stockport County v Chesterfield ....
Watford v Luton Town ....
Wrexham v Bury ....
York City v Wycombe Wanderers ....

Nationwide Football League Division 3

Carlisle United v Chester City ....
Colchester United v Exeter City ....
Darlington v Barnet ....

Doncaster Rovers v Lincoln City ....
Fulham v Scunthorpe United ....
Hartlepool United v Northampton Town ....
Hereford United v Cambridge United ....
Hull City v Cardiff City ....
Leyton Orient v Scarborough ....
Mansfield Town v Torquay United ....
Rochdale v Brighton and Hove Albion ....
Swansea City v Wigan Athletic ....

Wednesday, 30 October 1996

Nationwide Football League Division 1

Norwich City v Sheffield United ....
Queens Park Rangers v Ipswich Town ....
Swindon Town v West Bromwich Albion ....
Wolverhampton Wanderers v Huddersfield Town .

Nationwide Football League Division 2

Millwall v Blackpool ....

Saturday, 2 November 1996

FA Carling Premiership

Aston Villa v Nottingham Forest ....
Derby County v Leicester City ....
Leeds United v Sunderland ....
Manchester United v Chelsea ....
Sheffield Wednesday v Southampton ....
Tottenham Hotspur v West Ham United ....
Wimbledon v Arsenal ....

Nationwide Football League Division 1

Bolton Wanderers v Huddersfield Town ....
Bradford City v Oldham Athletic ....
Norwich City v Charlton Athletic ....
Oxford United v Ipswich Town ....
Port Vale v Birmingham City ....
Portsmouth v West Bromwich Albion ....
Queens Park Rangers v Stoke City ....
Southend United v Reading ....
Swindon Town v Manchester City ....
Tranmere Rovers v Crystal Palace ....
Wolverhampton Wanderers v Barnsley ....

Nationwide Football League Division 2

A.F.C. Bournemouth v Bury ....
Bristol Rovers v Gillingham ....
Crewe Alexandra v Wycombe Wanderers ....
Millwall v Walsall ....
Notts County v Shrewsbury Town ....
Peterborough United v Blackpool ....
Plymouth Argyle v Luton Town ....
Preston North End v Rotherham United ....
Stockport County v Bristol City ....
Watford v Brentford ....
Wrexham v Chesterfield ....
York City v Burnley ....

Nationwide Football League Division 3

Carlisle United v Wigan Athletic ....
Colchester United v Cardiff City ....
Darlington v Scarborough ....
Doncaster Rovers v Chester City ....
Fulham v Lincoln City ....
Hartlepool United v Brighton and Hove Albion .
Hereford United v Barnet ....
Hull City v Cambridge United ....
Leyton Orient v Torquay United ....
Mansfield Town v Scunthorpe United ....
Rochdale v Exeter City ....
Swansea City v Northampton Town ....

Sunday, 3 November 1996

FA Carling Premiership

Blackburn Rovers v Liverpool ....
Newcastle United v Middlesbrough ....

Nationwide Football League Division 1

Grimsby Town v Sheffield United ....

Monday, 4 November 1996

FA Carling Premiership

Everton v Coventry City ....

Friday, 8 November 1996

Nationwide Football League Division 1

Huddersfield Town v Bradford City ....

Saturday, 9 November 1996

Nationwide Football League Division 1

Barnsley v Norwich City ....
Birmingham City v Bolton Wanderers ....
Charlton Athletic v Grimsby Town ....
Ipswich Town v Southend United ....
Manchester City v Oxford United ....
Oldham Athletic v Portsmouth ....
Reading v Tranmere Rovers ....
Sheffield United v Swindon Town ....
Stoke City v Wolverhampton Wanderers ....
West Bromwich Albion v Port Vale ....

Nationwide Football League Division 2

Blackpool v A.F.C. Bournemouth ....
Brentford v Stockport County ....
Bristol City v Millwall ....
Burnley v Crewe Alexandra ....
Bury v York City ....
Chesterfield v Preston North End ....
Gillingham v Wrexham ....
Luton Town v Notts County ....
Rotherham United v Watford ....
Shrewsbury Town v Bristol Rovers ....
Walsall v Peterborough United ....
Wycombe Wanderers v Plymouth Argyle ....

Nationwide Football League Division 3

Barnet v Rochdale ....
Brighton and Hove Albion v Mansfield Town ...
Cambridge United v Swansea City ....
Cardiff City v Fulham ....
Chester City v Hull City ....
Exeter City v Leyton Orient ....
Lincoln City v Darlington ....
Northampton Town v Carlisle United ....
Scarborough v Hartlepool United ....
Scunthorpe United v Doncaster Rovers ....
Torquay United v Colchester United ....
Wigan Athletic v Hereford United ....

Sunday, 10 November 1996

Nationwide Football League Division 1

Crystal Palace v Queens Park Rangers ....

Friday, 15 November 1996

Nationwide Football League Division 1

Tranmere Rovers v Oldham Athletic ....

Saturday, 16 November 1996

FA Carling Premiership

Aston Villa v Leicester City ....
Blackburn Rovers v Chelsea ....
Everton v Southampton ....
Leeds United v Liverpool ....
Manchester United v Arsenal ....
Newcastle United v West Ham United ....
Tottenham Hotspur v Sunderland ....
Wimbledon v Coventry City ....

Nationwide Football League Division 1

Bolton Wanderers v Crystal Palace ....
Bradford City v Ipswich Town ....
Grimsby Town v Stoke City ....
Norwich City v Reading ....
Oxford United v Huddersfield Town ....
Port Vale v Sheffield United ....
Portsmouth v Manchester City ....
Queens Park Rangers v Charlton Athletic ....
Southend United v West Bromwich Albion ....
Swindon Town v Barnsley City ....
Wolverhampton Wanderers v Birmingham ....

Sunday, 17 November 1996

FA Carling Premiership

Derby County v Middlesbrough ....

Monday, 18 November 1996

FA Carling Premiership

Sheffield Wednesday v Nottingham Forest ....

Tuesday, 19 November 1996

Nationwide Football League Division 2

A.F.C. Bournemouth v Brentford ....
Bristol Rovers v Burnley ....
Crewe Alexandra v Bristol City ....
Notts County v Bury ....
Peterborough United v Gillingham ....
Plymouth Argyle v Chesterfield ....
Preston North End v Luton Town ....
Stockport County v Blackpool ....
Watford v Wycombe Wanderers ....
Wrexham v Rotherham United ....
York City v Walsall ....

Nationwide Football League Division 3

Carlisle United v Cambridge United ....
Colchester United v Scunthorpe United ....
Darlington v Exeter City ....
Doncaster Rovers v Northampton Town ....
Fulham v Barnet ....
Hartlepool United v Cardiff City ....
Hereford United v Lincoln City ....
Hull City v Torquay United ....
Leyton Orient v Wigan Athletic ....
Mansfield Town v Chester City ....
Rochdale v Scarborough ....
Swansea City v Brighton and Hove Albion ....

Wednesday, 20 November 1996

Nationwide Football League Division 1

Manchester City v Huddersfield Town ....

Nationwide Football League Division 2

Millwall v Shrewsbury Town ....

Friday, 22 November 1996

Nationwide Football League Division 3

Chester City v Colchester United ....

Saturday, 23 November 1996

FA Carling Premiership

Chelsea v Newcastle United ....
Coventry City v Aston Villa ....
Leicester City v Everton ....
Liverpool v Wimbledon ....
Middlesbrough v Manchester United ....
Nottingham Forest v Blackburn Rovers ....
Southampton v Leeds United ....
Sunderland v Sheffield Wednesday ....
West Ham United v Derby County ....

Nationwide Football League Division 1

Barnsley v Portsmouth ....
Birmingham City v Swindon Town ....
Charlton Athletic v Bradford City ....
Crystal Palace v Wolverhampton Wanderers ......

Huddersfield Town v Grimsby Town ....
Ipswich Town v Port Vale ....
Manchester City v Tranmere Rovers ....
Oldham Athletic v Oxford United ....
Reading v Queens Park Rangers ....
Sheffield United v Bolton Wanderers ....
Stoke City v Southend United ....
West Bromwich Albion v Norwich City ....

Nationwide Football League Division 2

Blackpool v Notts County ....
Brentford v Wrexham ....
Bristol City v Peterborough United ....
Burnley v A.F.C. Bournemouth ....
Bury v Plymouth Argyle ....
Chesterfield v Watford ....
Gillingham v York City ....
Luton Town v Bristol Rovers ....
Rotherham United v Millwall ....
Shrewsbury Town v Stockport County ....
Walsall v Crewe Alexandra ....
Wycombe Wanderers v Preston North End ....

Nationwide Football League Division 3

Barnet v Doncaster Rovers ....
Brighton and Hove Albion v Carlisle United .....
Cambridge United v Leyton Orient ....
Cardiff City v Hereford United ....
Exeter City v Hull City ....
Lincoln City v Mansfield Town ....
Northampton Town v Rochdale ....
Scarborough v Swansea City ....
Scunthorpe United v Darlington ....
Torquay United v Hartlepool United ....
Wigan Athletic v Fulham ....

Sunday, 24 November 1996

FA Carling Premiership

Arsenal v Tottenham Hotspur ....

Saturday, 30 November 1996

FA Carling Premiership

Aston Villa v Middlesbrough ....
Blackburn Rovers v Southampton ....
Derby County v Coventry City ....
Everton v Sunderland ....
Manchester United v Leicester City ....
Newcastle United v Arsenal ....
Sheffield Wednesday v West Ham United ....
Wimbledon v Nottingham Forest ....

Nationwide Football League Division 1

Bolton Wanderers v Barnsley ....
Bradford City v West Bromwich Albion ....
Grimsby Town v Crystal Palace ....
Norwich City v Birmingham City ....
Oxford United v Charlton Athletic ....
Port Vale v Huddersfield Town ....
Portsmouth v Stoke City ....

Queens Park Rangers v Sheffield United ....
Southend United v Oldham Athletic ....
Swindon Town v Reading ....
Tranmere Rovers v Ipswich Town ....
Wolverhampton Wanderers v Manchester City ..

Nationwide Football League Division 2

A.F.C. Bournemouth v Luton Town ....
Bristol Rovers v Bury ....
Crewe Alexandra v Shrewsbury Town ....
Millwall v Brentford ....
Notts County v Bristol City ....
Peterborough United v Rotherham United ....
Plymouth Argyle v Burnley ....
Preston North End v Gillingham ....
Stockport County v Walsall ....
Watford v Blackpool ....
Wrexham v Wycombe Wanderers ....
York City v Chesterfield ....

Nationwide Football League Division 3

Carlisle United v Barnet ....
Colchester United v Lincoln City ....
Darlington v Northampton Town ....
Doncaster Rovers v Cambridge United ....
Fulham v Brighton and Hove Albion ....
Hartlepool United v Exeter City ....
Hereford United v Chester City ....
Hull City v Wigan Athletic ....
Leyton Orient v Cardiff City ....
Mansfield Town v Scarborough ....
Rochdale v Scunthorpe United ....
Swansea City v Torquay United ....

Sunday, 1 December 1996

FA Carling Premiership

Leeds United v Chelsea ....

Monday, 2 December 1996

FA Carling Premiership

Tottenham Hotspur v Liverpool ....

Tuesday, 3 December 1996

Nationwide Football League Division 2

Blackpool v Plymouth Argyle ....
Brentford v Notts County ....
Bristol City v Watford ....
Burnley v Wrexham ....
Bury v Preston North End ....
Chesterfield v Peterborough United ....
Gillingham v Crewe Alexandra ....
Luton Town v York City ....
Rotherham United v Stockport County ....
Shrewsbury Town v A.F.C. Bournemouth ....
Walsall v Bristol Rovers ....
Wycombe Wanderers v Millwall ....

Nationwide Football League Division 3

Barnet v Leyton Orient ....
Brighton and Hove Albion v Darlington ....
Cambridge United v Mansfield Town ....
Cardiff City v Swansea City ....
Chester City v Fulham ....
Exeter City v Hereford United ....
Lincoln City v Carlisle United ....
Northampton Town v Hull City ....
Scarborough v Colchester United ....
Scunthorpe United v Hartlepool United ....
Torquay United v Rochdale ....
Wigan Athletic v Doncaster Rovers ....

Saturday, 7 December 1996

FA Carling Premiership

Arsenal v Derby County ....
Chelsea v Everton ....
Coventry City v Tottenham Hotspur ....
Leicester City v Blackburn Rovers ....
Liverpool v Sheffield Wednesday ....
Middlesbrough v Leeds United ....
Southampton v Aston Villa ....
Sunderland v Wimbledon ....

Nationwide Football League Division 1

Barnsley v Southend United ....
Birmingham City v Grimsby Town ....
Charlton Athletic v Swindon Town ....
Crystal Palace v Oxford United ....
Huddersfield Town v Norwich City ....
Ipswich Town v Wolverhampton Wanderers ......
Manchester City v Bradford City ....
Oldham Athletic v Queens Park Rangers ....
Reading v Port Vale ....
Sheffield United v Portsmouth ....
Stoke City v Tranmere Rovers ....
West Bromwich Albion v Bolton Wanderers ......

Sunday, 8 December 1996

FA Carling Premiership

West Ham United v Manchester United ....

Monday, 9 December 1996

FA Carling Premiership

Nottingham Forest v Newcastle United ....

Friday, 13 December 1996

Nationwide Football League Division 2

Preston North End v Blackpool ....

Nationwide Football League Division 3

Doncaster Rovers v Cardiff City ....
Swansea City v Barnet ....

Saturday, 14 December 1996

FA Carling Premiership

Arsenal v Southampton ....
Coventry City v Newcastle United ....
Derby County v Everton ....
Leeds United v Tottenham Hotspur ....
Liverpool v Nottingham Forest ....
Middlesbrough v Leicester City ....
Sheffield Wednesday v Manchester United ....
West Ham United v Aston Villa ....
Wimbledon v Blackburn Rovers ....

Nationwide Football League Division 1

Barnsley v Tranmere Rovers ....
Birmingham City v West Bromwich Albion ....
Bolton Wanderers v Ipswich Town ....
Bradford City v Reading ....
Charlton Athletic v Port Vale ....
Manchester City v Grimsby Town ....
Norwich City v Crystal Palace ....
Oxford United v Sheffield United ....
Portsmouth v Huddersfield Town ....
Queens Park Rangers v Southend United ....
Stoke City v Swindon Town ....
Wolverhampton Wanderers v Oldham Athletic ..

Nationwide Football League Division 2

A.F.C. Bournemouth v Millwall ....
Burnley v Brentford ....
Gillingham v Bury ....
Luton Town v Crewe Alexandra ....
Notts County v Rotherham United ....
Plymouth Argyle v Shrewsbury Town ....
Stockport County v Peterborough United ....
Walsall v Watford ....
Wycombe Wanderers v Chesterfield ....
York City v Wrexham ....

Nationwide Football League Division 3

Brighton and Hove Albion v Hull City ....
Cambridge United v Wigan Athletic ....
Chester City v Darlington ....
Fulham v Leyton Orient ....
Hereford United v Carlisle United ....
Lincoln City v Northampton Town ....
Mansfield Town v Colchester United ....
Rochdale v Hartlepool United ....
Scunthorpe United v Exeter City ....
Torquay United v Scarborough ....

Sunday, 15 December 1996

FA Carling Premiership

Sunderland v Chelsea ....

Nationwide Football League Division 2

Bristol City v Bristol Rovers ....

Wednesday, 18 December 1996

Nationwide Football League Division 2

Millwall v Luton Town ....

Friday, 20 December 1996

Nationwide Football League Division 2

Crewe Alexandra v Notts County ....
Peterborough United v Burnley ....

Nationwide Football League Division 3

Colchester United v Cambridge United ....
Northampton Town v Hereford United ....

Saturday, 21 December 1996

FA Carling Premiership

Blackburn Rovers v Middlesbrough ....
Chelsea v West Ham United ....
Everton v Leeds United ....
Leicester City v Coventry City ....
Manchester United v Sunderland ....
Nottingham Forest v Arsenal ....
Southampton v Derby County ....
Tottenham Hotspur v Sheffield Wednesday ....

Nationwide Football League Division 1

Crystal Palace v Charlton Athletic ....
Grimsby Town v Bradford City ....
Huddersfield Town v Queens Park Rangers ....
Ipswich Town v Stoke City ....
Oldham Athletic v Manchester City ....
Port Vale v Norwich City ....
Reading v Portsmouth ....
Sheffield United v Barnsley ....
Southend United v Birmingham City ....
Swindon Town v Bolton Wanderers ....
Tranmere Rovers v Wolverhampton Wanderers .
West Bromwich Albion v Oxford United ....

Nationwide Football League Division 2

Blackpool v York City ....
Brentford v Preston North End ....
Bristol Rovers v Wycombe Wanderers ....
Bury v Stockport County ....
Chesterfield v A.F.C. Bournemouth ....
Rotherham United v Plymouth Argyle ....
Shrewsbury Town v Walsall ....
Watford v Gillingham ....
Wrexham v Bristol City ....

Nationwide Football League Division 3

Barnet v Chester City ....
Cardiff City v Mansfield Town ....
Carlisle United v Scunthorpe United ....
Darlington v Torquay United ....
Exeter City v Swansea City ....
Hartlepool United v Lincoln City ....

Hull City v Doncaster Rovers ....
Scarborough v Fulham ....
Wigan Athletic v Rochdale ....

Sunday, 22 December 1996

FA Carling Premiership

Aston Villa v Wimbledon ....

Nationwide Football League Division 3

Leyton Orient v Brighton and Hove Albion ....

Monday, 23 December 1996

FA Carling Premiership

Newcastle United v Liverpool ....

Thursday, 26 December 1996

FA Carling Premiership

Aston Villa v Chelsea ....
Blackburn Rovers v Newcastle United ....
Leeds United v Coventry City ....
Liverpool v Leicester City ....
Middlesbrough v Everton ....
Nottingham Forest v Manchester United ....
Sheffield Wednesday v Arsenal ....
Sunderland v Derby County ....
Tottenham Hotspur v Southampton ....
Wimbledon v West Ham United ....

Nationwide Football League Division 1

Bradford City v Sheffield United ....
Grimsby Town v Bolton Wanderers ....
Ipswich Town v Crystal Palace ....
Manchester City v Port Vale ....
Oldham Athletic v Birmingham City ....
Portsmouth v Swindon Town ....
Queens Park Rangers v Norwich City ....
Reading v West Bromwich Albion ....
Southend United v Charlton Athletic ....
Stoke City v Barnsley ....
Tranmere Rovers v Huddersfield Town ....
Wolverhampton Wanderers v Oxford United .....

Nationwide Football League Division 2

A.F.C. Bournemouth v Bristol Rovers ....
Blackpool v Burnley ....
Bristol City v Shrewsbury Town ....
Bury v Crewe Alexandra ....
Chesterfield v Rotherham United ....
Gillingham v Luton Town ....
Millwall v Peterbough United ....
Plymouth Argyle v Brentford ....
Watford v Notts County ....
Wrexham v Stockport County ....
Wycombe Wanderers v Walsall ....
York City v Preston North End ....

Nationwide Football League Division 3

Barnet v Mansfield Town ....
Brighton and Hove Albion v Colchester United .
Cambridge United v Scunthorpe United ....
Cardiff City v Torquay United ....
Carlisle United v Hartlepool United ....
Chester City v Rochdale ....
Doncaster Rovers v Scarborough ....
Fulham v Exeter City ....
Hereford United v Swansea City ....
Hull City v Lincoln City ....
Leyton Orient v Northampton Town ....
Wigan Athletic v Darlington ....

Saturday, 28 December 1996

FA Carling Premiership

Arsenal v Aston Villa ....
Chelsea v Sheffield Wednesday ....
Coventry City v Middlesbrough ....
Derby County v Blackburn Rovers ....
Everton v Wimbledon ....
Leicester City v Nottingham Forest ....
Manchester United v Leeds United ....
Newcastle United v Tottenham Hotspur ....
Southampton v Liverpool ....
West Ham United v Sunderland ....

Nationwide Football League Division 1

Barnsley v Manchester City ....
Birmingham City v Tranmere Rovers ....
Bolton Wanderers v Southend United ....
Charlton Athletic v Wolverhampton Wanderers .
Crystal Palace v Stoke City ....
Huddersfield Town v Ipswich Town ....
Norwich City v Bradford City ....
Oxford United v Reading ....
Port Vale v Portsmouth ....
Sheffield United v Oldham Athletic ....
Swindon Town v Grimsby Town ....
West Bromwich Albion v Queens Park Rangers .

Nationwide Football League Division 2

Brentford v Chesterfield ....
Bristol Rovers v Millwall ....
Burnley v Gillingham ....
Crewe Alexandra v A.F.C. Bournemouth ....
Luton Town v Wycombe Wanderers ....
Notts County v Plymouth Argyle ....
Peterborough United v Wrexham ....
Preston North End v Bristol City ....
Rotherham United v Bury ....
Shrewsbury Town v York City ....
Stockport County v Watford ....
Walsall v Blackpool ....

Nationwide Football League Division 3

Colchester United v Fulham ....
Darlington v Leyton Orient ....
Exeter City v Cardiff City ....

Hartlepool United v Hereford United ....
Lincoln City v Chester City ....
Mansfield Town v Doncaster Rovers ....
Northampton Town v Barnet ....
Rochdale v Hull City ....
Scarborough v Brighton and Hove Albion ....
Scunthorpe United v Wigan Athletic ....
Swansea City v Carlisle United ....
Torquay United v Cambridge United ....

Wednesday, 1 January 1997

FA Carling Premiership

Arsenal v Middlesbrough ....
Chelsea v Liverpool ....
Coventry City v Sunderland ....
Derby County v Sheffield Wednesday ....
Everton v Blackburn Rovers ....
Leicester City v Tottenham Hotspur ....
Manchester United v Aston Villa ....
Newcastle United v Leeds United ....
Southampton v Wimbledon ....
West Ham United v Nottingham Forest ....

Nationwide Football League Division 1

Barnsley v Oldham Athletic ....
Birmingham City v Manchester City ....
Bolton Wanderers v Bradford City ....
Charlton Athletic v Ipswich Town ....
Crystal Palace v Reading ....
Huddersfield Town v Stoke City ....
Norwich City v Portsmouth ....
Oxford United v Grimsby Town ....
Port Vale v Southend United ....
Sheffield United v Wolverhampton Wanderers ..
Swindon Town v Queens Park Rangers ....
West Bromwich Albion v Tranmere Rovers ....

Nationwide Football League Division 2

Brentford v Wycombe Wanderers ....
Bristol Rovers v Plymouth Argyle ....
Burnley v Chesterfield ....
Crewe Alexandra v Millwall ....
Luton Town v Bury ....
Notts County v A.F.C. Bournemouth ....
Peterborough United v Watford ....
Preston North End v Wrexham ....
Rotherham United v Gillingham ....
Shrewsbury Town v Blackpool ....
Stockport County v York City ....
Walsall v Bristol City ....

Nationwide Football League Division 3

Colchester United v Leyton Orient ....
Darlington v Carlisle United ....
Exeter City v Barnet ....
Hartlepool United v Hull City ....
Lincoln City v Wigan Athletic ....
Mansfield Town v Fulham ....
Northampton Town v Cardiff City ....
Rochdale v Hereford United ....
Scarborough v Cambridge United ....

Scunthorpe United v Chester City ....
Swansea City v Doncaster Rovers ....
Torquay United v Brighton and Hove Albion ....

Saturday, 4 January 1997

Nationwide Football League Division 2

A.F.C. Bournemouth v Preston North End ....
Blackpool v Brentford ....
Bristol City v Rotherham United ....
Bury v Shrewsbury Town ....
Chesterfield v Luton Town ....
Gillingham v Walsall ....
Millwall v Notts County ....
Plymouth Argyle v Stockport County ....
Watford v Bristol Rovers ....
Wrexham v Crewe Alexandra ....
Wycombe Wanderers v Burnley ....
York City v Peterborough United ....

Nationwide Football League Division 3

Barnet v Lincoln City ....
Brighton and Hove Albion v Exeter City ....
Cambridge United v Northampton Town ....
Cardiff City v Scunthorpe United ....
Carlisle United v Scarborough ....
Chester City v Torquay United ....
Doncaster Rovers v Rochdale ....
Fulham v Swansea City ....
Hereford United v Darlington ....
Hull City v Colchester United ....
Leyton Orient v Mansfield Town ....
Wigan Athletic v Hartlepool United ....

Friday, 10 January 1997

Nationwide Football League Division 1

Tranmere Rovers v Swindon Town ....

Saturday, 11 January 1997

FA Carling Premiership

Aston Villa v Newcastle United ....
Blackburn Rovers v Coventry City ....
Leeds United v Leicester City ....
Liverpool v West Ham United ....
Middlesbrough v Southampton ....
Nottingham Forest v Chelsea ....
Sheffield Wednesday v Everton ....
Sunderland v Arsenal ....
Tottenham Hotspur v Manchester United ....
Wimbledon v Derby County ....

Nationwide Football League Division 1

Bradford City v Oxford United ....
Grimsby Town v Port Vale ....
Ipswich Town v Sheffield United ....
Manchester City v Crystal Palace ....
Oldham Athletic v Huddersfield Town ....
Portsmouth v Bolton Wanderers ....

Queens Park Rangers v Barnsley ....
Reading v Charlton Athletic ....
Southend United v Norwich City ....
Stoke City v Birmingham City ....
Wolverhampton v West Bromwich
    Wanderers   Albion ....

Nationwide Football League Division 2

A.F.C. Bournemouth v Rotherham United ....
Blackpool v Luton Town ....
Bristol City v Burnley ....
Bury v Walsall ....
Chesterfield v Bristol Rovers ....
Gillingham v Stockport County ....
Millwall v Preston North End ....
Plymouth Argyle v Crewe Alexandra ....
Watford v Shrewsbury Town ....
Wrexham v Notts County ....
Wycombe Wanderers v Peterborough United .....
York City v Brentford ....

Nationwide Football League Division 3

Barnet v Scunthorpe United ....
Brighton and Hove Albion v Northampton Town.
Cambridge United v Exeter City ....
Cardiff City v Lincoln City ....
Carlisle United v Torquay United ....
Chester City v Hartlepool United ....
Doncaster Rovers v Colchester United ....
Fulham v Darlington ....
Hereford United v Mansfield Town ....
Hull City v Swansea City ....
Leyton Orient v Rochdale ....
Wigan Athletic v Scarborough ....

Saturday, 18 January 1997

FA Carling Premiership

Arsenal v Everton ....
Chelsea v Derby County ....
Coventry City v Manchester United ....
Leicester City v Wimbledon ....
Liverpool v Aston Villa ....
Middlesbrough v Sheffield Wednesday ....
Nottingham Forest v Tottenham Hotspur ....
Southampton v Newcastle United ....
Sunderland v Blackburn Rovers ....
West Ham United v Leeds United ....

Nationwide Football League Division 1

Barnsley v Ipswich Town ....
Birmingham City v Reading ....
Bolton Wanderers v Wolverhampton Wanderers .
Charlton Athletic v Stoke City ....
Crystal Palace v Portsmouth ....
Huddersfield Town v Manchester City ....
Norwich City v Grimsby Town ....
Oxford United v Tranmere Rovers ....
Port Vale v Queens Park Rangers ....
Sheffield United v Southend United ....
Swindon Town v Bradford City ....
West Bromwich Albion v Oldham Athletic ....

Nationwide Football League Division 2

Blackpool v Crewe Alexandra ....
Brentford v Bristol City ....
Bristol Rovers v York City ....
Burnley v Bury ....
Luton Town v Wrexham ....
Notts County v Gillingham ....
Peterborough United v Plymouth Argyle ....
Preston North End v Watford ....
Rotherham United v Wycombe Wanderers ....
Shrewsbury Town v Chesterfield ....
Stockport County v Millwall ....
Walsall v A.F.C. Bournemouth ....

Nationwide Football League Division 3

Colchester United v Carlisle United ....
Darlington v Cambridge United ....
Exeter City v Wigan Athletic ....
Hartlepool United v Doncaster Rovers ....
Lincoln City v Brighton and Hove Albion ....
Mansfield Town v Hull City ....
Northampton Town v Chester City ....
Rochdale v Cardiff City ....
Scarborough v Barnet ....
Scunthorpe United v Hereford United ....
Swansea City v Leyton Orient ....
Torquay United v Fulham ....

Saturday, 25 January 1997

Nationwide Football League Division 2

Blackpool v Millwall ....
Brentford v Bristol Rovers ....
Bristol City v A.F.C. Bournemouth ....
Burnley v Preston North End ....
Bury v Wrexham ....
Chesterfield v Stockport County ....
Gillingham v Plymouth Argyle ....
Luton Town v Watford ....
Rotherham United v Crewe Alexandra ....
Shrewsbury Town v Peterborough United ....
Walsall v Notts County ....
Wycombe Wanderers v York City ....

Nationwide Football League Division 3

Barnet v Darlington ....
Brighton and Hove Albion v Rochdale ....
Cambridge United v Hereford United ....
Cardiff City v Hull City ....
Chester City v Carlisle United ....
Exeter City v Colchester United ....
Lincoln City v Doncaster Rovers ....
Northampton Town v Hartlepool United ....
Scarborough v Leyton Orient ....
Scunthorpe United v Fulham ....
Torquay United v Mansfield Town ....
Wigan Athletic v Swansea City ....

Tuesday, 28 January 1997

Nationwide Football League Division 1

Bradford City v Port Vale ....
Grimsby Town v Barnsley ....
Ipswich Town v West Bromwich Albion ....
Oldham Athletic v Charlton Athletic ....
Portsmouth v Oxford United ....
Reading v Huddersfield Town ....
Southend United v Crystal Palace ....
Tranmere Rovers v Norwich City ....

Wednesday, 29 January 1997

Nationwide Football League Division 1

Manchester City v Sheffield United ....
Queens Park Rangers v Birmingham City ....
Stoke City v Bolton Wanderers ....
Wolverhampton Wanderers v Swindon Town ....

Friday, 31 January 1997

Nationwide Football League Division 3

Colchester United v Torquay United ....
Swansea City v Cambridge United ....

Saturday, 1 February 1997

FA Carling Premiership

Aston Villa v Sunderland ....
Blackburn Rovers v West Ham United ....
Derby County v Liverpool ....
Everton v Nottingham Forest ....
Leeds United v Arsenal ....
Manchester United v Southampton ....
Newcastle United v Leicester City ....
Sheffield Wednesday v Coventry City ....
Tottenham Hotspur v Chelsea ....
Wimbledon v Middlesbrough ....

Nationwide Football League Division 1

Bolton Wanderers v Birmingham City ....
Bradford City v Huddersfield Town ....
Grimsby Town v Charlton Athletic ....
Norwich City v Barnsley ....
Oxford United v Manchester City ....
Port Vale v West Bromwich Albion ....
Portsmouth v Oldham Athletic ....
Queens Park Rangers v Crystal Palace ....
Southend United v Ipswich Town ....
Swindon Town v Sheffield United ....
Tranmere Rovers v Reading ....
Wolverhampton Wanderers v Stoke City ....

Nationwide Football League Division 2

A.F.C. Bournemouth v Blackpool ....
Bristol Rovers v Shrewsbury Town ....
Crewe Alexandra v Burnley ....
Millwall v Bristol City ....
Notts County v Luton Town ....

Peterborough United v Walsall ....
Plymouth Argyle v Wycombe Wanderers ....
Preston North End v Chesterfield ....
Stockport County v Brentford ....
Watford v Rotherham United ....
Wrexham v Gillingham ....
York City v Bury ....

Nationwide Football League Division 3

Carlisle United v Northampton Town ....
Darlington v Lincoln City ....
Doncaster Rovers v Scunthorpe United ....
Fulham v Cardiff City ....
Hartlepool United v Scarborough ....
Hereford United v Wigan Athletic ....
Hull City v Chester City ....
Leyton Orient v Exeter City ....
Mansfield Town v Brighton and Hove Albion ...
Rochdale v Barnet ....

Saturday, 8 February 1997

Nationwide Football League Division 1

Barnsley v Port Vale ....
Birmingham City v Portsmouth ....
Charlton Athletic v Tranmere Rovers ....
Crystal Palace v Bradford City ....
Huddersfield Town v Wolverhampton Wanderers .
Ipswich Town v Queens Park Rangers ....
Manchester City v Southend United ....
Oldham Athletic v Grimsby Town ....
Reading v Bolton Wanderers ....
Sheffield United v Norwich City ....
Stoke City v Oxford United ....
West Bromwich Albion v Swindon Town ....

Nationwide Football League Division 2

Blackpool v Peterborough United ....
Brentford v Watford ....
Bristol City v Stockport County ....
Burnley v York City ....
Bury v A.F.C. Bournemouth ....
Chesterfield v Wrexham ....
Gillingham v Bristol Rovers ....
Luton Town v Plymouth Argyle ....
Rotherham United v Preston North End ....
Shrewsbury Town v Notts County ....
Walsall v Millwall ....
Wycombe Wanderers v Crewe Alexandra ....

Nationwide Football League Division 3

Barnet v Hereford United ....
Brighton and Hove Albion v Hartlepool United .
Cambridge United v Hull City ....
Cardiff City v Colchester United ....
Chester City v Doncaster Rovers ....
Exeter City v Rochdale ....
Lincoln City v Fulham ....
Northampton Town v Swansea City ....
Scarborough v Darlington ....

Scunthorpe United v Mansfield Town ....
Torquay United v Leyton Orient ....
Wigan Athletic v Carlisle United ....

Friday, 14 February 1997

Nationwide Football League Division 3

Colchester United v Chester City ....

Saturday, 15 February 1997

FA Carling Premiership

Aston Villa v Coventry City ....
Blackburn Rovers v Nottingham Forest ....
Derby County v West Ham United ....
Everton v Leicester City ....
Leeds United v Southampton ....
Manchester United v Middlesbrough ....
Newcastle United v Chelsea ....
Sheffield Wednesday v Sunderland ....
Tottenham Hotspur v Arsenal ....
Wimbledon v Liverpool ....

Nationwide Football League Division 1

Bolton Wanderers v Sheffield United ....
Bradford City v Charlton Athletic ....
Grimsby Town v Huddersfield Town ....
Norwich City v West Bromwich Albion ....
Oxford United v Oldham Athletic ....
Port Vale v Ipswich Town ....
Portsmouth v Barnsley ....
Queens Park Rangers v Reading ....
Southend United v Stoke City ....
Swindon Town v Birmingham City ....
Tranmere Rovers v Manchester City ....
Wolverhampton Wanderers v Crystal Palace ......

Nationwide Football League Division 2

A.F.C. Bournemouth v Burnley ....
Bristol Rovers v Luton Town ....
Crewe Alexandra v Walsall ....
Millwall v Rotherham United ....
Notts County v Blackpool ....
Peterborough United v Bristol City ....
Plymouth Argyle v Bury ....
Preston North End v Wycombe Wanderers ....
Stockport County v Shrewsbury Town ....
Watford v Chesterfield ....
Wrexham v Brentford ....
York City v Gillingham ....

Nationwide Football League Division 3

Carlisle United v Brighton and Hove Albion .....
Darlington v Scunthorpe United ....
Doncaster Rovers v Barnet ....
Fulham v Wigan Athletic ....
Hartlepool United v Torquay United ....
Hereford United v Cardiff City ....
Hull City v Exeter City ....

Leyton Orient v Cambridge United ....
Mansfield Town v Lincoln City ....
Rochdale v Northampton Town ....
Swansea City v Scarborough ....

Saturday, 22 February 1997

FA Carling Premiership

Arsenal v Wimbledon ....
Chelsea v Manchester United ....
Coventry City v Everton ....
Leicester City v Derby County ....
Liverpool v Blackburn Rovers ....
Middlesbrough v Newcastle United ....
Nottingham Forest v Aston Villa ....
Southampton v Sheffield Wednesday ....
Sunderland v Leeds United ....
West Ham United v Tottenham Hotspur ....

Nationwide Football League Division 1

Barnsley v Wolverhampton Wanderers ....
Birmingham City v Port Vale ....
Charlton Athletic v Norwich City ....
Crystal Palace v Tranmere Rovers ....
Huddersfield Town v Bolton Wanderers ....
Ipswich Town v Oxford United ....
Manchester City v Swindon Town ....
Oldham Athletic v Bradford City ....
Reading v Southend United ....
Sheffield United v Grimsby Town ....
Stoke City v Queens Park Rangers ....
West Bromwich Albion v Portsmouth ....

Nationwide Football League Division 2

Blackpool v Stockport County ....
Brentford v A.F.C. Bournemouth ....
Bristol City v Crewe Alexandra ....
Burnley v Bristol Rovers ....
Bury v Notts County ....
Chesterfield v Plymouth Argyle ....
Gillingham v Peterborough United ....
Luton Town v Preston North End ....
Rotherham United v Wrexham ....
Shrewsbury Town v Millwall ....
Walsall v York City ....
Wycombe Wanderers v Watford ....

Nationwide Football League Division 3

Barnet v Fulham ....
Brighton and Hove Albion v Swansea City ....
Cambridge United v Carlisle United ....
Cardiff City v Hartlepool United ....
Chester City v Mansfield Town ....
Exeter City v Darlington ....
Lincoln City v Hereford United ....
Northampton Town v Doncaster Rovers ....
Scarborough v Rochdale ....
Scunthorpe United v Colchester United ....
Torquay United v Hull City ....
Wigan Athletic v Leyton Orient ....

Friday, 28 February 1997

Nationwide Football League Division 1

Tranmere Rovers v Stoke City ....

Nationwide Football League Division 3

Colchester United v Scarborough ....
Doncaster Rovers v Wigan Athletic ....

Saturday, 1 March 1997

FA Carling Premiership

Aston Villa v Liverpool ....
Blackburn Rovers v Sunderland ....
Derby County v Chelsea ....
Everton v Arsenal ....
Leeds United v West Ham United ....
Manchester United v Coventry City ....
Newcastle United v Southampton ....
Sheffield Wednesday v Middlesbrough ....
Tottenham Hotspur v Nottingham Forest ....
Wimbledon v Leicester City ....

Nationwide Football League Division 1

Bolton Wanderers v West Bromwich Albion ......
Bradford City v Manchester City ....
Grimsby Town v Birmingham City ....
Norwich City v Huddersfield Town ....
Oxford United v Crystal Palace ....
Port Vale v Reading ....
Portsmouth v Sheffield United ....
Queens Park Rangers v Oldham Athletic ....
Southend United v Barnsley ....
Swindon Town v Charlton Athletic ....
Wolverhampton Wanderers v Ipswich Town ......

Nationwide Football League Division 2

A.F.C. Bournemouth v Shrewsbury Town ....
Bristol Rovers v Walsall ....
Crewe Alexandra v Gillingham ....
Millwall v Wycombe Wanderers ....
Notts County v Brentford ....
Peterborough United v Chesterfield ....
Plymouth Argyle v Blackpool ....
Preston North End v Bury ....
Stockport County v Rotherham United ....
Watford v Bristol City ....
Wrexham v Burnley ....
York City v Luton Town ....

Nationwide Football League Division 3

Carlisle United v Lincoln City ....
Darlington v Brighton and Hove Albion ....
Fulham v Chester City ....
Hartlepool United v Scunthorpe United ....
Hereford United v Exeter City ....
Hull City v Northampton Town ....
Leyton Orient v Barnet ....
Mansfield Town v Cambridge United ....
Rochdale v Torquay United ....
Swansea City v Cardiff City ....

Tuesday, 4 March 1997

FA Carling Premiership

Arsenal v Manchester United ....
Sunderland v Tottenham Hotspur ....

Nationwide Football League Division 1

Barnsley v Swindon Town ....
Birmingham City v Wolverhampton Wanderers .
Charlton Athletic v Queens Park Rangers ....
Crystal Palace v Bolton Wanderers ....
Huddersfield Town v Oxford United ....
Ipswich Town v Bradford City ....
Oldham Athletic v Tranmere Rovers ....
Reading v Norwich City ....
Sheffield United v Port Vale ....
West Bromwich Albion v Southend United ....

Wednesday, 5 March 1997

FA Carling Premiership

Chelsea v Blackburn Rovers ....
Coventry City v Wimbledon ....
Leicester City v Aston Villa ....
Liverpool v Leeds United ....
Middlesbrough v Derby County ....
Nottingham Forest v Sheffield Wednesday ....
Southampton v Everton ....
West Ham United v Newcastle United ....

Nationwide Football League Division 1

Manchester City v Portsmouth ....
Stoke City v Grimsby Town ....

Friday, 7 March 1997

Nationwide Football League Division 3

Cambridge United v Colchester United ....

Saturday, 8 March 1997

FA Carling Premiership

Arsenal v Nottingham Forest ....
Coventry City v Leicester City ....
Derby County v Southampton ....
Leeds United v Everton ....
Liverpool v Newcastle United ....
Middlesbrough v Blackburn Rovers ....
Sheffield Wednesday v Tottenham Hotspur ....
Sunderland v Manchester United ....
West Ham United v Chelsea ....
Wimbledon v Aston Villa ....

Nationwide Football League Division 1

Barnsley v Sheffield United ....
Birmingham City v Southend United ....
Bolton Wanderers v Swindon Town ....
Bradford City v Grimsby Town ....
Charlton Athletic v Crystal Palace ....
Manchester City v Oldham Athletic ....

Norwich City v Port Vale ....
Oxford United v West Bromwich Albion ....
Portsmouth v Reading ....
Queens Park Rangers v Huddersfield Town ....
Stoke City v Ipswich Town ....
Wolverhampton Wanderers v Tranmere Rovers .

Reading v Bradford City ....
Sheffield United v Oxford United ....
Southend United v Queens Park Rangers ....
Swindon Town v Stoke City ....
Tranmere Rovers v Barnsley ....
West Bromwich Albion v Birmingham City ....

Nationwide Football League Division 2

A.F.C. Bournemouth v Chesterfield ....
Bristol City v Wrexham ....
Burnley v Peterborough United ....
Gillingham v Watford ....
Luton Town v Millwall ....
Notts County v Crewe Alexandra ....
Plymouth Argyle v Rotherham United ....
Preston North End v Brentford ....
Stockport County v Bury ....
Walsall v Shrewsbury Town ....
Wycombe Wanderers v Bristol Rovers ....
York City v Blackpool ....

Nationwide Football League Division 2

Blackpool v Preston North End ....
Brentford v Burnley ....
Bristol Rovers v Bristol City ....
Bury v Gillingham ....
Chesterfield v Wycombe Wanderers ....
Crewe Alexandra v Luton Town ....
Millwall v A.F.C. Bournemouth ....
Peterborough United v Stockport County ....
Rotherham United v Notts County ....
Shrewsbury Town v Plymouth Argyle ....
Watford v Walsall ....
Wrexham v York City ....

Nationwide Football League Division 3

Brighton and Hove Albion v Leyton Orient ....
Chester City v Barnet ....
Doncaster Rovers v Hull City ....
Fulham v Scarborough ....
Hereford United v Northampton Town ....
Lincoln City v Hartlepool United ....
Mansfield Town v Cardiff City ....
Rochdale v Wigan Athletic ....
Scunthorpe United v Carlisle United ....
Swansea City v Exeter City ....
Torquay United v Darlington ....

Nationwide Football League Division 3

Barnet v Swansea City ....
Carlisle United v Hereford United ....
Darlington v Chester City ....
Exeter City v Scunthorpe United ....
Hartlepool United v Rochdale ....
Hull City v Brighton and Hove Albion ....
Northampton Town v Lincoln City ....
Scarborough v Torquay United ....
Wigan Athletic v Cambridge United ....

Sunday, 16 March 1997

Nationwide Football League Division 3

Leyton Orient v Fulham ....

Friday, 14 March 1997

Nationwide Football League Division 3

Cardiff City v Doncaster Rovers ....
Colchester United v Mansfield Town ....

Friday, 21 March 1997

Nationwide Football League Division 3

Colchester United v Rochdale ....
Doncaster Rovers v Hereford United ....

Saturday, 15 March 1997

FA Carling Premiership

Aston Villa v West Ham United ....
Blackburn Rovers v Wimbledon ....
Chelsea v Sunderland ....
Everton v Derby County ....
Leicester City v Middlesbrough ....
Manchester United v Sheffield Wednesday ....
Newcastle United v Coventry City ....
Nottingham Forest v Liverpool ....
Southampton v Arsenal ....
Tottenham Hotspur v Leeds United ....

Saturday, 22 March 1997

FA Carling Premiership

Arsenal v Liverpool ....
Blackburn Rovers v Aston Villa ....
Coventry City v West Ham United ....
Derby County v Tottenham Hotspur ....
Everton v Manchester United ....
Middlesbrough v Chelsea ....
Sheffield Wednesday v Leeds United ....
Southampton v Leicester City ....
Sunderland v Nottingham Forest ....
Wimbledon v Newcastle United ....

Nationwide Football League Division 1

Crystal Palace v Norwich City ....
Grimsby Town v Manchester City ....
Huddersfield Town v Portsmouth ....
Ipswich Town v Bolton Wanderers ....
Oldham Athletic v Wolverhampton Wanderers ..
Port Vale v Charlton Athletic ....

Nationwide Football League Division 1

Birmingham City v Sheffield United ....
Bradford City v Wolverhampton Wanderers ......

Grimsby Town v Tranmere Rovers ....
Huddersfield Town v Barnsley ....
Manchester City v Stoke City ....
Norwich City v Bolton Wanderers ....
Oldham Athletic v Crystal Palace ....
Port Vale v Swindon Town ....
Queens Park Rangers v Portsmouth ....
Reading v Ipswich Town ....
Southend United v Oxford United ....
West Bromwich Albion v Charlton Athletic ....

Nationwide Football League Division 2

A.F.C. Bournemouth v York City ....
Blackpool v Bristol City ....
Bury v Chesterfield ....
Crewe Alexandra v Peterborough United ....
Gillingham v Wycombe Wanderers ....
Luton Town v Brentford ....
Millwall v Watford ....
Notts County v Stockport County ....
Plymouth Argyle v Wrexham ....
Shrewsbury Town v Rotherham United ....
Walsall v Burnley ....

Nationwide Football League Division 3

Brighton and Hove Albion v Cardiff City ....
Cambridge United v Chester City ....
Fulham v Hartlepool United ....
Hull City v Carlisle United ....
Leyton Orient v Lincoln City ....
Mansfield Town v Northampton Town ....
Scarborough v Exeter City ....
Swansea City v Darlington ....
Torquay United v Scunthorpe United ....
Wigan Athletic v Barnet ....

Sunday, 23 March 1997

Nationwide Football League Division 2

Bristol Rovers v Preston North End ....

Friday, 28 March 1997

Nationwide Football League Division 1

Ipswich Town v Manchester City ....

Nationwide Football League Division 2

Wrexham v Millwall ....

Nationwide Football League Division 3

Cardiff City v Scarborough ....

Saturday, 29 March 1997

FA Carling Premiership

Aston Villa v Sheffield Wednesday ....
Chelsea v Southampton ....
Leeds United v Derby County ....

Leicester City v Sunderland ....
Liverpool v Middlesbrough ....
Manchester United v Wimbledon ....
Newcastle United v Everton ....
Nottingham Forest v Coventry City ....
Tottenham Hotspur v Blackburn Rovers ....
West Ham United v Arsenal ....

Nationwide Football League Division 1

Barnsley v West Bromwich Albion ....
Bolton Wanderers v Port Vale ....
Charlton Athletic v Huddersfield Town ....
Crystal Palace v Birmingham City ....
Oxford United v Queens Park Rangers ....
Portsmouth v Bradford City ....
Sheffield United v Reading ....
Stoke City v Oldham Athletic ....
Swindon Town v Norwich City ....
Tranmere Rovers v Southend United ....
Wolverhampton Wanderers v Grimsby Town ....

Nationwide Football League Division 2

Brentford v Bury ....
Bristol City v Gillingham ....
Burnley v Luton Town ....
Chesterfield v Blackpool ....
Peterborough United v Bristol Rovers ....
Preston North End v Notts County ....
Rotherham United v Walsall ....
Stockport County v Crewe Alexandra ....
Watford v A.F.C. Bournemouth ....
Wycombe Wanderers v Shrewsbury Town ....
York City v Plymouth Argyle ....

Nationwide Football League Division 3

Barnet v Cambridge United ....
Carlisle United v Doncaster Rovers ....
Chester City v Brighton and Hove Albion ....
Darlington v Hull City ....
Exeter City v Mansfield Town ....
Hartlepool United v Colchester United ....
Hereford United v Fulham ....
Lincoln City v Torquay United ....
Northampton Town v Wigan Athletic ....
Rochdale v Swansea City ....
Scunthorpe United v Leyton Orient

Monday, 31 March 1997

Nationwide Football League Division 1

Birmingham City v Charlton Athletic ....
Bradford City v Stoke City ....
Grimsby Town v Ipswich Town ....
Huddersfield Town v Sheffield United ....
Norwich City v Oxford United ....
Oldham Athletic v Swindon Town ....
Port Vale v Tranmere Rovers ....
Queens Park Rangers v Wolverhampton Wanderers
Reading v Barnsley ....
Southend United v Portsmouth ....
West Bromwich Albion v Crystal Palace ....

Nationwide Football League Division 2

Blackpool v Rotherham United ....
Bristol Rovers v Wrexham ....
Bury v Wycombe Wanderers ....
Crewe Alexandra v Preston North End ....
Gillingham v Brentford ....
Notts County v Peterborough United ....
Plymouth Argyle v Watford ....

Nationwide Football League Division 3

Brighton and Hove Albion v Barnet ....
Cambridge United v Lincoln City ....
Colchester United v Darlington ....
Doncaster Rovers v Exeter City ....
Fulham v Rochdale ....
Hull City v Hereford United ....
Leyton Orient v Carlisle United ....
Mansfield Town v Hartlepool United ....
Scarborough v Scunthorpe United ....
Swansea City v Chester City ....
Torquay United v Northampton Town ....
Wigan Athletic v Cardiff City ....

Tuesday, 1 April 1997

Nationwide Football League Division 2

A.F.C. Bournemouth v Stockport County ....
Luton Town v Bristol City ....
Shrewsbury Town v Burnley ....
Walsall v Chesterfield ....

Tuesday, 2 April 1997

Nationwide Football League Division 2

Millwall v York City ....

Friday, 4 April 1997

Nationwide Football League Division 1

Tranmere Rovers v Bradford City ....

Saturday, 5 April 1997

FA Carling Premiership

Aston Villa v Everton ....
Chelsea v Arsenal ....
Leeds United v Blackburn Rovers ....
Leicester City v Sheffield Wednesday ....
Liverpool v Coventry City ....
Manchester United v Derby County ....
Newcastle United v Sunderland ....
Nottingham Forest v Southampton ....
Tottenham Hotspur v Wimbledon ....
West Ham United v Middlesbrough ....

Nationwide Football League Division 1

Barnsley v Birmingham City ....
Bolton Wanderers v Queens Park Rangers ....
Charlton Athletic v Manchester City ....
Crystal Palace v Huddersfield Town ....

Ipswich Town v Oldham Athletic ....
Oxford United v Port Vale ....
Portsmouth v Grimsby Town ....
Sheffield United v West Bromwich Albion ....
Stoke City v Reading ....
Swindon Town v Southend United ....
Wolverhampton Wanderers v Norwich City ....

Nationwide Football League Division 2

Brentford v Shrewsbury Town ....
Bristol City v Bury ....
Burnley v Millwall ....
Chesterfield v Gillingham ....
Peterborough United v A.F.C. Bournemouth .....
Preston North End v Plymouth Argyle ....
Rotherham United v Luton Town ....
Stockport County v Bristol Rovers ....
Watford v Crewe Alexandra ....
Wrexham v Walsall ....
Wycombe Wanderers v Blackpool ....
York City v Notts County ....

Nationwide Football League Division 3

Barnet v Hull City ....
Cardiff City v Cambridge United ....
Carlisle United v Fulham ....
Chester City v Wigan Athletic ....
Darlington v Doncaster Rovers ....
Exeter City v Torquay United ....
Hartlepool United v Leyton Orient ....
Hereford United v Colchester United ....
Lincoln City v Swansea City ....
Northampton Town v Scarborough ....
Rochdale v Mansfield Town ....
Scunthorpe United v Brighton and Hove Albion.

Wednesday, 9 April 1997

Nationwide Football League Division 1

Manchester City v Bolton Wanderers ....

Friday, 11 April 1997

Nationwide Football League Division 2

Rotherham United v Brentford ....

Nationwide Football League Division 3

Colchester United v Swansea City ....

Saturday, 12 April 1997

FA Carling Premiership

Arsenal v Leicester City ....
Blackburn Rovers v Manchester United ....
Coventry City v Chelsea ....
Derby County v Aston Villa ....
Everton v Tottenham Hotspur ....
Middlesbrough v Nottingham Forest ....
Sheffield Wednesday v Newcastle United ....
Southampton v West Ham United ....